NONDUALITY

NONDUALITY

A STUDY IN COMPARATIVE PHILOSOPHY

David Loy

Humanity Books

an imprint of Prometheus Books
59 John Glenn Drive, Amherst, New York 14228

Published by Humanity Books, an imprint of Prometheus Books

Inquiries should be addressed to
Humanity Books
59 John Glenn Drive
Amherst, New York 14228–2197.
VOICE: 716–691–0133, ext. 207. FAX: 716–564–2711.

06 05 04 03 02   9 8 7 6 5

Library of Congress Cataloging-in-Publication Data

Loy, David, 1947–
    Nonduality : a study in comparative philosophy / David Loy.
        p.   cm.
    Originally published in cloth: New Haven : Yale University Press, 1988;
Originally published in paper: Atlantic Highlands, NJ : Humanities Press
International, Inc., 1997
    Includes bibliographical references and index.
    ISBN 1–57392–359–1 (pbk.)
    1. Monism. 2. Philosophy, Comparative. 3. Philosophy, Oriental. I. Title.
[B105.M6L69   1999]
111′.82—dc21   99–10394
                                                                        CIP

Printed in the United States of America on acid-free paper

To my parents, Robert and Irene Loy

CONTENTS

ACKNOWLEDGMENTS

My deepest debt of gratitude is to my Zen teachers, Yamada Kōun-rōshi, director of the Sanbo Kyodan in Kamakura, Japan, and Robert Aitken Gyōun-rōshi, director of the Diamond Sangha in Hawaii. Without their personal examples and Zen guidance, this work would never have come to be written. Yet neither is a philosopher: these ideas have not been discussed with them, nor have they read the manuscript. So they cannot be held responsible for the conceptual proliferations that follow.

An earlier draft of this book was my doctoral dissertation, submitted to the National University of Singapore in 1984, while I was teaching in its department of philosophy. I am grateful to S. Gopalan and Goh Swee Tiang for their comments on the first draft. Robert Stecker also offered helpful suggestions on some of the early chapters. I am particularly grateful to Peter Della Santina and other members of the informal Mādhyamika Study Group that met in 1983–84, where many of these ideas were first discussed. The publication of this book owes much to the efforts of two people: Jeanne Ferris, editor at Yale University Press, who encouraged and nurtured the project, and John Koller, professor at the Rensselaer Polytechnic Institute, whose criticisms were both supportive and extremely helpful.

Parts of this book were first published in various journals. Passages from chapters 2 and 3 were in "The Difference between Saṁsāra and Nirvāṇa," *Philosophy East and West* 33, no. 4 (October 1983): 355–65, published by the University of Hawaii Press. An earlier version of the first section of chapter 3 appeared as "Wei-wu-wei: Nondual Action" in *Philosophy East and West* 35, no. 1 (January 1985): pp. 73–86, and an earlier version of the second section as "Chapter One of the *Tao Tê*

Ching: A 'New' Interpretation" in *Religious Studies* 21, no. 3 (September 1985), published by Cambridge University Press. Parts of chapter 4 appeared as "Nondual Thinking" in the *Journal of Chinese Philosophy* 13, no. 3 (September 1986). Some of the material in chapter 5 and the first two sections of chapter 6 was first presented as "Enlightenment in Buddhism and Advaita Vedanta: Are Nirvana and Moksha the Same?" in *International Philosophical Quarterly* 22, no. 1 (March 1982). An earlier version of the third section of chapter 6 appeared as "The Mahāyāna Deconstruction of Time" in *Philosophy East and West* 36, no. 1 (January 1986): pp. 13–23; much of the fourth section as "The Paradox of Causality in Mādhyamika" in *International Philosophical Quarterly* 25, no. 1 (March 1985); and an expanded version of the sixth section as "The Clôture of Deconstruction: A Mahāyāna Critique of Derrida" in *International Philosophical Quarterly* 27, no. 1 (March 1987). Some of the ideas discussed in chapter 8 were first published as "How Many Nondualities Are There?" (the title now given to chapter 1) in the *Journal of Indian Philosophy* 11, no. 4 (December 1983). A few pages from chapter 6 and from the conclusion were presented to the third Kyoto Zen Symposium and appeared in "Mu and Its Implications," *Zen Buddhism Today* 3 (1985), published by the Institute for Zen Studies, Kyoto, Japan.

I also thank Goh Boon Tay and Arlene Ho for their painstaking efforts in retyping various drafts, parts of which were barely legible, and Susan Hunston and Stephanie Jones for all their help with the manuscript.

Finally, deep and continuing gratitude to Linda Goodhew for taking care of me and putting up with me during this book's long gestation.

INTRODUCTION TO THE PAPERBACK EDITION

This paperback edition provides an opportunity to reflect back on the gestation of this book as well as its reception: in the light of both, how might it be different if written today? The importance of the topic, and the vast literature touching on it, continue to dwarf any attempt to provide a comprehensive overview, but the perspective of a few years allows a better understanding of how tentative the following chapters are and how they might have been improved.

It was with some reluctance that the chapter on nondual perception was placed so early, and the passage of time has reinforced those hesitations. My concern is that some readers may become stuck in the middle of that chapter and never get any further! The basic difficulty is that the epistemology of perception is notoriously and inescapably complicated, with the result that my treatment of those complications is sometimes in danger of losing the main thread of the argument. The comments I have received, however, have been more specific. Some Vedānta scholars have pointed out that there is no such thing as nondual perception in Advaita, which is true (and even emphasized within the text), but this does not obviate the main points that chapter two make about Vedānta: that understanding *nirvikalpa* experience as involving nondual perception illuminates many of the Advaitic claims about Brahman; and that reluctance to accept this touches upon the main problem with the Advaitic system, which is its inability to understand the relationship between *māyā* (the locus of perception) and *nirguṇa Brahman* (without perception).

The main difficulty with chapter two is elsewhere: the search for an unconditioned Reality "behind" concepts misses the essential point (emphasized in chapter six!) that the Unconditioned in Mahāyāna is to be found in the conditioned—more precisely, that the true nature of the conditioned is itself the unconditioned. Instead of looking for an Absolute usually obscured by conceptualization, it would be better to subject that distinction between the Real and whatever is opposed to it (thought? delusion? the phenomenal world?) to a deconstruction that inquires into why that duality has become so important to us.

To put it another way, the attempt in chapter two to dis-cover nondual perception has the effect of reifying another duality: that between Reality (usually accorded a capital R) and thought/language. This problem also applies, more or less, to the other chapters in Part One. It is addressed most directly in my essay in the book *Healing Deconstruction*, which is informed by a deeper appreciation of what Dōgen says about language.[1] Briefly, instead of rejecting language/thought (a response which is still dualistic), what is needed is an appreciation of the plurality of descriptive systems and the freedom to employ them according to the situation. As Dōgen might say, rather than eliminate concepts we need to "liberate" them!—which requires, of course, that we do not cling to any particular set.

In effect, however, this is less a critique of the arguments in Part One than it implies a more nuanced version of them.

I do not have as many reservations about any of the later chapters, and they are left to stand for themselves except for my concern to emphasize again the importance and centrality of chapter six "The Deconstruction of Dualism." Although this chapter serves a key role in the larger argument, it may be read by itself without reference to any of the other chapters.

Some readers have noticed problems with a few translated passages, which are more ambiguous than I have credited them for. In a book full of so many different quotations from so many different traditions and languages, this difficulty is not easily avoided—but my own linguistic skills (or lack thereof) have not helped, since they have made me largely dependent upon others' judgement. Nevertheless, I am not aware that this seriously impinges on *any* of the arguments offered. In cases where a particular translation is central—especially in chapter three, which considers at some length the first chapter of the *Tao Tê Ching*—my versions have of course been discussed with scholars more specialized in those fields.

Those familiar with *Lack and Transcendence: The Problem of Death and Life in Psychotherapy, Existentialism, and Buddhism,* published last year also by Humanities Press, may wonder about the relationship between that book and this one. The two are distinct, of course, in that neither requires any acquaintance with the other. There is nonetheless a connection, for the central theme of *Lack and Transcendence*—the sense-of-self's sense-of-*lack*—is prefigured in chapter four of this book, where the issue is raised why our minds seek a secure "home." In that sense the second book may be said to have grown out of the first and the two supplement each other.

It remains to thank Keith Ashfield and Humanities Press for making this book available again and at a more affordable price. The text remains unchanged from the original Yale University Press cloth edition, except for correcting some typographical errors. My hope remains that what follows will encourage other scholars to improve upon it, and, even more important, that it will encourage a new generation of readers to work toward overcoming their own sense of subject-object duality.

NOTE

1. "Dead Words, Living Words, and Healing Words: The Disseminations of Eckhart and Dōgen", in David Loy, ed., *Healing Deconstruction: Postmodern Thought in Buddhism and Christianity* (Atlanta, Georgia: Scholars Press, 1996), 33–51.

INTRODUCTION

In our self-seeing There, the self is seen as belonging to that order, or rather we are merged into that self in us which has the quality of that order. It is a knowing of the self restored to its purity. No doubt we should not speak of seeing; but we cannot help talking in dualities, seen and seer, instead of, boldly, the achievement of unity. In this seeing, we neither hold an object nor trace distinction; there is no two. The man is changed, no longer himself nor self-belonging; he is merged with the Supreme, sunken into it, one with it: centre coincides with centre, for on this higher plane things that touch at all are one; only in separation is there duality; by our holding away, the Supreme is set outside. This is why the vision baffles telling; we cannot detach the supreme to state it; if we have seen something thus detached we have failed of the Supreme which is to be known only as one with ourselves.

—Sixth Ennead IX.10

In case we miss the main point, Plotinus repeats it a sentence later: "There were not two; beholder was one with beheld; it was not a vision compassed but a unity apprehended."[1] The nonduality of seer and seen: there is no philosophical or religious assertion more striking or more counterintuitive, and yet claims that there is such an experience, and that this experience is more veridical than our usual dualistic experience, are not rare in the Western tradition. Similar statements have been made, in equally stirring language, by such important Western mystical figures as Meister Eckhart, Jakob Boehme, and William Blake, to name only a few. Philosophers have generally been more hesitant about committing themselves so decisively, but a claim regarding the nonduality of subject and object is explicit or implicit within such thinkers as Spinoza, Schelling, Hegel, Schopenhauer, Bergson, and Whitehead—again naming only a few; later I shall argue that similar claims may be found among important contemporary figures like Nietzsche, Heidegger, and perhaps Wittgenstein. We should not be surprised by the comparative reluctance of philosophers to commit themselves on this issue. Religious figures can be satisfied to rest the assertion of nonduality on faith or on their own experience, but philosophers must support their assertions with arguments; and what is reason to do with such an extraordinary claim, which (as Plotinus suggests) by its very nature is not susceptible even to adequate conceptual description, much less proof? It is not surprising that the mainstream of the Western intellectual tradition has not been sympathetic to such statements. Yet claims about subject–object nonduality, like the broad mystical tradition where they have found their most comfortable home, have survived as a puzzling subterranean undercurrent, sometimes attacked, at other times ridiculed.

The contemporary world prides itself on its pragmatism. This means, among other things, that most philosophers believe we have evolved beyond the abstract speculations of metaphysics by becoming self-critical and more sophisticated in the way we use language. But if traditional metaphysics is dead, metaphysics in the larger sense is inescapable. It ultimately refers to our basic understanding about the nature of the world, and some such understanding can always be extrapolated, if necessary, from our attitude toward the world we suppose ourselves to be "in." The farthest we can remove ourselves from metaphysics is to "forget" this metaphysical understanding in the sense of no longer being aware of our philosophical presuppositions about the world and ourselves. Today we are so impressed with the success of the physical sciences—originally derived from metaphysics—that we return a compliment and derive our metaphysics from natural science. But the scientific worldview has its own metaphysical presuppositions, which originated in ancient Greece, in ways of looking at the world that came to fruition in Plato and especially Aristotle. This dualistic view stands almost in diametric opposition to a worldview based on the nonduality of seer and seen. However, the Greek tradition of that time was a rich one, abounding in competing paradigms, and it is worthwhile to remind ourselves that, however inevitable it may seem in retrospect, the Aristotelian worldview which developed into the mainstream was not the only possible path. As we shall see, other important thinkers prior to Plotinus—such as Pythagoras, Heraclitus, Parmenides, and even Plato, according to how we interpret him—were more sympathetic than Aristotle to the metaphysical claim of nonduality, and what they thought on this matter may still have meaning for us today.

But my main concern is not the development of the Western philosophical tradition, although there will be many occasions to refer to it. In the West, the claim of subject–object nonduality has been a seed which, however often sown, has never found fertile soil, because it has been too antithetical to those other vigorous sprouts that have grown into modern science and technology. In the Eastern tradition—the rich yet dissimilar intellectual climates of India and China, in particular—we encounter a different situation. There the seeds of seer–seen nonduality not only sprouted but matured into a variety (some might say a jungle) of impressive philosophical species which have been attractive to many Westerners because they seem so exotic in relation to our own—and because they bear at least the promise of fruits which we Westerners lack yet still crave. By no means do all of these systems assert the nonduality of subject and object, but it is significant that three which do—Buddhism, Vedānta and Taoism— have probably been the most influential.

I should note at the outset that none of these three completely denies the dualistic "relative" world that we are familiar with and presuppose as "commonsense": the world as a collection of discrete objects, interacting causally in space and time. Their claim is rather that there is another, nondual way of experiencing the world, and that this other mode of experience is actually more veridical and superior to the dualistic mode we usually take for granted. The difference between such nondualistic approaches and the contemporary Western one (which, given its global influence, can hardly be labeled Western any more) is that the latter has constructed its metaphysics on the basis of dualistic experience only, whereas the former acknowledges the deep significance of nondual experience by constructing its metaphysical categories according to what it reveals.

But expressing the matter in this way is getting ahead of ourselves. That Buddhism, Vedānta and Taoism are basing their worldview on the experience of subject-object nonduality cannot be presupposed; it is one of the main concerns of this book to argue precisely that point. In so doing, the significant differences among these systems (and internally, for example, among different Buddhist systems) will receive our attention, and the basis for those disagreements will be considered. It is safe to say that those differences have not usually been overlooked. If anything, there has been more emphasis on disagreements than on similarities, which have tended to be passed over too quickly—perhaps because disagreements naturally provide more to discuss. The unfortunate result is that, even in Asian philosophy, this shared claim about the nonduality of subject and object has not received the philosophical attention that it merits. It is such an extraordinary claim, so much at variance with common sense, and yet so fundamental to all these systems, that it deserves careful investigation; and such investigation gives rise to a suspicion.

In all the Asian systems that incorporate this claim, the nondual nature of reality is indubitably revealed only in what they term enlightenment or liberation (*nirvāṇa, mokṣa, satori*, etc.), which is the experience of nonduality. That experience is the hinge upon which each metaphysic turns, despite the fact that such enlightenment has different names in the various systems and is often described in very different ways. Unlike Western philosophy, which prefers to reflect on the dualistic experience accessible to all, these systems make far-reaching epistemological and ontological claims on the basis of counterintuitive experience accessible to very few—if we accept their accounts, only to those who are willing to follow the necessarily rigorous path, who are very few. It is not that these claims are not empirical, but if they are true, they are grounded on evidence not readily available. This is the source of the difficulty in evaluating them. Plotinus has already drawn our attention to another characteristic of the nondual experience, which fully accords with Asian descriptions of enlightenment: the experience cannot be attained or even understood conceptually. We shall see that this is because our usual conceptual knowledge is dualistic in at least two senses: it is knowledge *about* something, which a subject *has*; and such knowledge must discriminate one thing from another in order to assert some *attribute* about some *thing*. Later I reflect on the isomorphism between our conceptual thought-processes and the subject–predicate structure of language. What is important at the moment is that the dualistic nature of conceptual knowledge means the nondual experience, if genuine, must transcend philosophy itself and all its ontological claims. And that brings our suspicions to a head: are these different philosophies based upon, and trying to point to, the same nondual experience?

During the experience itself there is no philosophizing, but if and when one "steps back" and attempts to describe what has been experienced, perhaps a variety of descriptions are possible. Maybe even contradictory ontologies can be erected on the same phenomenological ground. That suspicion is the motivation for this study.

Because nonduality is so incompatible with our usual experience—or, as the nondualist usually prefers, with our usual way of understanding experience—it is very difficult to grasp what exactly is meant when it is claimed that, for example, perception is or can be nondual. Clarifying those claims is the major concern of part 1. This is not to say that a dualistic claim is less problematic—the relation between subject and object has always been a (perhaps the) major epistemological problem—yet at least a dualistic approach seems to accord better with common sense, despite whatever puzzles arise when one tries to develop this belief philosophically. But that nonduality is difficult to understand is necessarily true, according to the various systems which assert it. If we did understand it fully we would be enlightened, which is not understanding in the usual sense: it is the experience of nonduality which philosophizing obstructs. From such a perspective, the problem with philosophy is that its attempt to grasp nonduality conceptually is inherently dualistic and thus self-defeating. Indeed, the very impetus to philosophy may be seen as a reaction to the split between subject and object: philosophy originated in the need of the alienated subject to understand itself and its relation to the objective world it finds itself in. But, according to the "nondualist systems" to be considered—Buddhism (especially Mahāyāna), Vedānta (especially Advaita) and Taoism—philosophy cannot grasp the source from which it springs and so must yield to praxis: the intellectual attempt to grasp nonduality conceptually must give way to various meditative techniques which, it is claimed, promote the immediate experience of nonduality. Of course, the shift of perspective from conceptual understanding to meditative practices is beyond the scope of this work, as it is beyond the range of philosophy generally. However, despite this attitude about the final inadequacy of philosophy—which means, among other things, that these systems are not philosophies at all in the Western sense—the various traditions have nonetheless made many specific claims about different aspects of the nondual experience. These claims provide the material for this work.

My approach is hermeneutical. I shall extract and elucidate a "core doctrine" of nonduality from these various claims. Such a project is ambitious enough, so let me emphasize that, despite the many references to Western parallels and contemporary theories, this work is not an attempt to establish, in some supposedly objective and rigorous fashion, whether our experience is or can be nondual. Instead, I shall construct a theory which is coherent in that it integrates a large number of otherwise disparate philosophical claims, and which is hence plausible as a systematic interpretation of these claims.

Such an approach is consistent with the attitude of the Asian traditions to be examined. Most of the passages I will quote offer assertions rather than arguments, a stance that is not atypical of the literature. When those claims were originally made, it was usually expected that they would be received reverently by those already committed to the tradition. In those whose minds were ripe (usually as a result of extensive meditation), a *mahāvākya* (great saying) such as "that thou art" or "mind is the Buddha" might be sufficient to precipitate the realization of nonduality. But logically compelling proofs of the possibility of nondual experience were not offered. The Upaniṣads include many claims about the nature of Ātman and Brahman, and analogies to help us understand those claims, but not arguments— which is to be expected, since they, like the classic texts of Taoism, are "pre-philosophical." Much later, Śaṅkara developed and systematized these claims with the help of many arguments, but most of these criticize other interpretations; his own views are defended apologetically as consistent with the Vedas and not contradicted by experience. The Pāli Canon does not offer proof that there is an escape from saṁsāra. Although many of the Buddha's doctrinal formulations are philosophically subtle, he intentionally avoided even describing what the state of nirvana is, other than characterizing it as the end of suffering and craving. Long afterwards, the Yogācāra philosopher Asaṅga pointed out that there are only three decisive arguments for transcendental idealism, and it seems to me that the same three arguments apply to the claim for nonduality. First, there is the direct intuition of reality (nonduality) by those who have awakened to it; second, the report that Buddhas (or other enlightened people) give of their experience in speech or writing; and third, the experience (of nonduality) that ocurs in deep meditative *samādhi*, when "the concentrated see things as they really are."[2] It is hardly necessary to point out that none of these three needs be accepted as compelling by anyone already skeptical. The third, meditative experience, may easily be criticized as abnormal and possibly delusive. The second is partly an appeal to authority, which is unacceptable as philosophical evidence, and partly a restatement of the first. This means that the argument for nonduality is actually reduced to the experience of nonduality—either our own or that of someone else whose testimony we may be inclined to accept.

W. T. Stace has argued that the "divine order" is "utterly other" to the natural order.[3] Whether or not this accurately describes Western mysticism, it is not the view of the nondualist philosophies we consider. Their general attitude is that one can realize the nature of the dualistic phenomenal world from the "perspective" of the nondual experience, but not vice versa. The Buddha did not describe nirvana because nirvana cannot be understood from the perspective of one still mired in *saṁsāra*, but full comprehension of the workings of saṁsāra—for example, the "dependent origination" (*pratītya-samut-pāda*) of all things—is implied by the experience of nirvana. In fact, full understanding of saṁsāra, of how craving and delusion cause rebirth, seems to constitute the nirvana of Pāli Buddhism, for that is how one is able to escape the otherwise mechanical cycle of birth and death. Śaṅkara would agree: *mokṣa*—the realization that "I am Brahman"—reveals the true nature of phenomena as *māyā*, illusion, but until that liberation one is blinded by māyā and takes the unreal as real, the real as unreal. In Taoism, the realization of Tao gives one insight into the nature of "the ten thousand things," but although some characteristics of the Tao (and the man of Tao) are expounded using parables and analogies, I am familiar with no serious attempt to prove the existence of the Tao.

That apparently dualistic phenomena can be understood from the perspective of nonduality, but not vice versa, appears to be necessarily true, due to the nature of understanding. What Sebastian Samay writes about Karl Jaspers' philosophy also applies here:

> Unlike science, which inquires into objects which are *in* the world, philosophy sets out to penetrate into the unity of all things by going back into their fundamental origin. Consequently, the object of phi-

losophy can permit nothing outside itself by means of which it might be "understood." Other objects are logically dependent on it, but it itself depends on nothing. Thoughts and statements about such an "object" are necessarily self-reflexive; while we explain everything by reference to this object, we must explain it by itself; it is self-explanatory, its own point of reference.[4]

This may be restated in our terms as follows: from the "perspective" of nonduality—that is, having experienced nondually—one can understand the delusive nature of dualistic experience and how that delusion arises, but not vice versa. There is no argument which, using the premises of our usual dualistic experience (or understanding of experience), can provide a valid proof that experience is actually nondual. All philosophy is an attempt to understand our experience, but here the critical issue is the type of experience that we accept as fundamental, as opposed to the type of experience that needs to be "explained." The Western epistemologist usually accepts as his data our familiar dualistic experience, dismissing other types (e.g., *samādhi*) as philosophically insignificant aberrations. In contrast, Asian epistemologists have placed more weight upon various "paranormal" experiences including samādhi, dreams, and what they consider to be the experience of liberation. The former approach accepts duality as valid and dismisses nonduality as delusive; the latter accepts nonduality as revelatory and criticizes duality as a more common but deluded interpretation of what we experience. Because it is a matter of premises, at this level there are no neutral or objective criteria by which we can evaluate these two views—indeed, the very concept of "objective criteria" is itself under question. In choosing between these approaches, cultural bias usually comes into play. Those raised in the classical Asian traditions are more inclined to accept the possibility of nonduality; those educated in the Western empiricist tradition are more likely to be skeptical of such an experience and prefer to "explain away" nonduality in terms of something else that they are able to understand—for example, as an "oceanic feeling" due to womb memory, Freud's formulation. The Western belief that only one type of experience is veridical is a post-Aristotelian assumption now too deeply ingrained to be easily recognized as such by many. Yet such skepticism is dangerously circular, using arguments based on one mode of experience to conclude that only that mode of experience is veridical.

This study divides naturally into two parts. Part 1 extracts various claims from the major nondualist traditions, Buddhism, Vedānta, and Taoism, in order to construct a "core doctrine" of nonduality largely consistent with all three. The process of selection is unsystematic, making use of assertions and arguments that provide helpful insights while ignoring most of the rest. This yields a theory about the nature of nondual experience that also explains the apparent "delusion" of our more usual way of understanding experience. But the disagreements among the nondualist systems—especially between Mahāyāna Buddhism and Advaita Vedānta—cannot be lightly dismissed. So part 2 works backward, using the core theory as a perspective from which to approach and resolve the disagreements. There we shall be able to understand how the same phenomenological experience may be subjected to different and even contradictory descriptions.

In this introduction, the term *nonduality* refers exclusively to the nonduality of (more narrowly) seer and seen, (more broadly) subject and object. Such nonduality is my main concern, but is by no means the only meaning of the term in the literature. At least five different meanings can be distinguished, all of them intimately related; three of those are of interest in part 1. Chapter 1 sets the parameters of the study by discussing the role of these three nondualities within Buddhism, Vedānta, and Taoism. It demonstrates their prevalence, importance, and relationships, dwelling particularly upon the third nonduality of subject and object, of self and nonself, of my consciousness and the world "I" find myself "in." Each of the following chapters of part 1 investigates what such nonduality might mean in one particular mode of our experience—perceiving, acting, and thinking, respectively. How can we understand the assertion that each of these is actually nondual?

In the case of perception, we will find general agreement that the act of perception is normally not simple but complex (*sa-vikalpa*), for a variety of other mental processes interpret and organize percepts. Through meditative practices, however, one can come to distinguish the bare percept from these other processes and experience it as it is in itself (*nir-vikalpa*); experiencing this way is without the distinction normally made between the perceived object and the subject that is conscious *of* it. As *The Awakening of Faith* (an important Mahāyāna text) says, "from the beginning, corporeal form and mind have been non-dual."[5] The meaning of this is discussed further, with particular reference to hearing and seeing, and is placed in the context of Western theories of epistemology as a version of phenomenalism. Two recent psychological experiments into meditation seem to provide empirical support for the possibility of such nondual perception.

We shall find a parallel in the case of action. Our normal experience of action is dualistic—there is the sense of an "I" that *does* the action—because the action is done to obtain a particular result. Corresponding to the usual tripartite division of perception into perceiver, perceived, and the act of perception, there is the agent, the action, and the goal of the action. Parallel to the superimposition of thought on percept, the mental "overlay" of intention also superimposes thought on action and thereby sustains the illusion of a separate agent; but without such thought-superimposition no distinction is experienced between agent and act, or between mind and body. Nondual action is spontaneous (because free from objectified intention), effortless (because free from a reified "I" that must exert itself), and "empty" (because one wholly *is* the action, there is not the dualistic awareness *of* an action). This perspective is derived from explaining the meaning of *wei-wu-wei*, the paradoxical "action of nonaction" of Taoism, and it is used to interpret the enigmatic first chapter of the *Tao Tĕ Ching*. It is also consistent with the emphasis, in some recent philosophy of mind, on intention as that which maintains the sense of self.

These accounts of nondual perception and nondual action seem to suggest that thought processes function only as an interference. Given also the emphasis on meditation in the nondualist traditions, one might conclude that thoughts are merely a problem to be minimized. But that is not the case. Even as thought processes may obscure the true nature of perception and action, so the nondual nature of thinking is obscured by its link with perception (hypostatizing percepts into objects) and action (providing intentions for action). The tripartite sense of a thinker who thinks thoughts is delusive, but there is a nondual alternative. We might suppose a thinker necessary in order to provide the causal link between various thoughts, to explain how one thought leads to another; but in fact there is no such link. In nondual thinking each thought is experienced as arising and passing away by itself, not "determined" by previous thoughts but "springing up" spontaneously. Such thinking reveals the source of creativity, as testified by the many writers, composers, and even scientists who have insisted that "the thoughts just came of themselves." It also provides a fruitful perspective for interpreting the later work of Martin Heidegger. The last section of chapter 4 suggests that Heidegger's "way" is best understood as nondual thinking and points out that the nonduality of consciousness and world is the central theme of his most important post-*Kehre* ("turning") essays.

The short summary concluding part 1 integrates these three studies into an understanding of a fourth nonduality, which may be called the nonduality of phenomena and Absolute, or, better, the nonduality of duality and nonduality. My approach supports the Mahāyāna claim that saṁsāra is nirvana. There is only one reality—this world, right here and now—but this world may be experienced in two different ways. Saṁsāra is the relative, phenomenal world as usually experienced, which is delusively understood to consist of a collection of discrete objects (including "me") that interact causally in space and time. Nirvana is that same world but as it is in itself, nondually incorporating both subject and object into a whole. If we can "interpolate" from nondual experience to explain duality, but not vice versa, this suggests that our usual sense of duality is due to the superimposition or interaction among nondual percepts, actions, and thoughts. The problem seems to be that these three functions somehow interfere with each other, thus obscuring the nondual nature of each. The material objects of the external world are nondual percepts objectified by superimposed concepts. Dualistic action is due to the superimposition of intention upon nondual action. Concepts and intentions are dualistic because thinking is preoccupied with percepts and actions rather than being experienced as it is in itself, when it springs up creatively.

Part 2 defends our core theory by considering the ontological differences among the nondual systems, for the conflict among their categories constitutes the major challenge to a study of this sort. Chapter 5 interprets the three major systems of Indian philosophy—Sāṅkhya-Yoga, Buddhism, and Advaita Vedānta—as the three main ways to understand the subject–object relation. The radical dualism of Sāṅkhya-Yoga is untenable, but several factors suggest that the claims of Buddhism and Advaita Vedānta are in fact quite compatible. Chapter 6—the most important of the book, in my opinion—provides a detailed analysis of five major issues on which Buddhism and Advaita seem diametrically opposed: no self versus all-Self, only-modes versus all-Substance, impermanence versus immutability, all-conditionality versus no-causality, and all path versus no-path. In each case, our nondualist approach leads us to conclude that the surface conflict of categories conceals a deeper agreement regarding the phenomenology of the nondual experience. When one wants to describe the nondual experience in the dualistic categories of language, two alternatives naturally suggest themselves: either to deny the subject or to deny the object; from this choice one's attitude toward the other disagreements follows. In both cases, what is more important than the choice between denial of subject or object is the denial common to both systems, of any bifurcation between self and non-self, and so on. The last section of chapter 6 employs the conclusions regarding time and causality to make a critique of Derrida's radical critique of Western philosophy, arguing that his deconstruction is incomplete because it is not radical enough to deconstruct itself; therefore it misses the possibility for a new, nonconceptual "opening" to something very different.

Chapters 7 and 8 test our core theory of nonduality in two ways. The first employs an analogy to demonstrate that the same experience can indeed result in incompatible descriptions, and in fact the "Mind-space" analogy seems to provide a common phenomenology for the major interpretations that we find in Indian philosophy. Chapter 8 uses the nondualist perspective to approach the two main philosophical issues raised by the *Bhagavad-gītā*: the relations among the various *margas* (spiritual paths), and the relationship between the personal (Saguṇa Brahman, God) and impersonal (Nirguṇa Brahman, Godhead) Absolutes.

The study concludes by considering, very briefly, the implications of subject–object nonduality for three other important areas of philosophy: the value-studies of ethics, aesthetics, and social theory. The nondual experience subverts the ground of the ethical problem, both by denying the existence of the ontological ego and, more radically, by challenging all moral codes as deluding superimpositions. Nonduality also gives us insight into the aesthetic experience, as Schopenhauer realized; we shall see that, finally, it becomes difficult to distinguish between aesthetic and "spiritual" experiences. We shall end by reflecting on a social parallel and its implications, for "the same dualism that reduces things to objects for consciousness is at work in the humanism that reduces nature to raw material for humankind."[6]

This introduction cannot end without an apologia. More than fifty years ago, Otto Rank temporarily gave up writing, complaining, "There is already too much truth in the world—an over-production which apparently cannot be consumed!" What would he say today? At the least no new book should be born without an *apologia pro vita sua*, an attempt to justify itself as more than a means for academic self-advancement. I write this book because I believe it is relevant to more than just our scholarly understanding of Asian philosophy: I hope that its critique of subject–object dualism helps to challenge the dualistic categories that have largely determined the development of Western civilization since Aristotle.

Today the Great Divide in Western philosophy is between those who see science as a model to be justified and emulated and those who see the scientific mode of knowledge—whose concern for objectivity makes it unavoidably dualistic—as only one mode of cognitive experience. Some of the most influential thinkers of the last century— Nietzsche, Wittgenstein, and Heidegger are the ones most often referred to in these pages—criticized these dualistic categories in various ways. But their critiques have been more influential than any positive vision that they and others have been able to offer. Despite increasing suspicion about the merits of technocratic society and the dualistic mode of experiencing that undergirds it, there is no agreement about what the root of the problem is and therefore what alternative there might be.

One way to become aware of our own presuppositions is to examine the worldviews of other civilizations. The philosophies of India and China are the most profound and subtle alternatives, but they present us with a profusion of systems which, despite some notable similarities, still seem to be poles apart in some important aspects of their understanding of reality. Their preoccupation with attaining another mode of experience stands in sharp contrast to the most influential strands of the Western tradition, which have rather sought to analyze and control our usual mode of experiencing. What is most promising about the Asian systems is that the alternative mode of experiencing they emphasize is understood to be not only revelatory but also personally liberating. Yet, as soon as we look more closely, the surface similarity among the systems seems to dissolve, for they characterize this other mode in very different ways. That is the point at which this study becomes relevant. If it can be demonstrated that beneath the clash of ontological categories there is a fundamental agreement about the nature of this alternative mode, our situation changes. In place of an internecine feud among rival opposition parties, which enervates them and keeps them from becoming genuine rivals to the the incumbent government, we have a united front which must be taken seriously. In my opinion, the nihilism of present Western culture means that we cannot afford to ignore what the greatest philosophical traditions of India and China may have to teach us.

PART ONE
TOWARD
A CORE
THEORY

CHAPTER I
HOW MANY NONDUALITIES
ARE THERE?

No concept is more important in Asian philosophical and religious thought than *nonduality* (Sanskrit *advaya* and *advaita*, Tibetan *gÑis-med*, Chinese *pu-erh*, Japanese *fu-ni*), and none is more ambiguous. The term has been used in many different although related ways, and to my knowledge the distinctions between these meanings have never been fully clarified. These meanings are distinct, although they often overlap in particular instances. This chapter distinguishes these different meanings, explores the relationships among them, demonstrates their importance for what I call "the nondualist systems," and reflects on the significance of all the above.

The following types of nonduality are discussed here: the negation of dualistic thinking, the nonplurality of the world, and the nondifference of subject and object. In subsequent chapters, our attention focuses primarily on the last of these three, although there will be occasion to consider two other nondualities which are also closely related: first, what has been called the identity of phenomena and Absolute, or the Mahāyāna equation of *samsāra* and *nirvāṇa*, which can also be expressed as "the nonduality of duality and nonduality"; second, the possibility of a mystical unity between God and man. No doubt other nondualities can be distinguished, but most of them can be subsumed under one or more of the above categories. As the negative construction of the word in all languages suggests, the meaning of each nonduality can be understood only by reference to the particular duality that is being denied. We shall quickly see that each of these negations has both an ontological and a soteriological function;

the term is used to criticize our usual dualistic experience (or understanding of experience) as both delusive and unsatisfactory, and the
corresponding nondual mode is recommended as both veridical and
superior.

THE NEGATION OF DUALISTIC THINKING

*It is because there is "is" that there is "is not"; it is because there is "is not" that there
is "is." This being the situation, the sages do not approach things on this level, but
reflect the light of nature.*

—Chuang Tzu[1]

Our first nonduality is a critique of "dualistic thinking," that is, of
thinking which differentiates that-which-is-thought-about into two
opposed categories: being and nonbeing, success and failure, life and
death, enlightenment and delusion, and so on. The problem with
such thinking is that, although distinctions are usually made in order
to choose one or the other, we cannot take one without the other since
they are interdependent; in affirming one half of the duality we
maintain the other as well.

> Without relation to "good" there is no "bad," in dependence on which
> we form the idea of "good." Therefore "good" is unintelligible. There is
> no "good" unrelated to "bad"; yet we form our idea of "bad" in depen-
> dence on it. There is therefore no "bad."   (Nāgārjuna)[2]

This abstract point becomes more relevant when, for example, we
consider the problem of how to live a "pure" life. The implication of
Nāgārjuna's argument is that attempting to live a pure life involves a
preoccupation with impurity. In order to have only pure thoughts and
actions, one must avoid impure ones, and this means determining to
which of the two categories each thought and action belongs. It is
generally claimed that this dichotomizing tendency of mind keeps us
from experiencing situations as they really are in themselves, when no
such dualistic categories as pure and impure, good and bad, and so
on, are applicable. These warnings are especially common in
Mahāyāna Buddhism:

> *Dānapāramitā* [literally, perfect or transcendental generosity] means
> relinquishment...of the dualism of opposites. It means total relin-
> quishment of ideas as to the dual nature of good and bad, being and

non-being, love and aversion, void and not void, concentration and distraction, pure and impure. By giving all of them up, we attain to a state in which all opposites are seen as void.

Thinking in terms of being and non-being is called wrong thinking, while not thinking in those terms is called right thinking. Similarly, thinking in terms of good and evil is wrong; not to think so is right thinking. The same applies to all the other categories of opposites—sorrow and joy, beginning and end... all of which are called wrong thinking, while to abstain from thinking in those categories is called right thinking. (Hui Hai)[3]

The second passage contains a claim which negates itself, as Hui Hai must have realized: dualistic thinking is criticized as wrong thinking, but the distinction between right and wrong thinking is itself dualistic. So, in fact, is the very distinction between dualistic and nondualistic thinking, or between duality and nonduality generally. Carried to this extreme, "the perfection of wisdom (*prajñāpāramitā*) should not be viewed from duality nor from non-duality."[4] Therefore such teaching naturally tends toward self-negation and paradox, due to its apparent violation of logic, especially the law of identity:

Q: The Vimalakīrti Nirdeśa Sūtra says: "Whosoever desires to reach the Pure Land must first purify his mind." What is the meaning of this purifying of the mind?
A: It means purifying it to the point of ultimate purity.
Q: But what does that mean?
A: It is a state beyond purity and impurity.... Purity pertains to a mind which dwells upon nothing whatsoever. To attain this without so much as a thought of purity arising is called absence of purity; and to achieve that without giving that a thought is to be free from absence of purity also. (Hui Hai)[5]

In other words, "purity is not purity; that is why it is purity." This paradox—A is not A, therefore it is A—is found in its clearest form in the Prajñāpāramitā literature. The Diamond Sutra, for example contains many instances:

Subhūti, the so-called good virtues, the Tathāgata says, are not good, but are called good virtues.

Subhūti, when [the Tathāgata] expounds the dharma, there is really no dharma to teach: but this is called teaching the dharma.[6]

This paradox finds its "purest" philosophical expression in Mādhyamika. Nāgārjuna insisted that the Buddha himself had no philosophical views, and his own approach was solely concerned to demonstrate
that all philosophical positions are self-contradictory and untenable.
In the process he had occasion to employ the term *śūnyatā* (emptiness),
but woe to him who grasps this snake by the wrong end and takes
śūnyatā as making some *positive* assertion about the nature of reality:
"The spiritual conquerors have proclaimed *śūnyatā* to be the exhaustion of all theories and views; those for whom *śūnyatā* is itself a theory
they declare to be incurable."[7] Insofar as the assertion of any philosophical position negates the opposite view, Mādhyamika may be said
to have developed the critique of dualistic thinking to its most extreme
philosophical conclusions. Ch'an (Zen) took this one step further and
eliminated even Nāgārjuna's anti-philosophy:

> The fundamental dharma of the dharma is that there are no dharmas,
> yet that this dharma of no-dharma is in itself a dharma; and now that
> the no-dharma dharma has been transmitted, how can the dharma of
> the dharma be a dharma?   (Huang Po)[8]

The result of this was that no teaching whatsoever—not even anti-
teaching—remained to be taught. Instead, Ch'an masters used various unconventional and illogical techniques to awaken a student,
which in this context means to make the student let go of any dualities
that he or she still clings to.

But isn't it the general nature of all reasoning to move between
assertion and negation, between "it *is*" and "it is *not*"? The critique of
dualistic thinking thus often expands to include all conceptual thinking or conceptualization.

> You can never come to enlightenment through inference, cognition, or
> conceptualization. Cease clinging to all thought-forms! I stress this,
> because it is the central point of all Zen practice....
>   ...You must melt down your delusions.... The opinions you hold
> and your worldly knowledge are your delusions. Included also are
> philosophical and moral concepts, no matter how lofty, as well as
> religious beliefs and dogmas, not to mention innocent, commonplace
> thoughts. In short, all conceivable ideas are embraced within the term
> "delusions" and as such are a hindrance to the realization of your
> Essential-nature.   (Yasutani)[9]

This expanded version of the critique seems to encompass all thinking whatsoever, obliterating Hui Hai's distinction between wrong thinking and right thinking. Now the problem with dualistic categories is that they are part of a conceptual grid which we normally but unconsciously superimpose upon our immediate experience and which deludes us by distorting that experience. Yasutani's admonition is so absolute that is seems to condemn all possible thought-processes, but such a radical "inflation" only strengthens the obvious objection to this type of critique: whether it is (more narrowly) dualistic thinking or (more generally) conceptual thinking that is problematic and to be rejected, what is the alternative? What kind of thinking remains? If all language seems to dualize, in distinguishing subject from predicate/attribute, how can there be such a thing as nondual, or nonconceptual, thinking? Can we get along without dualistic categories? And even if we can, is it desirable? The nature of any alternative—or is it no thinking whatsoever?—needs to be explained, and its feasibility defended. But the issue cannot be resolved at this stage in our inquiry. We return to the question of nondual thought in chapter 4.

THE NONPLURALITY OF THE WORLD

What is here, the same is there; and what is there, the same is here. He goes from death to death who sees any difference here.

By the mind alone is Brahman to be realized; then one does not see in It any multiplicity whatsoever. He goes from death to death who sees any multiplicity in It.
　　　　　　　　　　　　　　　　　　　　—Kaṭha Upaniṣad[10]

It is due to the superimpositions of dualistic thinking that we experience the world itself dualistically in our second sense: as a collection of discrete objects (one of them being *me*) causally interacting in space and time. The negation of dualistic thinking leads to the negation of this way of experiencing the world. This brings us to the second sense of nonduality: that the world itself is nonplural, because all the things "in" the world are not really distinct from each other but together constitute some integral whole. The relation between these two senses of nonduality is shown by Huang Po at the very beginning of his Chun Chou record:

All the Buddhas and all sentient beings are nothing but the One Mind, beside which nothing exists. This mind, which is without beginning, is unborn and undestructible. It is not green nor yellow, and has neither form nor appearance. It does not belong to the categories of things which exist or do not exist, nor can it be thought about in terms of new or old. It is neither long nor short, big nor small, for it transcends all limits, measures, names, traces and comparisons. It is that which you see before you—begin to reason about it and you at once fall into error.[11]

This asserts more than that everything is composed of some indefinable substance. The unity of everything "in" the world means that each thing is a manifestation of a "spiritual" whole because the One Mind incorporates all consciousness and all minds. This whole—indivisible, birthless, and deathless—has been designated by a variety of terms; as well as the One Mind, there are the Tao, Brahman, the Dharmakāya, and so on.

There is a beginning which contains everything.
Before heaven and earth it exists:
Calm! Formless!
It stands alone and does not change.
It pervades everywhere unhindered.
It might therefore be called the world's mother.
I do not know its name; but I call it the Tao.   (Tao Tê Ching)[12]

Now, all this [universe] was then undifferentiated. It became differentiated by name and form: it was known by such and such a name, and such and such a form. Thus to this day this [universe] is differentiated by name and form; [so it is said:] He has such a name and such a form."   (Bṛhadāraṇyaka Upaniṣad)[13]

Changes in one's train of thought produce corresponding changes in one's conception of the external world....
     As a thing is viewed, so it appears.
     To see things as a multiplicity, and so to cleave unto separateness, is to err.   (Padmasaṁbhava)[14]

The mechanism of differentiation identified in this passage from the Bṛhadāraṇyaka Upaniṣad—nāmarūpa (name and form), which is a common Vedāntic description of māyā—is also mentioned in the first chapter of the Tao Tê Ching (discussed in chapter 3), where it serves the same function in differentiating the Tao. Compare too the following quotation from Chuang Tzu:

The knowledge of the ancients was perfect. How perfect? At first, they did not know that there were things. This is the most perfect knowledge; nothing can be added. Next, they knew that there were things, but did not yet make distinctions between them. Next they made distinctions among them, but they did not yet pass judgements upon them. When judgements were passed, Tao was destroyed.[15]

Thus we have passages from four different traditions—the Upaniṣads, Tibetan Buddhism, Taoism, and Zen—which explicitly affirm the same relationship between these first two senses of nonduality: that dualistic conceptual thinking is what causes us to experience a pluralistic world.

If we compare the following two passages with the long quotation from Huang Po at the beginning of this section, we have our first encounter with a controversy that develops into a major theme of this book:

This Self is that which has been described as *not this, not this*. It is imperceptible, for It is not perceived; undecaying, for It never decays; unattached, for It is never attached; unfettered, for It never feels pain and never suffers injury. (Bṛhadāraṇyaka Upaniṣad)[16]

Gaze at it; there is nothing to see.
It is called the formless.
Heed it; there is nothing to hear.
It is called the soundless.
Grasp it; there is nothing to hold onto.
It is called the immaterial ....
. . . .
Invisible, it cannot be called by any name.
It returns again to nothingness.
Thus, we call it the form of the formless
The image of the imageless. (*Tao Tê Ching*)[17]

These selections claim that the Ātman/Tao is not perceptible. Huang Po agrees that the One Mind is formless, colorless, and without appearance, yet he also says "it is that which you see before you." In the next chapter Śaṅkara is quoted to the same effect: "the universe is an unbroken series of perceptions of Brahman." This brings us to the inevitable question about the relationship between the nonplural Ātman/Tao/One Mind and the multiple sensible particulars of this world. Are phenomena merely delusive māyā (illusions) that obscure this attributeless Mind, or are they manifestations of It? Strictly speaking, perhaps the former view cannot be said to maintain nonplurality as the unity of phenomena, but rather postulates a monistic ground that "underlies" them. This seems to create another duality—between phenomena and Mind, between duality and nonduality—which becomes problematic, as we shall see. In contrast, the latter view does not necessarily imply monism at all, depending on how monism is defined. A weaker version of pluralism, that there are many things, may be compatible with a weaker version of monism, that there is only one *type* of thing (e.g., Mind), of which the many particulars are manifestations—a perspective which is important for understanding Mahāyāna metaphysics.

The Upaniṣads and the *Tao Tĕ Ching* also contain passages which imply another intermediate position between monism and pluralism: that the Ātman/Tao functions as a first cause which created the phenomenal world and then pervades it as a kind of spiritual essence. The first passage quoted above from the Bṛhadāraṇyaka Upaniṣad continues:

> This Self has entered into these bodies up to the very tips of the nails, as a razor lies [hidden] in its case, or as fire, which sustains the world, [lies hidden] in its source.[18]

There is the same claim in the Kaṭha Upaniṣad:

> As the same nondual fire, after it has entered the world, becomes different according to whatever it burns, so also the same nondual Ātman, dewlling in all beings, becomes different according to whatever It enters. And It exists also without.[19]

Such a view may be criticized as incomplete—as tending toward, but stopping short of, complete nonduality in the second sense; despite differences in their perspective, neither Huang Po nor Śaṅkara would accept such a distinction between pervader and pervaded. Perhaps the difference is due to the unrigorous nature of these early works, for both the *Tao Tĕ Ching* and the Upaniṣads are collections of mystical insights rather than systematic philosophical works.

It is noteworthy that, although there are many references to the Tao in Taoist texts and to Ātman/Brahman in Vedānta, there are fewer such references in Buddhism. There is not even any agreed-upon term; a variety of expressions are used: *dharmadhātu, dharmakāya, tathatā, vijñāptimātratā,* and so on. These are all Mahāyāna terms; there is no good equivalent in Pāli Buddhism because early Buddhism is more pluralistic in its preoccupation with the interrelations of dharmas. Generally, Buddhism, with the exception of Yogācāra, is hesitant to assert a nondual whole in this second sense, preferring to emphasize that everything is empty *(śūnya)* while offering admonitions against dualistic thinking. This inverse proportion is quite logical: dualistic thinking in the broad sense includes any conceptual labeling, hence one should not name even the nondual whole. After all, any Tao that can be Tao'd is not the real Tao.

THE NONDIFFERENCE OF SUBJECT AND OBJECT

I came to realize clearly that mind is no other than mountains, rivers, and the great wide earth, the sun and the moon and the stars.

—Dōgen[20]

We have seen the connection between the first two dualities: it is because of our dualistic ways of thinking that we perceive the world pluralistically. The relationship between the corresponding nondualities is parallel: the world as a collection of discrete things (including *me*) in space and time is not something objectively given, which we merely observe passively; if our ways of thinking change, that world changes also for us. But there is still something lacking in this formulation. By itself it is incomplete, for it leaves unclarified the relation between the subject and the nondual world that the subject experiences. It was stated earlier that the nondual whole is "spiritual" because the One Mind includes my mind, but *how* consciousness could be incorporated has not been explained. The world is not really experienced as a whole if the subject that perceives it is still separate from it in its observation *of* it. In this way the second sense of nonduality, conceived objectively, is unstable and naturally tends to evolve into a third sense. This third sense, like the other two, must be understood as a negation. The dualism denied is our usual distinction between subject and object, an experiencing self that is distinct from what is experienced, be it sense-object, physical action, or mental event. The corresponding nonduality is experience in which there is no such distinction between subject and object. However extraordinary and counterintuitive such nonduality may be, it is an essential element of many Asian systems (and some Western ones, of course). Since the primary purpose of this work is to analyze this third sense of nonduality, it is necessary to establish in detail the prevalence and significance of this concept.

■

We begin with Vedānta. Several of the most important passages in the Upaniṣads assert this nonduality; for example, these famous ones from the Bṛhadāraṇyaka:

> Because when there is duality, as it were, then one smells something, one sees something, one hears something, one speaks something, one thinks something, one knows something. [But] when to the knower of Brahman everything has become the Self, then what should one smell and through what, what should one see and through what, [repeated for hearing, speaking, thinking and knowing]? Through what should one know That owing to which all this is known—through what, O Maitreyī, should one know the Knower?

> And when [it appears that] in deep sleep it does not see, yet it is seeing though it does not see; for there is no cessation of the vision of the seer, because the seer is imperishable. There is then, however, no second thing separate from the seer that it could see. [To emphasize the point, this verse is repeated, in place of seeing substituting smelling, tasting, speaking, hearing, thinking, touching and knowing.][21]

The nonduality of subject and object also constitutes the heart of the short Īśā Upaniṣad: "To the seer, all things have verily become the Self: what delusion, what sorrow, can there be for him who beholds that oneness?"[22] The Taittirīya Upaniṣad concludes with it:

> He [who knows Brahman] sits, singing the chant of the nonduality of Brahman: "Ah! Ah! Ah!"
> "I am food, I am food, I am food! I am the eater of food, I am the eater of food, I am the eater of food! I am the uniter, I am the uniter, I am the uniter!
> "... He who eats food—I, as food, eat him."[23]

So many other passages could be cited that I can say, with no exaggeration, that asserting this third sense of nonduality constitutes the central claim of the Upaniṣads. It is most often expressed as the identity between Ātman (the Self) and Brahman, implied by the most famous *mahāvākya* (great saying) of all: *tat tvam asi* (that thou art).[24] Such an interpretation is of course crucial to Advaita (lit., nondual) Vedānta, and the great Advaitin philosopher Śaṅkara devoted an entire work to expounding it, the short *Vākyavṛtti*. A stanza from the *Ātmabodha* gives a clear and succinct expression of his view:

> The distinction of the knower, knowledge, and the goal of knowledge does not endure in the all-transcendent Self. Being of the nature of Bliss that is Pure Consciousness, it shines of Itself.[25]

In his commentary on passages from the Bṛhadāraṇyaka quoted above, Śaṅkara insists that our usual sense of subject–object duality is delusive:

> When, in the waking or dream state, there is something else besides the self, as it were, presented by ignorance, then one, thinking of oneself as different from that something—though there is nothing different from the self, nor is there any self different from it—can see something.[26]

The phrase "as it were" (Sanskrit, *iva*) emphasizes that the appearance to the subject of something objective is what constitutes *avidyā*, ignorance or delusion. This claim is by no means unique to Vedānta; it is found in virtually all the Asian philosophies that assert this third sense of nonduality: our experience not only can be but already is and always was nondual; any sense of a subject apart from that which is experienced is an illusion. According to this view, it is not correct to say that our usual experience is dualistic, for all experience is actually nondual. The spiritual path involves eliminating only the delusion of duality. However variously the different systems may otherwise characterize this nondual reality, the goal is simply to *realize* and *live* this nondual nature.

The foremost Advaitin of the twentieth century supports and re-states the traditional Vedāntic position on nonduality:

> The duality of subject and object, the trinity of seer, sight and seen can exist only if supported by the One. If one turns inward in search of that One Reality, they fall away.

> The world is perceived as an apparent objective reality when the mind is externalized, thereby abandoning its identity with the Self. When the world is thus perceived the true nature of the Self is not revealed;

conversely, when the Self is realized the world ceases to appear as an objective reality.   (Ramana Maharshi)[27]

■

Advaita Vedānta clearly asserts nonduality in our third sense, to the extent of making it the central tenet. The case of Buddhism is more complicated. Ontologically, Pāli Buddhism, which bases itself on what are understood to be the original teachings of the Buddha, seems pluralistic. Reality is understood to consist of a multitude of discrete particulars (*dharmas*). The self is analyzed away into five "heaps" (*skandhas*) which the Abhidharma (the "higher dharma," a philosophical abstract of the Buddha's teachings) classifies and systematizes. So early Buddhism, while critical of dualistic thinking, is not nondual in the second, monistic, sense. Regarding the nondifference of subject and object, the issue is less clear. While the second sense of nonduality logically implies some version of the third, it is not true that a denial of the second sense implies a denial of the third. The world might be a composite of discrete experiences which are nondual in the third sense. I am not acquainted with any passage in the Pāli Canon that clearly asserts the nonduality of subject and object, as one finds in so many Mahāyāna texts. But I have also found no denial of such nonduality. One may view the *anātman* (no-self) doctrine of early Buddhism as another way of making the same point; instead of asserting that subject and object are one, the Buddha simply denies that there is a subject. These two formulations may well amount to the same thing, although the latter may be criticized as ontologically lopsided: since subject and object are interdependent, the subject cannot be eliminated without transforming the nature of the object (and vice-versa, as Advaita Vedānta was aware). This issue is discussed in chapter 6 as part of a broader consideration of the ontological differences between Buddhism and Vedānta.

Mahāyāna Buddhism abounds in assertions of subject–object nonduality, despite the fact that the most important Mahāyāna philosophy, Mādhyamika, cannot be said to assert nonduality at all, since it makes few (if any) positive claims but confines itself to refuting all philosophical positions. Mādhyamika is *advayavāda* (the theory of not-two, here meaning neither of two alternative views, our first sense of nonduality) rather than *advaitavāda* (the theory of nondifference between subject and object, our third sense).[28] *Prajñā* is understood to be nondual knowledge, but this again is *advaya*, knowledge devoid of views. Nāgārjuna neither asserts nor denies the experience of nonduality in the third sense, despite the fact that Mādhyamika dialectic criticizes the self-existence of both subject and object, since as relative to each other they must both be unreal.

> Nāgārjuna holds that dependent origination is nothing else but the coming to rest of the manifold of named things (*prapañcopaśama*). When the everyday mind and its contents are no longer active, the subject and object of everyday transactions having faded out because the turmoil of origination, decay, and death has been left behind completely, that is final beatitude. (Candrakīrti)[29]

In comparison, Yogācāra literature contains many explicit passages asserting the identity of subject and object. These from Vasubandhu are perhaps the best known:

> Through the attainment of the state of Pure Consciousness, there is the non-perception of the perceivable; and through the non-perception of the perceivable (i.e., the object) there is the non-acquisition of the mind (i.e., the subject).
> Through the non-perception of these two, there arises the realization of the Essence of Reality (*dharmadhātu*).[30]

> Where there is an object there is a subject, but not where there is no object. The absence of an object results in the absence also of a subject, and not merely in that of grasping. It is thus that there arises the cognition which is homogeneous, without object, indiscriminate and supermundane. The tendencies to treat object and subject as distinct and real entities are forsaken, and thought is established in just the true nature of one's thought. (Vasubandhu)[31]

The Yogācāra claim of *cittamātra* (mind-only), that only mind or consciousness exists, predictably gave rise to the misinterpretation (corrected in recent works) that Yogācāra is a form of subjective idealism. But subjectivism is not an aspect of any Buddhist school, nor, given the vital role of the anātman doctrine, could it be. As these two passages imply, for Yogācāra the apparently objective world is not a projection of my ego-consciousness. Rather, the delusive bifurcation between subject and object arises within nondual Mind. So in the *parinispanna-svabhāva* (absolutely accomplished nature), which is the

highest state of existence, experience is without subject–object duality.
In Yogācāra the claim that experience is nondual, in all three of our
senses, attains full development and explicitness, and so it is fitting
that with that claim Buddhist philosophy may be said to have reached
its culmination. What followed were derivative elaborations and syn-
theses (popular in Chinese Buddhism, e.g., T'ien T'ai and Hua Yen)
and the application of these philosophical perspectives to practice
(especially Pure Land, Ch'an, and tantric Buddhism). What is most
significant for us is that the third sense of nonduality, the nondifference between subject and object, was essential to all of them.
(Hereafter, unless otherwise noted, the term *nonduality* will always
refer to this third sense.)

The nonduality of subject and object is also the central concept of
both Hindu and Buddhist tantra, according to S. B. Dasgupta:

> The ultimate goal of both the schools is the perfect state of union—
> union between the two aspects of the reality and the realization of the
> nondual nature of the self and the not-self. The principle of Tantricism
> being fundamentally the same everywhere, the superficial differences,
> whatever these may be, supply only different tone and colour.

> The synthesis or rather the unification of all duality in an absolute unity
> is the real principle of union, which has been termed *Yuganaddha* . . . the
> real principle of *Yuganaddha* is the absence of the notion of duality as the
> perceivable (*grāhya*) and the perceiver (*grāhaka*) and their perfect syn-
> thesis in a unity.[32]

Evans-Wentz's translations of Tibetan Buddhist texts provide examples to support Dasgupta's view. From the "Yoga of Knowing the
Mind," attributed to Padmasaṁbhava:

> There being really no duality, pluralism is untrue.
> Until duality is transcended and at-one-ment realized, enlighten-
> ment cannot be attained.
> The whole *Sangsara* and *Nirvana*, as an inseparable unity, are one's
> mind. . . .
> The unenlightened externally see the externally-transitory dually.[33]

We find this exemplified in the *Mahāmudrā* (Yoga of the Great Symbol), which provides a set of graded meditations. The final two practices are, first, "the Yoga of Transmuting all Phenomena and Mind,

which are inseparable, into At-one-ment (or Unity)." This involves meditations on the nonduality between sleep and dreams, water and ice, water and waves. Finally, there is "the Yoga of Non-Meditation," which simply signifies the end of effort, since with the above transmutation into nonduality one has completed the Path: "one obtaineth the Supreme Boon of the Great Symbol, the Unabiding State of Nirvana."[34]

More recently, the Italian scholar Guiseppe Tucci has summarized the final objective of Tibetan Buddhist soteriology as follows:

Higher cognition is the penetrating to, and cognizing of, the true nature of these appearances, of these forms created by our discursive knowledge, these products of a false dichotomy between subject and object.... The final objective remains the awakening of that higher cognition, that *shes rab*, Sanskrit *prajñā*, in the adept's consciousness, which enables him to survey the ultimate nature of all things with the clarity of direct insight; in other words, the transcending of the subject–object dichotomy.[35]

In his voluminous writings on Zen, D. T. Suzuki repeatedly emphasized that the *satori* experience is the realization of nonduality. For example, in the first series of his *Essays on Zen Buddhism*, during a discussion of "original Mind," he states that "there is no separation between knower and known." Zen is "the unfolding of a new world hitherto unperceived in the confusion of the dualistically-trained mind."[36] There are many traditional Zen dialogues to support this:

Monk: "If Self-nature is pure, and belongs to no categories of duality such as being and non-being, etc., where does this seeing take place?"
Chih of Yun-chu (8th Century): "There is seeing, but nothing seen."
Monk: "If there is nothing seen, how can we say there is any seeing at all?"
Chih: "In fact there is no trace of seeing."
Monk: "In such a seeing, whose seeing is it?"
Chih: "There is no seer, either."

Another monk asked Wei-kuan: "Where is Tao?"
Kuan: "Right before us."
Monk: "Why don't I see it?"
Kuan: "Because of your egotism you cannot see it."

Monk: "If I cannot see it because of my egotism, does your reverence see it?"

Kuan: "As long as there is 'I and thou', this complicates the situation and there is no seeing Tao."

Monk: "When there is neither 'I' nor 'thou' is it seen?"

Kuan: "When there is neither 'I' nor 'thou', who is here to see it?"[37]

What is arguably the most famous of all Zen stories—purporting to describe how Hui Neng became the Sixth Patriarch—presents the Zen concept of "no mind" (Ch. *wu-hsin*, Jap. *mushin*), which asserts, in effect, the nonduality of subject and object. According to the auto-biographical first part of the Platform Sutra, Shen Hsiu, head monk at the Fifth Patriarch's monastery, submitted a stanza comparing the mind to a mirror which must be constantly wiped free of all concept-dust. In response, Hui Neng composed a stanza denying that there is any such mind-mirror: "since all is empty from the beginning, where can the dust alight?" The Fifth Patriarch publicly praised Shen Hsiu's verse as showing the proper way to practice, but privately criticized it as revealing that Shen Hsiu had not yet become enlightened. His view was still dualistic, conceiving of the mind as a mirror which reflects an external world. Hui Neng's verse points out that there is no such mind apart from the world.

In his explanation of "no mind," D. T. Suzuki emphasizes the significance of this story for Zen.

Hui Neng and his followers now came to use the new term *chien-hsing* instead of the old *k'an-ching* [to keep an eye on purity]. *chien-hsing* means "to look into the nature (of the Mind)." *K'an* and *chien* both relate to the sense of sight, but the character *k'an*, which consists of a hand and an eye, is to watch an object as independent of the spectator; the seen and the seeing are two separate entities. *Chien*, composed of an eye alone on two outstretched legs, signifies the pure act of seeing.... The seeing is not reflecting on an object as if the seer had nothing to do with it. The seeing, on the contrary, brings the seer and the object seen together, not in mere identification but the becoming conscious of itself, or rather of its working.[38]

The teachings of contemporary Zen masters also support the centrality of nonduality in Zen experience. Here are excerpts from Yasutani-rōshi's private interviews with Westerners during a meditation retreat:

There is a line a famous Zen master wrote at the time he became enlightened which reads: "When I heard the temple bell ring, suddenly there was no bell and no I, just sound." In other words, he no longer was aware of a distinction between himself, the bell, the sound, and the universe. This is the state you have to reach.

Kenshō [self-realization] is the direct awareness that you are more than this puny body or limited mind. Stated negatively, it is the realization that the universe is not external to you. Positively, it is experiencing the universe as yourself.[39]

Devotional Pure Land Buddhism, which emphasizes dependence upon Amitābha to help one be reborn in Sukhāvatī (the Western paradise of Mahāyāna), is not treated in detail in this work. But Shinran's development of Pure Land Buddhism into Shin Buddhism, a school that has been more popular in Japan than Zen, is relevant to my purpose. Shinran redefined Pure Land doctrine in the direction of nonduality. Rebirth in the Pure Land is not a stepping-stone to nirvana but is itself "complete unsurpassed enlightenment." Faith for Shinran was not merely belief in the power and benevolence of some external force; in the words of one commentator, "The awakening of faith in Shin Buddhism is an instant of pure egolessness."[40] This happens when we surrender to the infinite compassion of Amitābha, who is not an external God or Buddha but Reality itself, which is also our own true nature.

The Compassion of all the Buddhas, though transcending all the categories of thought, including those of subject and object, appears to our ego-oriented perception as a force which acts upon us externally— as the Other Power [*tariki*]. This Shinran makes quite clear when he says "What is called external power is as much as to say that there is no discrimination of this or that." To surrender to the Other Power means to transcend the distinction between subject and object. As we identify ourselves with Amida, so Amida identifies himself with us. (Sangharakshita)[41]

Unfortunately, the emphasis upon *tariki* (Other Power) has too often led to minimizing the importance of any personal meditation practice, continuing the traditional division between Pure Land and Zen, which emphasizes *jiriki* (self-effort). This disagreement is due to a misunderstanding: nonduality seems to imply the negation of the

opposition between tariki and jiriki in an effort which is not identified
as either mine or another's. We might say that the effort Amida exerts
to identify with me is at the same time my effort to identify with him.

●

None of the three classical Taoist texts—*Tao Tê Ching, Chuang Tzu*, and
Lieh Tzu—is as definitive as Vedānta and Mahāyāna in denying subject–object duality. There are several passages in the *Tao Tê Ching* (e.g.,
in chapter 13) which may hint at such nonduality, but they are unclear.
The *Chuang Tzu* is less ambiguous. "The perfect man has no self; the
spiritual man has no achievement; the true sage has no name." "If
there is no other, there will be no I. If there is no I, there will be none to
make distinctions."[42] In chapter 6, "The Great Teacher," Nu Chü
teaches the Tao to Pu Liang I:

> After three days, he [Pu Liang I] began to be able to disregard all
> worldly matters. After his having disregarded all worldly matters, seven
> days later he was able to disregard all external things; after nine days, his
> own existence. Having disregarded his own existence, he was
> enlightened ... was able to gain vision of the One ... able to transcend
> the distinction of past and present ... able to enter into the realm where
> life and death are no more.[43]

This and other passages refer to the negation of duality while in
meditative trance. We find the same in the *Lieh Tzu*, where Lieh Tzu
learns to "ride on the wind" by meditating until "Internal and External were blended into Unity."[44] Such passages strongly imply, but do
not explicitly state, that the goal, the resulting experience of Tao, is also
nondual. Some other *Chuang Tzu* passages, however, are more explicit.
The first quotation in this chapter is from the *Chuang Tzu*, criticizing
dualistic thinking; it continues:

> Thereupon, the "self" is also the "other"; the "other" is the "self". . . . But
> really are there such distinctions as "self" and "other", or are there no
> such distinctions? When "self" and "other" lose their contrareity, there
> we have the very essence of the Tao.

Chuang Tzu repeatedly urges: "Identify yourself with the infinite";
"hide the universe in the universe."[45] But how are we to do this? "With
the state of pure experience," explains Fung Yu-lan in the introduction to his translation of the *Chuang Tzu*:

In the state of pure experience, what is known as the union of the individual with the whole is reached. In this state there is an unbroken flux of experience, but the experiencer does not know it. He does not know that there are things, to say nothing of making distinctions between them. There is no separation of things, to say nothing to the distinction between subject and object, between the "me" and the "non-me." So in this state of experience, there is nothing but the one, the whole.[46]

Another contemporary commentator, Chang Chung-yuan, agrees: "the awareness of the identification and interpenetration of self and nonself is the key that unlocks the mystery of Tao."

Chih [intuitive knowledge] is the key word to understanding Tao and unlocking all the secrets of nonbeing. In other words, intuitive knowledge is pure self-consciousness through immediate, direct, primitive penetration instead of by the methods that are derivative, inferential, or rational. In the sphere of intuitive knowledge there is no separation between the knower and the known; subject and object are identified.[47]

Having established the significance of subject–object nonduality for Taoism, the presentation of nondualities comes to an end. I have offered a number of passages from Vedāntic, Buddhist, and Taoist sources and have referred to the opinions of many respected scholars commenting on these traditions. The point of this exercise has been to establish, indubitably and in detail, the central importance of the concept of nonduality for these three traditions, which we now see can well be called "nondualist traditions." Various meanings of the term nonduality have been determined. The chapter began by distinguishing five such meanings and has analyzed three of them: the negation of dualistic (more generally, conceptual) thinking, the nonplurality of the world, and the nondifference of subject and object. Given the interrelations among these three meanings, it is significant that all three of them are important for all three of our nondualist traditions, although there are differences in emphasis. For example, Buddhist texts contain more admonitions against dualistic thinking and fewer claims about the nonplurality of the world, as we have seen. Generally, explicit assertions of subject–object nonduality are less common in China than in metaphysical India, reflecting their different philosophical interests, and as a consequence Indian sources are cited more often in the chapters that follow. My emphasis continues to be on the third sense of nonduality, but the relationships among all three also continue to be important. Many other passages could be quoted, and other traditions incorporated, both non-Western (e.g., Sufism) and Western (e.g., Plotinus and other examples of the *philosophia perennis*). These are not included partly for reason of space but primarily because our three nondual philosophies are the ones that have developed the concept of nonduality in the greatest detail, providing more than sufficient material on the topic.

When we put together the claims embodied in these three meanings of nonduality, what do we end up with? Due to our dualistic, conceptual ways of thinking, we experience the world as a collection of discrete objects interacting in space and time. One of these objects is *me*: I experience myself as a subject looking out at an external world and anxious about my relationship with it. Expressed in this way, the peculiarity of such an understanding becomes more obvious, for certainly I must be "in" my world in a different way than this pen I am writing with. The nondualist systems agree that this way of experiencing is not the only posssible way, and not the best way, because it involves delusion about the true nature both of the world and of ourselves, and that delusion causes suffering. If our thinking changes, if our dualistic ways of thinking are transformed in some as yet unspecified manner, we shall experience the world as nonplural and, most important of all, we shall overcome our alienation in realizing our nondual unity with it. This spiritual experience will reveal to us for the first time our true nature, which is also the true nature of the world: formless, indivisible, birthless and deathless, and beyond the comprehension of the intellect. But we have also noticed what may be a serious disagreement about the precise relationship between this imperceptible One and sensible phenomena.

This is provocative, but of course it is not much. So far, it is too vague to be very meaningful, much less persuasive—only the bare bones of a hypothesis, which needs much fleshing in to become a living theory. Developing this hypothesis into a core doctrine of nonduality, finding the common ground largely agreeable to all three nondualist systems, is the concern of the next three chapters. Each one takes a specific mode of our experience—perceiving, acting, and thinking—and asks: what does the claim about nonduality actually mean in this context? For example, in the following chapter we attempt to determine what nondual perception is, by integrating what the nondualist systems say about perception and by considering in what ways this is or is not consistent with our own experience.

In these three chapters, I hope to describe a theory about nondual experience that not only is consistent with the major claims of Buddhism, Vedānta, and Taoism but also speaks to our condition.

CHAPTER 2
NONDUAL PERCEPTION

The eye that I see God with is the same eye God sees me with.
My eye and God's eye are one and the same.

God is abstract being, pure perception, which is perceiving itself in itself.

—Eckhart

THE REALITY OF APPEARANCE

Reality without appearances would be nothing, for there certainly is nothing outside appearances.

—F. H. Bradley, *Appearance and Reality*

According to many "illuminative" philosophies, both Eastern and Western, sense-perceptions are delusive and must in some way be transcended. This is particularly true for the nondualist Asian philosophies discussed in Chapter One. For Śaṅkara, the world as perceived, although not illusory from a phenomenal point of view, must ultimately be subrated and realized to be dream-like *māyā*, for only Brahman is really Real.[1] In the Fire Sermon, the Buddha states that his disciples should have aversion to sense-organs, sense-objects, sense-contact, and sense-consciousness, in which case passion will fade away and liberation occurs. Such claims seem to be recommending the negation of sense-phenomena in order to experience a Reality apart from them. This interpretation is consistent with a predisposition we have inherited from the Western metaphysical tradition, Parmenides through Kant, to distinguish between the constantly changing world of phenomena that the senses present to us and an unchanging Reality "behind" them; the former is usually devalued in favor of the latter, whose nature it is the task of philosophy to determine. Plato's Ideas (or Forms) are to be directly experienced by intellect alone, purified of any relationship with the senses, thus establishing a dichotomy that has had fateful consequences for Western philosophy and Western culture. It has been just as fateful for the Eastern tradition that this dichotomy did not occur, for as we shall see, the nondualist systems look upon the conceptualizing mind as a "sixth sense" which needs to be "transcended" at least as much as the other five—perhaps more.

The problem with this usual interpretation is that many puzzling passages, often attributable to the same sources, are incompatible with such a blanket rejection of sense-perception. In the *Vivekacūḍāmaṇi*, Śaṅkara makes a claim that seems inconsistent with his other views, but perhaps it is just inconsistent with others' views of him: "The universe is an unbroken series of perceptions of Brahman; hence it is in all respects nothing but Brahman."[2] In one of the Honeyball sutras, the Buddha teaches the monk Bahiya that the end of suffering—that is, nirvana—is to be found in training himself so that "in the seen there will be just the seen; in the heard, just the heard; in smelling, touching, tasting, just smelling, touching, tasting; in the cognized, just the cognized."[3] Both these passages suggest that sense-perception itself is not the problem: rather, Reality is staring us in the face all the time, but somehow we misperceive it.

How are we to reconcile these claims—by no means uncommon, as we shall see—with those critical of the senses? I argue in this chapter that what must be transcended is not sense-perception in toto but a certain type of sense-perception which, because we are not usually familiar with any alternative type, we tend to identify with sense-perception generally. As the Buddha recommends and Śaṅkara implies, another kind of sense-perceiving can be developed that reveals Reality—or, to be more exact, is Reality. (This is complicated by the fact, to be discussed later, that this other way of perceiving might not be termed sense-perception at all, since it can be argued that the act of perception is relative to perceiver and to sense-object, both of which are lacking in this other sense-perception. As a result, what might be called "only-perception" turns out to be equivalent to no perception. This is only the first example of a paradox that recurs many times in this book.) The difference between these two types of sense-perception is the difference between dualistic and nondualistic perception. The former, perception as we normally experience it (or interpret it), is sense-perception in which there is a distinction between the perceiver and the object perceived. The latter is nondual because there is no such distinction; therefore it has sometimes been described by denying (as Buddhism does) that there is a subject perceiving and sometimes by denying (as Vedānta does) that there is an external, objective world which is perceived. In such perception there is no longer any distinction between internal (mind) and external (world), or between consciousness and its object.

This chapter develops this conception of nondual perception. The second section examines in some detail the views of Buddhism and Advaita Vedānta on the nature of perception, and on the basis of those views constructs a theory or "core model" which, with some qualification, is consistent with both nondualistic systems. In the following section I ground these generalizations about perception with an examination of hearing and seeing, using Berkeley and Hume to develop this theory into a more coherent claim. The fourth section relates nondual perception to Western theories of perception, places it within contemporary epistemology as a version of phenomenalism, considers how it fares against the objections usually raised against phenomenalism, and reports on two psychological experiments into meditation that seem to support the possibility of nondual perception.

The implication of this view is that the commonsense, apparently objective world that we usually take for granted—which is understood to be composed of discrete material objects causally interacting in space and time—is a fiction the mind creates by superimposing its thought-constructions upon perceptions. Such an approach is not unfamiliar to modern Western philosophy, for it has some affinity with the basic stance of Kant's metaphysics. But there are two fundamental differences between such nonduality and Kantian metaphysics. First, whether this thought-construction is due completely to language acquisition and other socialization, or partly to innate faculties of the mind, the claim of the nondualist Asian systems is that this process can be undone—quite literally deconstructed or "de-automatized"—which is why their basic attitude is soteriological as much as philosophical. Such deconstruction is possible because of the second difference. One of the problems with Kant's distinction between *noumena* (things-in-themselves) and *phenomena* (things as we experience them) is that, while maintaining that causality is a category applicable only to phenomena, he also inferred that things-in-themselves must be the causes of phenomenal appearances. Nor can Kant easily escape this inconsistency, for without some such view there is no reason to postulate the existence of things-in-themselves at all, since he believed that they cannot in principle ever be directly experienced. The nondualist is not subject to such a criticism, since things-in-themselves—what I call nondual percepts, in the case of perception—are experienced immediately upon the cessation of thought-construction. Such a view avoids the postulation of a Reality "behind" Appearance. Rather, Reality is Appearance itself, although this of course cannot be appearance as we normally understand it, which is appearance *of* something. The nondualist explanation turns the usual view upside down: it is our normal, commonsense understanding—in which we distinguish between physical objects and their appearance to us—that is guilty (as Berkeley and Nietzsche realized) of metaphysically postulating a reality "behind" appearance. This was so obvious to Berkeley that he was surprised when others did not accept his critique of matter, that mysterious stuff we never actually experience. Like Vasubandhu long before him, he was denying not sensible qualities, such as impermeability, but the self-existing substratum to which they supposedly adhere. In this way the nondualist presents us with the possibility of actually returning to things-in-themselves, percepts as they are, before they have been thought-constructed into the dualistic world of a subject confronting a materialized world of discrete objects.

Soon after Berkeley there lived an English engraver and poet for whom this was not just philosophy but life itself, and we shall have occasion to quote him often in the pages that follow.

The whole creation will be consumed and appear infinite and holy, whereas it now appears finite and corrupt.

This will come to pass by an improvement of sensual enjoyment.

But first the notion that man has a body distinct from his soul is to be expunged . . . .

If the doors of perception were cleansed, everything would appear to man as it is, infinite. For man has closed himself up, till he sees all things thro' narrow chinks of his cavern.   (William Blake)[4]

PERCEPTION IN BUDDHISM AND ADVAITA VEDĀNTA

It was not until Kant that Western philosophy became truly aware of the role of the mind in sense-perception: how the mind does not just receive but interprets and synthesizes perceptions into the phenomenal world we experience. That perception involves conception is a commonplace of contemporary philosophy, although attention has shifted from Kant's Aristotelian categories to language as the means by which this organization occurs. But Indian philosophy has been aware of this since at least the time of the Buddha. After a brief introduction to the Indian distinction between *nirvikalpa* and *savikalpa* perception, I consider the view of Buddhism and Advaita Vedānta on this issue. We shall see that Pāli Buddhism emphasizes the need to distinguish the "bare percept" from its conceptual and emotional superimpositions. A more explicit statement that such a bare percept is nondual is found in Mahāyāna Buddhism: it is part of the Prajñāpāramitā claim that perception, like everything else, is *śūnya* (empty); it is implied in the Mādhyamika critique of all dualities, and it is clearest in the Yogācāra assertion that subject and object are not distinct. The same nondual claim will be found in Advaita, with a subtle but significant difference. Just as Vedānta distinguishes sharply between Brahman and the phenomenal world, so it distinguishes between our usual dualistic perception and the nondual experience of Brahman, which it does not call perception at all. We will need to consider how important this disagreement with Buddhism is, whether it points to a difference in experience or merely a difference in describing the same nondual experience.

With one important exception (Ch'an or Zen, which as a school of Mahāyāna was of course much influenced by Indian Buddhism), what follows deals solely with Indian philosophy. We do not find much reference to this topic in Taoism because Chinese philosophy, being generally more pragmatic than Indian philosophy, was not as interested in epistemological questions. A similar view is perhaps implicit in the first chapter of the *Tao Tê Ching*, but, since it is little more than a hint, discussion of that passage is postponed until the next chapter.

One of the main ways Indian philosophy acknowledges the role of conception in perception is by making a distinction between savikalpa and nirvikalpa perception. Our usual perception is *sa-vikalpa* (with thought-construction), but there is the possibility of *nir-vikalpa* perception, which is "without thought-construction" because the bare sensation is distinguished from all thought about it. The basis of both Sanskrit terms is *vikalpa*, a compound from the prefix *vi* (discrimination or bifurcation) and the root *kalpanā* (to construct mentally). This distinction is found in most of the important Indian systems, Jainism and the monotheistic schools of Vedānta being the main exceptions. There is of course much disagreement over the psychology and ontology of perception, but with the exception of Advaita Vedānta (examined later) it is agreed that nirvikalpa and savikalpa are not completely different types of perception, but earlier and later stages of a complex process. For example, the pluralistic Nyāya system, as developed by Gautama, defined nirvikalpa as "unassociated with a name" (*avyapadeśya*) and savikalpa as "well-defined" (*vyavasāyātmaka*). By its association with language all perception becomes "determinate," but this is necessarily preceded by an earlier stage when it is unassociated, a "bare sensation." "*Nirvikalpa* perception is the immediate apprehension, the bare awareness, the direct sense-experience which is undifferentiated and non-relational and is free from assimilation, discrimination, analysis and synthesis."[5] We can sense this bare sensation, but as soon as we try to know it, this "raw unverbalized experience" (William James) becomes associated with thought-conception and hence determinate (savikalpa).

This summary of the dualistic Nyāya position raises two issues important to the nondualist. First, what is the role of language in this distinction between nirvikalpa and savikalpa perception? Do we hypostatize a percept into an object by naming it, thus "identifying" it as a member of a certain class of objects? And does a sense of self arise in the same way—are the concepts of *I* and *mine* used to objectify ourselves? Second, we can readily see that this indeterminate/determinate distinction is not only epistemologically interesting but also obviously has ethical implications, among others. For example, there is a relationship between perception and the problem of craving. Due to mental tendencies accumulated from the past, the mind is prone to meddle with some percepts more than others and thus to activate certain predispositions. This suggests that a permanent resolution of the problem of craving might be related to an understanding of nirvikalpa perception and the process by which it becomes savikalpa.

In this section my main concern is naturally with Mahāyāna Buddhism and Advaita Vedānta, the two most important nondualistic systems in India. But here there also seems to be an important parallel with Yoga, which of the six orthodox Indian systems is the one most concerned with describing the path to liberation. Patañjali's *Yoga Sūtra* discusses the various stages of *samādhi* (yogic meditation) in great detail, and one could make a strong case that his four preliminary stages of *samprajñāta samādhi* actually "undo" savikalpa perception in order to return to the bare nirvikalpa percept. This suggests that, despite the overtly dualistic Sāṅkhya metaphysics that Patañjali adopts, the deeper *asamprajñāta samādhi* might actually be nondual, in the sense that the meditator is no longer aware of any distinction beween his own consciousness and the object of meditation. Sāṅkhya metaphysics will be discussed further in chapters 5 and 7, but we now return to our main concern. Since Vedānta as a system is antedated and influenced by Buddhism, we consider the latter first.

Perception in Early Buddhism

Because the Buddha's concern was almost exclusively soteriological, it is not surprising that the Pāli sutras present no single, developed theory of perception. However, they contain a wealth of epistemological material, much of it relating directly to perception, and, although the terms nirvikalpa and savikalpa are not used, the distinction between perception with and without thought-construction is clearly critical.[6]

A good account of this material is given in Edward Conze's *Buddhist Thought in India*. Conze summarizes the analysis of perception found in the Pāli Canon into "three levels of the apperception of stimuli, to which three kinds of 'sign' correspond—the sign as (1) an object of attention, as (2) a basis for recognition, and as (3) an occasion for entrancement." In the first stage, one "turns towards a stimulus"; attention is directed to what I call the "bare percept," an act both active and passive because one chooses to turn toward it but one cannot determine what the sensation will be. In the second stage, what has been perceived is recognized, "as a sign of its being such and such a part of the universe of discourse, and of habitually perceived and named things." So the "bare" visual percept is now seen *as* a woman, or a table, or whatever, with all the respective connotations. These connotations are elaborated in the third stage, which "is marked by the emotional and volitional adjustment to the 'sign.'" The sign is now interesting to us and awakens volitional tendencies; I am attracted to the woman and wonder how I can meet her.

Of course, the whole sequence usually occurs so quickly that one is unable to distinguish one stage from another. So we take this tripartite series of distinct impersonal processes to be one simple mental event: seeing an attractive woman. Normally we are not aware of what it is like to experience just the first stage, for we never have experienced just that by itself. But to build upon sense-perceptions in this way is undesirable, according to the Buddha, and in the Majjhima Nikāya he describes various methods for "restraining the senses." Conze summarizes:

> The task is to bring the process back to the initial point, before any "superimpositions" have distorted the actual and initial datum. The seemingly-innocuous phraseology of the formula which describes the restraint of the senses opens up vast philosophical vistas, and involves a huge philosophical programme which is gradually worked out over the centuries in the Abhidharma and the Prajna-paramita. "He does not seize on its appearance as man or woman, or its appearance as attractive, etc., which makes it into a basis for the defiling passions. *But he stops at what is actually seen.*" Taken seriously, this must lead to an attempt to distinguish the actual sense-datum from the later accretions which memory, intellect, and imagination superimpose upon it.... *"He seizes only on that which is really there."*... This is the starting-point of the considerations which in due course led to the concept of "Suchness" [*Tathatā*], which takes a thing just such as it is, without adding to it or subtracting from it.[7]

The second and third of Conze's stages of apperception describe how a "bare" nirvikalpa percept becomes savikalpa, and the process of "restraining the senses" is the means by which this apparently simple mental event may be broken up into its three impersonal component processes, thus deconstructing the savikalpa perception back into a nirvikalpa one. The second state, "recognition," obviously includes the application of language to what is immediately presented by the senses. The third stage, emotional and volitional response, will usually become expression of craving (*tṛṣṇa*). How these two factors interact requires some discussion.

According to Buddha, tṛṣṇa is the cause of our suffering, but the term refers not just to sensual desire but to attachment in general, whether to sense-experience or nonsensuous mental events. The above analysis of perception suggests that the fundamental problem with such craving is epistemological, since it distorts one's perception of things. However, such attachment seems limited to what is immediately presented to the senses. "I" can "seize on" a particular appearance only because that appearance is now appearing. How can I grasp at something that is not present any more? If there is some way to re-present the appearance, I can retain and refer to "It." Such "grasping at a distance" is enabled by a system of re-presentation, that is, a language. But language also widens the gulf between the I and the grasped-at objects, because when the percept again appears, the re-presentation ("urg," let us say) does not disappear as having no more function. It still represents the appearance. Now we know what the appearance is: it *is* "urg" (name) or "an urg" (particular instance of a universal). Now I experience the appearance *through* the representation, which is as it were superimposed upon it. The problem is that the more successfully a system of representation functions, the less likely we will be able to distinguish the representation from the appearance.

The above analysis presents a plausible view of how language functions, but it is naive and inadequate by itself. It is not really the case that the presented world is divided up into "objects" which we later represent. Rather, we divide up the world in the way that we do—that is, learn to notice what there is—using a system of representation. This is the point of the distinction between nirvikalpa and savikalpa perception: savikalpa determinations are not simply "added on" to nirvikalpa percepts, but they determine what the world is for us. John Searle, a contemporary philosopher of language, explains this well:

> I am not saying that language creates reality. Far from it. Rather, I am saying that *what counts* as reality ... is a matter of the categories that we impose on the world; and those categories are for the most part linguistic. And furthermore: when we experience the world we experience it *through* linguistic categories that help to shape the experiences themselves. The world doesn't come to us already sliced up into objects and experiences: what counts as an object is already a function of our system of representation, and how we perceive the world in our experience is influenced by that system of representation. The mistake is to

suppose that the application of language to the world consists of attaching labels to objects that are, so to speak, self-identifying. On my view, the world divides the way we divide it, and our main way of dividing things up is in the language. Our concept of reality is a matter of our linguistic categories.[8]

Like Kant, Searle doubts that it is possible to experience "things-in-themselves" apart from linguistic categories, but the linguistic approach seems to leave the door open in a way that Kant did not: since language is learned, isn't it possible to "unlearn" it, as the Buddha's program for "restraint of the senses" suggests? If so, and if Searle is right that language determines "what counts as reality," then the world experienced in such a way would be very different indeed from the world as we normally perceive and understand it. If we take Searle's phrase literally, then the nirvikalpa elimination of language implies that the category of *real* would no longer be applicable to any particular—just as Mahāyāna, Advaita, and Taoism insist.

Language must also be related to the third stage of apperception, which involves expressions of craving. In order to crave something I must be able to distinguish the object of my craving from other things, and in order to do this most successfully a system of representation is necessary. For example, it may be possible to crave a particular taste without being able to identify it, but such craving is more likely to be satisfied if I can re-present that flavor as "chocolate." Searle's account implies that it is doubtful whether I would even notice the subtle distinctions between types of chocolate without the vocabulary to represent those distinctions, just as I am likely to see only "snow" in Alaska, whereas an Eskimo would see a specific one of a dozen representable types of "snow." The vast number of possible conceptual distinctions can thereby increase and refine our cravings. This does not mean that craving is dependent upon our concept-formation. The general view of the nondualist philosophies is rather that our system of representation is at the mercy of our desires and in fact evolved to help us satisfy and elaborate them. The motivation behind the particular way we "divide up" the world through language (hence transforming nirvikalpa into savikalpa percepts) is, fundamentally, our craving. This does not obviate Searle's view. We do not first perceptually "pick out" objects and only later name them; rather, we learn to notice them by naming them, and the motivation behind that naming was originally the assistance it gave in satisfying desires. That is not contradictory to the nondualist view of perception, for what is important to the nondualist is that the association of percept with craving can be broken.

The passage from Conze quoted earlier seems to imply that stopping at the "bare" nirvikalpa percept *is* the goal. However, Conze's understanding of the "initial datum" stage is that it is still dualistic: "He seizes only on what is really there." As we shall see, the Mahāyāna view is that I can "let go" of the "seizing" too—that is, even the "I" can be let go—and what is experienced then is the original thing-in-itself, a nondual percept. The Abhidharmic view differs only in that the thing-in-itself is not explicitly nondual but seems to be a set of objectively existing dharmas. Conze does not see this because he follows other commentators and understands Buddhism to recommend a rejection of sense-experience. "Buddhism goes even further [than condemning sense desire] and regards even sense-perceptions as baneful." But instead of supporting this with an analysis of the Pāli sutras, he immediately relates this "distrust of sense-objects" to the European Neoplatonic tradition, quoting St. Gregory and St. Dionysius. In a footnote, he deals curtly with the fact that someone might respond with the injunction of Seng-ts'an (the third Ch'an patriarch) that we should "not be prejudiced against the six sense-objects." His answer is that Seng-ts'an is referring to a different and more advanced stage. "In terms of the five levels [which he has earlier] distinguished, we are here with the doors of deliverance on the third, whereas Seng-ts'an speaks of the fourth."[9] The quotation in question is from Seng-ts'an's *Hsin Hsin Ming* (Awakening Faith in Mind), the relevant lines of which are:

> If you pursue appearances
> You overlook the primal source
>
> If you would walk the Single Way
> Do not reject the sense domain
> Accepting the world of senses
> Conforms with true enlightenment[10]

Seng-ts'an himself draws no distinction between any such levels, nor do the many other Mahāyāna sources which, as we shall see, could also be cited to criticize Conze's rejection of sense-perception. Conze would have difficulty justifying his view with the Mahāyāna texts, but from the Pāli Canon he could (although he does not) cite the Fire Semon and the Sermon on the Marks of No-Self. Such passages do seem to reject sense-experience, but they must be set against many others in the Pāli canon that recommend not loathing or disgust but equanimity.[11]

Perhaps the strongest canonical evidence against Conze's rejection of the senses is in one of the Honeyball sutras where cognizing the "bare" percept is equated with "the end of duḥkha" (suffering).

> Then, Bahiya, thus you must train yourself: "In the seen there will be just the seen; in the heard, just the heard, in the *muta* [the sense impressions from smelling, tasting, and touching], just the *muta*; in the cognized, just the cognized." That is how, O Bahiya, you must train yourself. Now, when, Bahiya, in the seen there will be to you just the seen, in the heard . . . just the cognized, then, Bahiya, you will have no "thereby" (*na tena*); when you have no "thereby", then Bahiya, you will have no "therein" (*na tattha*); as you, Bahiya, will have no "therein" it follows that you will have no "here" or "beyond" or "midway-between". This is just the end of duḥkha.[12]

Traditional commentaries on this passage mention a number of conflicting interpretations, but it seems to be advocating a return to nirvikalpa perception to reach "the end of duḥkha"—which is the most common Pāli description of nirvana. The sutra continues by reporting that Bahiya, upon hearing this, attained nirvana almost immediately. Other passages which advocate equanimity toward the senses suggest that the return to "the first stage of apperception" is a necessary part of the meditative path, but this passage goes further to imply that such a return is sufficient for the attainment of nirvana. It is tempting to speculate on the meaning of *na tena* and *na tattha* and give them a nondualist interpretation: "If in the seen there is just the seen, then, O Bahiya, you will make no inferences on the basis of that 'seen,' and you will not see an object 'therein.'"

Passages such as these also shed a new light on the Buddha's repeated exhortation against "compounds" (*saṁskāra*), found even in his last words: "Impermanent are all compound things; attain perfection through diligence." After the Buddha passed away, the Abhidharma (higher dharma) developed his preference for the "noncompound" (asaṁskāra) into an ontology which classified everything that can be experienced into a fixed number of simple elements (dharmas). All compounds (for example, the five skandhas or "aggregates" that compose the self) may be deconstructed into these basic elements. This remains the most common interpretation of the saṁskāras, but perhaps the Buddha was actually making an epistemological point, criticizing compound savikalpa sense-experience in favor of the noncompound nirvikalpa "bare" percept.

Perception in Mahāyāna Buddhism

It must be emphasized that no passage has been referred to in the Pāli Canon which explicitly asserts the nonduality of perceiver and perceived, although I have tried to indicate some implications in this direction. What these passages add up to is the claim, not that perception must be "transcended" (as Conze maintained), but that we should return to the initial stage of perception, the unconstructed nirvikalpa percept. Since resting with this is "the end of duḥkha" and since the anātman doctrine of Buddhism denies any self, it would seem that such percepts must be nondual in the sense that there is no separate consciousness aware of them. We find clearer assertions to this effect in the paradoxical expressions of Mahāyāna, which uses the term śūnyatā to suggest strongly, and in some cases to state explicitly, that perception is nondual.

Prajñāpāramitā. Śūnyatā is perhaps the most important term in Mahāyāna, but it is not easy to translate. It comes from the root śū, which means "to swell" in two senses: hollow or empty, and also full, like the womb of a pregnant woman. Both are implied in the Mahāyāna usage: the first denies any fixed self-nature to anything, the second implies that this is also fullness and limitless possibility, for lack of any fixed characteristics allows the infinite diversity of impermanent phenomena. It has been unfortunate for Anglo-American Buddhist studies that "emptiness" captures only the first sense, but I follow the tradition.[13]

The term is used in both Pāli and Mahāyāna Buddhism, but differently. Śūnyatā in Pāli Buddhism generally means, first, that this world of saṁsāra is empty of value and should be negated in favor of nirvana; and second, that both saṁsāra and nirvana are empty of any self because all compounds are only clusters of dharma-elements. In Mahāyāna, śūnyatā means that the true nature of the world (*tathatā*) is empty of all description and predication; and that even all the dharma-elements are empty of any self-existence because all "things" are relative and conditioned by each other. The first Mahāyāna sense of śūnyatā is already familiar to us from the distinction between nirvikalpa and savikalpa perception. The second goes beyond the Abhidharmic critique of compounds and entails, among other things, the nonexistence of any self-subsisting object "behind" a percept.

> Mañjuśrī: "What is the root of the imagination which constructs something that is not actually there?"
> Vimalakīrti: "A perverted perception."
> Mañjuśrī: "And what is the root of the perverted perception?"
> Vimalakīrti: "The fact that it has no support."
> Mañjuśrī: "And what is the root of that?"
> Vimalakīrti: "This fact, that it has no support, it has no root at all. In this way all *dharmas* are supported on roots that have no support."

In itself, a perverted perception is śūnya because it has no support, which means that it refers to nothing else, neither a perceived object nor a perceiver. Such claims, which work out the implications of "the restraint of the senses" that Conze mentioned earlier, are common in the Prajñāpāramitā literature:

> Moreover, Subhūti, a Bodhisattva, beginning with the first thought of enlightenment, practices the perfection of meditation.... When he has seen forms with his eye, he does not seize upon them as signs of realities which concern him, nor is he interested in the accessory details. He sets himself to restrain that which, if he does not restrain his organ of sight, might give occasion for covetousness, sadness or other evil and un-wholesome dharmas to reach his heart. He watches over the organ of sight. And the same with the other five sense-organs—ear, nose, tongue, body, mind.
> ...he remains the same unchanged, neither elated not cast down, neither grateful nor thwarted. And why? Because he sees all dharmas as empty (*śūnya*) of marks of their own, without true reality, incomplete and uncreated.

This passage accords well with Pāli Buddhism until its last sentence, when it goes further to explain that the equanimity of the Bodhisattva is due to his seeing all dharmas (including percepts) as śūnya, without any reality of their own and referring to nothing else besides themselves. That is the experience of tathatā, the "suchness" of things.

> The Lord: ... This *prajñāpāramitā* cannot be expounded, or learnt, or distinguished, or considered, or stated, or reflected upon by means of the *skandhas*, or by means of the elements, or by means of the sense-fields. This is a consequence of the fact that all Dharmas are isolated, absolutely isolated. Nor can *prajñāpāramitā* be understood otherwise than by the *skandhas*, elements, and sense-fields. For just the very *skandhas*, elements, and sense-fields are *śūnya*, isolated, and calmly quiet. It is thus that *prajñāpāramitā* and the *skandhas*, elements and sense-fields are not two, nor divided. As a result of their emptiness, isolatedness, and quietude they cannot be apprehended. The lack of a basis of apprehension in all Dharmas, that is called *prajñāpāramitā*. Where there is no perception, appellation, conception or conventional expression, there one speaks of *prajñāpāramitā*.[14]

Dharmas, because they are empty, cannot even be apprehended: this seems to go beyond denying both perceiver and sense-object to deny even the act of perception. Such a claim seems odd, but we find it also in Nāgārjuna. In his case the denial of perception is based upon the fact that our understanding of perception is dependent upon the reality of the perceiver and the perceived, both of which he also denies. For Nāgārjuna, the relativity of perceiver, perceived, and the act of perception entails the unreality of all of them, that is, their lack of self-existence. This does not, however, support the claim that we must "transcend" perception for the sake of some other kind of apprehension. Nāgārjuna is rejecting perception as we understand it, the dualistic act in which two self-existing entities are related together. This raises the question whether what we have been describing as "nondual perception" should be called perception at all. If the bare nirvikalpa sensation does not provide some knowledge *to* someone *about* something (and it cannot, since any inference is savikalpa), perhaps the term *perception* no longer applies and should be reserved only for thought-determined savikalpa percepts. This may explain why some texts (such as the above) deny there is perception, some assert there is nondual perception, and others paradoxically recommend perceiving without perception—which may all be different ways of describing the same sense-experience. We return to this point at the end of this chapter.

> The comprehension which takes place as a result of perception does not imply an understanding of the reality (of the thing perceived). What you perceive without perceiving—that is Nirvāṇa, also known as deliverance. (*Śūraṅgama Sūtra*)[15]

Mādhyamika. The central tenet of Mādhyamika Buddhism, that saṁsāra is nirvana, is difficult to understand in any other way except as asserting the two different ways of perceiving, dually and nondually. The dualistic perception of a world of discrete objects (one of them being *me*) which are created and destroyed constitutes saṁsāra. Nāgārjuna describes the cessation of this way of experiencing the world in the last stanza of the *Mūlamadhyamikakārikā* chapter on nirvana: "Ultimate serenity is the coming to rest of all ways of taking things (*sarvopalambhopaśama*), the repose of all named things (*prapañcopaśama*)." In a footnote to his translation Sprung explains *sarvopalambhopaśama*: "It is not merely that ways of *thinking* about things change in nirvāṇa, but that the everyday way of *perceiving*, or 'taking', things ceases to function."[16]

This well-known verse—as close as Nāgārjuna comes to a "description" of nirvana—emphasizes the importance of ending *prapañca*. The Sanskrit term *prapañca* (Pāli, *papañca*) is important in both Buddhism and Vedānta, but its meaning is controversial. In Buddhism it refers to some indeterminate "interface" between perception and thought. Several times in the Pāli Canon the Buddha mentions papañca to describe what happens in the later stages of sense-cognition, and he says that his teaching is for those who delight in *nispapañca*, no prapañca. The Mahāyāna Laṅkāvatāra Sūtra says that Buddhas are "beyond all vikalpa and prapañca." Etymology yields *pra+pañc*, "spreading out" in the sense of expansion and manifoldness. This led the Theravadin scholar Ñānananda, in his book on prapañca, to define its primary meaning as "the tendency towards proliferation in the realm of concepts."[17] This is better than the ethical interpretations of the traditional Pāli commentaries,[18] but there remain two difficulties with such a definition: it loses any direct relation with perception, and prapañca becomes indistinguishable from vikalpa. Both the Tibetan and Chinese Mādhyamika exegetical traditions understand the relation between vikalpa and prapañca as the relation between the mental act of conceptualization, understood subjectively, and its crystallized, objectively experienced counterpart. Thus, in the terms of this chapter, prapañca might be defined as "the differentiation of the nondual world of nirvikalpa experience into the discrete-objects-of-the-phenomenal world, which occurs due to savikalpa thought-construction." This explains the important compound prapañca-nāmarūpa, since nāmarūpa (name and form) here can be understood to refer to the necessary relation between names and forms (the Buddha describes them as inseparable),[19] that we reify forms by naming them. We shall meet with this interpretation of nāmarūpa again, implied both in Śaṅkara's concept of adhyāsa (superimposition) and in the first chapter of the Tao Tê Ching.

It is significant that the earliest Vedāntic references to prapañca and prapañcopaśama are consistent with the above. The terms do not appear in the first Upaniṣads, such as the Bṛhadāraṇyaka and the Chāndogya, which are usually considered to be pre-Buddhistic. The two most important references are in the Śvetāśvatara, and the Māṇḍūkya. Śvetāśvatara VI.6 uses prapañca ontologically to denote the objectified universe, understood as a phenomenal world of manifoldness emanating from a creator God. Verse seven of the short Māṇḍūkya describes turīya, the fourth and highest state of experience, which is "all peace, all bliss, and nondual," as prapañcopaśama. "This is ātman, and this has to be realized."

The great importance of prapañcopaśama in Mahāyāna Buddhism is indicated by the fact that it is not only a term for nirvana but the preferred formulation for describing the Middle Way of Mādhyamika. In his commentary to Nāgārjuna's Mūlamadhyamikakārikā, Candrakīrti states and repeats that nirvana is the cessation and nonfunctioning of perceptions as signs of named things—in other words, that in nirvana perceptions do not refer to any hypostatized object "behind" the percept. "[When the wise are] cured by the balm of unmediated seeing that such things are irrefragably without substance, then they realize directly and for themselves that it is the true nature of such things not to be seen at all."[20] When we couple this with the general Buddhist denial of a self, it amounts to an assertion that nirvanic perception is nondual.

So nirvana is not even to be found "in" saṁsāra, for such a spatial metaphor is still dualistic. Rather, nirvana is the nondual "true nature" of saṁsāra. T. R. V. Murti expresses this well:

> The transcendence of the Absolute must not be understood to mean that there is an other that lies outside the world of phenomena. There are not two sets of the real. The Absolute is *the reality* of the apparent; it is their real nature.... The Absolute is the only real; it is identical with phenomena. The difference between the two is epistemic and not real.[21]

"The reality of the apparent" does not mean a reality *behind* appearance but that appearance is reality itself, as we realize if we do not use appearance as a basis for vikalpa thought-construction and prapañca thought-objectification. But we must be careful about accepting any distinction between epistemic and real. In the non-dualistic systems we are considering, epistemology and ontology cannot be so easily distinguished: epistemic changes in our experience amount to ontological changes as well, by revealing that things are (and perhaps always have been) very different from what we thought they were. In another well-known verse about the true nature of things, Nāgārjuna himself uses both prapañca and nirvikalpa: "Not dependent on anything other than itself, at peace, not manifested as named things (*prapañcairaprapañcitam*), beyond thought-construction (*nirvikalpa*), not of varying form—thus the way things are really is spoken of."[22]

Yogācāra. Despite the above, we do not find in Mādhyamika the clear statement that nirvana is nondual cognition. That is because Mādhyamika declines to give any positive account about the nature of reality. Reality is experienced when all dualizing categories—including, no doubt, duality and nonduality—cease to function, so Mādhyamika confines itself to making a critique of those dualities: cause and effect, perceiver and act of perception, saṁsāra and nirvana, etc. In the terms of this chapter, Mādhyamika is most aware of the paradox that any claim of nonduality amounts to a savikalpa attempt to describe the nirvikalpa. But it is not surprising that this exclusively negative critique should have been followed by an attempt to characterize nirvana in a more positive manner than just "the end of prapañca," and this we find in Yogācāra and Vijñānavāda Buddhism. It is significant, then, that the cognitive nonduality of subject and object constitutes the heart of the Yogācāra position. Passages from Vasubandhu denying the duality of perceiver and perceived are quoted in chapter 1. Here is a fuller version of his clearest statement:

> As long as consciousness does not abide in re-presentation-only, so long does one not turn away from the tendency towards the two-fold grasping [perceiver and perceived]. As long as he places something before him, taking it as a basis, saying: "This is just re-presentation-only", so long he does not abide in that alone.
>
> But when cognition no longer apprehends an object, then it stands firmly in consciousness-only, because, where there is nothing to grasp there is no more grasping. It is thus there arises the cognition which is homogeneous, without object, indiscriminate and supramundane. The tendencies to treat object and subject as distinct and real entities are forsaken, and thought is established in just the true nature of one's own thought.[23]

The most detailed discussion of perception is found in the logical treatises of the Sautrāntika-Yogācārins Dignāga and Dharmakīrti, which begin by analyzing the process of perception into two familiar moments: "the first indefinite (nirvikalpa) sensation and the following thought-construction of a definite (savikalpa) image or idea and then purposive action." According to them, problems arise because we confuse the two moments: mental construction converts the bare sensation, itself independent of any association with language, into an object that has a name. When one thinks he perceives such an object, "he simply conceals, as it were, his imaginative faculty and puts to the front his perceptive faculty," thus missing the fact that the object which is supposed to be immediately perceived is a creation of thought-construction.[24] According to Stcherbatsky, the distinction between these two moments is "one of the foundation stones upon which the whole system of Dignāga is built: Whatever is cognized by the senses is never subject to cognition by inference, and what is cognized by inference can never be subject to cognition by the senses." In accordance with this, Dignāga and his successors accept only these two pramāṇas (modes of knowledge): sensation, which directly cognizes ultimate reality, and inference, including all conception, which indirectly cognizes conditioned or empirical reality. The path to liberation is again a return to the bare thing-in-itself, exclusive of all its relations and characteristics, which is "sense-perception shorn of all its mnemic elements."[25]

This differs from Pāli Buddhism by explicitly claiming not only that such nirvikalpa sense-perception is the goal but also that is is nondual. Stcherbatsky concludes his translation of Dharmakīrti's "Short Treatise of Logic" with the following note:

> The trend of the discussion is to show that self-consciousness is not the attribute of a Soul, but it is immanent to every cognition without exception . . . our images are not constructed by the external world, but the external world is constructed according to our images, that there is no "act of grasping" of the object by the intellect, that our idea of the object is a unity to which two different aspects are imputed, the "grasping" aspect (grāhaka-akara) and the "grasped" aspect (grāhya).

The grasping aspect constitutes the sense of self, while the grasped aspect is the sense of a self-existing sense-object. How does this differentiation occur?

> From the standpoint of Tathatā, there is no difference at all! But hampered as we are by avidyā, all that we know is exclusively its indirect appearance as differentiated by the construction of a difference of a subject and an object. Therefore the differentiation into cognition and its object is made from the empirical point of view, but not from the point of view of Absolute Reality (yathātathatam). (Jinendrabuddhi)[26]

From the highest point of view there has never been a differentiation, which is why sense-perception has really always been nondual. This does not need to be accepted on faith, for the claim that Reality is composed of discrete moments of pure sensation is verifiable. Both Dharmakīrti and Kamalaśīla recommend that we prove this ourselves by the experiment of staring at a patch of color without thinking of anything else, thus reducing consciousness to immobility. This will give us the condition of pure sensation, although we can realize that only afterwards, when we begin to think again and reflect on what was experienced.[27]

Ch'an (Zen). Up to now, this chapter has discussed only Indian philosophy, but we will see that Ch'an Buddhism, which synthesized Mādhyamika and Yogācāra with the Taoism indigenous to China, is consistent with the above. Stanzas from the *Hsin Hsin Ming* of the third

Ch'an patriarch Seng-ts'an were quoted in response to Conze's treatment of "the three stages of apperception" in early Buddhism. Huang Po is also quoted, in chapter 1: "It [the One Mind] is that which you see before you—begin to reason about it and you at once fall into error." Another early Ch'an master, Fa-yen Wen-i, said the same thing: "Reality is right before you, and yet you are apt to translate it into a world of names and forms."[28] In the sermons recorded in the *Chun Chou Record* Huang Po elaborates on this:

> If you students of the Way seek to progress through seeing, hearing, feeling and knowing, when you are deprived of your perceptions, your way to Mind will be cut off and you will find nowhere to enter. Only realize that, though real Mind is expressed in these perceptions, it neither forms part of them nor is separate from them. You should not start *reasoning* from these perceptions, nor allow them to give rise to conceptual thought; nor should you seek the One mind apart from them or abandon them in your pursuit of the Dharma. Do not keep them nor abandon them nor cleave to them. Above, below and around you, all is spontaneously existing, for there is nowhere which is outside the Buddha-Mind.[29]

This passage is strikingly similar to what the Buddha said to Bahiya: do not reject perceptions, but do not infer any "therein" or "thereby" from them. This too stops short of clearly asserting nonduality, but elsewhere Huang Po denies any objective reality to sense-objects:

> If you understand that these eighteen realms [the six sense-organs, -objects and -fields] have no objective existence, you will bind the six harmoniously-blended "elements" into a single spiritual brilliance— which is the One Mind.

> It [the One Mind] is neither subjective nor objective, has no specific location, is formless, and cannot vanish.

> If an ordinary man, when he is about to die, could only see the five elements of consciousness as void . . . *his mind and environmental objects as one*—if he could really accomplish this, he would receive enlightenment in a flash.[30]

Similar passages from many other Chinese Ch'an and Japanese Zen masters could also be cited, but I confine myself to discussing the Ten Oxherding Pictures of the twelfth-century master Kuo-an Shih-yuan. These well-known pictures, which illustrate the various degrees of enlightenment using the analogy of searching for an Ox, are also explicit in claiming that what is sought is found in perception itself. The third stage, "first glimpse of the Ox," is the first "taste" of enlightenment. Kuo-an's commentary on this picture gives instructions on how this glimpse can be attained.

> If he will but listen intently to everyday sounds, he will come to realization and that instant see the very Source. The six senses are not different from this true source.... when the inner vision is properly focused, one comes to realize that that which is seen is identical with the true Source.[31]

It is because nondual perception *is* the Ox that the Ox has never been astray; as the verse says, "There stands the Ox, where could he hide?" The highest degree of enlightenment is reflected in the ninth picture, "Returning to the Source," in which one realizes, paradoxically, that one never left it. It depicts a flowering branch. "He observes the waxing and waning of life in the world while abiding unassertively in a state of unshakeable serenity. This [waxing and waning] is no phantom or illusion" but is how the empty Source expresses itself.[32] As the Prajñāpāramitā repeatedly says, form may be no other than emptiness but emptiness is also no other than form. However, the verse to this picture seems inconsistent with such a nondualist interpretation:

> It is as though he were now blind and deaf. Seated in his hut, he hankers not for things outside. Streams meander on of themselves, red flowers naturally bloom red.

"As if blind and deaf" is a common phrase in Ch'an literature. Sometimes it refers to the deluded man who has no insight, but often it praises those whose seeing and hearing are completely without any sense of duality—whose seeing and hearing are sometimes described as no-seeing and no-hearing. That is why the Ch'an master Hsiang-yen could be enlightened by the sound of a pebble striking a bamboo: he heard the nondual nirvikalpa sound, freed from any thoughts *about* it. It is when we do not use śūnya perceptions as a basis for thought-construction that nondual streams meander on and red flowers bloom by themselves.

In concluding this discussion of perception in Buddhism, we should notice a progression or development in the concept. The main theme, that the "bare concept" must be distinguished from its conceptual and emotional superimpositions, was established in the Pāli sutras. The claim that such perception is nondual becomes explicit in Mahāyāna, first negatively in the Mādhyamika critique of all dualities as relative and hence śūnya, then positively in the Yogācāra assertion that subject and object are not distinct. With Ch'an we see that philosophical claim put into practice. How meditation can lead to such nondual experience is discussed further in chapter 6. The same points could be made with reference to the tantric practices of Tibetan Buddhism, which rest upon the identical philosophical foundation of Mādhyamika and Yogācāra. It is no coincidence that the Vajrayāna technique of visualizing a deity is preliminary to the act of becoming that deity.

Perception in Advaita Vedānta

As if echoing Huang Po's declaration that the One Mind is what you see before you if you do not reason about it, Śaṅkara claims that our perception of the universe is a continuous perception of Brahman, although the ignorant do not know it. (*Vivekacūḍāmaṇi*, v. 521, quoted at the beginning of the chapter). Perhaps this is no coincidence, since Gauḍapāda and Śaṅkara are known to have been influenced by Mahāyāna to the extent that both have been accused of being "hidden Buddhists." Even more important for us, it is likely Vedānta borrowed the notion of prapañcopaśama to conclude that the thing-in-itself cognized in nondual nirvikalpa experience is Brahman.[33]

Although he had much to say about the pramāṇas (modes of knowledge), Śaṅkara, like the Buddha, developed no theory of perception. There are differences of opinion in Advaita over exactly how an object becomes manifest to a subject. The best traditional account, although unsophisticated and generally deemed unsatisfactory, is found in the *Vedānta-paribhāṣa* of Dharmarāja Adhvarīndra, which presents a theory of *abhedabhivyakti*—that the manifestation of the object is "non different" (*abheda*) from the consciousness underlying the subject. D. M. Datta summarizes that view as follows:

> The Advaitins view immediacy as the basic character of the Absolute Consciousness, of which the knower, the known, and the process or mechanism of knowledge are apparent differentiations due to ignorance. So, for them, immediacy is not generated by the knowing process. The self's knowledge of an external object is empirically

describable, of course, in terms of the function of the mind, or internal organ, and the sense concerned. In the light of this, the Advaitins say that in every perception the mind flows out to the object through the sense and assumes the form of the object and establishes thereby a sort of identity between the mind and the object. But this process does not generate consciousness or immediacy. It only destroys the imagined barrier between the knower (which is nothing but the basic consciousness delimited by the mind) and the object (which is also the same consciousness delimited by the objective form) by a kind of identity established between the two delimiting and differentiating factors.

So, for the Advaitin every sense perception is really the restoration of the basic identity between the knower and the known, and the allowing of the basic reality, i.e., consciousness, to reveal itself immediately.[34]

This Platonic view—in which "the mind flows out to the object through the sense"—is in striking contrast to the more dualistic modern understanding, according to which sense-data are processed and perceived in the brain. As such, Datta's account seems to support the claim that perception is originally nondual. But such a conclusion would be too quick. At least two qualifications are necessary.

First, the above account seems inconsistent in maintaining, on the one hand, that basic identity is "restored" by the mind flowing out through the senses, and, on the other, that this does not generate immediacy but only destroys an "imagined barrier." It would seem that *either* the basic nondual consciousness is delimited by mind and objective form, in which case there is a real barrier and restoration of identity is necessary, *or* that barrier is imaginary and nondual consciousness has never been delimited, which means that it is necessary only to remove the "veil of ignorance"—which sounds like what we have been describing as savikalpa thought-construction. According to Advaitins, however, this inconsistency is only apparent and is due to confusing the two standpoints or levels of truth basic to Advaita: the *vyāvahārika* (empirical) and the *paramārthika* (transcendental). That consciousness is delimited and restored is true only from the empirical standpoint; from the transcendental perspective there has never been any barrier or delimitation. Advaitins insist on distinguishing strictly between these two standpoints, which parallel (and were influenced by) the two truths of Mahāyāna, *samvrtajñāna* and *paramārthajñāna*. But solving the above problem by distinguishing these two standpoints just transposes the difficulty into another dimension, for what is the relationship between the two? The sharp distinction between them—so extreme that they cannot be related back together, as we shall see—brings us to the second qualification.

In the Advaita system, it would not be correct to say that perception is or can be nondual because *by definition* the nature of perception (*pratyakṣa*) is a vyāvahārika issue only. The Advaitin does not refer to nirvikalpa and savikalpa as two kinds of perception but reserves the term *pratyakṣa* for the latter only. Necessarily, then, perception is always dualistic. In response to Yogācāra "mentalism," which as we have seen denies the existence of an object distinct from our cognition, Śaṅkara defends a realistic epistemology: the object is independent of our knowlege of it, for the two are utterly different. Objects depend upon our awareness of them only to be revealed; that awareness does not constitute them. Knowledge is nothing other than the element of revelation in our experience, although the "essence" of that revelation is indeterminable since our very oneness with it means we are unable to understand it objectively. But we can see that our sense-cognition, like all cognition, is due to *vṛttis*, the modifications of the *buddhi* (the "internal organ" constituting the mind as we usually understand it). Because these vṛtti-modifications always constitute limiting conditions of one sort or another, the unlimited Brahman cannot be knowable through them. The only real (paramārthika) is Brahman, the thing-in-itself. Apparently turning the Yogācāra view upside down, Śaṅkara argues that anything dependent upon being known is unreal, mere appearance. The empirical world of appearances is real, but only *as* Brahman, only because it is grounded in Brahman.[35]

The rest strikes a more familiar note. The ideal of pure knowledge is to know the thing as it is, without the appearance of subjective representations, and this happens only in the knowledge of Brahman, when there is no distinction left between the knower and the known. Nirvikalpa awareness (the preferred Vedāntic term is *aparōkṣānubhūti*) is not intuition *of* Brahman but itself *is* Brahman. Then the distinction between knower, knowing, and known is realized to be delusive, but until then we must respect the empirical distinctions between them. Advaitins sometimes express this by saying that, although only Brahman is real, the empirical world nonetheless exists.

Thus the Advaitic view drives much more of a wedge than

Mahāyāna does between our usual sense-perception and the nondual experience. But how significant is this difference? Is it perhaps merely a linguistic one, over how to use the term *pratyakṣa*? In his critique of Yogācāra, Śaṅkara misses the point because he does not understand the function of the Yogācāra arguments. It has already been mentioned that Mahāyāna accepts the same distinction between empirical and transcendental that Advaita does (perhaps vice versa is more accurate, since the Mahāyāna version came first), which is important because it supports the possibility that both "two-truth" doctrines are based upon the same nondual experience. Where they do differ is on their attitude toward the empirical "lower truth."

Mādhyamika and Yogācāra are concerned to demonstrate the self-contradictory nature of our usual phenomenal world, including the pramāṇas, because such a logical refutation is their way of devaluing dualistic experience and paving the way for the nondual experience. Unlike some later Advaitins (e.g., Śrīharṣa, whose dialectic was much influenced by Mādhyamika), Śaṅkara is not interested in refuting the pramāṇas. He is content to accept them empirically and merely to state that they have no application in the sphere of ultimate knowledge, for when Brahman is realized the pramāṇas lose all authority as a means of right knowledge.[36] But Śaṅkara can do this only because he relies on *śruti* (the Vedic scriptures) to establish the existence of Brahman, whereas the Buddhist philosophers, not accepting such an appeal to authority, need to analyze the relation between the two levels of truth, logically refuting the lower for the sake of experiencing the higher.

This means that the epistemological difference between them is more apparent than real. Śaṅkara's defense of a realistic epistemology does not refute Yogācāra "mentalism," as he thinks, for what he criticizes is not the Buddhist empirical standpoint, but the Buddhist means of moving logically from the empirical to the transcendental. What is more important is the agreement of both sides that our usual empirical experience is a dualistic lower truth and that the transcendental is nondual. Advaitins often criticize Mādhyamika for dismissing this phenomenal world as "empty," whereas for them it exists; but this is the same confusion of standpoints, for Advaita makes the identical point in a different way by insisting that only Brahman is real. The difference between them comes down to the fact that, for Advaita, the two standpoints are so sharply distinguished that they have no commerce, whereas Mahāyāna—and this work, obviously—is more concerned to understand the relation between them.

A number of aspects of the Advaita Vedānta system reveal its otherwise deep affinity with Mahāyāna on this matter. A full consideration of the most crucial issue, the relation between śūnyatā and Brahman, is reserved for later chapters, but we now turn to consider some of those other aspects.

The veil of ignorance. The claim of Datta's passage, quoted above, is that the realization of nondual consciousness requires only that the "veil of ignorance" (*ajñāna*) be eradicated. As in Sāṅkhya-Yoga, this veil is destroyed by the buddhi in a mental modification (*Brahmātmakāra-vṛtti*) that realizes the identity between the self and Brahman. What distinguishes this vṛtti from other limiting vṛttis is that it then becomes extinct by consuming itself. "It is to the buddhi and not to the Self which is immutable that the knowledge 'I am Brahman' belongs" (Śaṅkara). But that knowledge is not yet the full nondual experience.

> Brahman being self-effulgent, nothing is needed for its manifestation. The mental mode coincident with It removes the veil of *ajñāna* but does not objectify it. By no means can Brahman be an object of cognition.
> . . . self-luminous Brahman is unveiled and is directly perceived as "I am Brahman"; instantly, the Self is realized as indivisible, limitless Pure Consciousness in *nirvikalpa samādhi*. This is illumination (*prajñā*), or immediate awareness (*aparōkṣānubhūti*) beyond the distinction of the knower and the known, the self and the not-self.[37]

The importance of this for us is its claim that in order to realize Brahman nothing needs to be gained or added; an obscuring veil needs only to be removed. Since this veil includes the Brahmāt-makāra-vṛtti of the buddhi, this amounts to eliminating all savikalpa thought-determinations. The result of this process is not a realization that the ego-self "has," for that would still be dualistic and Brahman is nondual.

Self-luminosity. One of the most common descriptions of Brahman, used twice in the previous quotation, is "self-luminous" (*svayaṃ-prakāśa*). According to Surendranath Dasgupta, *svayaṃprakāśa* in Vedānta refers to "that which is never the object of a knowing act but yet is immediate and direct with us. Self-luminosity thus means the capacity of being ever present in all our acts of consciousness without being an object of consciousness."[38] Discussing a related matter—the importance of luminosity (photism) in Tibetan Buddhism—Tucci elaborates on what this means:

> To understand these ideas better we need to recall the difference between the luminosity we are considering here and that of, for example, the sun's rays. The sun's rays enable us to see, in that they illuminate objects, but they do not see themselves. The luminous cognitive states on the other hand do not only illuminate what is cognizable inside and outside of us, they also illuminate themselves as objects of luminous cognition. Thus it comes about that in the cognitive process luminosity and cognition belong essentially to each other. If the luminous states as a result of adventitious defilements do not illuminate the objects proper to them, they still possess as cognitive states this power within themselves.[39]

Unlike Dasgupta, Tucci's explanation refers to objects, but the point is the same, since "objects that illuminate themselves" are not really objects as usually understood. It is rather Tucci's last sentence that illuminates where Vedānta and Mahāyāna differ, for Advaita distinguishes more sharply between self-luminous Brahman and perception which is dualistic because of adventitious defilements. Brahman is the self-luminous thing-in-itself because it is not dependent on anything else for its manifestation—unlike all supposed objects of consciousness, which, as dependent on a subject to be conscious *of* them, are mere appearances. But what if "I" were to realize that is true for all "my" experience *right now*?

Superimposition. In his discussion of the "three stages of apperception" in Pāli Buddhism, Conze twice uses the term "superimposition" to describe the relation between the initial (nirvikalpa) sensation and the succeeding thought-constructions of recognition and volitional reaction. *Superimposition* is a fortuitous term for this tripartite process, since one of Śaṅkara's major contributions is that he uses it to describe the "relation" between Brahman and the phenomenal world.[40] "*Adhyāsa* [superimposition] is the apparent presentation by the memory of something previously perceived elsewhere." This seems to echo Dignāga's emphasis on the role of the mnemic function in transforming nirvikalpa into savikalpa. To understand adhyāsa, there are the well-known analogies of a snake that on closer inspection turns out to be a coiled rope, and a silver coin that is actually a piece of mother-of-pearl shell. The point of the analogy is that the phenomenal world may be viewed as due to such a superimposition. Taking the pluralistic universe of material objects to be real—which constitutes māyā—is like seeing a rope as a snake. Just as we would say afterward that we had really been seeing a rope, so "we" must actually be perceiving (or "experiencing") Brahman all the time, although we are ignorant of it—exactly what Śaṅkara says in the *Vivekacūḍāmaṇi* verse quoted at the beginning of this chapter. The analogy would further seem to imply—indeed, it can hardly be meaningful otherwise—that Brahman should not be characterized as transcendental to sense-perception, although of course "It" cannot be perceived as an *object*.

In one sense, *superimposition* is an unfortunate term, since it suggests the Platonic Form or Kantian noumenon dualistically "behind" phenomena—and that is the way it has sometimes been understood. For example: "*Māyā* is energized and acts as a medium of the projection of this world of plurality on the nondual ground of Brahman."[41] Perhaps "on" here is meant only metaphorically, but it is a dangerous metaphor. If Brahman is a nondual ground, the realization of which is characterized by self-luminous immediacy, then it cannot be projected *upon* because it is not something objective—an objection that Śaṅkara was quick to raise against his own definition of adhyāsa in the preamble of the *Brahmasūtrabhāṣya*. He replies that, although Brahman cannot be an object of pure consciousness, it can still be the apparent object of empirical (i.e., dualistic) consciousness. It is difficult to understand what this could mean except as asserting the nonduality of enlightened cognition.

Māyā. Since māyā is "the chief characteristic of the Advaita system" (Radhakrishnan), it is significant for the claim of this chapter that, although māyā is said to be indeterminable (*anirvacya*), it is nonetheless identified with "names and forms" (nāmarūpa) that in their evolved state constitute the phenomenal world.[42] "All variations are due to the superimposition of names and forms by māyā on immutable Brahman."[43] This conception of māyā is so similar to the Buddhist usage of prapañca that it suggests the former, like the latter, might be understood to be due to the savikalpa determination of nirvikalpa percepts. In such statements as māyā "is an appearance only" and "the whole phenomenal world is the appearance of Brahman," the fact that appearance must ultimately be negated may be taken not as referring to some transcendental realm apart from sensory experience but as denying the apparent "objectivity" of sense-experience, that there are discrete, self-existing objects.

Although scholars may argue about who influenced whom, the cross-fertilization of the nondualist systems is undeniable here. Not only do we find the term prapañca in the post-Buddha Upaniṣads, but māyā is also an important term in Mahāyāna. Mādhyamika understands māyā in its more original meaning of "magic trick" and then applies this to the world, whose objectivity is as delusive as the illusions of a magician. Śaṅkara makes māyā more "concrete" when he also describes it as a positive, beginningless material causal force responsible for creating the world. But, again, this may not be a significant difference; in fact, it may clarify our understanding of prapañca. To identify māyā and prapañca need not reduce māyā to our imagination: it may serve the opposite function of expanding the effects of our thought. If the objectivity of the world—that is, the objective world—is due to our ways of thinking about it, it suggests that the significance of our thought-processes is much greater than we usually believe, in a way which also makes sense out of the doctrine of *karma*. Śaṅkara agrees with Buddhism not only that avidyā never belongs to anyone or anything, but also (unlike Gauḍapāda) he seems to identify māyā and avidyā. If there is no self that is deluded, if on the contrary the sense of self is due to delusion, then avidyā must be "transpersonal" and is elevated to a more cosmic role; it is no longer merely our own personal ways of thinking. Thus māyā refers to the fact that the delusive objectification of the world has a "collective" dimension which transcends the delusion of particular individuals.

Four important aspects of the Advaita system have been briefly discussed: the realization of Brahman as requiring only the eradication of the veil of ignorance, the nature of Brahman as "self-luminous," and Śaṅkara's concepts of adhyāsa and māyā. In all four cases we see significant parallels between the Advaita position and that already developed in the Buddhist sections of this chapter. The disagreements seem to concern linguistics—for example, how to use the term *pratyakṣa*—more than the relationship between dualistic savikalpa perception and nondual nirvikalpa perception/intuition. But in fact the linguistic issue is only the surface of a more profound difference to which we now return.

A person's main character weakness is often the other side of his greatest character asset. For instance, someone who shows great determination when that is necesssary is also likely to be unreasonably stubborn when it is not. Sometimes the same is true for philosophical systems. The strong point of Advaita is its uncompromising solution to the problem of the relation between the Absolute and the phenomenal world (a problem which does not exist for Mahāyāna, for it understands the Absolute as nothing other than the "emptiness" of phenomena). For Śaṅkara, the problem of how the world was created does not arise because, as for Nāgārjuna, there never was a creation. But unlike Mahāyāna, Śaṅkara does away with this issue by sublating the phenomenal world into illusory māyā, which is completely devalued in comparison with Brahman. The corresponding problem that arises with this solution is the difficulty of characterizing the nature of māyā, which is neither real (since it has no existence apart from Brahman) nor unreal (since it does project the world of appearance). It is not surprising that māyā is ultimately deemed indeterminable and indefinable, which in my opinion amounts to an admission of failure. The problem has merely been pushed back one step: that which has been postulated to understand the "relation" between the Absolute and the phenomenal world cannot itself be understood. That Brahman both does and does not incorporate māyā is a problem that cannot in principle be resolved in Advaita, but conceiving of Brahman as the self-luminous nirvikalpa percept, the view defended in this chapter, provides an explanation: the difference between māyā and Brahman is the difference between percepts bifurcated into subject and object and those same percepts experienced nondualistically. This is why Mahāyāna could equate saṁsāra and nirvana. According to Mahāyāna, the nirvikalpa ground of perception remains the same whether perceptions are "grasped" dualistically or realized to be nondual. But Advaita Vedānta would not accept this form of "nonduality," preferring to characterize Brahman as nirguṇa and beyond all perception.

In the end, it turns out to be difficult to distinguish such an unqualified being as Brahman from the śūnyatā of Mahāyāna, as we shall see in chapters 5–6. But there is still an important difference. For Mahāyāna, śūnyatā is not a category distinct from phenomena but a statement about their lack of self-nature. As the Prajñāpāramitā Heart Sutra says, emptiness is not other than form. In Advaita, however, a wedge has been driven between attributeless Being and phenomena, between the higher and the lower truths. For Mādhyamika, the "two-truths" doctrine is a shorthand way of expressing a difference between two modes of experience: what we normally experience as real is, from the perspective of another experience, unreal. The two levels of truth salvage the truth of both experiences by subsuming the one below the other. From the viewpoint of nondual experience, the dualistic lower truth is untrue, but nonetheless we must all dwell in that delusion to some extent in our everday lives—which is why it is not *merely* delusion. As my analysis has shown, the problem with the Advaitic position is that these two truths have been sundered; that version of the doctrine has since become reified into a orthodoxy which paralyzes the possibility of developing fresh ways to understand the old truths. Anyone who accepts the "perennial philosophy" will accept some verson of the two-truths doctrine, but the challenge for philosophy is elucidating the relation between them. The simplest refutation of such a split is to realize that there must be some relation or liberation would not be possible, because we could never make the transition (or "leap") from delusion to enlightenment. This is not to overlook the importance of the distinction between the two levels. The point of that distinction is that we must not attempt to understand the transcendental from the relative or empirical perspective. But that is not the function of Mahāyāna analysis, which rather demonstrates the self-contradictions of our empirical experience in order to undermine our committment to it. Nor is this world liable to such an objection, for my project is not to "extrapolate" from the lower truth to the higher, but to "interpolate" by using the traditional nondualist claims about the higher truth to examine our understanding of the lower.

NONDUAL HEARING AND SEEING

The Eye of Man, a little narrow orb, clos'd up & dark,
Scarcely beholding the Great Light, conversing with the ground:

The Ear, a little shell, in small volutions shutting out True
Harmonies & comprehending great as very small...
— William Blake, *Milton*

The previous section established that the nonduality of perception is a central tenet of some important Asian philosophies, particularly Buddhism and (with some qualifications) Advaita Vedānta. But it did little to reduce the oddity of that claim, so incongruous with all our common sense. We need to elaborate on what such a claim might mean, although without any hope of being able to grasp this matter completely. We cannot hope to understand nondual perception clearly through concepts if our usual dualistic perception is delusive precisely because it is conceptualized.

Almost everything said so far has referred to sense-perception in general. These generalizations must now be grounded in a discussion of the two most important senses. Since hearing is the easier of the two to "understand" nondualistically, it is examined first. Although nondual hearing is by no means common, music is probably the medium of most nondual experiences. The "silence" that nondual hearing reveals will help us to understand better the difference in perspective between Mahāyāna Buddhism and Advaita Vedānta, which are so similar and yet also diametrically opposed. Our discussion of nondual seeing will use the arguments of Berkeley and Hume to help us understand the nondualist critique of the visual object as material, discrete, and self-existing. In contrast, the nondual "Light-object" is a śūnya, self-luminous event.

■

        ... music heard so deeply
That it is not heard at all, but you are the music
While the music lasts.
— T.S. Eliot, "The Dry Salvages"

Chapter 1, in a discussion of nonduality in Zen, included some quotations from a contemporary Japanese Zen master, Yasutani Hakuun. These were from his *dokusan* (private interviews) with Western students. One of those statements dealt specifically with the nature of hearing:

> There is a line a famous Zen master wrote at the time he became enlightened which reads: "When I heard the temple bell ring, suddenly there was no bell and no I, just sound." In other words, he no longer was

aware of a distinction between himself, the bell, the sound, and the universe. This is the state you have to reach.

Yasutani elaborates on this in another dokusan with a different student.

Usually when you hear a bell ringing you think, consciously or unconsciously, "I am hearing a bell." Three things are involved: I, a bell, and hearing. But when the mind is ripe, that is, as free of discursive thoughts as a sheet of pure white paper is unmarred by a blemish, there is just the sound of the bell ringing. This is *kenshō* [enlightenment or self-realization.][44]

While such nondual hearing can hardly be said to be common, neither is it confined to adherents of the nondualist Asian traditions. The lines from T. S. Eliot quoted above clearly allude to a very similar experience, and other examples could be cited. Eliot's is especially interesting because it refers to the medium by which most nondual experiences probably occur. The experience described is unmistakably nondual. Not only is there no hearer, but there is no objective music that is heard. It doubtless records an experience that Eliot had, perhaps many times, and that I suspect many people have had occasionally. One literally becomes "absorbed" into the music; the sense of a self that is doing the hearing fades, and at the same time the music ceases to be something "out there." Especially if the musical work is a familiar one, we normally (and dualistically) hear each note or chord in the context of the whole phrase, by remembering the previous notes and anticipating the ones to come, as if the whole phrase were simultaneously present before us and we "read" it from beginning to end. But this is an example of mnemic savikalpa determination of the nirvikalpa sound. This changes in the nondual hearing: No matter how well I may know the work, I cease to anticipate what is coming and become that single note or chord which seems to dance "up and down." Music is the ideal medium for nondual experience, since we listen to it for enjoyment—that is to say, we listen for no other reason or intention outside itself; we do not need to assign the sounds a meaning, which is to have them refer to something else. The sound need not be a sound *of* something, and without any such thought-construction we have "a pure sound, a bark without its dog" (Neruda). For those of religious inclination, like Eliot, such moments of nondual hearing have a spiritual or mystical quality, but I suspect that for all those who have had them they are cherished as a "heightening of consciousness." This is despite the fact that at the time one cannot be said to be aware of oneself "enjoying" the music, for when I do become aware of myself as enjoying, the nonduality of the experience has already faded away into dualistic hearing and it cannot be brought back by any effort of will or attention. Nondual experience cannot be repeated or produced by the self because it is something that happens to the self—the sense of self evaporates temporarily. One can only create conditions where this is more likely to occur (e.g., meditation), but even then the expectation of such an experience will interfere with its occurrence, as experienced meditators know.

There is another aspect to nondual hearing, which is brought out clearly in a letter by the recent French philosopher Simone Weil. She wrote tht she was in the habit of reciting the "Our Father" in Greek each morning with absolute attention—in other words, her prayer was a meditation exercise.

> At times the very first words tear my thoughts from my body and transport it to a place outside space where there is neither perspective nor point of view. The infinity of the ordinary expanses of perception is replaced by an infinity to the second or sometimes the third degree. At the same time, filling every part of this infinity of infinity, there is a silence, a silence which is not an absence of sound but which is the object of a positive sensation, more positive than that of sound. Noises, if there are any, only reach me after crossing the silence.[45]

It is not clear from this account whether Weil's experience can be called nondual, but it contains an aspect that pertains to nondual hearing: along with the sound there is also an awareness of that which is beyond the sound, which in the context of sound is silence, but it is a silence that is "heard"—"the sound of no sound," we might say. (We shall meet with this curious paradox in later chapters also. For example, nondual action is "the action of nonaction"—Chinese, wei-wu-wei—and nondual thinking has been called "the thought of no thought.") This is part of what Mahāyāna means by the "emptiness" of phenomena: when a sound is experienced as not referring to anything else (not the sound of a barking dog), then "in place of" (we might say) an awareness of the thought-constructed referent (dog), there is instead an awareness of silence. This is how one is able to "stop the sound of that distant temple-bell" (a common Zen koan); when one *becomes* that nondual "bong!" one also becomes aware of that silence "beyond"—that is, the "emptiness of"—the sound. (This paragraph has thrice referred to an "awareness of silence," but of course this dualistic mode of expression should not be taken as implying that the experience of the silence is dualistic. Rather, the nondualist position is that the silence and the consciousness *of* the silence are not two.)

What is the relation between the nondual sound and this silence that is also "heard"? The answer to this question reveals the difference in perspective between Advaita and Mahāyāna. In Weil's account the two seem to be distinct: noises must cross this silence in order to be heard. Advaita, which distinguishes the attributeless Absolute from all ephemeral phenomena, would agree with that: in this case, Brahman corresponds to the "heard silence" and noise serves as an example of delusive phenomena to which we cling by superimposing names-and-forms, with the consequence that we never "hear the silence" which is always there, unchanging. The answer of Mahāyāna is slightly but significantly different. It accepts the above analysis with the proviso that noise is not merely something that conceals silence but is itself an expression or manifestation of the silence. Mahāyāna allows no duality between the silence and the sound. From one perspective, we may say that noise (or sound) is how the silence manifests itself; from another perspective, that silence is the "underside" of the sound, revealing that the sound has no "self-essence" (*svabhāva*). What is important is that the same nondual experience can lend itself to both interpretations— and others as well (discussed at greater length in chapters 6 and 7.)

∎

For many years snow has covered the mountain,
This year the snow is the mountain.

—Dōgen

Vision, by far the most important sense, is also the most difficult one to understand nondualistically. That our understanding of experience is dualistic may be due to the fact that vision has tended to serve as the "standard case" for perception generally and therefore as the measure for all the other senses—and for knowledge as well, which is why most languages abound in visual similes for knowing. We are

inclined to distinguish the "sound heard" from the "objective sound
over there," because we follow the model of vision, which seems to
require a tripartite ontology, distinguishing the one who sees from the
visual appearance (which changes according to perspective) as well as
from the visual object (which is understood to persist unchanged).
Vision provides us with a "co-temporaneous manifold," whereas all
other senses construct their perceptual "unities of a manifold" out of a
temporal sequence of sensations. The predominance of vision thus
gives us a different sense of time than that of all the other senses: the
present is not just the passing *now* but also a dimension where things
can be observed to remain the same. "Only sight therefore provides
the sensual basis on which the mind may conceive the idea of the
eternal, that which never changes and is always present."[46] This makes
possible the philosophical distinction drawn by Plato and Advaita
between Being and Becoming, the former conceived of as an immutable reality that persists "behind" the deceptive world of change.

What do we actually *see*? This question throws us into the long-
raging philosophical controversy over whether it is correct to say that
we see physical objects or whether in fact there are only "sense-data"
(e.g., an elliptical visual image) from which the physical object (a
round plate) is mentally constructed. It is important not to settle this
question linguistically by appealing to the ordinary usage of language, for whether or not the bare nirvikalpa percept can be properly
said to be what we see, the issue is the relation between eye-con-
sciousness and thought: whether and in what way the apparently
objective physical world is constructed by their prapañca-interaction.

Normally—that is, in a nonphilosophical context—we know how to
answer readily enough: we see pens, cups, books...physical objects,
which have weight, color, and so forth. If we delve into the meaning of
what it is for something to be a physical object, we find three characteristics which are important to the nondualist because he wants to
deny them all:

Matter. An equivalent for the "physical" in "physical object" is "material." That objects are material means that they are composed of
matter. We take matter to be an independent, self-existing stuff, which
is real if anything is real, but our experience of this matter is largely
confined to two of its aspects: that it is the source of visual images and
that it is impermeable. One material object is usually impermeable to

another. The cup is solid to my touch; neither my finger not water can penetrate through it, which is why it can function as a cup.

Self-existence. A physical object is self-existent. It has an existence of its own which is not dependent on other objects or on subjects (a consciousness that is aware "of" it), although it may be affected by them. The cup conditions other objects and is affected by them, but it still has its own existence until it is destroyed. This concept of svabhāva differs from that of Mādhyamika, according to which nothing that has self-existence could ever be changed or destroyed, but it does embody the commonsense notion. The bubble may have a very short life, but it nonetheless exists until it pops.

Persistence. A corollary of the previous characteristic is that the object tends to persist unchanged unless affected externally by something else. It is easy to think of counterexamples to this, but they do not refute the fact that this describes our usual notion of what an object is like: it stays the same unless interfered with. The cup does not change unless someone else chips it or drops it on the floor.

When the key characteristics of the visual object are specified in this way, the arguments of the nondualist against its objectivity are predictable.

Against matter. Following the example of Berkeley, the nondualist can deny that we ever *see* such a thing as matter or a material object; given the nature of the eyes, all we can ever see is light. As Berkeley maintained in his *New Theory of Vision*, the notion of matter is a thought-construct created by combining the perceptions due to sight (that is, light) and touch (impermeability, etc.)[47] Strictly speaking, we can never see the impermeability of any object. That I see it *as* impermeable is part of the savikalpa determination of the luminous nirvikalpa percept. In his discussion of causality, Hume remarked that Adam could not have inferred from the fluidity and transparency of water that it would suffocate him.[48] The nondualist would add that Adam could not have inferred from the sight of water how it would feel to the touch. Of course this relating-together of the senses must occur quite early and is now so automatized or "subconscious" that it is normally impossible to see "objects" as other than impermeable. Nonetheless, the nondualist claims that this thought-constructed "unity of apperception" can be undone.

Such undoing must include eliminating the subject of perception. From his claim that we do not "see" distance, Berkeley too quickly inferred that all visual objects are really in the mind, which he understood subjectively. He would have done better to argue as Hume did, that in experience itself there is nothing corresponding to a self:

> "I never catch *myself* at any time without a perception, and can never observe anything but the perception.... All our particular perceptions are different, and distinguishable... and may exist separately, and have no need of anything to support their existence."[49]

By combining these two empiricist arguments—Berkeley against the material object that is perceived, Hume against the subject that perceives—the meaning of the claim that perception is nondual emerges more clearly.

If there is only light, with no physical objects to be seen and no seer to see them, then light must be very different from what we normally take it to be and from the way phenomenalists usually describe sense-data. Our usual understanding of light is dependent upon a dualistic ontology, which relegates it to the role of medium between object and subject, mechanistically reflecting off the one into the eye of the other. But if there is no such subject–object ontology, light must be reevaluated to incorporate not only the object that it is believed to refer to, but also the consciousness which is usually believed to be aware of it. This means that visual "things" are composed not of matter but of something which we might term "Light," and such "Light-things" are śūnya because they do not "refer" to anything else (e.g., a material substratum) when they are experienced as they are in themselves, nondually.

The many references to light in the religious and "illuminative" traditions suggest this. For example, there is the "self-luminosity" (*svayaṁprakāśa*) of Brahman:

> The sun does not shine there, nor the moon and the stars, nor these lightnings—not to speak of this fire. He shining, everywhere shines after Him. By His light all this is lighted.

> [Brahman] is the Light of lights; It is that which they know who know the Self.

> They [knowers of Brahman] see everywhere the Supreme Light, which shines in Brahman, which is all-pervading like the light of day.[50]

A similar view of luminosity is central to the Tibetan tradition:

> In the entire course of the religious experience of Tibetan man, in all of
> its manifestations from *Bon* religion to Buddhism, a common funda-
> mental truth is evident: photism, the great importance attached to light,
> whether as a generative principle, as a symbol of supreme reality, or as a
> visible, perceptible manifestation of that reality; light from which all
> comes forth and which is present within ourselves.
>   ... the connection between light and mind, which is defined as "non-
> duality of the profound and the luminous," characterizes the state of
> transcendent consciousness.... the connection between *sems* [transcen-
> dent nondual consciousness] and light, and the identity of these two
> terms, forms the basis of Buddhist soteriology in Tibet.[51]

Such luminosity of Mind is inconsistent with most Pāli interpretations
of Buddhism, but in the *Dīgha Nikāya* there is a curious passage where
the Buddha says that in nirvana "there is this consciousness, without a
distinguishing mark, infinite and shining everywhere." In the *Aṅguttara Nikāya* also the Buddha describes this consciousness as "luminous" (*pabhassara*) and freed from adventitious defilments.[52] Many
other references, both Eastern and Western could of course be cited.
There is not a lack of such allusions but rather so many that we no
longer notice them and their significance is lost. We take the reference
as metaphoric, but perhaps it is literal. Maybe "the Great White Light"
of Bon and Tibetan Buddhism is nothing other than what light really
is, if it were "seen" as it is.

Against self-existence. If visually there is only nondual Light and if
everything we now consider to be a material object is self-luminous,
this explains why according to the nondualist traditions there are no
sentient beings: there is *only* sentience. The concept of a sentient
being has meaning only in contrast to something nonsentient. In
place of this negated dualism (and its negated corollary, life versus
death), "all phenomena are like a dream, an illusion, a bubble and a
shadow, like dew and lightning," as the Diamond Sutra concludes.
The Bodhisattva does not really save any sentient beings, because
there are none to save. On this point Śaṅkara, Lao Tzu, and the
Christian mystic Eckhart agree with Mahāyāna. Eckhart: "All creatures in so far as they are creatures, as they 'are in themselves' (*quod sunt
in et per se*) are not even illusion, they are pure nothing." Śaṅkara: "This

whole multiplicity of production existing under name and form, in so far as it is Being itself is true. Of itself (*svatas tu*—that is, as self-existing) it is untrue.[53] Chapter 5 of the *Tao Tê Ching* describes the sage as not humane, for he regards the people as "straw dogs"; there is only the Tao, itself void like a bellows. There is still some difference, sharpest between Vedānta and Mahāyāna. For Śaṅkara, creatures are true insofar as they are Being (Brahman)—a formulation Mahāyāna would not accept since it denies any Being. Both explanations may be viewed as opposite solutions to the old problem of how something (in this case, consciousness) can arise out of nothing (nonconscious matter). In fact, their answers are the only two possible solutions: either there never was a "nothing"—that is, "matter" was never nonconscious because it was always self-luminous (the Advaitic solution)—or sentient beings are still nothing (the śūnyatā of Mahāyāna). As we shall see later, these two formulations are not really opposed, for in the final analysis the choice between them becomes linguistic. "It is difficult indeed to distinguish between pure being and pure non-being as a category" (Dasgupta).[54]

Against persistence. We usually distinguish between the visual appearance of an object, which changes as our perspective or the light changes, and the object, which is believed to persist unchanged. If there is no physical object, then there is nothing to "stay the same" and the distinction we make between objects and their interactions—between things and events—crumbles. It might be objected that nondual Light may remain constant, but the sense of *the same* is different in the two cases. It is part of what we mean by a material object that its staying-the-same does not need to be explained, for it is the nature of what we understand as matter to do that unless disturbed in some way. But the staying-the-same of a Light-thing must be an *active* persistence or enduring; its continued presence is an act, we might say. This notion some Buddhist schools attempted to express in the claim that Reality is momentary (*kṣaṇika*)—a formulation which, I argue later, is only half true. Perhaps Heidegger makes the same point better when he said that "things 'thing.'" The nondualist experience is not self-existing objects that interact causally, but empty events or processes. The cup "dwells" on my desk. The concept of an object is a "shorthand" way of accounting for the fact that certain Light-events tend to persist and change in a predictable pattern. This stablity allows us to relate these events causally and form expectations. In itself, such a shorthand is obviously very useful, but when it becomes so auto-matized that we forget it is shorthand, then we mis-take the persisting event (e.g., the self-luminosity of Brahman) as a physical object (self-existing matter).

According to the nondualist, then, what is *seen?* Instead of a self-existing, material object, which passively persists unchanged, there is śūnya, self-luminous sentience, which actively dwells.

NONDUAL PHENOMENALISM

This chapter cannot conclude without showing the place of this theory of nonduality in the context of Western epistemology and indicating, although briefly, how it meets some objections that may be raised against it. We will see that, in the terms of modern epistemology, nondual perception is best understood as a version of phenom-enalism. Nondual phenomenalism escapes some of the objections that have been raised against other phenomenalistic theories, but not the main difficulty: how to account for the role of the sense-organs. Responding to this problem propels us into a deeper understanding of the issues involved. But first I consider some contemporary objec-tions to the notion of "pure sensation" without any conceptual super-imposition.

■

Although twentieth-century epistemology accepts that perception involves conception, many philosophers have objected to the implica-tion (e.g., in sense-datum theories) that our primary level of experi-ence is composed of "pure sensations" stripped of any reference to objects in the perceived world. They claim that such "bare percepts" do not constitute the building blocks of our lived-in-world, for they are the artificial products of intellectual analysis and could never be used to reconstruct the intentional structures of conscious experience. According to this view, introspection gives us no evidence of such indeterminate percepts distinguishable from perceived objects, and it is therefore correct to say that what we do immediately intuit in per-ception *is* objects. This is in criticism of claims such as this one by Berkeley:

> When I hear a coach drive along the street, immediately I perceive only the sound; but, from the experience I have had that such a sound is connected with a coach, I am said to hear a coach. It is nevertheless evident that, in truth and strictness, nothing can be *heard* but *sound* and the coach is not then properly perceived by sense, but suggested from experience."[55]

Heidegger disagrees with Berkeley: "what we hear in the first instance is never noises and sound-complexes, but the creaking wagon, the motorcycle.... It requires a very artificial and complicated frame of mind to 'hear' a 'pure noise'."[56] Yet (to make Berkeley's point), had I never seen or heard one before, I would not be able to say that what I am hearing is a motorcycle. So the issue is whether, once I am familiar with motorcycles, there is a conscious inference from sensation to perception, an inference that I can recognize through introspection. Then the negative answer of Merleau-Ponty and Heidegger is certainly the correct one: once I am familiar with "the sound of a motorcycle," that sound is normally not distinguishable from its source; so what I hear *is* the motorcycle. But rather than argue over the correct use of the word *hear*, what is important here is that inference cannot be denied; it is simply that the inference is so automatic that it is unconscious.

> Normally ... perceptual consciousness seems intuitive—that is, without interpretation and quite unanalyzable; except in perceptual reduction its content almost always consists of ostensible objects. All the same, psychological evidence shows that there is a range of subjective processes.... Perceptual consciousness is introspectively a whole but must be supposed to be a product of a range of selective, supplementary, integrative or organizational, and quasi-interpretative processes acting on a supposed basic sentience. But—and this is the point—both processes and sentience are *unconscious* and so may plausibly be regarded as cerebral activities or adjustments of the nervous system. However, since we cannot as yet give any precise neurological statement of these processes, we have to describe them as if they were conscious, basing the description on the difference between the input to the senses and the finished product, but this product (perceptual consciousness) does not reveal within itself the processes that may be supposed to form it. (R. J. Hirst)[57]

Here philosophy yields to psychology, and it is significant that one recent scientific study concludes that in perception the conceptual element plays an even larger role than sensation:

> Perception seems to be a matter of looking up information that has been stored about objects and how they behave in various situations. The retinal image does little more than select the relevant stored data.... We can think of perception as being essentially the selection of the most appropriate stored hypothesis according to current sensory data. (Richard Gregory)[58]

Evaluated according to our everyday experience, this is not implausible. Our minds are usually so preoccupied with various intentions that we do not so much observe objects as infer their presence on the basis of the most cursory glance. Another way to describe such "intentional perception" is to say that normally observation is selective.

> It needs a chosen object, a definite task, an interest, a point of view, a problem.... A hungry animal...divides the environment into edible and inedible things. An animal in flight sees roads to escape and hiding places.... Generally speaking, objects change according to the needs of the animal.   (Karl Popper)[59]

But what happens if one simply observes without any task, point of view, or needs—as occurs during some types of meditation? If one were able to let go of all intentions, might one come to perceive in a very different way and realize something hitherto unnoticed about those perceptions? It may be granted that the inferences we undeniably make are unconscious at the moment we make them, for they are not observable through normal introspection; but that does not imply that they must remain unconscious and that there are no techniques by which they may be brought to consciousness. We know from psychoanalysis that it is possible to re-expose to consciousness memories and emotional responses which have been long repressed. There is no reason to assume, as Hirst does, that the same is not true of perception. This of course does not settle the issue but makes it one that can be resolved only empirically—that is, experientially—a turn which is agreeable to the nondualist, who invites us to realize this for ourselves in meditative samādhi.

Most of the scientific research into meditation and samādhi has been concerned with its physiology, but I am acquainted with two scientific experiments whose results seem to support the possibility of nondual perception. These experiments were conducted by Dr. Arthur J. Deikman, of the Austen Riggs Medical Center in Stockbridge, Massachusetts, and he reported on them in the April 1963 and February 1966 issues of *The Journal of Nervous and Mental Disease* (from whch I quote below).

In both experiments the subjects (four in the first, six completed the second) sat in a simple room with subdued lighting and were asked to concentrate on a blue vase ten inches high; the number and length of the sessions varied. After excluding those percepts readily explicable in terms of such familiar concepts as after-images, phosphenes, and stabilized retinal images, there remained certain unfamiliar phenomena experienced by all the subjects. The color of the vase shifted to a deeper and more intense blue, frequently described as "more vivid." "The adjective 'luminous' was often applied to the vase, as if it were a source of light." "It was as if light were coming from it." "It started radiating. I was aware of what seemed like particles... [that] seemed to be coming from the highlights there and right at me." Another effect was an instability in the shape of the vase. Its size and/or shape changed; it appeared to become two-dimensional; and there was "a diffusion or loss of its perceptual boundaries." Often the vase appeared to move: "rocking," "drifting," "wavering." "The outlines of the vase shift. At that point they seem almost literally to dissolve entirely...and for it to be a kind of fluid blue... a *very* fluid kind of thing...kind of moving." "...Things seem to sharpen and there is a different nature to the substance of things. It's as though I'm seeing between the molecules...the usual mass of solidity loses its density or mass and becomes separate."

> Solid material such as myself, the vase and the table...seem to be attributed then with this extra property of flexibility such as in its natural, fluid state. It's almost as though we are, myself and the vase and the door, a form which has lost its fluidity the way water loses its property of fluidity when it's frozen.

All Deikman's subjects reported that the vase lost its solidity and rigid boundaries, becoming more fluid and formless; yet, paradoxically, this made it seem even more vivid and real to them. Subjects often used the term "feeling" to describe these experiences, meaning not touch or emotion, "but rather perception that cannot be located in the usual perceptual routes of sight, hearing, and the like." The phenomena observed were not replicable at will. "On different occasions subjects would try to repeat an experience they had had and usually found this very difficult, if not impossible. Indeed such attempts were found to be an interference in the concentration process."

The phenomenon most significant for us is also the one most interesting to Deikman, for it is the first of the individual phenomena discussed in the first report: the "merging experience" of Subject A, who "from the very beginning reported striking alterations in her perception of the vase and her relation to it."

> "One of the points that I remember most vividly is when I really began to feel, you know, almost as though the blue and I were perhaps merging, or that vase and I were. I almost got scared to the point where I found myself bringing myself back in some way from it.... It was as though everything was sort of merging and I was somehow losing my sense of consciousness almost." This "merging" experience was characteristic of all her meditation sessions, but she soon become familiar with it and ceased to describe it as anything remarkable. Following the sixth session she reported, "At one point it felt...as though the vase were in my head rather than out there: I know it was out there but it seemed as though it were almost a part of me." "I think that I almost felt at that moment as though, you know, the image is really in me, it's not out there." This phenomenon of "perceptual internalization" did not recur although she stated that she hoped it would.

In later sessions Subject A described a "film of blue"—later, a "mist" and then "a sea of blue"—that developed as the boundaries of the vase dissolved, covering the table on which the vase sat and the wall behind it, giving them all a blue color. She experienced some anxiety in that "it [this sea of blue] lost its boundaries and I might lose mine too.... I was swimming in a sea of blue and I felt for a moment that I was going to drown..." Her anxiety seems similar to that often experienced by Zen students just before self-realization (as we shall see in chapter 6). The Zen solution is to "let go" and merge with that sea, which is the ego-death that leads to enlightenment. Deikman adds: "despite the anxiety it occasioned, she felt that the experience was very desirable." Deikman mentions a later session, conducted after the end of the experimental series, in which Subject A "reported that a diffuse blue occupied the entire visual field and that she felt merged completely with that diffuseness."

Deikman's second paper reports on another instance of "breakdown in the self-object distinction":

> It was also as though we were together, you know, instead of being a table and a vase and me, my body and the chair, it all dissolved into a bundle of something which had ... a great deal of energy to it but which doesn't form into anything but it only feels like a force.

Subject B in the first study experienced a different sequence of perceptions that Deikman describes as "de-differentiation" and then "transfiguration." Looking out of the window after his sixth session, he was unable to organize his visual impressions:

> I don't know how to describe it, it's scattered. Things look scattered all over the lot, not being together in any way. When I look in the background there is much in the foreground that is kind of drawing my attention.... [later:] The view didn't organize itself in any way. For a long time it resisted my attempt to organize it so I could talk about it. There were no planes, one behind the other. There was no response to certain patterns. Everything was working at the same intensity.... I didn't see the order to it or anything and I couldn't impose it, it resisted my imposition of pattern.

Deikman comments that this description "suggests that the experience resulted from a de-automatization of the structures ordinarily providing visual organization of a landscape (30–50 feet)." But during the next day's session, Subject B's perception of the landscape "might be termed 'transfigured.'" He mentioned very few objects or details but instead talked in terms of pleasure, luminescence, and beautiful movements. For example:

> ... the building is a kind of very white ... a kind of luminescence that the fields have and the trees are really swaying, it's very nice ... lean way over and bounce back with a nice spring-like movement ...
> ... It's a perception filled with light and movement both of which are very pleasurable. Nobody knows what a nice day it is except me.

Subject B later added: "It was coming in to me in a sense, I wasn't watching myself watching.... the antithesis of being self-aware."

In evaluating these results, Deikman considers a number of hypotheses that might be advanced to account for the phenomena: projection, hypnagogic state, hypnosis, sensory translation, sensory deprivation, and unconscious suggestion (but "the very striking phenomena reported were quite unexpected to the experimenter"). He rejects these in favor of "de-automatization":

> Hartmann explicates the concept of automatization as follows: "In well established achievements they (motor apparatuses) function automatically: the integration of the somatic systems involved in the action is automatized, and so is the integration of the individual mental acts involved in it. With increasing exercise of the action its intermediate steps disappear from consciousness ... not only motor behaviour but perception and thinking too show automatization." "It is obvious that automatization may have economic advantages in saving attention cathexis in particular and simple cathexis of consciousness in general...." ... de-automatization is the undoing of automatization, presumably by *reinvesting actions and percepts with attention.*

To this may be added Deikman's summary of the implications of the first experiment.

> The meditation procedure described in this report produces alterations in the visual perception of sensory and formal properties of the object, and alterations in ego-boundaries—all in the direction of fluidity and breakdown of the usual subject–object differentiation. The phenomena are consistent with the hypotheses that through contemplative meditation de-automatization occurs and permits a different perceptual and cognitive experience.... De-automatization is here conceived as permitting the adult to attain a new, fresh perception of the world by freeing him from a stereotyped organization built up over the years and by allowing adult synthetic and associative functions access to fresh materials, to create with them in a new way that represents an advance in mental functioning.... The struggle for creative insight in all fields may be regarded as the effort to de-automatize the psychic structures that organize cognition and perception.

In his second study, Deikman concludes:

> If, as evidence indicates, our passage from infancy to adulthood is accompanied by an organization of the perceptual and cognitive world that has as its price the selection of some stimuli to the exclusion of others, it is quite possible that a technique could be found to reverse or undo, temporarily, the automatization that has restricted our com-

munication with reality to the active perception of only a small segment of it. Such a process of de-automatization might then be followed by an awareness of aspects of reality that were formerly unavailable to us.

If automatization provides a satisfactory account of the perceptual process, then the claim of Merleau-Ponty and Heidegger that what we do immediately hear *is* a motorcycle turns out to be not only consistent with but even implied by the claim that nirvikalpa perception is nondual. From the perspective of the nondualist, it is necessarily true of the phenomenal everyday world that we do not distinguish between the sound and the visual object, for that is part of what we mean by the avidyā (delusion) of dualistic perception. Then the difference between the nondualist and most Western epistemologists is not over the thought-constructed nature of phenomenal experience but over what de-automatization (if that is possible) leads to—whether a merely inexpressible sensation of no interest, or another mode of perceiving that reveals something otherwise overlooked about the nature of sense-perception. Deikman's experiment suggests the latter.

Much of twentieth-century Western philosophy has been concerned with this issue. For example, Husserl realized that all our explicit experience of objects takes for granted an "unthought background" of practices and relations to other objects—a "basic horizon," as it were—and Wittgenstein came to the same conclusion regarding the functioning of language. The usual response is epitomized by Husserl's attempt to analyze that horizon phenomenologically, which, however understandable the effort may be, would amount to bringing that background into the foreground, a feat no less extraordinary than levitating by pulling on one's shoelaces. For the nondualist traditions, this analytic approach is self-defeating, since the prapañca-attempt to grasp that background objectively also hypostatizes the subject in his act of constituting the object. In such a manner we will never be able to experience the nondual ground underlying them both. But if the "unthought background" was once "thought"—if that horizon is a sedimented set of beliefs, inferences, practices, and so on, that were once conscious—then the possibility of de-automatization opens up a completely different approach. Again, the best way to settle the issue is not logically but experientially.

•

By definition, nonduality escapes the main problem for most Western theories of perception: how I can ever have knowledge of things if those things are separate from my mind. For example, direct realism, which claims that we immediately perceive physical objects, cannot account for how the subject (understood as mental) can reach something outside it and completely independent of it. It also cannot explain error and illusion—why some perceptions are veridical and some not, how the plate can be both round and oval. Illusion is not a problem for the nondualist, for the nirvikalpa percept is neither veridical nor nonveridical; like the sense-datum, it cannot appear to be anything other than it is. Questions of error and illusion arise only with savikalpa determination—that is, in the phenomenal world.

Representational realism and causal theories wreck on the same rock: having driven a wedge between what is actually experienced and the object represented or causing the experience, they cannot thereafter bridge that gap to establish the independent existence of perceived objects. Nonduality as developed in this chapter might be viewed as an "idealist" theory of perception, for it denies the existence of objects independent of the mind. But we must remember to distinguish such nonduality from subjective idealism, which reduces the object to the subject, whereas our theory of nonduality denies the one as much as the other. It is as wrong to say that the object is "in" the mind as to say that consciousness resides "in" all physical objects. So subjective idealism is no better a label than realism. I think that nondual perception is better understood as a version of phenomenalism: if we accept that (as Mahāyāna insists) emptiness does not exist apart from form, then there are only nondual appearances.

Having come to this conclusion, I hasten to add that nonduality must be distinguished from other phenomenalisms (e.g., sense-datum theories) which take for granted a naive understanding of the subject. Despite Hume, most versions tend to question only the ontological status of the object and fail to realize that in perception the nature of the perceiver is just as problematic. Because of this, the nondualistic theory of perception avoids some of the difficulties that plague other phenomenalistic accounts. A good example is the issue of solipsism: the view that nothing exists except the self—which thus can be aware only of its own experience—is a problem that lurks for all theories denying objectivity. Traditionally, to be argued into solipsism is equivalent to being checkmated at chess, but the nondualist escapes the mating net. Like subjective idealism, phenomenalism seems to imply solipsism because it isolates the observer by deconstructing other sentient beings into his own sense-data. But such a reduction is not objectionable to the nondualist since the subject is also deconstructed into "sense-data." This avoids the problem of all the data of consciousness becoming private: I may be the only one in the universe, but only because I *am* the universe.

The phenomenalist must also answer difficult questions about the status of the unmediated "sense-data" that the "self" is believed to "have." Are they physical or mental? Spatial and temporal? How long do they last? The nondualist response is that such questions presuppose there are such "things" as "sense-data," but to understand them as something presented to a subject means the nirvikalpa percept has already been processed into objectified savikalpa. Something about nondual perception is always indeterminable by intellectual analysis, for the presupposition of all such analyses is the dualistic need to objectify what in this case cannot be grasped objectively. One question that is meaningful is whether nondual percepts are physical or mental. The nondualist answer is that they can be neither because they are prior to the delusive bifurcation of mind from matter, which suggests comparisons with the "neutral monism" of William James and Bertrand Russell.

A third and more contemporary objection to phenomenalism transforms the phenomenalist's ontological claim into a conceptual thesis about language. Since (according to the argument) we cannot determine the nature of perception empirically, what is at stake must be what we mean when we talk about physical objects. Phenomenalism then becomes the claim that statements about physical objects are (or should be) sets of conditional statements about "what we would see if..." But it is impossible to convert statements about physical objects into hypothetical ones without losing an important part of the meaning. The nondualist answer to this is, first, that nondualistic phenomenalism in the Asian traditions is a claim which can be and is settled empirically every time someone becomes enlightened. Nonduality is not a theory about language but about how the world is experienced without the superimpositions of language. Second, it may readily be granted that our normal beliefs about physical objects extend beyond any translation into nondual percepts, for that additional belief in the self-existence of the perceived object (and the perceiver) constitutes the delusion that needs to be overcome.

The Problem of Sense-Organs

This Life's dim Windows of the Soul
Distorts the Heavens from Pole to Pole
And leads you to Believe a Lie
When you see with, not thro', the Eye
That was born in a night to perish in a night
When the Soul slept in the beams of Light
                    —William Blake, *The Everlasting Gospel*

One difficulty for phenomenalism that nonduality does not escape is accounting for the causal processes apparently involved in the physiology of perception. When physical objects are deconstructed into sensations (or bundles thereof), experience seems to be fragmented: the Light-objects in this room persist only while there is cognition "of" them, and they immediately disappear when my head turns the other way—to reappear when I turn back. In order to avoid this implausibility, phenomenalists sometimes postulate what Bertrand Russell termed *sensibilia*—"objects which have the same metaphysical and physical status as sense-data without necessarily being data to any mind"—which Russell at one time considered to be "the ultimate constituents of matter."[60] Sensibilia of some sort are implied by the nondualist claim that objects are self-luminous. But if nondual sensibilia are self-luminous, why are sense-organs necessary at all? And their necessity is hard to deny: if one has no eyes one cannot see at all, dually or nondually.

This objection is too obvious to have been overlooked. Although the nondualist's answer is implied by everything else discussed in this chapter, it still comes as a shock, revealing more clearly than anything else how alien nondualist perception is, not only to Western epistemology but to all our common sense. For the nondualist bites the bullet and denies that physiological processes are causes of perceptions. More baldly, sense-organs are no more necessary to perception than sense-objects are, because both are śūnya. As the Heart Sutra says, "there are...no eyes, ears, nose, tongue, body or mind." A philosophical exposition and defense of this view is found in the third chapter of the *Mūlamadhyamikakārikā*, where Nāgājuna refutes the reality of sense-organs, sense-objects, and the act of perception by demonstrating their relativity to each other. Since they are all śūnya, to believe that we perceive *with* the sense-organs is a delusion. Rather than dismiss such a conclusion out of hand as nonsense (and at first encounter it could have seemed no less so to Nāgājuna and his contemporaries), we should consider whether our usual understanding of the physiology of perception does in fact prove dualism, or whether that understanding *is* the delusion which perpetuates our sense of dualism.

To begin, let us remind ourselves that in nondual perception there is no awareness that one is seeing *with* the eyes or hearing *with* the ears. According to the ninth Oxherding Picture, the perceiving of an enlightened person is "as though he were blind and deaf" in the sense that "he absorbs himself so unselfconsciously in what he sees and hears that his seeing is no-seeing and his hearing no-hearing." To be simultaneously aware of the sense-organ would mean that attention is divided, hence the experience is dualistic and the Light-object (for example) could not be completely self-luminous. This view is equally agreeable to both Mahāyāna and Advaita, but Advaita quite understandably wants to distinguish between such transcendental experience and our usual perception, in which sense-consciousness is dependent upon the contact between organ and object. But the only way we can avoid splitting experience into two radically different types, thus severing saṁsāra from nirvana, is to make the extraordinary claim that we do not actually perceive with the sense-organs even now.

How could anyone dare to suggest such a thing? The crucial point is that the necessity of eyes for visual perception (for example) is not something immediately experienced (nirvikalpa) but is an inference (hence savikalpa)—however unavoidable that inference may be every time I close my eyes. Wittgenstein made a similar claim in the *Tractatus*:

> Where *in* the world is a metaphysical subject to be found?
> You will say that this is exactly like the case of the eye and the visual field. But really you do *not* see the eye.

And nothing *in the visual field* allows you to infer that it is seen by an eye.[61]

Of course Wittgenstein is not arguing for nondual perception, but his quotation may nonetheless shed light on Nāgājuna's otherwise peculiar refutation of the sense-faculties: "Vision (*darśana*) does not see itself. How can something which does not see itself see other things?"[62] This odd argument is open to several interpretations, perhaps none of which is immediately convincing. The obvious response is that it is only because the eye does not see itself that is *can* see other things—an objection that Nāgārjuna immediately considers. But I think that Wittgenstein points to what Nāgārjuna is getting at: since the eye does not see itself seeing other things, how do we know that we see *with* the eye? It is circular to make my seeing dependent upon my eye, when the conclusion that I see with my eye is an inference dependent upon my seeing. We can never immediately see that it is the eye that is seeing, but only infer it in various ways (e.g., from looking in a mirror). However deeply automatized such a basic inference may be, still it is nothing more than a savikalpa thought-construct. This argument also implies something else important to the nondualist: that we have never had any dualistic sense-experience. The sense of duality can only be thought-constructed by juxtaposing one nondual experience (e.g., an eye opening) with another (the experience of a self-luminous Light-object).

Then to "transcend" all savikalpa-determinations is also to "transcend" the sense-organs, but—we cannot stop yet— to transcend the sense-organs becomes equivalent to transcending sense-perception altogether. Our understanding of sense-perception is so relative to sense-organs and sense-objects that if those are completely denied then the concept of perception loses all meaning. Perception thus inflated becomes perception denied: if (as this chapter argues) there is what might be called *perceiving-only* (without sense-objects and sense-organs), then there is no such thing as perception, and never has been.

Though there is no being of an object because of the knowledge of perception-only, through this knowledge that there is no object, "perception-only" is also refuted. When there is no being (of an object), perception is not possible, so these are alike in this way. (Vasubandhu)[63]

So we end up with what was denied at the beginning of this chapter: the necessity to transcend perception. But our route has been a backward one; on this account, the way to transcend perception is to nondually become it. We are not to negate perception for the sake of some other faculty (e.g., intuition) but to realize that what we have understood as perception (the act of relation between sense-organ and sense-object) is in fact something very different. In other words, what transcends perception is nothing other than the true nature of perception itself.

What does such nondual perception/nonperception leave us with? According to Mahāyāna and Advaita the world is māyā because it is like dreams and a magic show. As the Diamond Sutra concludes:

> All phenomena are like a dream
> An illusion, a bubble and a shadow,
> Like dew and lightning.
> Thus should you meditate upon them.

Other Prajñāpāramitā texts compare perception to a mirage, for nothing is ever created or destroyed. Māyā, dreams, mirages, and magic all have the same characteristic of seeming to be different than they are, of presenting us with something that appears real when it is really śūnya. While sleeping we may dream that we are "in" a body and using its sense-organs, but they are not actually necessary for the dream experience. If that were also true for our "waking" lives, it would explain the nondualist claim that the universe is Mind. It is also consistent with the visualization exercises in Tibetan Vajrayāna Buddhism. It is common to meditate first on a physical object (e.g., a deity depicted on a *thangka* mandala) and then to develop the ability to visualize it in detail in the mind. Enlightenment occurs when the student realizes that the physical object in the visual world and the mentally visualized object in his or her mind are not essentially different from each other. Nondual perception, in refuting the self-existence of Light-objects, implies that the physical object is no more real than the visualized one. Denying the bedrock of objectivity removes our grounds for distinguishing one from the other. According to our sympathies, either this is a self-refuting absurdity or it points to the root of subject–object, mind–body dualism: the sharp but delusive distinction we make between physical objects and mental events. Perhaps material objects are only thoughts that have been concretized in some way.[64] Such speculations are hardly original, but the claim of nondual perception gives us a different mode of approach to them.

Yet to follow this logic too far and completely deny the role of the sense-organs would be one-sided, to say the least. Like Advaita, Buddhism also stresses the sense-organs' phenomenal (saṁvṛti, "lower truth") necessity. The doctrine of pratītya-samutpāda (interdependent origination), which explains all phenomena by relating them in a causal continuum, identifies sensation as the effect of contact between sense-organ and object. The crucial problem then becomes how to understand the connection between these lower-truth, cause-and-effect relationships and the higher-truth claim that nondual experience is unconditioned (nirvikalpa, tathatā) without bifurcating the two as Advaita does. Expressed in this way, the question becomes part of the larger issue of causality. (A full examination of it is reserved for Chapter 6.)

The problem we face in trying to understand the role of sense-organs cannot be distinguished from the more general difficulty of understanding nondual perception philosophically. Because our usual understanding of experience is dualistic, we can "think" nonduality only in one of two incompatible ways. Either we conceive of consciousness materialistically, as panpsychically residing "in" physical objects, or we idealistically reduce the object to an image "in" the mind. It is the first conception, in which the object somehow incorporates consciousness, that falters before the causal processes of the sense-organs. The second conception, in explaining the sense-organs too as objectified mental experience, reduces the material sense-organs to mental percepts that are no more privileged than any other percepts, thus escaping the difficulty. This is not to claim that the second conception is valid whereas the first is not. Both are inadequate because they are based upon dualistic categories of understanding, which unfortunately philosophy cannot hope to escape completely. But the second conception does seem to shed more light upon this problem. Like most philosophical answers, it also raises another question: if it is true that sense-organs are not necessary, then why have they materialized? What has caused their objectification?

This chapter concludes by offering a speculative answer to that question.

The problem of sense-organs could be overlooked until now because the approach used has been almost completely "mentalist," the second of the two conceptions above. It is thought-construction that transforms nirvikalpa into savikalpa perception, and so on. But even a purely mentalist analysis can be accused of taking for granted a Cartesian-type (now commonsense) mind-body dualism, for both the idealist and the materialist starting-points presuppose the very dualism they try to eliminate. As the previous paragraph implies, such a mental–physical dualism is a corollary of the subject–object duality being denied. The claim of subject–object nonduality is more consistent with different approaches to the mind–body problem, such as the neutral monism of James and Russell or Spinoza's double-aspect theory, according to which mind and body are different aspects of the same substance. Adopting such a double-aspect approach would require us to consider the process of thought-construction-and-projection from the material side as well. Does it have a physical correlate?

Man has no Body distinct from his Soul; for that call'd Body is a portion of Soul discern'd by the five Senses, the chief inlets of Soul in this age.
                                                                                    (William Blake)[65]

As soon as we ask the question in this way, something falls into place. For what if not the sense-organs function to condition sensations? To think that the sense-organs must merely receive sensations passively, and that thought-construction occurs only in the brain, is an assumption that, however deeply engrained, seems to presuppose some form of mind–body dualism. A Spinozan double-aspect account raises the possibility that our sense-organs are objectifications of our prapañca—of our tendencies to thought-condition sensations. This is consistent with the view of Tibetan Buddhism, according to which the body is understood as what might be called *materialized karma-potential* and the sense-organs are those parts of the body where such saṁskāras (karmic tendencies) tend to concentrate. That does not mean one's saṁskāras are fixed, for body as well as mind changes, but it does suggest that vikalpa and prapañca may be more deeply ingrained and more difficult to overcome than a purely mentalist analysis would suggest—just as the Advaita conception of māyā as materialized avidyā suggests.

If this speculation is correct, then as the sense-organ changes so the world will change. "The eye altering alters all.... The sun's light when he unfolds it, depends upon the organ that beholds it."[66] Such a claim is not original to Blake, but is part of the Neoplatonic tradition:

> For one must come to sight with a seeing power akin and like to what is seen. No eye even saw the sun without becoming sun-like, nor can a soul see beauty without becoming beautiful. (Plotinus)[67]

That belief is consistent with the tantric emphasis on the body as the means of liberation, as the microcosm of the macrocosm. The Buddha said that the whole world is in this fathom-long body. More recently, Merleau-Ponty has argued that the human body and the perceived world form a single system of intentional relations, that to experience one is to experience the other, and that the body's presence to the world is what enables things to exist.[68] Probably the most interesting implication of such a double-aspect approach is that it gives us a different perspective on the possibility of disembodied existence. If the body and its sense-organs are objectifications of the ways we tend to thought-condition perceptions, it raises the question whether a mind which has freed itself from such automatized tendencies might be able to function without a body.

CHAPTER 3
NONDUAL ACTION

> . . . at the still point, there the dance is,
> But neither arrest nor movement. And do not call it fixity,
> Where past and future are gathered. Neither movement from nor towards,
> Neither ascent nor decline. Except for the point, the still point,
> There would be no dance, and there is only the dance.
> —T. S. Eliot, "Burnt Norton"

If we are to find a parallel to nondual perception in nondual action, then it must be action in which there is also no bifurcation between subject and object. Such nondual action requires that there be no differentiation between agent and act; in other words, no awareness of an agent as distinct from its actions. This chapter explores what that might mean. The first section argues that the Taoist paradox of *wei-wu-wei* (the action of nonaction) is a description of such nondual action. It is highly significant that the same paradox is found in the other two nondualist traditions, clearly enunciated in the *Bhagavad-gītā* and more fully developed in the Buddhist account of the Bodhisattva's path. Comparing these, we discover that the difference between dualistic and nondualistic action involves intention. The mental process of intending a result *from* an action devalues that act into a means and functions as a superimposition that bifurcates the nondual "psychic body" into a mind inhabiting a body, "a ghost in a machine." The second section supports this by demonstrating that the bifurcating role of intentionality is one of the crucial claims in the first chapter of the *Tao Tê Ching*; that chapter is explicated in detail. The third section makes comparisons with some recent analytic work in Western philosophy of mind and suggests that, contrary to first appearances, its conclusions are consistent with and even support the claim that action can be nondual. The last section evaluates two objections that might be raised against this concept of nondual action.

WEI-WU-WEI

Nondual action has just been defined as action in which there is no awareness by an agent, the subject that is usually believed to *do* the action, of being distinct from an objective action that is *done*. Chapter 2 gave us occasion to notice that nondual experience tends to be described in one of two ways: either the subject incorporates the object, or vice versa. In the present case the first alternative amounts to denying that any action is performed. It can hardly be a coincidence that we find precisely this claim in the wei-wu-wei of Taoism. Wei-wu-wei is the central paradox of Taoism and as a concept is second in importance only to the Tao itself, which incorporates it: Lao Tzu describes the activity of someone who has realized the Tao as wu-wei.

> Thus, the wise man deals with things through wu-wei and teaches through no-words.
> The ten thousand things flourish without interruption.
> They grow by themselves, and no one possesses them.   (Chap. 2)

> The Tao is constant and wu-wei, yet nothing remains undone.
> If rulers abide with it, all things reform themselves.   (Chap. 37)

> The highest virtue [*tê*] is wu-wei and is purposeless [*wei*].   (Chap. 38)

> To learn, one accumulates day by day.
> To study Tao, one reduces day by day.
> Less and less is done
> Until wu-wei is achieved.
> When wu-wei is done, nothing is left undone.   (Chap. 48)[1]

That other Taoist paradoxes are susceptible to parallel expression—"the morality of no morality," "the knowledge of no knowledge," and so on—suggests that they derive from wu-wei, perhaps as more specific manifestations of its general pattern. As a paradox, wei-wu-wei seems to be as difficult to understand as the ineffable Tao itself. A number of interpretations have been offered, but they are unsatisfactory without the more radical understanding of wu-wei as nondual action. This is not to claim that nondual action is the only correct meaning, for it may be a mistake to assume that any one particular interpretation must be *the* meaning of wu-wei. Here we might have a case of what Wittgenstein called "family resemblances"; rather than any one characteristic being common to all instances, sometimes there is a cluster of overlapping characteristics.[2]

■

The simplest interpretation of wei-wu-wei is that it means doing nothing, or, more practically, as little as possible. This may be understood either politically or personally. The political interpretation sees wu-wei as "the main precept behind the *Lao Tzu's* conception of government as the minimum amount of external interference projected onto the individual from those in power combined with an environment most conducive to the individual's quest for personal fulfilment."[3] If one leaves the people alone and lets them live their own lives, social problems will resolve themselves—perhaps because political interference is more often the cause of such problems than their solution, as was certainly the case during the Warring States period when Lao Tzu is believed to have lived. Such an explanation of wu-wei is often part of a more general political interpretation of Taoism, which however fits the *Tao Tê Ching* better than the *Chuang Tzu*.[4] This view of wu-wei is also consistent with the sole recorded reference to wu-wei by Confucius:

> The Master said, "If anyone could be said to have effected proper order while remaining inactive [wu-wei], it was Shun. What was there for him to do? He simply made himself respectful and took up his position facing due south."[5]

By regulating his own conduct so that it reflects the moral order, the Confucian ruler sets a positive example and thus is able to influence his subordinates without coercing them. But this does not necessarily imply wu-wei toward the people. The emphasis in Confucianism is that the king reigns but does not rule. In the ideal administration, the ruler does not personally attend to matters of government but depends upon the charismatic influence of his virtue (*tê*); this does not mean that the king's ministers do not need to act. In Taoism the emphasis shifts from this need for a personal example to an anarchism that allows all social and political organization to evolve according to the Tao. Unfortunately, both approaches are faced with the same problem. Despite the hopes of utopian anarchists and economic conservatives, neither of these philosophies of government is very practicable today. Perhaps such government might work in an unthreatened traditional society, but I do not see how it could have been successful in the cutthroat Warring States period, nor do I see a place for it in our contemporary interdependent world, given its complexity and rapid transformation.

The personal interpretation of wei-wu-wei as literally "doing nothing" does not fare much better, and in fact this approach does not seem to have been very common. In his commentary on the *Chuang Tzu*, Kuo Hsiang criticized this view: "Hearing the theory of wu-wei, some people think that lying down is better than walking. These people are far wrong in understanding the ideas of Chuang Tzu."[6] Nevertheless, Fung Yu-lan, after quoting this, went on to add: "despite this criticism, it would seem that in their understanding of Chuang Tzu such people were not far wrong."[7] This reveals more about Fung than Chuang, but I think that Fung is not completely wrong. In fact, such a reading is consistent with the nondual interpretation offered later, since complete "not acting" requires eliminating the sense of self, which is inclined to interfere. Noninterference is not really possible unless one has dissipated the fog of expectations and desires that keeps us from experiencing the world as it is in itself (Tao), and the judgement that "something must be done" is usually part of that fog. Josh Billings said that he was old and had had lots of troubles—most of which never happened. Many, perhaps most of our problems originate in our own minds, in an anxiety projected outward into the environment.

What might be seen as a corollary of "doing nothing" is knowing when to stop. Chapter 77 of the *Tao Tê Ching* compares the course of nature to a bow: "That which is at the top is pulled down; that which is at the bottom is brought up. That which is overfull is reduced; that which is deficient is supplemented." Thus the man who abides in the Tao never wants to reach an extreme, and because he knows the right time to stop he is free from danger (chaps. 15 and 44). Nature, here including man, is a succession of alternations: when one extreme is reached a reversal occurs (chap. 40), as we see in such natural phenomena as day/night and summer/winter—an insight later elaborated into the complexities of the Yin–Yang school.

A more common interpretation of wei-wu-wei sees it as action that does not force but *yields*. This might be called "the action of passivity." Under the weight of a heavy snowfall, pine branches break off, but by bending, the willow can drop its burden and spring up again. Chuang Tzu gives the example of an intoxicated man who is not killed when he falls out of his carriage because he does not resist the fall. This would seem to be an argument for alcoholism, but "if such integrity of the spirit can be got from wine, how much greater must be the integrity that is got from Heaven."[8] So wu-wei is a recommendation to be soft and yielding, like water—Lao Tzu's favorite metaphor. Often the character I translated as "yielding," *joh*, is translated as "weakness,"[9] but "weakness" has unavoidably negative connotations that do not seem right in this context—especially since *joh* is usually (although not always; see chaps. 8 and 66) a means to conquer in the end. It is because water is the softest and most yielding thing that it is able to overcome the hard and strong.

A corollary to this is that a very slight action may be enough to have extraordinary results, if done at the right time. This is "contemplating the difficult with the easy, working on the great with the small" (chap. 63). In particular, one should deal with potentially big problems before they become big (chap. 64). The growth of the sapling is easy to affect, but not that of a mature tree. Both of these points seem undeniable, if limited, truisms. The challenge is knowing when and how to apply them.

Probably the most common interpretation of wei-wu-wei is action that is *natural*. Herlee G. Creel quotes several examples:

> The natural is sufficient. If one strives, he fails.   (Wang Pi)

> The Taoist saint chooses this attitude in the conviction that only by so doing the "natural" development of things will favour him.
>
> (Duyvendak)

> According to the theory of "having-no-activity," a man should restrict his activities to what is necessary and what is natural. "Necessary" means necessary to the achievement of a certain purpose, and never over-doing. "Natural" means following one's *Te* with no arbitrary effort.   (Fung Yu-lan)[10]

The problem with such explanations is that they do not explain very much. As Creel asks, how can we distinguish natural from unnatural action? The term is so pliable that it ends up meaning whatever one wants it to mean, as those who check the ingredients in "natural food" products know. Fung's use of *arbitrary* just pushes the question one step back, for how shall we distinguish arbitrary from not arbitrary? Isn't the passing of such dualistic judgement condemned in Taoist literature? Wang Pi equates the natural with not striving, and others with not making willful effort,[11] but this too begs the question unless some criterion is offered for distinguishing willful from nonwillful action; otherwise we are left, like Fung, lying down. One suggested criterion is spontaneity,[12] but at best that can be only a necessary and not a sufficient condition. The anger I spontaneously feel when someone steps on my toe, or runs off with my wife, is not necessarily a case of wu-wei.

None of the above is a refutation of the view that wei-wu-wei is natural, nonwillful action and so on. The problem is rather that such descriptions do not in themselves go far enough. But allied with the proper criterion they may be valuable. In fact, the concept of nondual action can be seen as such a criterion. The root irruption and disturbance of the natural order of things is man's self-consciousness, and the return to Tao is conversely a realization of the ground of one's being, including one's own consciousness. If consciousness of self is the ultimate source of unnatural action, then natural action must be that in which there is no such self-consciousness—in which there is no awareness of the agent as being distinct from "his" act.

The main problem with understanding wei-wu-wei is that it is a genuine paradox: the union of two contradictory concepts, nonaction ("nothing is done...") and action ("...and nothing remains undone"). The resolution of this paradox must somehow combine both, but how this can be anything other than a contradiction in terms is difficult to understand. Some scholars have concluded that it *is* an unresolvable contradiction. Creel, for example, decided that this greatest Taoist paradox was probably unintentional, due to the juxtaposition of two different aspects in early Taoism: an original "contemplative aspect" and a subsequent "purposive aspect." The first denotes "an attitude of genuine non-action, motivated by a lack of desire to participate in the struggle of human affairs," while the second is "a technique by means of which one who practices may gain enhanced control over human affairs." The former is merely passive (hence "nonaction"), the latter is an attempt to act in and reform the world ("action"), and as Creel emphasizes, these are not only different but "logically and essentially they are incompatible." Creel admits that this interpretation is not to be found within the Taoist texts themselves, and he further recognizes that this puts him in the awkward position of claiming that the more contemplative *Chuang Tzu* is earlier than the compilation of the more purposive *Lao Tzu*. What is worse, he must acknowledge that "we find 'contemplative' Taoism and 'purposive' Taoism lying cheek by jowl, and sometimes scrambled in a grand mixture, in the *Lao Tzu* and the *Chuang Tzu*," which he tries to justify by saying that men are seldom wholly governed by logic.[13] I think the problem is rather that, because Creel here is wholly governed by logic, he cannot understand that the paradox is resolved by a particular experience—the realization of Tao—which cannot be grasped so logically. As with the Vedāntic realization of Brahman and the Buddhist attainment of nirvana, this experience is nondual in the sense that there is no differentiation between subject and object, between self and world. The implication of this nonduality for action is that there is no longer any bifurcation between an agent and the objective action that is done. As usually understood, "action" requires an active agent; "nonaction" implies a passive subject that does nothing and/or yields. The "action of nonaction" occurs when there is no "I" to be either active or passive, an experience that can be expressed only paradoxically: "nothing is done, yet nothing remains undone." The simpler interpretations of wu-wei as noninterference and yielding view not-acting as a kind of action; nondual action reverses this and sees nonaction—that which does not change—"in" the action.

That wei-wu-wei means nondual action is suggested in the *Chuang Tzu*, although less by its references to wu-wei than by its description of another, very similar, paradox. In contrast to the twelve instances of wu-wei in the *Tao Tê Ching*, there are some fifty-six occurrences in the *Chuang Tzu*, but only three of these occur in the seven "inner chapters." It is significant that two of these clearly describe more than noninterference or yielding:

Now you have a large tree and are anxious about its uselessness. Why do you not plant it in the domain of non-existence, in a wide and barren wild? By its side you may wander in nonaction [wu-wei], under it you may sleep in happiness.

Tao has reality and evidence, but no action [wu-wei] or form.

Unconsciously, they stroll beyond the dirty world and wander in the realm of nonaction [wu-wei].

Even more important is the paradox we find in chapter 6, where Nu Chü teaches the Tao to Pu Liang I:

Having disregarded his own existence, he [Pu Liang I] was enlightened ... gained vision of the One ... was able to enter the realm where life and death are no more. Then, to him, the destruction of life did not mean death, nor the prolongation of life an addition to the duration of his existence. He would follow anything; he would receive anything. To him, everything was in destruction, everything was in construction. This is called tranquillity-in-disturbance. Tranquillity in disturbance means perfection.[14]

Here "tranquillity-in-disturbance" (or "Peace-in-Strife")[15] cannot mean a lack of activity. Rather, there is an unchanging sense of peace in the midst of continual destruction and construction—in that ceaseless transformation which includes Pu Liang I's own activity. This is possible only because Pu Liang I first "disregarded his own existence," thus overcoming the duality between self and nonself and "gaining vision of the One."

It can hardly be a coincidence that we find precisely the same paradox in the other traditions which maintain the nonduality of subject and object. Not surprisingly, it is most common in Chinese Buddhism, where Taoist influence is to be expected. But that wei-wu-wei is a paradoxical synthesis of nonaction *in* action is more clearly recognized in Buddhism. Seng Chao maintained in the *Chao Lun* that action and nonaction are not exclusive: things in action are at the same time always in nonaction; things in nonaction are always in action.[16] This claim is expounded in the first chapter, "On the Immutability of Things," but the point is so important to him that he repeats it in chapter 4, "Nirvāṇa is Nameless": "Through nonaction, movement is always quiescent. Through action, everything is acted upon, means that quiescence is always in motion."[17] One of the earliest Ch'an texts,

the *Hsin Hsin Ming* of the third patriarch, Seng-ts'an, states twice that
the awakened mind transcends the duality of rest and nonrest:

> When rest and no rest cease to be,
> Then even oneness disappears.
> From small mind comes rest and unrest
> But mind awakened transcends both.[18]

Niu-t'ou Fa-yung, an important disciple of the fourth Ch'an
patriarch, expressed the same paradox using the Ch'an concept of
"no mind" (*wu-hsin*), in answer to the question whether the mind
should be brought to quiescence:

> The moment when the mind is in action is the moment at which no-
> mind acts. To talk about names and manifestations is useless, but a
> direct approach easily reaches it. No-mind is that which is in action; it is
> that constant action which does not act.[19]

Although this understanding may be derived from Taoism, the Buddhist conception of no-mind shows more clearly that such action
involves the denial of a subjective agent.

There are other instances of the paradox that definitely do not
derive from Taoism. Seng-ts'an's poem echoes chapter 2 of Nāgārjuna's *Mūlamadhyamikakārikā*, which concludes that both motion and
rest are incomprehensible and unreal (śūnya). Given the seminal role
of this text, which became the most important work of Mahāyāna
philosophy, it is possible that all subsequent Buddhist references are
traceable to it. (Full discussion of this claim must be reserved for
chapter 6, where it forms part of a larger examination of causality.) Yet
Nāgārjuna did not write in isolation. His works are usually understood to be a more systematic exposition and defense of claims found
in the Prajñāpāramitā, and we find the same paradox there. Just as all
dharmas are said to be unproduced and unborn, so suchness (tathatā)
does not become, nor does it cease to become. A Bodhisattva neither
comes nor goes, for his coursing is a noncoursing. According to both
the *Daśabhūmika Sūtra* and Candrakīrti's *Madhyamakāvatara*, beginning with the eighth of the ten *bhumis* (the stages of a Bodhisattva's
career), which is called *acalā* (the immovable), the Bodhisattva works
without making any effort, just like the moon, the sun, a wishing
jewel, or the four primary elements. A characteristic of the tenth stage

is that such a "celestial Bodhisattva" is both active and inactive: although results are produced, he does nothing.[20]

In Tibetan Buddhism, the "Yoga of the Mahāmudrā" (already quoted in chapter 1) describes "the final state of quiescence" as follows:

> Although while thus quiescent there is cognition of the [mental] motion [of thoughts arising and vanishing], nevertheless, the mind having attained its own condition of rest or calmness and being indifferent to the motion, the state is called "The state wherein falleth the partition separating motion from rest."
>
> Thereby one recognizeth one-pointedness of mind.

This state is followed by an "Analysis of the 'Moving' and the 'Non-Moving,'" as a result of which

> One cometh to know that neither is the "Moving" other than the "Non-Moving," nor the "Non-Moving" other than the "Moving."
>
> If the real nature of the "Moving" and the "Non-Moving" be not discovered by these analyses, one is to observe:—
>
> Whether the Intellect, which is looking on, is other than the "Moving" and the "Non-Moving";
>
> Or whether it is the very self of the "Moving" and the "Non-Moving."
>
> Upon analysing, with the eyes of the Self-Knowing Intellect, one discovereth nothing; the observer and the thing observed are found to be inseparable.[21]

Finally, probably the best-known example from India is a passage in the *Bhagavad-gītā* that explicitly describes action which is yet no-action:

> He who in action sees inaction and action in inaction—he is wise among men; he is a *yogin*, and he has accomplished all his work.
>
> Having abandoned attachment to the fruit of works, ever content without any kind of dependence, he does nothing though he is ever engaged in work.[22]

The Sanskrit word for action, *karma*, suggests that we might interpret these verses to recommend action which does not bring karmic results. In answer to the Buddhist and Yogic emphasis on withdrawal from the world of social obligation, the *Gītā* claims that action too may lead to Krishna because no karma accrues if an act is performed "without attachment to the fruit of action." This does not disagree with a nondualist interpretation of these verses but rather supplements it. Lao Tzu, the Buddhists, and the *Gītā* may be seen to be describing different aspects of the same experience of nondual action. The difference between the descriptions of Lao Tzu and the Buddhists is in which half of the dualism of agent ←→ action is eliminated. The Taoist wei-wu-wei is the denial of objective action, while the Indian Buddhist concept of anātman and the no-mind of Ch'an emphasize the denial of an agent. The Taoist denies that I *act*; the Buddhist denies that *I* act. But to deny a subjective agent or to deny an objective action amounts to the same thing, since each half of the polarity is dependent on the other. The *Gītā* passage implies how this bifurcation occurs. The sense of dualism arises because action is done with reference to the fruit of action—that is, because an act is performed with some goal or aim in mind: I act *in order to* gain some particular result. The *Gītā* may be understood either (more narrowly) as proscribing selfish action in favor of work "for the maintenance of the world" or (more broadly) as showing the problem with all intentional action. The Buddhist concept of karma, which emphasizes intention, is another expression of the latter view: although "good actions" may lead to pleasurable rebirth in the *deva* (god) realm, that is still saṁsāra. One must act in such a way as to escape both good and bad karmic consequences. Both good and bad karmic acts originate from dualism. In the former, the self manipulates the world for its own advantage; in the latter, the self consciously works for the benefit of something or someone else. The only way to transcend the dualism between the self and the other is to act without intention—that is, without attachment to some projected goal to be obtained from the action—in which case the agent can simply *be* the act.

According to Pāli Buddhism, one of the three "doors to deliverance" (*vimokṣa-mukhāni*) is "wishlessness" or "aimlessness." The other two, śūnyatā and *animitta* ("signlessness," referring to perception without thought-construction) are discussed in chapter 2. The Sanskrit term for the third, *apraṇihita*, literally means that one "places nothing in front"; this is understood to recommend the absence of intentions (*āśaya*) or plan (*praṇidhāna*). Mahāyāna retained all three "doors": "He [the Bodhisattva] should cognize the wishless, in that no thought proceeds in him concerning the triple world" (*Śat-

asāhasrikā).[23] For the dedicated Buddhist, the most problematic intention—in one way necessary, but as self-defeating as any other—is the desire for enlightenment itself. "Do not seek for Buddha outside" emphasizes Ch'an, because as long as one seeks Buddha the true Buddha cannot self-awaken. "If you seek a Buddha, you will be seized by a Buddha-devil; if you seek a patriarch, you will be bound by a patriarch devil; if you seek at all, all is suffering" (Rinzai).[24]

The problem is that intentions are thoughts, which are "superimposed" upon actions in much the same way that thoughts are superimposed upon perception, as discussed in chapter 2. When superimposed upon perception, the superstructure of thought is delusive because it causes a polarization between the subjective consciousness that perceives and the external world that is perceived. In the present case, the attachment to and identification with thought (i.e., the projected goal) gives rise to a sense of duality between the mind that intends (agent) and the body that is used to attain the intended result.

But how does the nonduality of agent and act resolve the paradox of "the action of nonaction"? One may accept the negation of a subject, in the absence of which the action can no longer be called something "objective"; yet there is still an action of some sort. The answer is that, when one completely *becomes* an action, there is no longer the awareness that it is an action. Buber saw this:

> For an action of the whole being does away with all partial actions and thus also with all sensations of action (which depend entirely on the limited nature of actions)—and hence it comes to resemble passivity.
> This is the activity of the human being who has become whole: it has been called not-doing, for nothing particular, nothing partial is at work in man and thus nothing of him intrudes into the world.[25]

As long as there is the sense of oneself as an agent distinct from one's action, that act can be only partial and there will be a sensation of action due to the relation between them. In such a case there is a perspective from which an act is observed to occur (or not to occur), whereas in nondual action there is no sense of an ego-consciousness outside the action. When one *is* the action, no residue of self-consciousness remains to observe that action objectively. Then there is wu-wei: a quiet center that does not change although activity constantly occurs, as in Chuang Tzu's tranquillity-in-disturbance. Just as in nondual hearing there is awareness of an unchanging silence as the ground from which all sounds arise, so in nondual action the act is experienced as grounded in that which is peaceful and does not act. In both these cases (and others to follow), to forget oneself and completely become something is also to realize its "emptiness" and thus to "transcend" it.

Such an action can be experienced as nondual because it is complete and whole in itself. It cannot be related to anything else, for such relating is an act of thought, which shows that there is thinking as well as acting and hence the action is only "partial." If the nondual act is complete in itself and does not refer to something else, then it is also meaningless: that is, it simply is what it is, which is suchness (tathatā). This pinpoints the problem with intention, since it is the reference to some goal to be derived from the act that gives the act meaning. In contrast, the dānapāramīta (perfection of generosity) of Mahāyāna is a complete giving in which the giver, the gift, and the recipient are all realized to be empty (śūnya):

> The supramundane perfection of giving . . . consists in the threefold purity. What is the threefold purity? Here a Bodhisattva gives a gift, and he does not apprehend a self, a recipient, a gift; also no reward of his giving. He surrenders that gift to all beings, but he apprehends neither beings nor self.   (Pañcavimśatisāhasrikā) [26]

Such a "giving of no-giving" (as it might be termed) can be done "without leaning on something" because there is no intention tied to it. The best giving, like the best action generally, is so "free from traces" (Tao Tê Ching) that there is not even the sense that it is a gift. Developing this "intentionless activity" (anābhogacārya) constitutes an important part of the path of the Bodhisattva.

Nondual action becomes effortless because there is not the duality of one part of oneself pushing another part—in the case of physical activity, of an "I" which needs to exert itself in order to get the muscles to move. Rather, I am the muscles. This gives insight into a number of Zen koans, such as the following from the Mumonkan:

> Master Shōgen said, "Why is it that a man of great strength cannot lift up his legs?"
> And he also said, "We do not use the tongue to speak." [or: "It is not the tongue that we speak with."] [27]

This amounts to a denial of the mind–body dualism. However, this is not materialism or behaviorism. Rather than negating the psyche, this claims that the body itself is wholly psychic.

> Yun Yen asked Tao Wu, "What does the Bodhisattva of Great Compassion use so many hands and eyes for?"
> Wu said, "It's like someone reaching back grasping for a pillow in the middle of the night."
> Yen said, "I understand."
> Wu said, "How do you understand it?"
> Yen said, "All over the body are hands and eyes." (*The Blue Cliff Record*)[28]

The Heart Sutra says that one who has realized the emptiness of all things acts freely because he is "without hindrance in the mind." Clearly this is one way in which mental events interfere with nondual action, by sometimes keeping one's physical actions from responding naturally to the situation. All athletes are aware of how anxiety can cause a self-consciousness that interferes with the spontaneity of one's bodily reactions to the movement of a football or tennis ball, for example. The nondual "psychic body," which knows how to react perfectly well by itself, suffers a kind of paralysis due to psychological hindrances. Asian martial arts usually include some meditation in their training in order to avoid this, so students can react spontaneously to attack without being paralyzed by fear and without needing to deliberate first. Acccording to some Zen masters, the first aim of zazen (Zen meditation) is to develop such a "power of concentration" (joriki).

> *Joriki* ... is the power or strength which arises when the mind has been unified and brought to one-pointedness through concentration. This is more than the ability to concentrate in the usual sense of the word. It is a dynamic power which, once mobilized, enables us even in the most sudden and unexpected situations to act instantly, without pausing to collect our wits, and in a manner wholly appropriate to the circumstances. (Yasutani)[29]

However, the problem with dualistic action is not just "hindrance in the mind" but intention in general:

Cultivation is of no use for the attainment of Tao. The only thing that one can do is to be free from defilement. When one's mind is stained with thought of life and death, or deliberate action, that is defilement. The grasping of Truth is the function of everyday-mindedness. Everyday-mindedness is free from intentional action, free from concepts of right and wrong, taking and giving, the finite and the infinite.... All our daily activities—walking, standing, sitting, lying down—all response to situations, our dealing with circumstances as they arise: all this is Tao.   (Ma-tsu)[30]

"Ordinary mind is the Tao" because, when daily activities are "free from intentional action," they are realized to be nondual. This gives insight into how the "mindfulness of body" described in the *Sati-paṭṭhāna Sūtra*, and Theravāda *vipassanā* practice in general, might function. In the slow "walking meditation" of *vipassanā*, for example, one lets go of all intentions by concentrating on the act of walking itself. This also suggests why Zen koans that ask "Why?" (e.g., "Why did Bodhidharma come from the West?") never receive a straight answer. "Unmon said, 'The world is vast and wide like this. Why do we put on our seven-panel robe at the sound of the bell?'" (*Mumonkan*, case 16). A contemporary Zen master commented thus on this koan:

> Some of you are familiar with the last line of the mealtime sutra, "We and this food and our eating are equally empty." If you can acknowledge this fact, you will realize that when you put on your robe, there is no reason or "why" in it.... Try to search out this "why". There is no reason for the "why" in anything! When we stand up, there is no reason "why". We just stand up! When we eat, we just eat without any reason "why". When we put on the *kesa* [seven-piece robe], we just put it on. Our life is a continuous just...just...just.[31]

This passage clarifies what *intentionless activity* means. From the usual perspective, it seems impossible to avoid intentions. We eat to satisfy our hunger, for example, and even taking a walk can be said to have relaxation as its purpose. In this way it is possible to find a purpose in every activity. But the claim above is that even now actions such as dressing and eating are not purposive. Intentionless activity does not mean merely random and spontaneous action; it involves realizing the distinction between thought (intention) and action. The thought (for example, "time to eat") is whole and complete in itself; the act (eating) is also whole and complete in itself. It is when each is not

experienced wholly and discretely but only in relation to the other, the
first as if "superimposed" upon the second, that action seems intentional and there is the sense of an agent/mind that uses the act/body
for the sake of something.

In answer to such stock questions as "What is the first principle of
Buddhism?" Zen masters such as Ma-tsu, Huang Po, and Lin Chi were
apt to strike the student or shout in his ear. If the Tao is nonintentional everyday-mind, such responses are not evasive. They are answers
to the question, demonstrations of "why" because they exemplify
nondual action, complete and whole in itself.

> One day the World-Honoured One [Śākyamuni Buddha] ascended his
> seat. Mañjuśrī struck the gavel and said, "Clearly behold the Dharma of
> the King of the Dharma; the Dharma of the King of Dharma is 'just
> this!'" (*The Blue Cliff Record*)[32]

In his lecture on the first case of the *Mumonkan*, Yasutani-rōshi
describes the actions of someone who has attained kenshō:

> Wherever you may be born, and by whatever means, you will be able to
> live with the spontaneity and joy of children at play—this is what
> is meant by a "samādhi of innocent delight." Samādhi is complete
> absorption.[33]

Complete absorption means that the self is completely absorbed in play,
in which case the self and its activity are nondual. The Sanskrit word
for play, *līlā*, is often used in Vedānta to describe Saguṇa Brahman's
purpose in creating the phenomenal universe: that is, there is no
purpose outside the process itself. The dialectic of ignorance-and-
liberation is God playing hide-and-seek with Himself. The Semitic
religions, which do not accept reincarnation, generally look upon
spiritual life as a more serious business, our "one chance" to prepare
ourselves for God's judgment. But the experience of some Western
mystics led them to a conclusion similar to that of the nondualists:

> When [Jakob] Boehme is speaking of God's life as it is in himself he
> refers to it as "play." . . . Adam ought to have been content to play with
> nature in Paradise. (*Mysterium Magnum* 16:10) Adam fell when this play
> became serious business, that is, when nature was made an end instead
> of a means.[34]

Meister Eckhart echoes the Zen masters:

Do all you do, acting from the core of your soul, without a single "Why." . . . Thus, if you ask a genuine person, that is, one who acts from his heart: "Why are you doing that?"—he will reply in the only possible way: "I do it because I do it!"

[The just man] wants nothing, seeks nothing, and has no reason for doing anything. As God, having no motives, acts without them, so the just man acts without motives. As life lives on for its own sake, needing no reason for being, so the just man has no reason for doing what he does.[35]

CHAPTER ONE OF THE *TAO TÊ CHING*

> *. . . contracting our infinite senses*
> *We behold multitude, or expanding, we behold as one,*
> *As One Man all the Universal Family . . .*
>
>   —William Blake, *Jerusalem*

The previous section developed the view that the difference between dualistic and nondualistic action is intentionality. That intentionality is the "hinge" between duality and nonduality is also emphasized in the difficult first chapter of the *Tao Tê Ching*, according to the traditional interpretation. Despite its ambiguity, this succinct chapter (only fifty-nine Chinese characters) is clearly the most important passage in all of Taoism.[36] Scholars such as Wing-tsit Chan and Chang Chung-yuan[37] go further to claim that chapter 1 is the key to the entire *Tao Tê Ching*; all the rest may be inferred from it. Therefore it is all the more unfortunate that the importance of the concept of intention has been obscured in some recent translations. To correct this, and to show how well a nondualistic interpretation of this chapter works, I present a line-by-line explication of this crucial passage, demonstrating that the first eight lines are in a parallel structure because they refer to two different ways of experiencing: lines 1, 3, 5, and 7 refer to the nondual experience of Tao, and lines 2, 4, 6, and 8 to our more usual dualistic way of experiencing the world. This parallel structure unfolds dialectically: each succeeding pair of lines elaborates upon the issues that are raised by the preceding pair. In the process of showing this, I discuss the two main controversies over this chapter: first, whether it should be interpreted cosmologically or ontologically/epistemologically; second, whether lines 5 and 6 should be punctuated to translate *yü* as "desire/intention." My main point is that the traditional understanding of *yü* as "desire" or "intention" is an essential part of the meaning. This is not an original claim, but *why* it is so important does not seem to have been noticed. Wing-tsit Chan's criticism of such an interpretation, that "intention interrupts the thought of the chapter," is a serious misreading of the text.[38]

But, when dealing with so laconic a passage, one must be especially cautious about declaring any interpretation to be "the correct one." Of no text are deconstructive qualifications more relevant, and perhaps the most we can ever expect to have are "strong misreadings." In justification of what follows—indeed, of this whole work—I can do no better than cite Heidegger: "Every interpretation is a dialogue with the work, and with the saying. However, every dialogue becomes halting and fruitless if it combines itself obdurately to nothing but what is directly said."[39]

> The Tao that can be Tao'd is not the constant Tao
> The name that can be named is not a constant name
> Having-no-name is the source of heaven and earth
> Having-names is the mother of the ten thousand things
> Therefore always do not have intention in order to see the wonder
> Always have intention in order to see the forms
> These two thing have the same origin
> Although different in name
> Their sameness is called the mystery
> From mystery to mystery: the gate of all wonder![40]

How to translate *Tao* is a question which need not detain us, since Chinese thought is now familiar enough that we can leave the term untranslated and let it reverberate according to its usage in various contexts. Literally, *Tao* combines the character for "head" with a radical meaning "the way" or "the path"; thus a literal translation is "the Supreme Way." As one would expect, the earliest sense of the radical seems to have been a road or path, and only later did the more metaphoric and metaphysical meanings arise, enabling Tao (like its Greek counterpart *logos*) to be translated, although not very well, as Truth, Reason, Nature, and so on. The philosophical issue of what the Tao is cannot, of course, be evaded and will need to be discussed.

A common translation of the first line is: "The Tao that can be spoken of is not the eternal Tao." There are two problems with such a rendering. First, translating *ch'ang* as "eternal" implies a metaphysical bias toward unchanging permanence which is not in the original. *Eternal* would be a suitable characterization of the Indian *puruṣa* or Nirguṇa Brahman, but, given the Chinese emphasis on the reality of changing phenomena, not for the Tao. The word *constant* (or *invariable*) is preferable because it is more ambiguous, leaving more possibilities open—for example, that the Tao is to be understood not diachronically but synchronically, as some pattern in the flux of change. This brings us to the second point. To describe the Tao as an ineffable metaphysical principle is to exclude another part of the meaning, that the path (here temporal as much as spatial) which can be followed is not the true path. Putting these two together, we have something like: "The Tao which is spoken about/followed is not the real Tao." Why not? Why cannot the Tao be Tao'd? This is answered in the second line, which drives a wedge between the Tao and all attempts to characterize it. Names—later it becomes clear that this means language generally—are not "constant" in the way that the Tao is; so, conversely, that which can be named can't be the Tao. The namelessness of the Tao, our inability to characterize it, is declared to be its primary characteristic—a paradox that is self-stultifying only insofar as we are confined within the bounds of language, whereas the claim is evidently that there is a reality "outside" language which is inaccessible to it but not necessarily to us. That the Tao is unnameable is repeatedly emphasized in later chapters; for example, 32 ("The constant Tao is unnameable") and 41 ("The Tao, when hidden, has no name").

This issue of the ineffability of the Tao has been much discussed.[41] It is clear that Lao Tzu is, among other things, denying a representative theory of truth.[42] But so, for example, does Wittgenstein, without postulating any spiritual Absolute. So it is necessary to say more to uncover the meaning of Lao Tzu's claim. Given the brevity of this chapter, and the "pre-philosophical" nature of the whole work, one cannot expect any textual exegesis to reveal a complete metaphysical theory implicit in this passage or in the ones that follow. So here we may benefit from a comparison with the other nondualist systems discussed in this work, which also emphasize the ineffability of the Absolute and go further to link that ineffability with the nonduality of subject and object—a nonduality that is also found in Taoism, especially in Chuang Tzu, but which is not explicit in the *Tao Tê Ching*. As discussed in chapter 2, Mādhyamika characterizes (or, more precisely, explains why we cannot characterize) nirvana as "the coming-to-rest of the manifold of named things," in which we realize that our usual way of perceiving the world—as a collection of discrete named things—is just one way of "taking" it. Yogācāra Buddhism is more explicit in asserting that the true nature of things is nondual. The apparent bifurcation of subject from object is due to grasping at phenomena: that-which-is-grasped is reified into an object, and that-which-grasps becomes the sense of an autonomous self. What is most relevant to us at the moment is that our main way of grasping is through language. The object is a creation of thought-construction, which converts the bare nirvikalpa sensation into a determinate image associated with a name. We have understood Śaṅkara's explanation of māyā as adhyāsa—name and form superimposed upon Brahman—in the same way. Ch'an Buddhism too asserts nonduality and criticizes language as deceptive: "Reality is right before you, and yet you are apt to translate it into a world of names and forms" (Fa-yen Wen-i). With the exception of Vedānta, all of the above were well-received in China and greatly influenced its thought—largely because the similarities between Buddhism and Taoism were so deep. Ch'an, of course, was a result of their convergence and as a living tradition is therefore especially valuable in interpreting Taoism "after the fact."

The factor common to all these schools is that they link the ineffability of the Absolute (however otherwise "characterized") with its nonduality: the problem with any attempt to describe the nondual Absolute is that it amounts to dualistically separating oneself from it. Later I argue that the above nondualities are phenomenologically equivalent; here the important point is that, although we do not find an explicit denial of subject–object duality in the *Tao Tê Ching*, such a claim is quite consistent with its claims and is particularly helpful in explicating the first chapter. The Tao can then be understood as the totality of what-is, which is both ontologically and epistemologically prior to any duality that arises within it. Then to give the Tao a name is to try to determine that whose nature is indeterminate, to objectify that which cannot be objectified because it is what there is before any bifurcation into subject and object. If the goal is to experience that nondual Tao, this also amounts to an indictment of all philosophy. Philosophy originates in the awareness that the apparently objective and matter-of-fact reality of the world is in fact problematical, and in our uncertainty as to how we relate to it. We realize that our everyday understanding of the world is just an understanding, and philosophy is the resulting search for the correct understanding, an attempt to construct that set of categories which when superimposed upon reality will "mirror" it precisely. Thought thus distinguishes itself from the world in order to divine the world's structure—but in the process it perpetuates the dualism between "inner" conscious mind and "outer" objective world, which dualism is the root problem to be overcome, according to our nondualist systems. The "spirituality" of the Tao, like the Brahman of Vedānta and the Dharmakāya, and so on, of Mahāyāna, arises from the fact that these nondual Absolutes cannot be understood reductively as some material substratum but are the source of all consciousness as well. All of these negate ego-self because the individual consciouness usually understood to be the essence or property of that self is finally realized to be but an aspect or "reflection" of an all-encompassing consciousness.

If the first line is understood as "the Path that can be followed," the emphasis becomes different. The problem with attempting to "follow" the Tao is the self-conscious and hence dualistic effort involved. If one is truly harmonized—that is, one—with the nondual Tao, the Way will not be experienced as something external to oneself, as a path that either is or is not being followed. From this perspective, the Tao should be understood not as a timeless Absolute but as the natural course of things; and *trying* to follow the natural course of things is to be no longer natural. That is the point of the famous *mondo* between Ch'an masters Chao-chou (Jap., Jōshū) and Nan-ch'üan (Nansen):

Chao-chou: "What is the Tao?"
Nan-ch'üan: "Ordinary mind is the Tao."
Chao-chou: "How should I try to follow it [more literally, 'turn towards it']?"
Nan-ch'üan: "If you try to turn towards it, it will turn away from you."[43]

In summary, I am suggesting that the first two lines be taken as describing two different ways of experiencing—nondual and dual, respectively. The role of language in the bifurcation of the Tao into subject and object is elaborated in lines 3 and 4:

> Having-no-name is the source of heaven and earth
> Having-names is the mother of the ten thousand things

Since the Tao is what has no name, these two lines parallel the first two. But they are more controversial. Should they be taken cosmologically, as a cosmogonic myth describing the creation of the phenomenal world, or ontologically/epistemologically, as I have been doing?[44] Given that the ambiguity of this laconic text is obviously intentional, I see no reason to conclude that these interpretations must be mutually exclusive. But the ontological/epistemological approach does seem more revealing. That the Tao is the source of heaven and earth means that the Tao is everything, a totality which incorporates the entire universe. In contrast, "having-names" is the mother of "the ten thousand things," the common Chinese idiom for all the things *in* the world—that is, the sum total of all the particulars that exist. At first glance the distinction between the two is not clear. But if the "source" of line three is understood as what heaven and earth really *are*, then the Tao as their source is the universe apprehended nondually; the claim is that this is how the universe may be experienced when we "take" it without names. In contrast to this, language-acquisition is identified as the process that gives birth to our phenomenal world of multiplicity, breaking up the primordial whole into objects—one of which is the subject, since the sense of self is also reified in the process. These objects are then perceived as distinct from each other but as interacting causally *in* space and time. This interpretation is obliquely supported by another term for the Tao, used in later chapters: *p'o,* or "the Uncarved Block," to use Waley's felicitous expression; chapter 37 refers twice to "the unnameable *p'o.*" So lines 3 and 4 make another distinction between nonduality and duality, contrasting the nameless "ground" of everything with the multiplicity of various objects "in" the world. But, as I pointed out in chapter 1, this nonduality also implies the nondifference of subject and object, for "my" world cannot be a whole unless it incorporates "my" consciousness as well.

But why do we name? What motivates us to carve up the Uncarved Block? This is explained in the next pair of lines:

> Therefore always do not have intention in order to see the wonder
> Always have intention in order to see the forms

More idiomatically: whenever you let go of all intentions, you will
experience the wonder; whenever you have intentions, you will see
forms. These lines are the heart of the chapter. The parallel structure
continues: the first concerns the Tao and the second refers to the
manifold phenomenal world. This becomes evident when we clarify
the meaning of the key terms. "Wonder" is *miao*, also translated
"subtlety" (Wing-tsit Chan, following Wang Pi), "secrets" (D. C. Lau),
and "inner wonders" (Charles Fu). What is unquestionable in all cases
is that *miao* has connotations of spirituality and holiness. It refers to
the "spiritual" way of apprehending reality, which is the experience of
Tao, or, better (because less dualistic), Tao-experience. "Forms" is
chiao, which has been translated in even more different ways: "out-
come" (Wing-tsit Chan), "manifestations" (Chang Chung-yuan),
"manifest forms" (Lin Yutang), "outer fringe" (Giles), "borders"
(Bodde), "ultimate results" (Waley), "the obvious" (Nagatomo). That
the original image for *chiao* seems to have been "edges" is felicitous for
my interpretation, for how do we divide up the undifferentiated Tao
into multiple forms? We distinguish one thing from another by determining it, in the etymological sense of perceiving where it termi-
nates. The edge is where an object comes to an end. To de-fine
something is to differentiate its form from another form, or from the
formless. But the Tao itself has no edges or borders. The Tao is
infinite and in-determinate, because it is all-encompassing. So *miao* is a
spiritual experience of the Tao, and *chiao* is the world experienced as a
collection of discrete forms.

   "Intention," *yü*, is often translated "desire," but I think "intention" is
to be preferred because it is more general and captures a meaning that
"desire" misses—unless one understands the term broadly, as in
"desiring to do something." Yet lines 5 and 6 are susceptible to an
entirely different translation, according to how they are punctuated.
If a comma is read between the *wu* and *yü*, rather than after the *yü*,
they become:

> Therefore let there always be nonbeing, so one may see the wonder
> Let there always be being, so one may see the forms

The former version, using "intention/desire," is more traditional, deriving ultimately from Wang Pi and Ho-shang Kung. Recently Wing-tsit Chan has followed Wang An-shih and Su Ch'ê in preferring the latter version: "I have also departed from tradition because the idea of desires interrupts the thought of the chapter."[45] But this misses Lao Tzu's point. As Chang Chung-yuan points out:

> Su Ch'ê did not understand that through *wu yü*, or without intention or non-willing, one is freed from conceptualization and released to the total identity of the seer and the seen, which is the highest stage of the mystery of Tao.... Then one will achieve what Taoists call "*wu o chu wang*" or "both things and myself are forgotten." Once one is free from both subjectivity and objectivity, one can enter the gate of Tao.[46]

Before elaborating on this, it is important to designate the limits of the controversy. Both readings are possible because both are consistent with other claims made in subsequent chapters. More than consistent, both claims are essential to Lao Tzu's conception of the Tao. For example, chapters 11 and 40 both refer to nonbeing as in some sense prior to being,[47] and "no intention" is emphasized in chapters 34 and 37. So the controversy is reduced to the less significant issue of whether, as Wing-tsit Chan claims, the concept of desire/intention disrupts the meaning of the first chapter. In what follows I argue that, on the contrary, *yü* as "intention" is essential for a full understanding of Lao Tzu's point.

Let me summarize where we are. What is it that keeps me from experiencing the "wonder" (*miao*) of Tao? Lao Tzu has already pointed to names. In naming, I determine something as a thing, distinguishing it both from its contextual ground and from me, its "grasper." If the name itself is not part of the thing, but something subjective, then I do not apprehend just the thing, as it is in itself, when I see it *as* "a pen" or *as* "a cup." Then why do I name? What is the link between naming and intentions? In order to answer this, we need to understand the relationship between language and causality: how causality is built into language itself.

In chapter 2, John Searle was quoted to point out that naming is not just a matter of pinning labels on self-identifying objects. "The world doesn't come to us already sliced up into objects and experiences: what counts as an object is already a function of our system of representation, and how we perceive the world in our experiences is influenced by that system of representation." When naming, I do not first see a thing and then decide to call it a "door"; learning to call it a door is how I pick it out from the nirvikalpa visual manifold and notice it. We divide up the world and come to see it as a collection of objects by giving names to those objects. But now we may take a further step. How does language "mean"? As Wittgenstein has shown, a name should not be understood merely as a label. Names usually imply functions, because we cannot understand how language works until we see its connection with our behavior. The meaning of a word is usually to be discovered in how it is used, what "form of life" it is part of. "We may say: only someone who already knows how to do something with it can significantly ask a name."[48] Since language is an integral part of our life, the only way we can determine whether a person truly "understands" certain language patterns is by observing his behavior. A person shows that he understands the meaning of *door* not by being able to give a verbal definition, but by being able to use it in the appropriate way for going in and coming out. To understand that "that" (pointing) is "a door" includes understanding the function of a door, which defines one's causal relationship with "that."

In looking about my office, I see many things—books, blackboard, cup, pens, chalk, chairs, and so on. To experience the room in this way (an effect of prapañca) is to perceive it as a set of things ready-to-hand to be used in the appropriate ways. Heidegger's concept of *zuhanden*[49] (utensils) is helpful here. In our usual day-to-day living what we experience are not objects just "simply there," but utensils available to be used. The full nondual presence of a pen is not perceived as it is in itself because "I" am busy utilizing "it" to write these words, and the paper is also not perceived fully but just utilized as something to write on, the desk is used to support the paper, the cup to drink from when I am thirsty, and so on. As soon as I identify something as, for example, "a piece of chalk," its function—that is, my relationship with it, where it fits into my web of intentions—is established, and at that point I usually put it in its "place" and then pay no more attention to it until I need to write on the blackboard. As I argued in chapter 2, seeing in this way is something we have learned to do, although we are not usually aware of the fact. We are not normally conscious of the difference between that which is actually perceived by the eye and the functions subjectively implied by the name; the two are experienced together.[50] Only with the "wondrous experience" of Tao do I realize that I have been seeing things *as* . . . , rather than as they are in themselves, which is Tao.

Heidegger concludes that we most immediately experience the world as a "totality of destinations" (purposes) which ultimately refers back to *me*. But it is important not to hypostatize this *me*. If the Tao is nondual, it is not the "I" that names and intends, but rather the reverse: subjectivity—the sense of a subjective consciousness that is *doing* the seeing, acting, and so on—arises because of the naming and intending. Without these activities—for example, in Taoist "mind-fasting"—the self evaporates. (Such mind-fasting is discussed in the *Chuang Tzu*—for example, that of Pu Liang I in chapter 6—but there are only oblique references to meditation in the *Tao Tê Ching*—e.g., in chapter 10.)

Why do we tend to see objects as utensils—that is, causally? Insofar as I have desires and intentions, I will need to manipulate the world in order to get what I want. Such manipulation requires me to ask what will produce the desired effect. In fact, that tendency to manipulation may be seen as the root of the concept of causality.

> The idea of cause has its roots in purposive activity and is employed in the first instance when we are concerned to produce or to prevent something. To discover the cause of something is to discover what has to be attested by our activity in order to produce or to prevent that thing; but once the "cause" comes to be applied to natural events, the notion of altering the course of events tends to be dropped. "Cause" is then used in a non-practical, purely diagnostic way in cases where we have no interest in altering events or power to alter them.   (Nowell-Smith)[51]

So causality is built into language. Names do not simply cover things like a blanket of snow resting on the roof of a house. Learning a language is learning to make causal connections, learning to see the world as a collection of utensils used to accomplish certain ends. The same point may be made in terms of conceptualizing: thought-construction (vikalpa, prapañca) is also causality-construction. In this way, craving, conceptualizing, and causality work together to sustain the dualistic sense of a self "in" an objective world (fig.1). Further

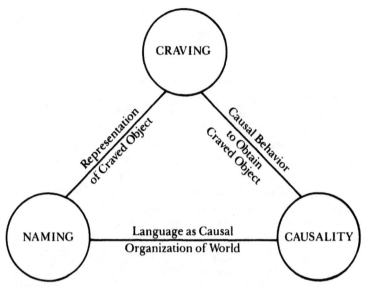

Figure 1

development of this is reserved for the discussion of causality in chapter 6; now we return to the *Tao Tê Ching*.

If the above is true, and intentions are "built into" language, then the concept of intention by no means interrupts the thought of the first chapter, as Wing-tsit Chan claims. On the contrary, intention becomes the crucial point. To ignore this is to miss Lao Tzu's logic. The first two lines distinguish the ineffable Tao from the everyday world of named things. The second pair declare that the Tao is what everything really *is*, but that language splits up this whole by distinguishing one thing from another. The third pair explain why we name by connecting language with our web of intentional action and they claim that we can return to the nondual Tao-experience by letting go of our intentions.

Having completed differentiating these two modes of experience, the next two lines emphasize their unity:

> These two things [*miao* and *chiao*] have the same origin
> Although different in name

There is no specifiable difference between nirvana and the everyday world, said Nāgārjuna; the limits of the one are also the limits of the other.[52] The same is true for the Tao and our world of multiplicity. They are two ways of apprehending the same reality. To experience the wonder of Tao is to apprehend this reality nondually. To experience the world as we usually do is to perceive that reality fragmented into the ten thousand things, one of which is *me*, the subject who is really the first hypostatized object. There are other similarities between the Tao and the nondual Absolutes of Indian philosophy, but we should also notice an important difference. For Vedānta, ultimately only Brahman is real, for the changing phenomenal world is eventually subrated into illusory māyā. But Lao Tzu grants reality to the forms also, since the world of named things is one way the Tao manifests itself. Indian philosophy generally is more "otherworldly" in wanting to negate completely the phenomenal world for the sake of a changeless Absolute, whereas the more pragmatic Chinese ideal, as in this passage, is to understand the relation between both ways of experiencing so as to be able to move back and forth freely from one mode to the other.

Yet this very distinction between two modes of experience, and their subsequent identification, is valid only from the perspective of one of those modes. That they are different only in name shows this, for names do not apply to the Tao itself. This means that the sage who is fully harmonized with the Tao will see only the Tao and everything as a manifestation of the Tao. One who has realized the Tao may feel alienated from it, but from his perspective there is always only the Tao and we have never been apart from it.

> Their sameness is called the mystery
> From mystery to further mystery: the gate of all wonder!

The relation between these two modes, the nondual Tao and named multiplicity, the fact that reality has two aspects and yet is one, is here declared to be a great mystery. Perhaps there is a hint too that this is an essential mystery which can never be fathomed. For in order to understand it, would we not need to stand outside the relation and see it objectively? And according to this chapter we cannot do that: there is no third mode.

To conclude this section, the first chapter of the *Tao Tĕ Ching* may be summarized as follows. Lines 1, 3, 5, and 7 describe the nameless Tao, the source of heaven and earth, which is reality apprehended as a "spiritual" (*miao*) whole. Such Tao-experience can occur when one has no intentions, in which case there is no self in the usual sense and experience is nondual. Lines 2, 4, 6, and 8 refer to the dualistic everyday world, which is perceived as a collection of interacting but discrete things. We experience the world in this way due to language and intention, which mental processes are not the activities that a self does but rather are what create and sustain the illusory sense of a self.

INTENTIONALITY AND FREEDOM

Recent Western work in the philosophy of mind has developed the view that the continuity of consciousness is maintained not by memory, as the earlier empiricists believed, but by the stream of intentional action. Stuart Hampshire argues for this in *Thought and Action*:

> British empiricists since Hume have tried, to their own dissatisfaction, to represent the continuity of a person's consciousness as some binding thread of memory running through the separate data of consciousness. But within the trajectory of an action, with its guiding intention, there is already a continuity through change, and, if it is true that a conscious person is necessarily engaged upon some action, however trivial, this known continuity is interrupted only by sleep and by other forms of unconsciousness.... I do distinguish myself, as the inner core that is the source of directed effort, from all my passing states, and it is this sense of myself as the source of meaningful action that gives me the sense of my continuity from the present into the future.
> ... a conscious mind is always and necessarily envisaging possibilities of action, of finding means towards ends, as a body is always and necessarily occupying a certain position. To be a conscious human being, and therefore a thinking being, is to have intentions and plans, to be trying to bring about a certain effect. We are therefore always actively following what is happening now as leading into what is to happen next. Because intentional action is ineliminable from our notion of experience, so also is temporal order.[53]

This seems to contradict what was maintained in the first two sections of this chapter, but the disagreement masks a deeper agreement. If we take the "conscious mind" of the second passage to mean "consciousness (or awareness) of self," then such a view about the relation between "the sense of myself" and intentional action is consistent with what has been claimed in this chapter. The only significant difference is that, because Hampshire believes intentional action to be "ineliminable from our notion of experience," he does not envision the possibility of nondual action as a result of eliminating "the source of directed effort." If intentional action were eliminable, then the implication of Hampshire's position is that the sense of self is also thus eliminable—precisely what I have argued. Hampshire is wrong when he claims that "a conscious mind is always and necessarily envisaging possibilities of action," for there is the counterexample of meditation—an example very much to the point, since it is generally agreed to be a very important part, perhaps the most important part, of the path for those who wish to experience nonduality. It may be objected that even in meditation one has intentions and makes efforts to concentrate on something, but, as we shall see later, this is no longer the case in the deeper stages of meditation, for in samādhi the sense of self evaporates, precisely because all effort and intention cease. Hampshire's account seems valid as an explanation of the usual dualistic way of understanding experience, but it does not amount to a critique of nonduality. On the contrary, if one accepts (as Hampshire would not) a distinction between sense of self and nondual experience, then his account would agree with this chapter in explaining the difference between dualistic and nondual experience as due to intentionality. In this sense, Hampshire's view of action as intentional corresponds to Wittgenstein's and Heidegger's view of perception as conceptual (discussed in chapter 2). Both are consistent with—indeed, implied by —the account of nonduality presented here, for they are descriptions of everyday experience that account for why experience seems dualistic. They should not be taken *prima facie* as refutations of the possibility of nondual experience.

There is still a serious problem with Hampshire's account. Explaining the continuity of consciousness as due to intentionality takes for granted what we usually take for granted, some sort of causal relationship between intentions and actions. However, Hume pointed out, as a corollary to his critique of the causal relation, that no one can hope to understand how volition produces motion in our limbs: "That their motion follows the command of the will is a matter of common experience, like other natural events: but the power or energy by which this is effected, like that in other natural events, is unknown and inconceivable."[54] In other words, the relationship between intention and action, which normally we readily accept, is really inexplicable. The implication of this is that intentionality—the sense of myself as the source of meaningful action, to use Hampshire's words—cannot provide my continuity through change, for that continuity between guiding intention and an action is itself philosophically problematical. One might be inclined to say that only consciousness *can* bridge the gap; however, then one has not explained the continuity of consciousness but merely postulated it ad hoc to resolve the difficulty.

This gap is a problem for those who, like Hampshire, presuppose a dualistic account of experience and therefore must attribute some type of reality to "the sense of myself"—thus reifying consciousness into a self, in effect. But having accepted Hume's critique, one cannot thereafter bring back the self through the back door, as it were, as "continuity of consciousness." This inexplicable relation between intention and action is not a problem for the nondualist, who accepts that the consciousness of the self is actually illusory and agrees that a fictive self has been postulated in order to bridge the "gap." The nondualist can accept this "gap" between thought and action—in fact he can deny any causal link, as we see in chapter 6—and this is why actions have always been nondual, even when not realized as such.

Hampshire might try to bridge that gap between thought and action by agreeing on the one hand that the relation is incomprehensible yet asserting on the other that, as we experience in daily life, it is undeniable. As Hume said, "That their motion follows the command of the will is a matter of common experience." But that this is undeniable is not true, as the history of the mind–body problem indicates. Nietzsche, for example, denies that intention is the cause of an event, and he reverses Hume by extrapolating this denial of volition into a denial of the causal relation generally:

> *Critique of the concept "cause"* . . . We have absolutely no experience of a cause; psychologically considered, we derive the entire concept from the subjective conviction that we are causes, namely, that the arm moves—But that is an error. We separate ourselves, the doers, from the deed, and we make use of this pattern everywhere—we seek a doer for every event. What is it we have done? We have misunderstood the feeling of strength, tension, resistance, a muscular feeling that is

already the beginning of the act, as the cause, or we have taken the will
to do this or that for a cause because the action follows upon it . . .
—*In Summa*: an event is neither effected nor does it effect. *Cause* is a
capacity to produce effects that has been super-added to the events—

. . . Only because we have introduced subjects, "doers", into things does
it appear that all events are the consequences of compulsion exerted
upon subjects—exerted by whom? again by a "doer". Cause and
effect—a dangerous concept as long as one thinks of something that
causes and something upon which an effect is produced.
. . . When one has grasped that the "subject" is not something that
creates effects, but only a fiction, much follows.
It is only after the model of the subject that we have invented the
reality of things and projected them into the medley of sensations. If we
no longer believe in the effective subject, then belief also disappears in
effective things, in reciprocation, cause and effect between those phenomena that we call things. . . . At last, the "thing-in-itself" also disappears, because this is fundamentally the conception of a "subject-in-
itself". . . . If we give up the concept "subject" and "object", then also the
concept "substance"—and as a consequence also the various modifications of it, e.g., "matter", "spirit", and other hypothetical entities, "the
eternity and immutability of matter", etc. We have got rid of *materiality*.

As soon as we imagine someone who is responsible for our being thus
and thus, etc. (God, nature), and therefore attribute to him the intention that we should exist and be happy or wretched, we corrupt for
ourselves the *innocence of becoming*. We then have someone who wants to
achieve something through us and with us.[55]

Nietzsche is quoted at some length because these passages not only
deny intention but also relate that denial to the negation of other
entities whose existence the nondualist also rejects: cause and effect,
subject and object, substance, matter, personal God. Our sense of
being a subject is connected with the discrimination that intentionality
"causes" certain events but not others. The point most immediately
relevant is that, for Nietzsche, intention and the will in general are
epiphenomena and not the true cause of an action.

Such a denial of volition (by no means uncommon)[56] is usually
understood to imply determinism, but the concept of nondual action
suggests an alternative that escapes the usual dilemma of freedom
versus determinism. The usual formulations of that problem are

dualistic in presupposing a conscious subject whose actions either are completely determined by a causal chain (the strongest causal influence reaps the effect) or are free from a causal chain (or rather free from complete determination, since totally uncaused, random choice does not seem to provide freedom in any meaningful sense). Both alternatives assume the existence of a conscious self distinct from its actions and existent outside the causal chain, although its actions may be totally determined by external causes. But the nondualist claim that there is no self does not imply unimpeded determinism, for if there is no subject then there are also no "objective" causal factors. The deterministic view implies a self helpless before causal influences that struggle among themselves to see which is strongest, rather like medieval knights competing to see who will win the hapless lady; but if there is no hapless consciousness here then the situation must be understood differently. Hobbes said that "liberty or freedom signifies properly the absence of opposition"[57] and that captures our common-sense notion of freedom *from*. This means that the concept of freedom is dualistic in two senses. *Free* is dependent upon its opposite, becoming the negation of unfree, and moreover that opposite is dualistic in the sense that one thing constrains another. If there is no "other" to be opposed, as in nondualistic experience, such dualistic concepts do not apply. In later chapters I argue that the nondualist denial of self (as in Buddhism) is equivalent to asserting that there is only the Self (as in Vedānta). We would normally infer that the former implies complete determinism, the latter absolute freedom. However, if the universe is a whole (Brahman, Tao, Vijñaptimātratā, etc.) and if, as Hua Yen Buddhism develops in its image of Indra's Net, each particular is not isolated but contains and manifests that whole, then whenever "I" act it is not "I" but the whole universe that acts—or, rather, *is* the action. And if we accept that the universe is self-caused, then it acts freely whenever anything is done. Thus, from the nondualist perspective, complete determinism turns out to be equivalent to absolute freedom.[58]

But a disclaimer is necessary. Despite everything argued in this chapter about nondual action, I do not want to deny that, from another point of view, thoughts and actions are related to each other causally. From a "phenomenal" perspective they certainly condition each other. My point is that, when one "forgets oneself" and *becomes* a nondual action, there is no longer any awareness that the action is determined: it is experienced as spontaneous and "self-caused." The paradoxical relationship between these two viewpoints is discussed in chapter 6, which evaluates the implications of nonduality for causation generally by considering the Mādhyamika equivalence between seamless conditionality and unconditioned freedom.

TWO OBJECTIONS CONSIDERED

We cannot conclude without evaluating two objections against the concept of nondual action as it has been developed in this chapter. The first is a critique of the notion of *anābhogacārya* (Sanskrit, "intentionless activity"), while the second questions the value and indeed the possibility of *acintyakarma* (Sanskrit, "activity transcending thought").

The first objection is that blanket recommendation of intentionless activity overlooks a distinction, at least as old as Aristotle, between two different types of activity, which he calls *poiesis* and *praxis*. *Poiesis* refers to the productive arts, which are engaged in means directed toward an end (e.g., flute-making), whereas *praxis* describes the performing arts, in which the activity is an end in itself (e.g., flute-playing).[39] This distinction is valid for all activity, and all discussion of intentionless activity can apply only to the latter. If one is to make good flutes, then one's actions must be directed towards an end—that is, must be intentional.

The reply to this objection is that the distinction between poiesis and praxis, although valuable up to a point, becomes questionable when pushed. The result is that the distinction between them may be located within intentionless activity, within praxis in the broad sense. Even flute-playing may be understood as a means to an end, such as making money or impressing others, but of course it may be an end in itself. However, poiesis may be viewed in the same way. If the flute-maker is not thinking about the money to be made from selling the flute or about impressing others with his craftsmanship, then his work can be praxis too. Drilling a perfectly sized hole can be an end in itself just as playing a perfectly pitched note can be. In both cases we can imagine an audience of apprentices admiring their master's skill. This is not to deny that there is a different kind of "product" in the two cases, but if the flute-maker is not thinking about the finished product and what will be done with it, then there is no relevant difference in the acts themselves. From the nondualist standpoint, the experienced flute-maker can become one with the act of flute-making just as the master flutist can become one with his flute-playing.

There are a number of passages in the *Chuang Tzu* that illustrate the nondual *tê* of such craftspeople—butcher, wheelwright, boatman, and so forth. For example:

> Ch'ing, the chief carpenter, was carving wood into a stand for hanging musical instruments. When finished, the work appeared to those who saw it as though of supernatural execution. And the prince of Lu asked him, saying, "What mystery is there in your art?"
>
> "No mystery, Your Highness," replied Ch'ing; "and yet there is something. When I am about to make such a stand, I guard against any diminution of my vital power. I first reduce my mind to absolute quiescence. Three days in this condition, and I become oblivious of any reward to be gained. Five days, and I become oblivious of any fame to be acquired. Seven days, and I become unconscious of my four limbs and my physical frame. Then, with no thought of the Court present in my mind, my skill becomes concentrated, and all disturbing elements from without are gone.... I bring my own natural capacity in relation with that of the wood.[60]

One might expect some such process of preparation by a flute-player before an important concert, but here it is experienced by the equivalent of a flute-maker. It supports the idea that the distinction between poiesis and praxis is one that is to be found within the intentionless activity of praxis in the broad sense.

This answer contains the seeds of a reply to the next objection. The second objection is that eliminating intention—driving a wedge between action and all thought—seems hardly possible and is certainly not desirable. To act in such a way would mean to live aimlessly, with no direction or meaning at all. Moreover, "activity transcending thought" is likely to be more willful and selfish, giving greater freedom to instinctive and indiscriminate drives, than action that has been deliberated and mediated by moral principles. We need intentions because we must reflect on what we do, and before we act.

However, as mentioned earlier, nondual action does not imply wanton, merely spontaneous activity like that of a spoiled child. The point is more subtle. The objection assumes that acculturation introduces ethical factors (e.g., a superego) that condition our instinctive selfishness, but nonduality, in denying an ego-self, eliminates the basis of selfishness. (This is the essence of the Taoist response to Confucian morality.) It is true that "activity transcending thought" negates any meaning to life, in the sense that life's acts do not gain their meaning from referring to something outside themselves. But from another perspective, that meaning may be found within the action and perceptions themselves, which are experienced as fully satisfying. Only thus can each moment be complete in itself.

In order to determine whether nondual life may be said to have any goal or direction, we must again distinguish between two perspectives. From one perspective it is true that life does not have a direction, but then, as above, life does not need a direction. The present may be fulfilling without deriving its meaning from being projected toward some future state of affairs. From another perspective, however, life can still have a pattern without having a direction dualistically imposed upon it. As Unmon said, when the bell sounds we put on our robes and go to the meditation hall. There is the nondual sound "bong!", there is the nondual thought "time to sit," and there is the nondual activity of dressing and walking. I venture to suggest that those who learn to live in such a way often become aware of a pattern developing in their lives which is more profound and meaningful than any they could have created for themselves.

It may be objected here that, while such "activity transcending thought" may be possible in the protected environment of a monastery, where the sequence of activities is determined, it is not possible for the rest of us, who as laypeople are constantly required to make decisions and choose between possible intentions. This issue will be taken up in the following chapter. But here it is necessary to say that for the person who experiences nondually, decisions too are made differently. Choosing between pros and cons is not such a problem because the appropriate choice is much clearer, perhaps arising more spontaneously from what are normally called "subconscious" parts of the mind. Of course, to express the matter in this way is to take for granted the causal relation between decision and actions that was questioned earlier. We may make the same point in a less dualistic way by pointing out that how decisions are actually made is no less mysterious than how intentions "cause" actions. Seng-ts'an's *Hsin Hsin Ming*, cited in the first section of this chapter, begins with the much-quoted lines: "The Supreme Way [Tao] is not difficult, it simply dislikes choosing." But how can we escape the dilemma of choice? Only if nondual decisions make themselves. That brings us to the topic of the next chapter.

CHAPTER 4
NONDUAL THINKING

I never think—my thoughts think for me.

—Lamartine

Chapters 2 and 3 constitute a radical critique not only of perception and action but also of thinking. Chapter 2 discussed how language and thought usually distort our perception by reifying nondual percepts into an objective world distinct from the perceiving consciousness. Chapter 3 argued that intention bifurcates the nondual action of our "psychic body" in a similar way. In both cases it has been claimed that the superimposition of thought obscures the true nature of the experience. If one also considers the emphasis on meditation in the nondualist Asian traditions, one might conclude that the act of thinking is nothing but an interference that distorts reality; therefore we should strive to eliminate or minimize it. But this inference would be just as wrong as believing that sense-perception or physical activity must be "transcended." None of these should be rejected, but their actual nature must be realized. The linkage between perception/ conception and action/intention may be explored from either side. If concepts veil the nondual nature of percepts, and if intentions do the same for nondual actions, perhaps percepts and actions also obscure the true nature of thinking. When the thought-forming activity of the mind is used primarily in a system of representation and intention, then something fundamental about the nature of thoughts is obscured too. Our thought-processes are usually preoccupied with creating and maintaining the apparently objective world, with physically and psychologically protecting the sense of self, and with obtaining desired objects, but we should not assume that these indicate the limits of thought processes. Perhaps such dualistic activites tell us nothing about the nature of thinking in itself. "Thought is best when the mind is gathered into herself, and none of these things trouble her—neither sounds nor sights nor pain, nor any pleasure—when she has as little as possible to do with the body and has no bodily sense or feeling, but is aspiring after being" (Plato).[1] Just as there is nondual perception and action, so there may be nondual thinking—which also would be radically different from our usual understanding of thinking.

In Zen, the fifth of the Ten Oxherding Pictures describes a stage of enlightenment in which one realizes that thoughts too should not be rejected. "Enlightenment brings the realization that thoughts are not unreal since even they arise from our True-nature. It is only because delusion still remains that they are imagined to be unreal."[2] A Zen master once began a sesshin I attended by saying that those striving for enlightenment should look upon thoughts as the enemy to be fought, but then he qualified this by adding that thoughts were not really an enemy, as we would understand when we came to self-realization; only temporarily in our meditation practice must they be treated as such. This implies that the problem is, not thoughts per se, but a certain *way* of thinking. According to the record of his own enlightenment experience, the same Zen master struck his bed and exclaimed: "Ha, ha, ha! There's no reasoning here, no reasoning at all!"[3] But what kind of thinking is left if we eliminate reasoning? Sometimes the type of thinking that is criticized is called *conceptual thinking* or *conceptualizing*, but exactly what these terms refer to is not clear, especially if an alternative mode of thinking is supposed. If conceptual thinking means "thinking that uses concepts," it is difficult, indeed impossible to conceive of what thinking without concepts could be, and it is unlikely that that would be satisfactory even if it were possible. The main concern of this chapter, then, is to characterize the difference between reasoning/conceptualizing and whatever type of thinking is supposed to occur after enlightenment.

In the previous two chapters, nondual perception and nondual action were elucidated by taking familiar concepts from the non-dualist traditions and interpreting them nondualistically. In the case of perception these were prapañca and the common Indian distinction between savikalpa and nirvikalpa perception. In the case of action, there was the Taoist paradox of wei-wu-wei. In this chapter the equivalent is the Mahāyāna concept of prajñā, which is discussed in the first section. The second section argues that thinking may be realized to be "unsupported" (without a think*er*) when thoughts do not "link up in a series" (Hui Neng). Just as dualistic perception and action are both due to thought-superimposition, so the "empty" nature of thoughts and their true origin are overlooked as long as thoughts are *superimposed upon each other*—which is what we understand as the act of thinking that "I" dualistically *do*. The third section uses this view to understand the creative process in art and science, and the fourth discusses parallels to prajñā in Western philosophy, focusing on the later work of Martin Heidegger. The conclusion reflects briefly on the implications of nondual thinking for philosophy.

PRAJÑĀ

By now the parallel pattern is clear. In order to conflate the subject—object relation, nondual thinking must negate any thinker distinct from the thoughts that are thought. When we look for an equivalent to such nondual thinking in Asian thought, the term which comes closest is *prajñā*, a Sanskrit term used to describe the "wisdom" that is said to come with enlightenment or to constitute enlightenment. This wisdom is not something that can be gained or grasped, however, for it has no objective content; instead, it is often described as knowing in which there is no distinction between the knower, that which is known, and the act of knowing. This concept of prajñā was developed most in Mahāyāna Buddhism, especially in the vast prajñāpāramitā ("transcendental prajñā") literature. Yet, despite innumerable references to it, prajñā was treated much like its counterpart in early Buddhism, nirvana: both were recommended more than explained. For an analysis of the concept we turn to D. T. Suzuki, who begins his paper on "Reason and Intuition in Buddhist Philosophy" by distinguishing between prajñā and the more usual *vijñāna*:

> *Prajñā* goes beyond *vijñāna*. We make use of *vijñāna* in our world of the senses and intellect, which is characterized by dualism in the sense that there is the one who sees and there is the other that is seen—the two standing in opposition. In *prajñā* this differentiation does not take place: what is seen and the one who sees are identical; the seer is the seen and the seen is the seer.[4]

Prajñā is indeed the most fundamental experience. On it all other experiences are based, but we ought not regard it as something separate from the latter which can be picked out and pointed to as a specifically qualifiable experience. It is pure experience beyond differentiation.[5]

In a chart he lists the various counterbalancing characteristics of prajñā and vijñāna, the "non-duality" of the former contrasting with the "duality" of the latter.[6] The title of Suzuki's paper derives from his translation of these terms. Vijñāna, which is sometimes rendered as "conceptual thinking" or "conceptualizing," he translates as "reason or discursive understanding." In contrast, prajñā is translated, perhaps unfortunately, as "intuition." The philosophical meaning of intuition is "the immediate apprehension of an object by the mind without the intervention of any reasoning process"[7]—as in Spinoza's *scientia intuitiva*, the third and highest form of knowledge, the perception of a thing "through its essence alone," which does not consist in being convinced by reasons but in an immediate union with the thing itself. In this sense Suzuki's term is appropriate and even fortuitous for the viewpoint of this chapter. However, "intuition" is unfortunate in the sense that it more commonly suggests another faculty of mind apart from the intellect, whereas the function of the "intuition" here is nothing more than the function of the intellect when it is experienced nondually. As Suzuki repeatedly emphasizes, prajñā underlies vijñāna:

> If we think that there is a thing denoted as *prajñā* and another denoted as *vijñāna* and that they are forever separated and not to be brought to the state of unification, we shall be completely on the wrong track.
>
> *Vijñāna* cannot work without having *prajñā* behind it; parts are parts of the whole; parts never exist by themselves, for if they did they would not be parts—they would even cease to exist.[8]

The etymologies of vijñāna and prajñā are revealing. They have the same root *jñā* (to know). The *vi-* prefix of vijñāna (also in *vi-kalpa* and *vi-tarka*) signifies "separation or differentiation." Hence vijñāna refers to knowing that functions by discriminating one thing from another. In contrast, the *pra-* prefix of prajñā means "being born or springing up"—presumably referring to a more spontaneous type of knowing in which the thought no longer seems to be the product of a subject but is experienced as arising from a deeper nondual source. In such knowing the thought and that which thinks the thought are not distinguishable. This claim is explicit in the *Mahāmudrā* passage quoted in chapter 3, that the Moving (the thought, according to Evans-Wentz's commentary) and the Non-Moving (mind) are one:

> One cometh to know that neither is the "Moving" other than the "Non-Moving," nor the "Non-Moving" other than the "Moving"....
> If the real nature of the "Moving" and the "Non-Moving" be not discovered by these analyses, one is to observe:—
> Whether the Intellect, which is looking on, is other than the "Moving" and the "Non-Moving";
> Or whether it is the very self of the "Moving" and the "Non-Moving".
> Upon analysing, with the eyes of the Self-Knowing Intellect, one discovereth nothing; the observer and the thing observed are found to be inseparable.[9]

This passage was cited in chapter 3 as another example of the wei-wu-wei paradox; later we shall see in what way nondual thinking might also be an instance of wu-wei, paradoxically being both active and passive.

If thought and thinker are indistinguishable, then it is impossible to observe one's own thoughts objectively. The *Śikṣāsamuccaya* of Śāntideva contains a meditation on thought that dwells on this point:

> For thought, Kāśyapa, cannot be apprehended, inside or outside, or in between both. For thought is immaterial, invisible, non-resisting, inconceivable, *unsupported* and homeless. Thought has never been seen by any of the Buddhas, nor do they see it, nor will they see it.... A thought is like the stream of a river, without any staying power; as soon as it is produced it breaks up and disappears.... A thought is like lightning, it breaks up in a moment and does not stay on ....
> Searching for thought all round, he does not see it within or without.... Can then thought review thought? No, thought cannot review thought. As the blade of a sword cannot cut itself, as a finger-tip cannot touch itself, so a thought cannot see itself.[10]

But this seems contradicted by our experience. Surely thought can review itself, for that happens often, whenever we ponder the logical implications of some thought as part of a sequence of reasoning. The point of the passage must be that the various thought-elements of such a sequence do not coexist at the same time. At any moment there can be only one thought. A "review" of that thought, or any other thought that arises, is a completely new thought. The next section explores the implications of this.

AN UNSUPPORTED THOUGHT

It thinks, one ought to say. We become aware of certain representations which do not depend on us; others depend on us, or at least so we believe; where is the boundary? One should say, it thinks, just as one says, it rains.

—Lichtenberg

In the Western philosophical tradition, the self as thinker has been considered even less dubitable than the self as perceiver or agent, which means that the corresponding denial of a thinker is even more radical than the denial of a perceiver or an agent. Modern philosophy begins with Descartes' postulation of the subject which functions autonomously as its own criterion of truth, and this subject is founded on the fact that the act of thinking requires a thinker, an "I" to be doing it.

> What of thinking? I find here that thought is an attribute that belongs to me: it alone cannot be separated from me. I am, I exist, that is certain. But how often? Just when I think; for it might possibly be the case if I ceased entirely to think, that I should likewise cease to exist. . . . I am, however, a real thing and really exist; but what thing? I have answered: a thing which thinks.[11]

Descartes argues that it is self-contradictory to doubt one's own existence. "For it is so evident of itself that it is I who doubts, who understands, and who desires, that there is no reason here to add anything to explain it."[12] But as a proof, this begs the question: to assume that "I" am doubting my own existence is to go beyond what is empirically given. What is experienced is thoughts, some of which involve the concept "I," but from this it is illegitimate to infer a thinker distinct from the thought. No *cogito* can be derived from *cogitans*.

In reaction, Hume's conception of the mind (quoted in chapter 2) denies the existence of any identifiable self and emphasizes the "intentionality" of all consciousness, by which he means that consciousness always has a *content*:

> I never catch *myself* at any time without a perception, and can never observe anything but the perception. When my perceptions are

removed for any time, as by sound sleep, so long am I insensible to myself, and may truly be said not to exist.[13]

That the "I-consciousness" is intentional in this sense (not the same sense of "intentionality" discussed in chapter 3) is a notion essential to the nondualist position, for this is implied by the nondualist's claim that there is no autonomous self ("I...") distinguishable from its experience ("I am aware *of*..."). John Levy has elaborated this concept of intentionality into what is perhaps the classic argument against subject–object duality. The importance of the following passage can hardly be overemphasized:

> When I am conscious of an object, that is, of a notion or a percept, that object alone is present. When I am conscious of my perceiving, what alone presents itself to consciousness is the notion that I perceive the object: and therefore the notion of my being the perceiver also constitutes an object of consciousness. From this, a most important fact emerges: the so-called subject who thinks, and its apparent object, have no immediate relation.
>
> ...the notion, I am reading, does not occur while we are thus absorbed [in reading a book]: it occurs only when our attention wavers....a little reflection will show that even when we are not thus absorbed for any appreciable lapse of time, the subject who afterwards lays claim to the action was not present to consciousness when the action was taking place. The idea of our being the agent occurs to us as a separate thought, which is to say that it forms an entirely fresh object of consciousness. And since, at the time of the occurrence, we were present as neither the thinker, the agent, the percipient, nor the enjoyer, no subsequent claim on our part could alter the position. ...
>
> If the notions of subject and object are both the separate objects of consciousness, neither term has any real significance. An object, in the absence of a subject, cannot be what is normally called an object; and the subject, in the absence of an object, cannot be what is normally called the subject. It is in memory that the two notions seem to combine to form an entirely new notion, *I am the perceiver or the thinker.*[14]

From this, Levy later concludes: "Memory and the consciousness of individual existence are therefore synonymous."[15]

When I am conscious of a percept, only the percept is present, and when I am conscious of a thought, there is only that thought: from this modest and undeniable premise, the most extraordinary consequences follow. It implies what the Japanese Zen master Dōgen claimed to have realized, that "mind is no other than mountains, rivers, and the great wide earth, the sun and the moon and the stars."[16] Originally, there is no distinction between "internal" (mental) and "external" (physical), which means that trees and rocks and clouds, if they are not juxtaposed in memory with the "I" concept, will be experienced to be as much "my mind" as thought and feelings.

Levy develops a point stressed in Advaita but often misunderstood: although there is *only* the Self, that Self cannot be known, for to *know* it is to make it into an object. What is usually overlooked about this point is that our usual sense of self is the result of just such an objectification. The sense of subject–object duality arises not only from a simple bifurcation between grasper and grasped. The subject must also be "grasped" in an objectification whereby I identify my consciousness with thought (including memory), a body, and its possessions—all of which are objects lacking the most essential characteristic of Self, consciousness. According to Śaṅkara this is the primary superimposition, the fundamental ignorance that needs to be overcome.

Levy's emphasis on memory as the source of duality is consistent with Śaṅkara's reference to it in his definition of adhyāsa, quoted in chapter 2 and restated here: Superimposition is the apprehension of something in the present as different than it actually is, due to the interference of memory-traces. There is a parallel in the *Laṅkāvatāra Sūtra*: "When the triple world is surveyed by the Bodhisattva, he perceives that its existence is due to memory [literally, 'perfuming'] that has been accumulated since the beginningless past, but wrongly interpreted."[17] The usual function of memory as superimposition is to interpret the perception so that it is seen *as*—in this case, *as* an object presented to a subject. Levy's argument is of paramount importance for the nondualist. We have already applied it, in effect, in developing models of nondual perception (memory-superimposition as savikalpa determination) and nondual action (memory-superimposition as intention) in the two previous chapters. But the most important implications of Levy's argument are for nondual thinking. For what if memory were *not* there to relate together the distinct notions of percept and subject? Or (it amounts to the same thing) if the memory-trace were experienced as it is, "an entirely fresh object of consciousness" quite distinct from the other thoughts and percepts upon which it is usually superimposed? The significance of the *Śikṣāsamuccaya* passage quoted at the end of the section on prajñā becomes obvious. If memory "wrongly interpreted" is equivalent to what Levy calls individual existence because it is a case of "thought reviewing thought," then the experience of each thought as autonomous will eliminate that sense of individual existence—in our terms, would dissolve the sense of subject–object duality.

Nietzsche came to the conclusion that each thought is autonomous by developing the implications of his remarks (quoted in chapter 3) on intention and causality:

> "Causality" eludes us; to suppose a direct causal link between thoughts, as logic does—that is the consequence of the crudest and clumsiest observation.
>
> "Thinking", as epistemologists conceive it, simply does not occur: it is quite an arbitrary fiction, arrived at by selecting one element from the process and eliminating all the rest, an artificial arrangement for the purpose of intelligibility—
>
> The "spirit", something that thinks: . . . this conception is a second derivative of that false introspection which believes in "thinking": first an act is imagined which simply does not occur, "thinking", and secondly a subject-substratum in which every act of thinking, and nothing else, has its origin: that is to say, both the deed and the doer are fictions.
>
> We believe that thoughts as they succeed one another in our minds stand in some kind of causal relation: the logician especially, who actually speaks of nothing but instances which never occur in reality, has grown accustomed to the prejudice that thoughts *cause* thoughts . . .
>
> *In summa*: everything of which we become conscious is a terminal phenomenon, an end—and causes nothing; every successive phenomenon in consciousness is completely atomistic.[18]

Nietzsche relates the denial of a think*er* to a denial of the process of think*ing*. Why, after all, do we believe that there is an act of thinking? Because that act is what the thinker *does*: stringing thoughts together by forming new thoughts on the basis of the old thoughts. If there is no such thinker then there need be no such act. That leaves only thoughts, one at a time, although the succession may be rapid.

The significance of Nietzsche's remarks for us is that we find the same claim in the Asian nondualist philosophies, particularly evident in Mahāyāna. In the Platform Sutra, the Sixth Ch'an Patriarch Hui Neng explains what prajñā is:

> To know our mind is to obtain liberation. To obtain liberation is to attain Samādhi of Prajñā, which is "thoughtlessness". What is "thought-lessness"? "Thoughtlessness" is to see and know all Dharmas [things] with a mind free from attachment. When in use it pervades everywhere, and yet it sticks nowhere.... When our mind works freely without any hindrance, and is at liberty to "come" or to "go", we attain Samādhi of Prajñā, or liberation. Such a state is called the function of "thoughtless-ness". But to refrain from thinking of anything, so that all thoughts are suppressed, is to be Dharma-ridden, and this is an erroneous view.[19]

The term *thoughtlessness* would seem to recommend a mind free from any thoughts, but Hui Neng denies this. Instead, thoughtlessness is the function of a mind free from any attachment. The implication is that for someone who is liberated thoughts still arise, but there is no clinging to them when they do. Why the term thoughtlessness can be used to characterize such a state of mind will become clear in a moment. But the question that arises first is how one can ever be attached to thoughts if, as the *Śikṣāsamuccaya* says, a thought has no staying power, if like lightning it breaks up in a moment and disappears. Hui Neng answers this later when he says more about "how to think":

> In the exercise of our thinking faculty, let the past be dead. *If we allow our thoughts, past, present and future, to link up in a series, we put ourselves under restraint.* On the other hand, if we never let our mind attach to anything, we shall gain liberation.[20]

We cling to a thought by linking up thoughts in a series, rather than letting each thought arise spontaneously and independently. The effect of such linking is that the nondual nature of each individual thought is obscured. This is not to deny that thoughts also stand in a causal relationship; from another point of view, it is undeniable that previous thoughts somehow condition later ones. But when one "forgets oneself" and *becomes* a nondual thought, there is no longer any awareness that the thought is caused. Then it arises spontaneously, as if "self-caused." (This relationship is discussed further in chapter 6, which considers the paradoxical Mādhyamika equivalence between *pratītya-samutpāda* conditionality and the Unconditioned.)

According to the autobiographical first part of the Platform Sutra, Hui Neng became deeply enlightened and realized that all things in the universe are his self-nature when his teacher read him a line from the Diamond Sutra: "Let your mind (or thought) arise without fixing it anywhere."[21] The passage just prior to this one—which Hui Neng must also have heard—puts this in context. Edward Conze translates it as follows:

> Therefore then, Subhūti, the Bodhisattva should produce an unsupported thought, a thought which is nowhere supported, which is not supported (*apratiṣṭhiti*) by forms, sounds, smells, tastes, touchables, or objects of mind. . . . And why? What is supported has no support.[22]

A thought is "unsupported" when it is not experienced as arising in dependence upon anything else. It is not experienced as "caused" by another thought (which is a "mind-object") and of course it is not "produced" by a thinker, since the Bodhisattva realizes that "thinkers" (like ego-selves generally) do not exist. Such an "unsupported thought," then, is prajñā, arising by itself nondually.

Hui Neng's grandson-in-the-Dharma Ma-tsu agrees with Hui Neng and the Diamond Sutra: "So with former thoughts, later thoughts, and thoughts in between: the thoughts follow one another without being linked together. Each one is absolutely tranquil."[23] That each such unsupported thought is absolutely tranquil is a new point, although perhaps implicit in Hui Neng's use of the term thoughtlessness. When one loses sense of self and completely becomes an unsupported thought, there is again the paradox of wei-wu-wei, in which action and passivity are combined. As the Mahāmudrā claims, there is the movement of nondual thought, but at the same time there is an awareness of no movement. That is why such an experience can just as well be described as thoughtlessness. The later Ch'an master Kuei-shan Ling-yu referred to this as "thoughtless thought": "Through concentration a devotee may gain thoughtless thought. Thereby he is suddenly enlightened and realizes his original nature."[24] *Thoughtless thought* is not a mind completely void of any thoughts. Rather, "one (nondual) thought is thoughtless thought," just as one nondual sound is soundless sound (chap. 2) and one nondual action is actionless action (chap. 3).

Buddhism describes this awareness of that-which-does-not-change as realization that the thought is śūnya (empty). In chapter 6 I argue that the Vedāntic equivalent of śūnyatā is its concept of Nirguṇa Brahman, that knowing but attributeless consciousness which cannot itself be known. If this is true, we can see a parallel to the Buddhist account in the Advaita claim that "unvaried consciousness penetrates the modifications of the mind like the thread in a string of pearls."[25] This consciousness is not a thinker in the dualistic Cartesian sense, but is, like the *puruṣa* of Sāṅkhya, that which never changes.

An even more striking parallel is found in this statement by the great twentieth-century Advaitin Ramana Maharshi:

> The ego in its purity is experienced in the interval between two states or between two thoughts. The ego is like the worm which leaves one hold only after it catches another. Its true nature is known when it is out of contact with objects or thoughts. You should realize this interval as the abiding, unchangeable Reality, your true Being.[26]

The image of the ego as a worm that leaves one hold only after catching another might well have been used by Hui Neng and Ma-tsu to describe the way thoughts are linked up in a series. The difference is that Mahāyāna Buddhism encourages the arising of an "unsupported" thought, whereas Ramana Maharshi understands unchangeable Reality as that which is realized only when it is out of contact with all objects and thoughts. This is consistent with the general relation between Mahāyāna and Advaita: as we have seen, Mahāyāna emphasizes realizing the emptiness of all phenomena, whereas Advaita distinguishes between empty Reality and phenomena (both physical and mental), thus devaluing the latter more.

The image of a worm hesistant to leave its hold was used in a conversation I had in 1981 with a Theravada monk from Thailand, a meditation master named Phra Khemananda. What he said was not prompted by any remark of mine; it had been taught to him by his own teacher in Thailand. He began by drawing the diagram illustrated in figure 2.

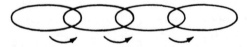

Figure 2

Each oval represents a thought, he said. Normally we leave one thought only when we have another one to go to (as the arrows indicate), but to think in this way constitutes delusion. Instead, we should realize that thinking is actually as shown in figure 3.

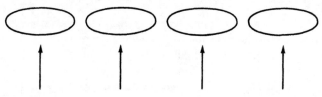

Figure 3

Then we will understand the true nature of thoughts: that thoughts do not arise from each other but by themselves.

This understanding of thoughts not linking-up-in-a-series but springing up nondually is consistent with D. T. Suzuki's conception of prajñā:

> It is important to note here that *prajñā* wants to see its diction "quickly" apprehended, giving us no intervening moment for reflection or analysis or interpretation. *Prajñā* for this reason is frequently likened to a flash of lightning or to a spark from two striking pieces of flint. "Quickness" does not refer to progress of time; it means immediacy, absence of deliberation, no allowance for an intervening proposition, no passing from premises to conclusion.[27]

This offers insight into the many Zen dialogues in which students are criticized for their hesitation or praised for their apparently nonsensical but immediate replies. That the reply is immediate is not itself sufficient; what is important is that each response be experienced as a nondual "presentation of the whole." Hesitation reveals lack of prajñā because it indicates either some logical train of thought or the self-conscious paralysis of all thought.

Even more important, this also explains how meditation functions, since letting go of thoughts breaks up the otherwise habitual linking of thoughts into a series. Huang Po:

> Why do they [Zen students] not copy me by letting each thought go as though it were nothing, or as though it were a piece of rotten wood, a stone, or the cold ashes of a dead fire?[28]

Working on a Zen koan such as Jōshū's Mu (discussed in chapter 6) can be understood in this way, for the end of the process is to experience Mu precisely as such an unsupported thought—which is important because it leads to experiencing everything else as unsupported too.

We are now in a position to answer the problem posed at the beginning of this chapter: how to characterize the difference between reasoning/conceptualizing/dualistic thinking and the type of thinking that occurs after deep enlightenment. The problem with reasoning/conceptualizing is that it involves thinking as a logical process leading to a conclusion—that is, as a series of linked thoughts. The thought elements of such thinking never stand unsupported by themselves but are understood only with reference to previous thoughts, apparently "caused" by them and having no meaning apart from them. The experience of prajñā seems to be that, instead of my laboriously extracting the logical implications of one thought for another (for which process a self is assumed to be necessary), thoughts spring up full-grown, like Minerva from the forehead of Zeus.

But something is still unclear. If the sense of self is a result of this reflective linking of thoughts together, it cannot also be postulated as the cause. "I" can't cling to thoughts if the "I" is a consequence of the clinging. Then precisely *who* is this "I" that links thought in a series? If we answer that it must be Mind itself, the nondual Absolute, this just pushes the problem back one step, for *why* does Mind need to link thoughts together delusively, when It presumably lacks nothing?

Insofar as this involves looking for a "first cause"—in this case, the origin of delusion—no definitive answer is given in the nondualist traditions, presumably because none can be given. What can be provided is the phenomenology of the process as we experience it now. The second noble truth of Pāli Buddhism identifies the cause of our suffering as craving. This refers to more than physical desire. The common ground between such desire and most of our other mental processes, including philosophizing, is *seeking*. Why does the mind seek? Because it is trying to fix itself, to find a secure home. The mind tries to objectify itself because it experiences its own formlessness, its emptiness, as uncomfortable. That the ego-self is a fiction is not something that we need to learn from an exotic philosophy, for we all experience it. But we experience it as a lack, a bottomless hole which, try as we may, can never be filled up. The frustration of our lives is that there is always something which needs to be done. The emotional equivalent is the feeling of inadequacy; psychologically it is guilt. We constantly feel the need to validate our existence in some way, which is self-defeating because the preoccupation with gaining something or proving something is what keeps mind from noticing its own nongaining, nonlosing nature. This resolves the problem of how there can be such a *thing* as a sense of self: there isn't. The sense of self can be understood only as a process that continually but vainly attempts to secure itself in one way or another. The ego tries to deny its emptiness in a way which just reveals its obsession with that emptiness, by always needing to get ahead of itself, by grasping at the next thought, and so on. The ego *is* this constant thrust into the future—a thrust which, more precisely, generates the future, as we see in chapter 6. By definition, the self is that which is "deferred." That is why the prospect of physical death can so often lead to ego-death: Death is the end of all deferral.

Now we see why prajñā does not have any content, why it cannot involve grasping anything mentally: because the compulsion to grasp something is just as problematic whether it is a craving for sense-objects or the spiritual need To Know The Truth. But the solution to this is not a quietism that dwells peacefully in blankness of mind: "The Way is not a matter knowing *or not knowing*. Knowing is delusion; not-knowing is a blank consciousness" (Nan-ch'üan).[29] When we look for another alternative, the "middle way" between these two extremes, we resolve another dualism: that between enlightenment and delusion. Yung Chia's "Song of Enlightenment" begins:

> Have you not seen a man of Tao at his ease
> In his non-active (wu-wei) and beyond learning states
> Who neither suppresses thoughts nor seeks the real? To him
> The real nature of ignorance is Buddhatā
> And the non-existent body of illusion is Dharmakāya.[30]

To reject delusion and accept truth is just another form of delusion, Yung Chia says later, for such discrimination between rejecting and accepting is still dualistic; one who practices in this way mistakes a thief for his own son. The Way is not a matter of escaping delusion, because there is nowhere to escape except to an equally delusive quietism. It is rather a matter of *liberating* delusion, as Dōgen might say. What distinguishes liberated delusion is the utter freedom of the mind to dance freely from one śūnya thing to another, from one set of concepts to a different and perhaps contradictory set. The difference is not necessarily in the concepts themselves—they may be the same—but how effortlessly the mind is able to play with them without getting stuck. To the extent that the mind thinks there is an objectifiable Truth (whether already grasped or not yet), or to the extent that it thinks dwelling in blankness of mind is the Truth, this freedom is not realized: the mind trips over itself, sticks at this, jumps to that, and doesn't want to let go because it still understands its fundamental task as finding and dwelling in a secure "home" for itself.

> Should your mind wander away, do not follow it, whereupon your wandering mind will stop wandering of its own accord. Should your mind desire to linger somewhere, do not follow it and do not dwell there, whereupon your mind's questing for a dwelling-place will cease of its own accord. Thereby, you will come to possess a non-dwelling mind—a mind which remains in the state of non-dwelling. If you are fully aware in yourself of a non-dwelling mind, you will discover that there is just the fact of dwelling, with nothing to dwell upon or not to dwell upon. This full awareness in yourself of a mind dwelling upon nothing is known as having a clear perception of your own nature. A mind which dwells upon nothing is the Buddha-Mind, the mind of one already delivered, Bodhi-Mind, Uncreate Mind... you will have attained to understanding from within yourself—an understanding stemming from a mind that abides nowhere, by which we mean a mind free from delusion and reality alike.   (Hui Hai)[31]

Because of its preoccupation with various types of seeking, because of its identification with various types of phenomena, the mind does not realize its formless, nondwelling nature. It is not the case that the mind wants something in particular, for as soon as mind obtains what is wanted it wants something else, as we know. Most of all, mind wants *itself*, but the great irony is that this is the one thing it can never *have*. This does not stop mind from trying to grasp itself, however, and the result of that reflexivity is ego or sense of self. This gives a kind of security, but at a tragic cost, because fear is generated at the same time: anything grasped can also be lost. No objectifications are stable enough, for "all things pass away"—fortunately, since success here would be a sort of petrification. But fear of loss of self—which we experience in many forms, most notably as fear of death—becomes a suffering which pervades life, sometimes consciously, more often unconsciously. It results in the sometimes desperate attempt to find a kind of "substitute immortality" through symbols—for example, by collecting money or possessions (equals accumulating life) or by creating culture-objects (e.g., books, artworks) that will be gratefully appreciated by posterity (equals surviving death in symbolic form).[32]

Chapter 6 discusses the solution to this problem, which is simple but not easy. In order for formless mind to realize its formlessness and its corollary freedom, the reflexively objectified sense of self and all its projections must collapse. The difficulty is how to approach that without making this collapse into nonseeking just one more thing the the ego seeks, which as we shall see later is what happens with the usual spiritual dualism between practice as means and enlightenment as goal. The alternative is not to willfully abandon the spiritual search, for the value of that search is that it is able to take all the desires and attachments wherein the mind is dispersed and concentrate them into one; it is the evaporation of that one which can then put all seeking to rest. Unless the empty, unborn nature of mind is clearly realized and not just conceptually grasped, the unconscious search for symbolic self-validation and substitute immortality continues, because the fear of loss of self has not been fully resolved. The only true solution is for the mind to let go and indeed lose itself. "Men are afraid to forget their minds, fearing to fall through the Void with nothing to stay their fall. They do not know that the Void is not really void, but the realm of the real Dharma" (Huang Po).[33]

An objection may arise spontaneously in reaction to this conception of nondual thinking, along the same lines as the objection raised in the previous chapter about the desirability of non-intentional action: without the direction of a thinker to organize one's thought into some order, thoughts would arise randomly and chaotically and one could not function in any meaningful way. This objection gains its force from our experience of the free-association that occurs during daydreaming, when the conscious controls that normally direct (or seem to direct) our thinking are relaxed. But we should not equate concentration of mind with a thinker. The former—"one-pointed mind"—is much recommended in Zen, for example, even though the ego-self is denied. Prajñā is an instance of the first *because* there is not the self-conscious "reviewing" of the second. A manifestation of this occurs in the dharma-combat which advanced Zen monks were expected to engage in as a way to test and "polish" their own realization. When a monk was challenged with a "Zen question," his answer needed to be both immediate and appropriate to the situation, since these are the publicly observable criteria for nondual thinking. The point here is that, contrary to our usual understanding, it is not necessary for reasoning to mediate by choosing the most appropriate response from among various alternatives, for what arises spontaneously and nondually in "prajñā-intuition" will be appropriate if self-hesitation does not interfere.

This is no special process of "intuiting"; it is the natural function of mind for someone without the delusion of duality. But if nondual thinking is to parallel the other types of nondual experience, then there has never been a thinker creating and linking thoughts. There is certainly a pattern in the organization of "my" mental life, but it is not something that "I" have imposed upon it. The difference between a "tip-of-the-tongue" *kenshō* and the *anuttara-samyak-sambodhi* of a Buddha is that the former is only a first glimpse of nondual experience in which the sense of self lets go but quickly reconstitutes, so that the *sense* of duality returns even though the realization that it is delusive persists. With nonregressive satori, the core of one's being remains empty and there is nothing to obstruct the "welling up" of nondual thought, and so on, from an innermost source unfathomably deep. That welling up brings us to the topic of creativity.

CREATIVITY

The Eternal Body of Man is the Imagination: that is God himself/
The Divine Body... We are his Members. It manifests itself in his
Works of Art (In Eternity All is Vision).
                                                           —William Blake, *The Laocoön Plate*

In chapter 3 Hume was quoted as pointing out that the power or energy by which we move our limbs, like that in other natural events, is unknown and inconceivable. This is implied by his view of causality; another corollary, which Hume discusses immediately after that passage, is that we cannot even understand how the mind can create an idea.

> This is a real creation; a production of something out of nothing: which implies a power so great, that it may seem, at first sight, beyond the reach of any being, less than infinite. At least it must be owned, that such a power is not felt, nor known, nor even conceivable by the mind. We only feel the event, namely the existence of an idea, consequent to a command of the will: but the manner, in which this operation is performed, the power by which it is produced, is entirely beyond our comprehension.[34]

There is something mysterious about how any thought arises, all the more so if thoughts are believed to spring up (*pra-*) nondually instead of each conditioning the subsequent thought in a sequence. Because we experience the latter frequently, or think we do, it loses its mysterious quality until someone like Hume draws our attention to it. Nondual thinking seems more essentially mysterious; do we have any experience of it, or is it a mere possibility, a mystical light at the end of a meditative tunnel? The answer is that we glimpse it in what is normally expressed by the term *creativity*. Nondual thinking is the source of the creative process, which does not "explain" creativity but rather explains why creativity is so essentially mysterious.

Many examples could be given of the emphasis on egoless spontaneity in Asian art and literature (e.g., Zen brush painting and haiku composition); the reader is referred to D. T. Suzuki's *Zen and Japanese Culture* and Chang Chung-yuan's *Creativity and Taoism* for detailed discussions of this subject.[35] But few are aware how widespread this phenomenon is, especially among those acknowledged to be the most creative—the famous composers, writers and, as we shall see, scientists as well. That nondual thinking is the source of creativity is important for illustrating what was discussed in the previous section, so I shall devote a few pages to examples of the nondual creative process.

■

We begin with the creative experience of composers. Musical composition is an instance of thinking which, although not conceptual in the usual sense, is yet "logical" in that we would normally expect it to be determined by the various rules of harmony, key change, sonata or fugue structure, and so on. All of this, we might well assume, would require the direction of a "thinker" highly trained in such technical skills and able to apply them consciously in working on his thematic material. How unexpected then that such a "formal" composer as Mozart should have written a letter describing his creative technique thus:

> All this fires my soul and, provided I am not disturbed, my subject enlarges itself, becomes methodized and defined, and the whole, though it be long, stands almost complete and finished in my mind, so that I can survey it, like a fine picture or a beautiful statue, at a glance. . . . All this inventing, this producing, takes place in a pleasing, lively dream.[36]

This passage contains two points we encounter repeatedly: that the subject enlarges—that is, creates—itself, and that this process is "dreamlike." These two points are two sides of the same coin. The process is dreamlike because it is without the sense of a directing ego, which is why the thought processes can occur nondually. Of course, there is still a pattern to the sequence of these notes and chords—without that it would not be music—but this is not inconsistent with the claim of nondual thinking. The important point is that the succeeding measures are experienced as arising *by themselves*, without a "thinker" linking them together and creating that pattern. The structure is not something that the "thinker" imposes. Tschaikovsky's description agrees with Mozart's:

> Generally speaking, the germ of a future composition comes suddenly and unexpectedly. . . . It takes root with extraordinary force and rapidity, shoots up through the earth, puts forth branches and leaves, and finally blossoms. I cannot define the creative process in any other way than by this simile. . . . I forget everything and behave like a madman: everything within me stands pulsing and quivering; hardly have I begun the sketch before one thought follows another. In the midst of this magic process, it frequently happens that some external interruption awakes me from my somnambulistic state. . . . such dreadful interruptions break the thread of inspiration.[37]

Sometimes there is the sense that one is communicating with another consciousness that is dictating the music. Richard Strauss described the composition of his operas *Elektra* and *Der Rosenkavalier* thus: "While the ideas were flowing in upon me—the entire musical, measure by measure—it seemed to me that I was dictated to by two wholly different Omnipotent entities.... I was definitely conscious of being aided by more than an earthly Power." Since many composers were Christians, it is not surprising that they explained their inspiration in more conventional theistic terms. Puccini: "The music of this opera [*Madame Butterfly*] was dictated to me by God; I was merely instrumental in putting it on paper and communicating it to the public."[38] Brahms:

> When I feel the urge I begin by appealing directly to my Maker... I immediately feel vibrations which thrill my whole being... then I feel capable of drawing inspiration from above as Beethoven did.... Those vibrations assume the form of distinct mental images.... Straightaway the ideas flow in upon me, directly from God, and not only do I see distinct themes in the mind's eye, but they are clothed in the right forms, harmonies, and orchestration. Measure by measure the finished product is revealed to me when I am in those rare, inspired moods.... I have to be in a semi-trance condition to get such results—a condition when the conscious mind is in temporary abeyance, and the subconscious is in control, for it is through the subconscious mind, which is a part of Omnipotence, that the inspiration comes.[39]

Both "God" and "the subconscious mind" are what might be called "theoretical constructs" which are ready at hand in Western culture to account for what I am alternatively describing as examples of "nondual thinking." It is not surprising that contemporary Western descriptions of the creative process often prefer "the subconscious" explanation to the theistic one. So Elgar looked upon himself as "the all but unconscious medium" through which his works were created.[40]

Brahms's passage contains a significant new element: references to feeling "vibrations," which Puccini also mentions (although not in the passage quoted above). Wagner was also convinced that "there are universal currents of Divine Thought vibrating the ether everywhere.... I feel that I am one with this vibrating force."[41] Brahms's description makes explicit what was implicit in all the earlier quotations: the vibrations from God provide not only the theme or basic material but "the right forms, harmonies, and orchestration"—in other words, all the details, everything. Many more examples could be cited, but our last will be Stravinsky, who said "I heard, and I wrote what I heard. I am the vessel through which *The Rite of Spring* passed."[42]

•

We find the same themes when we turn to literature, despite the fact that literature is more "conceptual" and hence should offer more resistance to nondual thinking. Nietzsche again:

> Has anyone at the end of the nineteenth century a clear idea of what poets of strong ages have called *inspiration*? If not, I will describe it.—If one had the slightest residue of superstition left in one's system, one could hardly reject altogether the idea that one is merely incarnation, merely mouthpiece, merely a medium of overpowering forces. The concept of *revelation*—in a sense that suddenly, with indescribable certainty and subtlety, something becomes visible, audible, something that shakes one to the last depths and throws one down—that merely describes the facts. One hears, one does not seek; one accepts, one does not ask who gives; like lightning, a thought flashes up, with necessity, without hesitation regarding its form—I never had any choice....
>
> Everything happens involuntarily in the highest degree but as in a gale of a feeling of freedom, of absoluteness, of power, of divinity.—The involuntariness of image and metaphor is strangest of all; one no longer has any notion of what is an image or a metaphor: everything offers itself as the nearest, most obvious, simplest expression. It actually seems, to allude to something Zarathustra says, as if the things themselves approached and offered themselves as metaphors.[43]

Notice how Nietzsche identifies conditionality ("involuntarily in the highest degree") and the unconditioned ("a gale of a feeling of freedom") in the same sentence; in chapter 6 we shall have occasion to reflect on this. *Beyond Good and Evil* describes a philosopher as a man "who is struck by his own thoughts as though they were external to him, as though they struck him from above and from below, who is struck by *his* type of events as though by lightning."[44] With typical modesty Nietzsche concludes the above passage from *Ecce Homo* with the claim that one would need to go back thousands of years to find the same experience. However, Thomas Wolfe's experience in the writing of his first novel, *Look Homeward, Angel*, which catapulted him to fame, sounds similar:

> "I cannot say the book was written. It was something that took hold and possessed me.... Upon that flood everything was swept and born along

as by a great river. And I was borne along with it." He likened his mental processes to "a huge black cloud" that was "loaded with electricity ...with a kind of hurricane violence that could not be held in check much longer."[45]

Apparently unlike the work of the composers cited earlier, all of Wolfe's novels needed considerable editing afterward. This seems to be the pattern rather than the exception for writers generally: the light of their inspiration later needs to be refracted through a critical lens. But the point remains that the lens of critical reflection remains powerless if the light of genius—what I have called nondual thinking—is not strong enough.

The sense of being possessed is common among mystical writers and, more surprisingly, among many nonmystical ones as well. Jakob Boehme always believed that his first book, *Aurora*, had been dictated to him as he passively held the pen that wrote it.

> Art has not written here, neither was there any time to consider how to set it down punctually, according to the understanding of the letters, but all was ordered according to the direction of the Spirit, which often went in haste....the burning fire often forced forward with speed, and the hand and pen must hasten directly after it; for it goes and comes like a sudden shower.[46]

In *Paradise Lost* Milton refers to his "Celestial Patroness, who...unimplor'd...dictates to me my unpremeditated Verse" even as he dictated it to his daughters.[47] In a letter William Blake described the composition of his *Milton* likewise: "I have written this poem from immediate dictation twelve or sometimes even twenty or thirty lines at a time, without premeditation and even against my will."[48] Goethe also said his poems came to him of themselves and sometimes against his will: "The songs made me, and not I them; the songs had me in their power." Dickens said that when he sat down to write, "some beneficent power" showed it all to him. George Eliot told a friend "that, in all she considered her best writing, there was a 'not herself' which took possession of her and that she felt her own personality to be merely the instrument through which the spirit, as it were, was acting."[49] It is well known that Coleridge composed *Kubla Khan* in an opium-induced sleep "at least of the external senses," which he afterwards described in the third person: "if that indeed can be called composition in which all the images rose up before him as *things* with a parallel production of the correspondent expressions, without any sensation or consciousness of effort."[50] Unfortunately, what survives is only a fragment of the "not . . . less than from two to three hundred lines," due to that bane of all such creation, the interruption of a visitor. Again, the reference to absence of effort makes explicit what is implicit in the other accounts.

Apparently of less mystical origin, but equally relevant for our purposes, is Lewis Carroll's account of how he wrote his children's books.

> *Alice* and *Looking Glass* are made up almost wholly of bits and scraps, single ideas which came of themselves. In writing it out, I added many fresh ideas, which seemed to grow of themselves on the original stock; and many were added when, years afterwards, I wrote it all over again for publication; but (this may interest some readers of *Alice* to know) every such idea and nearly every word of the dialogue *came of itself*. Sometimes an idea comes at night, when I have had to get up and strike a light to note it down—sometimes when out on a lonely winter walk, when I have had to stop and with half-frozen fingers jot down a few words which should keep the new-born idea from perishing—but whenever or however it comes, it *comes of itself*.[51]

The emphasis is Carroll's. As one commentator has observed, "The point was apparently so important for Lewis Carroll that he had to say it four times in one paragraph and italicize it twice as well."[52] Similarly, A. E. Housman reported that snatches of lines would "bubble up" after a beer and a walk "with sudden and unaccountable emotions"; such poems then "had to be taken in hand and completed by the brain."[53]

Finally, some reference to the apparently independent life of characters. Thackeray wrote in the *Round-About-Papers*, "I have been surprised by the observations made by some of my characters. It seems as if an occult Power was moving the pen. The personage does or says something and I ask: how the dickens did he come to think of that?" Echoing Thackeray is the prolific children's writer Enid Blyton:

> I shut my eyes for a few minutes . . . make my mind a blank and *wait*—and then, as clearly as I would see real children, my characters stand before me in mind's eye. . . . The story is enacted almost as if I had a private cinema screen there. . . . I don't know what is going to happen. I

am in the happy position of being able to write a story and read it for the first time at one and the same moment.... Sometimes a character makes a joke, a really funny one that makes me laugh as I type it on my paper and I think, "Well, I couldn't have thought of that one by myself in a hundred years!", and then I think: "Well, *who* did think of it?"[54]

In looking back over all these passages, we seem to find a wide variety of explanations for the creative process: musical subjects that take root and enlarge themselves in a dream or are dictated by God and/or the subconscious, with or without vibrations; pregnant storms of inspiration that sweep one away; books and poems immediately transmitted by God and songs that write themselves; "beneficent Powers" that show everything or take possession of one; characters that take their lives into their own hands; and, more humbly, bits and scraps of ideas and dialogue that, take note, *come of themselves*. Despite this plethora of interpretations, I suggest that all of these are descriptions of the same mental process, which I have called nondual thinking, experienced as more or less spiritual according to the artist's religious convictions. That there is such a diversity of descriptions for this process is to be expected, for in trying to understand such an extraordinary experience one will naturally tend to use the explanation that is most familiar, be it spirit possession, dictation by God, or an irruption of the unconscious. The undeniable differences between the extremes of Boehme and Blake on the one side and Lewis Carroll on the other may be viewed as differences in depth which are quantitative rather than qualitative. For Carroll the experience was comparatively shallow, manifesting itself only as fragmentary nondual thoughts that he later put together. For Boehme and Blake, the process is so deep and automatic that it seems as if whole poems are being dictated to them. Perhaps it is relevant here that the former was a mathematician (who, as we shall shortly see, normally needs only "sparks" of inspiration) and the latter two primarily mystics and only derivatively writers.

An objection may be raised here that, while the people mentioned do speak of works apparently writing themselves, none of them explicitly denies the self. In fact many of them refer to an "I" that is observing the process, and so these do not constitute cases of thought transcending subject–object duality. My answer is that none of the people cited is a philosopher (except Nietzsche, who does deny a thinker), and so we should not expect them to derive such philosophical conclusions from their experience. Yet the references often made to "daydreaming" and the like suggest the equivalent, in which the sense of self as we normally experience it, controlling and directing the thought processes, is suspended. In the nondual experience consciousness does not disappear but becomes one with its "object": I *am* the thought processes, and it is this negation of the usual duality of "thinker–thinking–thought" that has been described in the passages quoted above.

•

Those not familiar with the methods of scientific investigation and discovery might suppose its procedure to be radically different from what has been described above. Unlike the purely "subjective" material that the creative artist works with, the scientist is trying to extract the laws of "objective reality," by which all his theories must be verified. Yet the procedures employed in science require a creativity which has some similarity to that of the writer or composer.

> There are, then, no generally applicable "rules of induction," by which hypotheses or theories can be mechanically derived or inferred from empirical data. The transition from data to theory requires creative imagination. Scientific hypotheses and theories are not *derived* from observed facts, but *invented* in order to account for them. They constitute guesses at the connections that might obtain between the phenomena under study, at uniformities and patterns that might underlie their occurrence. "Happy guesses" of this kind require great ingenuity, especially if they involve a radical departure from current modes of scientific thinking, as did, for example, the theory of relativity and quantum theory. (Hempel)[55]

The composer or writer requires constant or repeated "inspiration," but the creativity that the scientist needs is just a spark—the "Eureka!" experience—to bridge the gap between the accumulated data and the rough idea, or metaphor, for a theory. Rigorous logical thinking is necessary but not sufficient here; something extra is needed that cannot be derived mechanically. One of the most eloquent descriptions of creativity in the history of science is that of the French mathematician Henri Poincaré:

> For fifteen days I strove to prove that there could not be any functions like those I have since called Fuchsian functions.... One evening,

contrary to my custom, I drank black coffee and could not sleep. Ideas
rose in crowds; I felt them collide until pairs interlocked, so to speak,
making a stable combination. By the next morning I had established
the existence of a class of Fuchsian functions....

Just at that time I left Caen, where I was then living to go on a
geologic excursion under the auspices of the school of mines. The
change of travel made me forget my mathematical work. Having
reached Coutances, we entered an omnibus to go some place or other.
At the moment I put my foot on the step the idea came to me, without
anything in my former thoughts seeming to have paved the way for it,
that the transformations I had used to define the Fuchsian functions
were identical with those of non-Euclidean geometry....

Then I turned my attention to the study of some arithmetical questions apparently without much success and without a suspicion of any
connection with my preceding researches. Disgusted with my failure, I
went to spend a few days at the seaside, and thought of something else.
One morning, walking on the bluff, the idea came to me, with just the
same characteristics of brevity, suddenness, and immediate certainty,
that the arithmetical transformations of indeterminate ternary quad-
ratic forms were identical with those of non-Euclidean geometry.[56]

Poincaré gives further examples, but it is important to cite other sources too. Here is another French mathematician, Andrew Marie Ampère:

The matter often returned to my mind and I had sought twenty times
unsuccessfully for this solution. For some days I had carried the idea
about with me. At last, *I do not know how*, I found it, together with a large
number of curious and new considerations concerning the theory of
probability.[57]

A third mathematician, Karl Gauss, described in a letter how he
proved a theorem he had been working on for four years:

At last two days ago I succeeded, not by dint of painful effort but so to
speak by the grace of God. As a sudden flash of light, the enigma was
solved.... For my part I am unable to name the nature of the thread
which connected what I previously knew with that which made my
success possible.[58]

The experiences of all three mathematicians apparently occurred in
full waking consciousness. A fourth, Jacque Hadamard, described his
as "the sudden and immediate appearance of a solution at the very
moment of sudden awakening. On being very abruptly awakened by

an external noise, a solution long searched for appeared to me at once without the slightest instant of reflection on my part."[59]

When we turn to other scientific fields, we find the curious phenomenon that many of the more celebrated discoveries were inspired by dreams. Kekule dreamed of snakelike atoms, one of which bit its tail, providing the image for the atomic composition of benzene, which he had been searching for. Bohr devised his model for the atom from dream-images of planets whirling around a sun. Frederick Banting won his Nobel Prize by dreaming of the physiological process that causes diabetes. Elias Howe, wondering how to construct a sewing machine, dreamed he was in a mob of savages, whose swords all had holes in their tips and went up and down, up and down...[60]

Arthur Koestler's own researches into this phenomenon led him to the following conclusion:

> All the biographical evidence indicates that such a radical re-shuffling operation as occurs in "creative originality" requires the intervention of mental processes beneath the surface of conscious reasoning, in the twilight zone of awareness. In the decisive phase of the creative process the rational controls are relaxed and the creative person's mind seems to *regress* from disciplined thinking to less specialized, more fluid ways of mentation.[61]

Koestler implicitly assumes the prevalent (although not unchallenged) "conscious/subconscious" model to explain "creative originality." But if we take conscious reasoning to be thinking in which thoughts are linked together in a series, and if the "twilight zone of awareness" is a twilight zone (cf. "a dreamlike state") because there is no sense of a self directing the mental processes, then this passage can stand as a description of nondual "prajñā-intuition," from which the more familiar vijñāna processes derive. This differs from "the subconscious" in that prajñā-intuition can be experienced more consciously, although not *self*-consciously.

Two qualifications regarding scientific inspiration must be made. First, apparently unlike musical and literary creativity, it normally requires a great amount of preliminary conscious work—that is, vijñāna. "Saturate yourself through and through with your subject...and wait."[62] Second, there is no guarantee that when such inspirations occur they will be correct. There is nothing in the inspiration itself to differentiate true from false hunches. Faraday, Darwin, Huxley, Planck, Einstein (who lost "two years of hard work" due to a false inspiration) and Poincaré have all commented on this.[63] A scientific hypothesis is either verified or refuted by its accuracy in predicting what will happen, unlike sonatas or poems, which cannot be evaluated in this way because they are not simply true or false. Yet with the latter too, the fact that a work arises "nondually" is no guarantee of its value. Enid Blyton's children's books, although popular, are not expected to endure as immortal literature. One might try to account for the difference in value by variations in the "depth" or "intensity" of the nondual experience, but in order to avoid nonfalsifiability one would need an independent criterion of intensity. It is unlikely that a criterion of sufficient rigor could be found, and the examples that come to mind seem to invalidate the attempt. *Alice in Wonderland* survives because of an inventive charm that Enid Blyton's books lack, and Mozart is "greater" than Puccini; but the inspiration for *Alice*, apparently unlike Blyton's, came only in bits and pieces, and unlike Puccini, Mozart apparently did not feel that his music was dictated to him by God. I think one must accept that nondual thinking does not always produce inspirations of enduring value.

The implications of this are important. Since the nonduality of the creative process does not guarantee the truth of the solution or the value of an artistic work, more discursive and "reflective" thought-processes—Suzuki's vijñāna and our "thoughts linked in a series"—are necessary as well. As mentioned earlier, creative inspiration often needs to be reflected through a critical lens. Just as vijñāna without prajñā becomes sterile, so nondual prajñā without vijñāna is often blind.

THE WAY OF THINKING

We never come to thoughts.
They come to us.

—Heidegger

In the West as in the East, a distinction between types of thinking is practically as old a philosophy itself. But what is probably the most influential example is comparatively modern: Kant's discrimination between *Vernunft* and *Verstand*. "Concepts of reason (*Vernunft*) serve us to conceive (*begreifen*), as concepts of the intellect (*Verstand*) serve us to apprehend perceptions."[64] There is no parallel here to prajñā and vijñāna, but the distinction between Vernunft and Verstand was not original to Kant. It goes back at least as far as Jakob Boehme, whose interpretation was indubitably nondual. According to Boehme, Vernunft "comprehends nothing of the kingdom of God but the husk" and "always goes round in a circle on the outside of things"; it "stands always in doubt" and "out of it comes all strife." This will of Vernunft "rules the outward world without the spirit and will of God, according to its own self-will," so it "must be broken: it must be a living movement of the will which breaks through *Vernunft* and which strives against *Vernunft*." Howard Brinton comments on this: "On the whole Reason [Vernunft] in Boehme's writings seems to be condemned for partial truth rather than untruth.... *Vernunft* wholly isolated from *Verstand* becomes evil."[65] All of this could be used to describe vijñāna, just as Verstand's transcendence of duality seems identical to that of prajñā:

> In *Vernunft* subject and object are separated. Accordingly *Vernunft* is doubtful knowledge. In *Verstand* the subjective–objective distinction has been transcended, therefore Boehme held *Verstand* is sure knowledge, for knower and known are one.
>
> Volition is an identification of subject and object in an action where all sense of otherness is lost because each penetrates and determines the other.
>
> *Vernunft* struggles in vain from multiplicity to unity, *Verstand* beginning at unity sees reality as a whole filled with interrelated forms. Thus *Vernunft* is conceptual thought and *Verstand* is mystical experience. *Verstand* internalizes the external. It sinks into the lowest depths of the dark abyss within the soul, and rises up with God's life to a deeper understanding of the same objects dealt with by *Vernunft*. It can see the meaning of things because it has come out of the source of all meanings. (Brinton)[66]

This description of Vernunft and Verstand agrees so completely with D. T. Suzuki's account of the distinction between vijñāna and prajñā that one could substitute the Sanskrit words for the German ones. I wonder if Suzuki was familiar with Boehme's work or Brinton's study of it (published in 1930).

The distinction between Vernunft and Verstand originally derives from the Neoplatonic distinction between the Aristotelian *ratio* and a faculty of intuition or intelligence superior to reason termed *intellectus*. The Greek equivalent to these Latin terms is found in the distinction Plotinus makes between *logismos*, mere understanding, and *nous*, the superior faculty of Intellect. For Plotinus the understanding sees the Forms separately from each other, but the Intellect sees them all together. According to Nicolas of Cusa it is by means of intellectus that we rise above the principle of noncontradiction and see the unity and coincidence-of-opposites in reality. Eckhart also distinguishes between them, interpreting intellectus more generally as a faculty for the transcendental which for him, like Boehme, was nondual: "the eternal process is a self-revealing of God in pure knowledge where the knower *is* that which is known."[67] But an equally striking parallel is to be found much closer to home.

If philosophy in the nineteenth century became historically conscious, philosophy in the twentieth century has become self-conscious. Attention has shifted from the construction of metaphysical systems to the *act* of philosophizing, that is, thinking itself. This has taken different directions in Anglo-American and continental European philosophy. The former grasps the nature of thinking more objectively, by identifying it with language, and has become sensitive to the ways in which philosophical problems arise due to the misuse of words; many problems are "dissolved" by uncovering the linguistic confusions at their root. On the continent, some phenomenology has continued the traditional pursuit of a scientific "presuppositionless" philosophy, but the influential writings of Heidegger, Jaspers, and more recently Gadamer and Derrida, have shifted attention to the "subjective" act of thinking itself. Their continually evolving work may best be understood as "process philosophies" of philosophizing rather than as the construction of systems that offer something objectively fixed; their most important insights concern the nature of philosophical reflection as such. Thus it is significant that the work of Martin Heidegger (the most influential of the four), and particularly his enigmatic later writings, provides some profound parallels to the account of nondual thinking presented in this chapter. Heidegger has little to say about the problem of perception and almost nothing about the body; rather, he meditated primarily on the nature of thinking. A comprehensive development of this subject would be a book in itself, but a few pages will be enough to point out that Heidegger's general concern was to overcome subject–object duality and that his conclusions bear some similarity to those of the nondualist traditions.

It is not possible to discuss Heidegger's "system" because, like Nāgārjuna, he has none. For Heidegger thinking is not a means to gain knowledge but both the path and the destination.[68] Many of his titles are of peregrination: "Unterwegs zur Sprache" (On the way to language), "Der Feldweg" (The field path), "Wegmarken" (Way-markers), "Holzwege" (Forest paths), and so on. He ends his papers, not with summaries and conclusions but with further questions. In so far as Heidegger has a goal, it is simply to continue questioning and to think more deeply. "I have left an earlier standpoint, not in order to exchange it for another one, but because even the former standpoint was merely a way-station along a way. The lasting element in thinking is the way."[69] This is not, as one would expect, because we can always progress further, but just the opposite: because there is no such thing as progress in thinking.

> When philosophy attends to its essence it does not make forward strides at all. It remains where it is constantly to think the same. Progression, that is, progression forward from this place is a mistake that follows thinking as the shadow which thinking itself casts.[70]

It is hard to conceive of a more radical challenge to our ambitious Western philosophy, but such a denial of progress is also implied by the "empty tranquility" of nondual thinking.

Socrates is praised by Heidegger as "the purest thinker of the West."

> All through his life and right into his death, Socrates did nothing else than place himself into this draft of thinking, this current and maintain himself in it. . . . That is why he wrote nothing. For anyone who begins to write out of thoughtfulness must inevitably be like those people who run to seek refuge from any draft too strong for them.[71]

This is also why Socrates, according to Plato's *Apology*, insisted that he knew nothing, for those sucked into the draft of nondual thinking must let go of that which they "know"—that is, they must not cling to any conclusions as final. Hannah Arendt, a student of Heidegger, described Socrates' method as "unfreezing frozen thoughts." "The word 'house' is something like a frozen thought that thinking must unfreeze whenever it wants to find out the original meaning."[72] That thinking can be "frozen"—reified into concepts and ideas which become *things* retained and used—parallels the "frozen percepts" of chapter 2. If visual objects are reified percepts, perhaps concepts and ideas are reified thoughts. Unstable, fluid thought, which in itself breaks up instantly (*Śikṣāsamuccaya*), may be held only by being petrified into an idea, and that-which-holds-it becomes the "thinker." Whether or not Socrates himself was drawn into "the draft of thinking," certainly that is Heidegger's method and goal, and this requires that one not "freeze" any thoughts that arise but use them as a departure for further questioning.

In *Was Heisst Denken?*—the book that, as its name suggests,[73] deals most specifically with what it means to think—Heidegger finds most "thought-provoking" the fact that we are still not thinking. Heidegger's style in this book is exasperating to anyone looking for an answer. He clearly delights in the sheer movement of thought itself, leisurely exploring all the byways that his thinking encounters, and obviously feeling no necessity to reach a conclusion. The title question is designed not to elicit an answer but to effect a transformation, a deepening of thought.

> The question "What is called thinking," therefore, does not aim to establish an answer by which the question can be disposed of as quickly and conclusively as possible. On the contrary, one thing and one thing only matters with this question: to make the question problematical....
> The question cannot be settled, now or ever....
> To answer the question "What is called thinking?" is itself always to keep asking, so as to remain underway.[74]

Heidegger's intention in *Being and Time*, his first important work, was to reawaken the question of the meaning of Being, which Western philosophy has neglected in its preoccupation with beings. Heidegger began by analyzing the Being of a particular being, of that being whose nature it is to raise the question of the meaning of Being—man (*Dasein*). Having grasped Being in this way, he then intended to turn around and redo the whole analysis from the perspective of Being itself. Instead of this, Heidegger's thinking underwent a crucial shift in the 1930s. The nature and significance of this "turning" or "reversal" (*Kehre*) is controversial, but in any case it marked a radical change not only in many of Heidegger's philosophical views but most of all in his attitude toward the process of thinking. In *Being and Time* Heidegger stated that he wanted to "overcome" metaphysics, but the turning included a realization that his own thinking had still been metaphysical in form. He was still dualistically using thoughts in an attempt to "re-present" Being, still trying "to grasp Being in the network of his concepts."[75] This was replaced by a kind of thinking which has been "claimed by Being" and therefore serves Being: "Before he speaks man must first let himself be claimed again by Being."[76]

> Thinking . . . lets itself be claimed by Being so that it can say the truth of Being. . . . Thinking accomplishes this letting. Thinking is *l'engagement par l'Etre pour l'Etre . . . penser, c'est l'engagement de L'Etre*. Here the possessive form "de l' . . ." is supposed to express both subjective and objective genitive. [Heidegger explains later that this "thinking *of* Being" means both "Being is what is thought about" and "Being is what is doing the thinking."] In this regard, "subject" and "object" are inappropriate terms of metaphysics, which very early on in the form of Occidental "logic" and "grammar" seized control of the interpretation of language. We today can only begin to descry what is concealed in that occurrence.[77]

It seems then that in the most important sense Heidegger accomplished the project he set out for himself in *Being and Time*—he "turned around" and was thinking from the perspective of Being—but in order to do this his conception of that task (and of the means necessary for it) needed a revolutionary transformation. Only thinking that is "an event of Being" can be both means and goal, for only such thinking is sufficient unto itself and needs to accomplish nothing else. "Such thinking has no result. It has no effect. . . . for it lets Being—be." Heidegger distinguishes such *ursprüngliches Denken* from the more calculative, re-presentational *vorstellendes Denken*. The latter includes the "technical interpretation" of thinking: thinking, as Plato and Aristotle (but evidently not Socrates) took it to be, as *technē*, "a process of reflection in service to doing and making."[78] Thinking can begin only when we realize that reason, glorified for centuries as man's highest faculty, is actually the most obstinate opponent of true thinking. The obvious parallel with prajñā and vijñāna is strengthened by the etymological similarities. *Ur-sprüng-liches Denken* is literally "primal-springing-up" thinking (similar to the *pra-* in *prajñā*) and *vorstellendes Denken*, often translated as "re-presentational thinking," is literally "before-placing" thinking, which places one thing in front of something else. Like prajñā and vijñāna, ürsprungliches Denken is discontinuous with ordinary vorstellendes Denken: "The leap alone takes us into the neighborhood where thinking resides."[79] And like prajñā, this leap is not the attainment of something new or adventitious but a "step back":

> Because there is something simple to be thought in this thinking it seems quite difficult to the representational thought that has been transmitted as philosophy. But the difficulty is not a matter of indulging in a special sort of profundity and of building complicated concepts; rather, it is concealed in the *step back* that lets thinking enter into a questioning that experiences—and lets the traditional opining of philosophy fall away.[80]

Philosophy faces the same difficulty with, and is likewise the obstacle to, the simplicity of prajñā. In order to experience either, the philosophizing intellect must be shattered.

> As long as philosophy merely busies itself with continually obstructing the possibility of admittance into the matter for thinking, i.e., into the truth of Being, it stands safely beyond any danger of shattering against the hardness of that matter. Thus to "philosophize" about being shattered is separated by a chasm from a thinking that is shattered. If such thinking were to go fortunately for a man no misfortune would befall him. He would receive the only gift that can come to thinking from Being.[81]

As Mehta explains, such thinking is not the act of a supposedly independent agent called man directed toward or against some other entity distinct from him. I do not see how such thinking, "claimed by Being" and "an event of Being," can be anything *except* nondual thinking as it has been described in this chapter. Heidegger terms the "standing in the lighting of Being" that occurs as a result of being claimed by Being "the ek-sistence of man." What is Being? "The farthest and yet the nearest" because "man at first clings always and only to beings"; thus he "forgets the truth of Being in favor of the pressing throng of beings unthought in their essence." But what is the relation between Being and man's ek-sistence? "Being itself *is the relation* to the extent that It, as the location of the truth of Being and beings, gathers to itself and embraces ek-sistence in its existential, that is, ecstatic essence."[82] Later in the same essay, Heidegger expresses the same point more clearly:

> Man is never first and foremost man on the hither side of the world, as a "subject," whether this is taken as "I" or "We." Nor is he ever simply a mere subject which always simultaneously is related to objects, so that his essence lies in the subject–object relation. Rather before all this, man in his essence is ek-sistent into the openness of Being, into the open region that lights the "between" within which a "relation" of subject to object can "be."[83]

Heidegger concludes "Letter on Humanism" as follows:

> The thinking that is to come is no longer philosophy, because it thinks more originally than metaphysics—a name identical to philosophy. However, the thinking that is to come can no longer, as Hegel demanded, set aside the name "love of [in the sense of "striving for . . .", "pursuit of . . . "] wisdom" and become wisdom itself in the form of absolute knowledge. Thinking is on the descent to the poverty of its provisional essence. Thinking gathers language into simple saying. *In this way language is the language of Being, as clouds are the clouds of the sky.*[84]

●

To follow one star, only this. To think is to concentrate on one thought, motionless like a star in the heavens above the world.

—Heidegger

Heidegger's way of thinking has been compared with the nondual thinking of prajñā, but we may develop the parallel further, for Heidegger's "conclusions" have an affinity not only to nondual thinking but to subject–object nonduality generally. Most of Heidegger's later work is a series of attempts to express the "thought" of nonduality, which we will identify within four of Heidegger's most important essays: "On the Essence of Truth," "Letter on Humanism," "Gelassenheit" ("Conversation on a Country Path about Thinking") and "The End of Philosophy and the Task of Thinking." The context within which this "thought" occurs is different in each essay, but in every case there is the same central point, around which the meditation revolves. And in retrospect we can see premonitions of that thought even in Heidegger's 1929 inaugural lecture "What Is Metaphysics?"

In a later postscript to "On the Essence of Truth" (first given as an address in 1930), Heidegger states that the *Kehre* (turning) occurs in it and evaluates its significance by claiming that "in its decisive steps . . . it accomplishes a change in the questioning that belongs to the overcoming of metaphysics." Not only is all metaphysical subjectivity left behind and "the truth of Being sought as the ground of a transformed historical position," but also "the movement of the lecture is such that *it sets out to think from this other ground. The course of the questioning is intrinsically the way of a thinking which, instead of furnishing representations and concepts, *experiences and tries itself as a transformation of its relatedness to Being.*"[85]

Heidegger's original intention in *Being and Time* had been to redo in part 2 the Dasein-analysis of part 1 from the perspective of Being itself. As we have seen, this failed because the approach of *Being and Time* was still metaphysical in its attempt to re-present what-is. Subjectivity is still implicit in conceiving of philosophy as an activity that man uses in order to grasp Being. In order to accomplish the intention of part 2, a turning away from this subjective conception of thinking was necessary. One must "think from this other ground"—that is, from the perspective of Being itself. What might be termed the "presubjective ground" of Being must be identified and "yielded to" in order for thinking to take place *from* or rather *in* that ground. That presubjective ground is first articulated in "On the Essence of Truth" and is the hinge upon which the essay turns.

In it, Heidegger begins by questioning the conventional definition of truth, more precisely, the relation that obtains between a statement and the thing referred to. As long as the nature of this relation remains undetermined and is taken for granted, as Heidegger believes it has been, all discussion about the correspondence theory must lose its way. So Heidegger looks at this relation. What a statement states is about something presented to us, that is, something that is opposed to us as an object.

What stands opposed must traverse an open field of opposedness

(*Entgegen*) and nevertheless must maintain its stand as a thing and show itself as something withstanding. This appearing of the thing in traversing a field of opposedness takes place in an open region, *the openness of which is not first created by the presenting but rather is only entered into and taken over as a domain of relatedness.*[86]

Here, for the first time, appears "the thought" that Heidegger restates again and again in his later essays, devising new contexts and vocabularies to express it, constantly circling around it as a moth around a flame. Translated into our nondualist terms, Heidegger says that the "openness" of the traversed region—the world of our surroundings, which each of us is most immediately "in"—is "not . . . created," in that it is prior to our dualistic understanding of an object presented to a subject. Heidegger challenges the notion that consciousness is the attribute of a discrete subject observing a nonconscious external world. That usual dualistic understanding is only one historically determined interpretation of the "open region." Here Heidegger goes beyond speculation about the nature of Being and for the first time tries to point directly to the presubjective ground that *is* Being.

The rest of "On the Essence of Truth" follows from this point. The correctness of a statement depends upon an "openness of comportment" in this open region, which allows Heidegger to locate the essence of truth in freedom—on "*being free* for what is opened up in an open region." But man overlooks this openness and "clings to what is readily available and controllable even where ultimate matters are concerned." Our mistake is that we "hold fast to what is offered by beings, *as if they were open of and in themselves.*"[87] This is "the fall": by clinging to particular beings as if they were self-existent, one misses the predualistic openness of Being that makes them possible.

The "Letter on Humanism" develops the implications of this insight by using it to reinterpret the *Being and Time* categories of Dasein, ek-sistence, "the fall," authenticity, Being, and especially language and thinking. Humanism does not go deep enough to inquire into the nature of this opening, but tends to accept the given interpretation of the relation between Being and man. Dasein's "being-there" now means our being thrown by Being into its illumined openness, and Dasein's ek-sistence is our essential exposure to this disclosure of

Being, into which we have been summoned. Dasein's "fall" is failure to recognize this disclosure, oblivious to it in Dasein's clinging to particular beings. Authenticity is fulfilling one's essence by answering this "call of Being" and becoming "the shepherd of Being," but modern man has fallen and hence is homeless.

The most radical shift in this essay is a new view of language and thinking, which are now understood to originate from this presubjective opening. We miss the essence of language if we treat it merely as a means of communication, as a tool that man possesses. Language is "the house of Being" within which man dwells as its caretaker rather than its owner. The new understanding of thinking parallels this: the presubjective opening of Being is also the source of all essential (ürsprungliches) thinking, as we have seen. These insights about language and thinking are the logical development of Heidegger's earlier "thought" about the "open region" whose openness is not created in the dualistic relation but exists prior to it. Just as men generally miss the openness of Being by clinging and trying to possess particular beings as if "they were open in and of themselves," so thinkers tend to do the same with their "own" thoughts, thus missing that presubjective opening from which thoughts arise. This realization negates all metaphysical system-building and led to the Way of nondual thinking discussed above. It is through such "essential thinking" that the thinker dwells in the "open region" of Being.

"Gelassenheit"[88] begins by asking whether the question about man's nature is in fact *not* a question about man, and (as in "Letter on Humanism") the essay concludes that man's nature is indeed determined in what is beyond man. The topic is again thinking but includes what we would normally call perception. Thinking is usually understood as "transcendental-horizontal re-presenting," which, for example, places before us ("re-presents") what is *typical* of a tree "as that view into which we look when one thing confronts us in the appearance of a tree." But then both horizon and transcendence are experienced only in relation to what we re-present as objects opposing us.

> What lets the horizon be what it is has not yet been encountered.... We say that we look into the horizon. Therefore the field of vision is something open, *but its openness is not due to our looking*. Likewise we do

not place the appearance of objects, which the view within a field of vision offers us, into this openness . . . *rather that comes out of this to meet us.*

Here again is "the thought." "On the Essence of Truth" said that the openness of the open region is not created by the presenting of some object to us; here we are told that the openness is also not due to *our* looking. Again, this is the central point around which the conversation turns. The horizon can now be understood as only the side facing us of an openness that surrounds us. That openness is termed "an enchanted region," a "regioning," and finally "that-which-regions" (*die Gegnet*). This region is more than just some "place": while resting in itself, it gathers each thing into its "re-sheltering abiding." Nonwilling thinking becomes meaningful as a presubjective thinking in which willing has been renounced in favor of a "waiting" that releases oneself from all transcendental-horizontal re-presenting into the openness of this Gegnet and in so doing lets die Gegnet "reign purely as such." This waiting is not waiting *for* "releasement" but *is* releasement, for it is not the subject that is responsible for this waiting but die Gegnet itself. So "the nature of thinking lies in the regioning of releasement by that-which-regions," hence the nature of thinking is indeed determined through something other than itself.

"The End of Philosophy and the Task of Thinking" discusses the two questions suggested by the title. Philosophy has entered its final stage because it is equivalent to metaphysics, and "metaphysical thinking, starting from what is present, represents it in its essence and thus exhibits it as grounded by its ground."[89] In other words metaphysics, in its search for the ground of what is present, does not let a tree in bloom present itself to us but always re-presents it, to cite the example that Heidegger uses in *What Is Called Thinking?*

> When we think through what this is, that a tree in bloom presents itself to us so that we can come and stand face to face with it, the thing that matters first and foremost, and finally, is not to drop the tree in bloom, but for once let it stand where it stands. Why do we say 'finally'? Because *to this day, thought has never let the tree stand where it stands.*

> The presence of what is present is not finally and also something we face, rather *it comes before. Prior to all else it stands before us*, only we do not see it because we stand within it. *It is what really comes before us.*[90]

Yet another kind of thinking besides metaphysics is possible. Two recent attempts to return to "the things themselves," those of Hegel and Husserl, were still subjective heirs to the dualistic legacy of Descartes. Heidegger reflects on what remains "unthought" in their methods. In Hegel's speculative dialectic, philosophy presents itself by appearing of itself and for itself. Such an appearance must occur in some light, for only through brightness can what shines show itself. But that brightness depends upon something open and free which "grants to the movement of speculative thinking the passage through what it thinks." This logic provides the opportunity, albeit a rather strained one, to approach "the thought" again. Heidegger calls "this openness that grants a possible letting-appear" the "opening" (*Lichtung*) and then makes—and remakes—his point:

> Light can stream into the clearing, into its openness, and let brightness play with darkness in it. But light never first creates openness. Rather, light presupposes openness.

> In the Greek language, one is not speaking about the action of seeing, about *videre*, but about that which gleams and radiates. But it can radiate only if openness has already been granted. The beam of light does not first create the opening, openness, it only traverses it.

> We have already reflected upon the fact that the path of thinking . . . needs the opening. But in that opening rests possible radiance, that is, the possible presencing of presence itself.[91]

Heidegger uses this point to redefine *aletheia*: no longer understood as truth, it is now that opening which first grants the possibility of truth. He concludes by defining "the task of thinking." Metaphysics asks about this Being (i.e., the ground) of beings, but "does not ask about Being as Being, that is, . . . how there can be presence as such. *There is presence only when opening is dominant.*" To "think this opening" is the future task for thought.

It comes as no surprise that the same point is fundamental to Heidegger's interpretation of the history of philosophy: that the Greek concepts of *physis* and *hypokeimenon* ("that which lies before") embodied some naive understanding of this "thought," later lost when they were transformed into *technē* and the self-conscious *subiec-*

tum, respectively. Less obvious is the fact that in retrospect we can see anticipations of Heidegger's "thought"—not a rudimentary form, but its birth pangs—in his 1929 inaugural lecture "What Is Metaphysics?" The new perspective in Heidegger's later works was not due merely to an abstract philosophical insight, the result of objective reflection. The change is more profound than just a new style of thinking. Heidegger implied later that his thinking had been "shattered," and "What Is Metaphysics?" seems to be a record of this transition to a new way of *being*.

The lecture is concerned with a particular metaphysical question: the nature of transcendence, taken to be identical to the problem of Nothingness. Science is concerned with investigating the various types of beings and, taking the objectivity of these beings for granted, "wants to know nothing of the nothing." But the Nothing is revealed in the fundamental mood of anxiety, in which our preoccupation with grasping objects fades away. This Nothing, although it is "the complete negation of the totality of beings," is not an annihilation but a "slipping away of the whole," which includes oneself—that is, one's own subjectivity. In this receding, things do not disappear but turn toward us and close in on us because we can get no hold on them. We "hover" in an anxiety that is yet "a kind of bewildered calm" which brings us "for the first time before beings as such." Dasein means "being held out into the nothing" and this being "already beyond beings as a whole" is what Heidegger calls our transcendence. "Without the original revelation of the nothing, no selfhood and no freedom."[92]

What Heidegger here presents philosophically seems to be a description of the difficult process of losing his subjectivity (in the Cartesian sense) and letting in or surrendering himself to the presubjective "opening" of Being, which at this point is experienced incompletely as a numbing Nothingness. While he denies any dualism between Nothing and beings ("the Nothing does not merely serve as the counterpart of beings; rather it originally belongs to their essential unfolding as such"), yet some such dualism is implicit in this lecture because there is not yet a clear understanding of Being as simply the opening for the un-represented "presencing" of those beings. Hence this experience is, as we can see in retrospect, transitional. So are the categories used to express this experience: for example, the terms "metaphysics" and "transcendence," both of which are subsequently rejected. Here man is necessarily metaphysical because of the transcendence of beings in Nothingness. In terms of the later Heidegger, this transcendence is metaphysical in a pejorative sense because there is still the representational attempt to "ground" beings—in this case, in their Nothingness. The re-presented tree in bloom recedes and closes in on Heidegger because he can get no hold on it, but he has not yet realized how the subjective tendency to grasp and re-present is all that separates him from the Being he seeks. Later Heidegger realizes that there is no metaphysical need to transcend the presencing of a tree in bloom, and then that anxious Nothing becomes the abiding opening within which all presencing radiates.

•

So perhaps we should take William Barrett's story seriously: "A German friend of Heidegger told me that one day when he visited Heidegger he found him reading one of D. T. Suzuki's books; 'If I understand this man correctly,' Heidegger remarked, 'this is what I have been trying to say in all my writings.'"[93] But if there is such similarity between the paths of Heidegger and the nondualist Asian philosophies, where do they differ? For differ they clearly do. Heidegger, if not a philosopher, is still a "thinker," which the Zen student is not. I think that both affirm a paradox which might be called "the thinking of no-thinking." But they emphasize different aspects of it. The meditative traditions emphasize the no-thinking, Heidegger the thinking. In meditation, one is concerned to dwell in the silent, empty source from which thoughts spring; as thoughts arise, one ignores them and lets them go. Heidegger is interested in the thoughts arising from that source—although not stopping with any particular thoughts by freezing them into a system, but staying in the "draft of thinking" itself. The question that remains is whether Heidegger himself went into the draft far enough to reach that tranquility where no wind ever blows. Did he "step back" far enough for his thinking to be completely shattered? Did it ever descend into the poverty of truly simple saying?

A monk earnestly asked Jōshū, "I have just entered this monastery. I beg you, master, please instruct me." Jōshū asked: "Have you eaten your rice porridge yet?" "Yes, I have." "Then wash your bowls." The monk realized something.[94]

How satisfactory can a theory be that purports to show why all theories must be unsatisfactory? Like Wittgenstein in the *Tractatus*, have we climbed up a ladder which must now be kicked out from beneath us? Or, to use the more appropriate Zen koan, how do we keep going when we have reached the top of a hundred-foot pole?[95] Not that we are in any danger of becoming Cretan liars. The problem here is not semantic but soteriological. If the view of nondual thinking developed in this chapter is true, then everything written herein is subrated to thought-linked-in-a-series vijñāna and condemned as the primary obstacle to the realization of prajñā. This means that any theory of nonduality, if it is to retain the prescriptive aspect of the nondualist philosophies, must be paradoxical and self-negating. As in the Prajñāpāramitā, what one hand offers, the other takes back. We cannot avoid the Mādhyamika distinction between two levels of truth, and all philosophy is on the lower. The only way to experience the higher is to throw out the baby with the bathwater.

In Suzuki's terms, all this chapter is vijñāna vainly attempting to comprehend prajñā, the source underlying it. Like Heidegger in *Being and Time*, we have dualistically tried to "grasp" what nondual thinking is. What is unique to thinking about the nature of thinking is that what is to be grasped and what is to grasp it are the same thing— yet another type of "nonduality." This makes thinking both the easiest thing to comprehend and the most difficult. In the usual sense it becomes impossible, just as the hand cannot grasp itself and the eye cannot see itself.

> Hsüan-tse told Master Fa-yen that when he was with his first teacher, he learned that to seek for Buddhahood would be just as if Ping-ting T'ung-tsu were to ask for fire. He explained that Ping-ting T'ung-tzu was the god of fire; this god's asking for fire would be like being oneself a Buddha and seeking Buddha. Fa-yen remarked that his understanding was completely off the track. Hsüan-tse was extremely offended and left the temple. But when he came back to the master and asked for another statement, to Hsüan-tse's surprise the Master said, "Ping-ting T'ung-tzu asks for fire." This immediately awakened Hsüan-tse.[96]

The monk was "correct" the first time, but this "fact" had to be experienced fully, not just grasped as something conceptually true. To miss this truth by an inch is to be off by a thousand miles, just as all philosophizing about being shattered against the hardness of this matter is separated by a chasm from thinking that has been shattered. The question about the nature of nondual thinking must finally be answered on a different level than that of other questions. As Heidegger said in response to a related question, "if the answer could be given it would consist in a transformation of thinking, not in a propositional statement about a matter at stake."[97]

SUMMARY OF THE
CORE THEORY

This study of subject–object nonduality has reached its midpoint, for part 2 offers a different approach to the topic. The analyses of nondual perception, nondual action, and nondual thinking have given us a theory that part 2 defends and elaborates. We must prepare for what is to follow by summarizing what has been done.

We began by noticing something interesting. Several important Asian philosophical systems, which have many similarities and many differences, make the same claim that the true nature of reality is nondual. Then are they perhaps referring to the same experience? Chapter 1 distinguished five different meanings of nonduality and discussed three of them: thinking that does not employ dualistic concepts, the nonplurality of phenomena "in" the world, and the nondifference of subject and object. We observed that all three claims are found in Mahāyāna Buddhism, Advaita Vedānta, and Taoism, which we have since referred to as "nondualistic systems." These three nonduality claims are closely related. The critique of thinking that employs dualistic categories (being vs. nonbeing, pure vs. impure, etc.) usually expands to encompass all conceptual thinking, for such thinking acts as a superimposition which distorts our immediate experience. That is why we experience the world dualistically in the second sense, as a collection of discrete objects (including *me*) interacting causally in space and time. Negating dualistic thinking leads to experiencing the world as a unity, variously called Brahman, Dharmakāya, Tao, the One Mind, and so on. But what is the relationship between this whole and the subject that experiences it? The Whole is not truly whole if the subject is separate from it. This leads to the third sense of nonduality, the denial that subject and object are truly distinguishable. The rest of this work is devoted to understanding that extraordinary and counterintuitive claim, which is not just an objective evaluation; the nondualistic systems also agree that our usual sense of duality—the sense of separation (hence alienation) between myself and the world "I" am "in"—is the root delusion that needs to be overcome.

The preceding three chapters have explored what the claim of subject–object nonduality means in three different modes of our experience. It is significant that in each case we were able to utilize concepts ready at hand in the nondualist traditions. In chapter 2 it was the Indian epistemological distinction between savikalpa and nirvikalpa perception (prapañca is a related term); in chapter 3 it was the wei-wu-wei of Taoism; and in chapter 4 it was the prajñā of Mahāyāna Buddhism. In the process of unpacking the unfamiliar and counterintuitive implications of these concepts—clarifying what the claim is and using comparisons to situate it in Western thought—we have been in danger of losing the forest for the trees. We must see clearly the relationships among these three in order to attain an overview. The "architectonic" of their parallels is as important as the sum of their individual claims. If, as discussed in the introduction, the nondualistic perspective is able to understand dualistic experience, but not vice versa, then evidently we can "interpolate" from these nondual claims to explain our usual dualistic experience as due to superimposition or interaction among these three.

Chapter 2 argued that, according to both Buddhism and Advaita, the distinction between savikalpa (with thought-construction) and nirvikalpa (without thought-construction) is equivalent to the distinction between the dualistic and nondualistic modes of perception. When the percept is differentiated from all its thought-superimpositions, there is no awareness of any duality between that which is perceived and that which perceives. Our usual understanding hypostatizes such percepts into material objects, but in themselves they are empty (śūnya) because they have no self-nature (svabhāva). They are only the phenomenal manifestation, according to Advaita, of a qualityless (nirguṇa) Mind; according to Buddhism, of *nothing*. I argued that the most satisfactory presentation of this view is found in Mahāyāna: negatively, in the Mādhyamika refutation of any possible conceptual superimpositions, for the critique of prapañca shipwrecks any possibility of philosophy providing a "mirror of nature"; positively, in the explicit subject–object nonduality of Yogācāra. It was suggested (and the argument will be developed in subsequent chapters) that this view is also implicit in the early Buddhist denial of a self (anātman) and in the Advaitic assertion of all-Self (ātman). But both views suffer from an inadequate account of the nature of phenomena: early Buddhism tends to accept uncritically the objectivity of dharmas, while Advaita takes an ambivalent attitude toward māyā. What nondual hearing and seeing might be was developed by referring to Berkeley's denial of the material object and Hume's critique of the ontological subject, and placed in the context of Western epistemology as a version of phenomenalism. The contemporary Western view that perception is always "thought-constructed" does not necessarily constitute an argument against such nondual perception but rather indirectly supports its possibility, since the nirvikalpa claim is not about our usual perception but about a special case not often experienced, in which perception has been "de-automatized." The possibility of such de-automatization thus becomes an issue that can be settled only empirically—exactly what the nondualist traditions claim to happen in the enlightenment experience.

Parallels to this, too striking to be coincidental, were found in the Taoist paradox of wei-wu-wei, which is interpreted to mean not just passivity or noninterference, but action that may be realized to be nondual when it is distinguished from the superimposition of intentions. Just as linguistic superimposition delusively bifurcates perceiver from perceived, so intention-superimposition bifurcates agent from act—splitting what might be called the "psychic body" and giving rise to the mind–body distinction, the sense of being "a ghost in a machine." Nondual actions are experienced as no action at all (wu-wei) because wholly to *be* an action is to lose the perspective of an agent distinct from it and thus to eliminate the sensation that an action is occurring. This paradox is all the more significant because we found precisely the same to be true of nondual perception and nondual thinking: "one sound is soundless sound," "one thought is thought-less thought." Such an understanding of wei-wu-wei was used to explicate the first chapter of the *Tao Tê Ching*, whose cryptic lines lend themselves to such a nondualistic interpretation. This critique of intentionality was further developed by reference to Western theories about mind and action. The relationships among craving, conceptualizing, and causality were explored, using ideas of Heidegger and Wittgenstein that enable us to see how causal relationships are "built into" language. Recent work in the philosophy of mind, pointing to intentionality as that which maintains the sense of self, was (just as in the previous case of Western theories of perception) shown not to refute the possibility of nondual action but rather indirectly to support it, for if the sense of self is maintained by intention, then eliminating intention will also eliminate that sense of self. But, following Hume, one should not assume a causal link between intention and action, for any "link" between them, like causal links generally, is essentially mysterious. Causality, as usually experienced, is part of our interpretative filtering, which must be distinguished from the "thing in itself." On one side, the lack of any causal link between intention and action amounts to a refutation of volition and implies determinism. One could argue, conversely, that the elimination of all savikalpa thought-constructions (which include all causal inferences) rather refutes determinism. But the problem of freedom versus determinism is dualistic in presupposing a self whose actions are either free or determined, and the nondualistic denial of an ontological self resolves that bifurcation: if I am the universe, then complete determinism becomes equivalent to absolute freedom. This issue of causality is perhaps the most crucial one of all, and is discussed further in part 2.

We found the equivalent nondual thinking in the Mahāyāna concept of prajñā, that knowing in which there is no distinction between the knower, the act of knowing, and that which is known. Such knowing is sometimes understood quite broadly to describe all nondual experience, but with reference to thinking it means that there is no thinker (consciousness) apart from the thought. For both perception and action, the difference between dualistic and nondualistic experience was seen to be due to the superimposition of thought-constructions. Again, it can hardly be a coincidence that we find a similar parallel with thinking: that thoughts are superimposed upon each other, in effect. An important passage by John Levy argues that the sense of subject–object duality is due to the mental juxtaposition of different experiences—that is, the superimposition of memory-traces onto a new experience. Then to eliminate or distinguish the memory-trace (in the case of thinking, the previous thought) from that which it conditions (the new thought) will eliminate the sense of subject–object duality. This explains the importance Mahāyāna places upon not letting thoughts link up in a series (making a chain by superimposing one on the other) but rather allowing an "unsupported thought" to arise spontaneously. This also connects with the previous critique of causality. From the highest (paramārtha) point of view, just as intentions do not "cause" actions, so earlier thoughts do not "cause" subsequent ones; "everything is its own cause and its own effect" (Blake). On this account, the difference between our more usual ways of thinking and the special cases of creativity and inspiration is the difference between dualistic thinking—in which there is clinging to familiar and comfortable thoughts—and a more open, receptive thinking in which thoughts spring up (pra-) nondually. Because the latter thoughts cannot be accounted for causally—as the effects of previous causes—there is something essentially inexplicable and mysterious about the creative process. This gave us a fruitful perspective for interpreting the later work of Heidegger.

The significance of these individual studies increases as we notice the parallels among our conclusions. Probably the most important parallel concerns the emptiness (śūnyatā) of experience. Each mode of experience was found to be empty in at least three related senses. First, of course, each is empty of subject–object duality, for when distinguished from thought-superimpositions there is no awareness of a discrete consciousness separate from the experience. It is argued in part 2 that to inflate either the subject or the object by eliminating the other cannot be satisfactory. Both must be denied, since as relative to the other each is meaningless without the other. Second is the paradox that to "forget yourself" and nondually "become" something is to gain an awareness (of) that (which) transcends any particular experience, (of) what may be called an emptiness because it cannot be grasped objectively. This implies the third sense. None of these three modes has any reality or self-nature of its own, for each is only a phenomenal manifestation of what part 2 argues is an all-encompassing, attributeless Mind, which can be phenomenologically experienced only as a *nothingness* that is creative because it is the source of all phenomena.

This understanding allows us to account for the difference between dualistic and nondualistic experience without needing to add anything extraneous. If perception, action, and thinking are in themselves nondual, then we can understand our usual sense of duality as due to their superimposition and interaction. As an example of such interaction, we have discussed the relations among craving, conceptualizing, and causality (chapter 3). The general problem seems to be that the three modes of experience interfere with each other and thus distort or obscure each other's nondual nature. The material objects of the external world are nondual percepts objectified by thought-superimposition and by our attempts to "grasp" them. Dualistic action is due to the superimposition of intention upon nondual action, and that network of intentions both presupposes and reinforces the objectivity of its field of play. Both concepts and intentions occur when nondual thinking is related to percepts and actions rather than experienced as it is in itself (fig. 4).

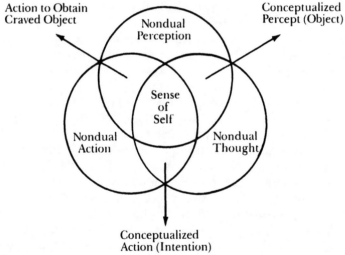

Figure 4

Such a nondualistic interpretation implies a critique of several stereotyped misunderstandings about the nature of spirituality. The most important one is that enlightenment does not involve transcending the world and attaining some other, nonsensuous realm, for on this account the transcendental is nothing other than the "empty" nature of this world. As Mahāyāna emphasizes, saṁsāra is nirvana: "Nothing of saṁsāra is different from nirvāṇa, nothing of nirvāṇa is different from saṁsāra. That which is the limit of nirvāṇa is also the limit of saṁsāra; there is not the slightest difference between the two" (MMK, XXV, 19–20). In this way we come to an understanding of this fourth sense of nonduality, mentioned at the beginning of chapter 1.

Another misunderstanding sees the spiritual path as quietistic and requiring a withdrawal from activity (e.g., physical labor, sex, political involvement). There may well be periods when such a retreat is valuable, but the possibility of wei-wu-wei means that eremiticism, asceticism, and so on should not be understood as inherently superior. (Gandhi may be a model in this regard.)

Finally, the emphasis on meditative techniques in the nondualist traditions has sometimes resulted in an anti-intellectualism which dismisses the higher thought-processes as obstructive, but in fact the nondual intellect is our most creative faculty. Each of these misunderstandings may now be seen to be an overreaction against its respective dualistic mode of experience. This work implies that a better solution is not to try to negate each dualistic mode but to transform it into the nondualistic mode.

We have just seen how part 1 attempted to construct a core theory of nonduality by extracting and synthesizing claims from a variety of Asian traditions—primarily, but not exclusively, Mahāyāna Buddhism, Advaita Vedānta, and Taoism. There have also been numerous references to the Western tradition—particularly to Blake, Nietzsche, Wittgenstein, and Heidegger—but these have played a supportive role. The method of extraction has been unsystematic and intuitive: claims supportive to this enterprise have been used, while others have been ignored. This means that similarities and congruences have been emphasized while disparities have seldom been remarked. But these differences among the various traditions—in particular, the contradictory ontological claims—cannot simply be swept away. They provide the most serious challenge to this inquiry. If behind each philosophy is the same nondual experience, as I have been suggesting, then why do the various systems end up with such different ontologies? As soon as we turn to the question of what is Real, our tidy core doctrine dissolves into a hotbed of controversy. For example, Advaita Vedānta is monistic, Sāṅkhya-Yoga is dualistic, early Buddhism seems to be pluralistic, and Mādhyamika denies both that things exist and that they do not exist.

The purpose of part 2 is to deal with these conflicting ontological claims. The approach is that these differences do not in fact negate the core theory constructed in part 1, for these ontological differences arise not from different experiences but from emphasizing different aspects of the same nondual experience. The experience itself involves no claims, ontological or otherwise, for it transcends philosophy; yet when one tries to satisfy the inevitable philosophical demand for an ontology, one may make different and inconsistent inferences by dwelling upon different aspects of that experience, according to one's cultural or personal dispositions.

Part 2 argues for this in various ways. Chapter 5 examines the relationships among what are perhaps the three most important Indian systems (or sets of systems): Sāṅkhya-Yoga, Buddhism, and Vedānta. We shall see that each develops one of the three primary ways of understanding the subject–object relation. Since the radical dualism of Sāṅkhya-Yoga is untenable, chapter 6 focuses on the curious relationship between the other two, whose categories are so diametrically opposed that each is the mirror image of the other. For the purpose of analysis, their conflict will be reduced to five sets of categories: all-Self versus no-self, substance versus modes, immutability versus impermanence, no-causality versus all-conditionality, and no-Path versus only-Path. I argue that in each case one extreme is phenomenologically equivalent to the other if the dualism between them is truly negated. The implication of this is that the nondual experience "behind" these contradictory systems is the same, and that the differences between them may be seen as due primarily to the nature of language: linguistic categories being inherently dualistic, the natural tendency is for descriptions of nonduality to eliminate one or the other of the dualistic pair.

But there is much more to Indian philosophy than Buddhism and Vedānta. Other ontological views must be dealt with. Chapter 7 attempts to make much the same point analogically, by presenting a "nondual experience" that is subject to a variety of interpretations. By no coincidence, these interpretations happen to correspond to the ontological claims of the major systems. Finally, chapter 8 tests our core theory by demonstrating how it helps us to understand the *Bhagavad-gītā*. We will see that a nondualist approach can explain the relations among its various *margas* (spiritual paths) and perhaps even resolve the relationship between personal (God, Krishna) and impersonal (Brahman, etc.) Absolutes.

PART TWO
RESOLVING
ONTOLOGICAL
DIFFERENCES

CHAPTER 5
THREE APPROACHES TO THE SUBJECT–OBJECT RELATION

In the Himalaya of Indian thought, three mountain ranges tower above the rest: Sāṅkhya-Yoga, Buddhism, and Vedānta. Rather than argue that this is so, let us consider *why* it is so. What is it that causes these three systems (or sets of systems) to stand out as the most important? This short chapter answers that question by demonstrating their relationship. What is special about these three is that they elaborate the three primary responses to the epistemological problem of the subject–object relation—an issue that is fundamental to any metaphysical system and is especially crucial for any philosophy that purports to explain the experience of enlightenment.

Sāṅkhya-Yoga presents the most radical dualism possible by completely sundering subject and object. The separation between the two is so extreme that, as is generally accepted, the system fails because there can be no communication or cooperation between them.

Early Buddhism conflates subject into object. Consciousness is something conditioned, arising only when certain conditions exist. The self is merely an illusion created by the interaction of the five aggregates. The self shrinks to nothing and there is only a void, but the Void is not a thing: it expresses the fact that there is absolutely nothing, no-thing at all, which can be identified as the self.

Advaita Vedānta conflates object into subject. There is nothing external to Brahman, the One without a second. Since Brahman is a nondual consciousness, consciousness may be said to expand and encompass the entire universe, which is but the appearance of

Brahman. Everything is the Self. One important consequence of this is that we all have (or rather *are*) the same Self.[1]

Of these three, only Advaita Vedānta is obviously an attempt to describe the experience of subject–object nonduality. With Buddhism one must be more careful about such a generalization: it seems true for Mahāyāna, but not for Pāli Buddhism, at least not explicitly (an issue we return to). In the case of Sāṅkhya-Yoga, which is unequivocably dualistic, there seems to be no ground whatsoever for claiming that it is an attempt to describe the nondual experience. But chapter 7 suggests that Sāṅkhya-Yoga may be viewed as such an attempt, although an unsatisfactory one. Here it is necessary to summarize the claims of Sāṅkhya metaphysics, which will enable us to see why it is inadequate.

SĀṄKHYA-YOGA

Sāṅkhya is dualistic because it explains the subject–object relation by postulating two basic substances: *puruṣa*, pure unchanging consciousness, and *prakṛti*, the natural world that encompasses everything else. It is significant that this is not a Cartesian dualism: prakṛti includes all mental as well as physical phenomena; what we experience as our mind (buddhi) and all its mental phenomena are evolutes of prakṛti too. Anything that can be experienc*ed* is prakṛti. Thus puruṣa is reduced to a pure "seer" which actually does nothing, although its presence is necessary not only for there to be awareness but also to act as a catalyst for the evolutes of prakṛti. In our usual deluded condition we are not able to distinguish between these two substances. Pure consciousness mistakenly identifies itself with its reflections; that is, I cling to "my" mental panorama and "my" body and its possessions. The puruṣa is so attenuated that it is not even able to realize the distinction between itself and prakṛti. As in Advaita, it is actually the buddhi, the most rarified part of the prakṛti, that realizes the distinction, whereupon it abdicates by itself and the puruṣa is established in its own true nature as solitary and independent, indifferently observing the natural world.

The main problem is that the polarity between puruṣa and prakṛti is so great that they are unable to cooperate. Puruṣa is so indifferent and prakṛti so mechanical that they cannot function together. The common simile to explain their interaction is that of a blind man of good foot carrying a cripple of good eye; but this is not a good analogy because in order to interact both men must have intelligence, whereas prakṛti does not. The simile would fit better if the cripple has no desire to go anywhere and so says and does nothing, while the blind man literally has no mind at all. Clearly, in such a case they would not cooperate, yet Sāṅkhya-Yoga claims that the whole universe evolved out of the interaction arising from the introduction of puruṣa to prakṛti.

Whereas Sāṅkhya is a metaphysical system, Yoga deals mainly with the yogic path which one follows in order to attain kaivalya, the "liberated isolation" of the puruṣa. It is significant that there is nothing within the eight limbs of yoga practice antithetical to Vedānta. In fact the yogic path seems to fit an Advaitic metaphysics better than a Sāṅkhya one. In samādhi, the eighth and highest limb, the mind loses ego-awareness and becomes one with its object of meditation, but this nondualistic experience can be described only as "as if one" in Yoga, since the ultimate goal is understood to be the discrimination of pure consciousness from all those objects it usually identifies with. But of course this nondual experience accords very well with the Advaitic aim of "realizing the whole universe as the Self."

Yet what is the most interesting is that the puruṣa, like the jīva of Jainism and the ātman of Vedānta and Nyāya-Vaiśeṣika, is eternal and omnipresent; it has no particular locus but is ubiquitous, pervading everywhere. So the puruṣa is very different from consciousness as we normally understand it, an "internal world" counterposed to the external world. Clearly Sāṅkhya is far from capturing commonsense duality. That the puruṣa is so emptied of any function—it has almost nothing to do except to be unvarying consciousness—is also significant. In this respect it is similar to the Nirguṇa Brahman of Vedānta, which is also devoid of any attributes in itself, or one might characterize puruṣa with the Buddhist term śūnya, as empty. But that the puruṣa is all-pervading leads to problems for Sāṅkhya, since there is supposedly an infinity (or at least a very large number) of completely distinct, unrelated puruṣas. How can they all occupy the same infinite space without affecting each other in some way? Given that they are all devoid of any attributes, how are they to be distinguished from each other? A corollary problem is that each undifferentiated puruṣa has a relationship with only one particular buddhi. Furthermore, each liberated puruṣa, being ubiquitous, must coexist with all of prakṛti, yet be completely unaffected by it.

For these and other reasons, this most extreme dualism between subject and object fails. The failure of Sāṅkhya-Yoga, it should be noted, is not incidental but is due to a basic inadequacy: the duality is so radical that it precludes any cooperation between the two categories. In accord with this, there are two ways one might try to resolve the problem. One could conceive of all puruṣas as various reflections of one unified consciousness and subsume prakṛti as another aspect or manifestation of this consciousness. Or, given the functionlessness of the puruṣa, one could eliminate it altogether and incorporate consciousness into prakṛti. Either solution, of course, transforms Sāṅkhya into a completely different system, because the root dualism has been abandoned. The first alternative makes Sāṅkhya into Vedāntic monism, and the second makes it into the anātman pluralism of Pāli Buddhism. If, as some scholars believe, Sāṅkhya is the oldest Indian metaphysical system, this may well have been what happened historically: when its dualism came to be recognized as an unsatisfactory description of the enlightenment experience, Indian philosophy developed the diametrically opposed alternatives of Vedānta and Buddhism. The conflict between these two alternatives is our main concern, but I refer to Sāṅkhya-Yoga again when we return in chapter 7 to the question of whether all these systems might be responding to the same nondual experience.

BUDDHISM

The nature of nirvana is the greatest problem of Buddhist philosophy, probably because the Buddha himself refused to speculate on it. His attitude was, in effect, that if you want to know what nirvana is, then you must attain it. But clearly nirvana does not involve the isolation of a Sāṅkhya-like pure consciousness, because there is no such thing in Buddhism. The unique feature of Buddhism is that there is no self at all, and never was; there are only five skandhas, aggregates or "heaps" of elements which constantly interact. These skandhas do not constitute a self; the sense of a self is merely an illusion created by their interaction. The Buddha emphasized that we should not identify anything as the self.

Thus nirvana is probably best characterized as the realization that there is no self, although this by itself is not much help because what that means—what there is that realizes this—is still unclear. The Buddha compounded the mystery by emphasizing that nirvana is neither annihilation nor eternal life. Clearly this is necessary since there never was a self to be destroyed or to live eternally, but it is confusing in so far as our thinking naturally tends to dichotomize into one or the other.

Yet there are a few pasages in the Pāli Canon that contradict the usual Theravāda interpretation. In the *Brahmanimaṇtanika Sūtra* (*Majjhima-Nikāya*), the Buddha says: "Do not think that this [nirvana] is an empty or void state. There is this consciousness, without a distinguishing mark, infinite and shining everywhere (*Viññānam anidassanaṁ anantaṁ sabbatopabhaṁ*); it is untouched by the material elements and not subject to any power." The passage reappears in the *Kevaddha Sūtra (Dīgha Nikāya* I. 213) with an addition: "here it is that conditioned consciousness ceases to be."[2] This distinction between conditioned consciousness and an infinite consciousness, shining everywhere, is inconsistent with the usual view in early Buddhism that consciousness is the result of conditions and does not arise without these conditions. Needless to say, it accords very well with the Vedāntic position regarding "self-luminous" Brahman. Elsewhere in the same *Brahmanimaṇtanika Sūtra* the Buddha criticizes the idea of an omnipotent Brahma, but it is significant that within the Pāli Canon "there is no expressed contradiction *or even recognition* of the Vedānta theory of an ātman or brahman as the one ultimate reality."[3]

It is also significant that much the same controversy between early Buddhism and Vedānta is found internally within Buddhism. Abhidharma, the philosophical branch of early Buddhism, analyzed reality into a set of discrete dharmas whose interaction creates the illusion of a self. Nirvana in Pāli Buddhism seems to have been understood as the cessation of cooperation among these various dharmas, leading to their quiescent isolation from each other.[4] Since consciousness is conditioned, existing only as a result of their interaction, this would seem to be the cessation of all consciousness as well. But insofar as these dharmas are believed to exist objectively, such a view may be criticized as ontologically lopsided; although the self has been analyzed away, the reality of the world as objective has been left largely unaffected. Yet the elimination of consciousness requires a redefinition of what it means for something to exist. What remains must somehow incorporate consciousness (or what we have understood as consciousness) within itself. Our usual dualistic understanding of self-confronting-object may be likened to a scale balancing two weights; one weight cannot be removed without affecting the other side of the balance. A basic principle of this book is that we cannot change one pole of any duality without transforming the other just as much. It is not possible to deconstruct one half of the consciousness/matter duality by simply absorbing it into the other, undeconstructed half. If we deny mind as an ontological category then we must redefine matter as other than inert and find what we have understood as mind within it.

Mahāyāna accepted the theory of dharmas—an important point often overlooked—but not their objective reality. It expanded the denial of the self (*pudgalanairātmya*) into a denial of the reality of dharmas (*dharmanairātmya*) because all dharmas are relative and hence śūnya. There is a higher, absolute truth (*paramārtha*), which cannot be described (according to Mādhyamika) but which (according to Yogācāra) comes close to the nondual attributeless consciousness of Advaita Vedānta. The relation between Mādhyamika and Yogācāra, the two main philosophical systems of Mahāyāna, is of considerable relevance to this work. Significant and unresolvable differences between them would constitute a challenge to our defense of a core doctrine of nonduality. So it is noteworthy that the weight of scholarly opinion favors the view that they complement much more than they contradict each other. On this matter, it is worth our while to quote three of the twentieth century's greatest Western scholars of Buddhism. First, Guiseppe Tucci, perhaps the foremost student of Tibetan Buddhism:

> It is generally said that Mahāyāna may be divided into two fundamental schools, viz., Mādhyamika and Yogācāra. This statement must not be taken literally. First of all it is not exact to affirm that these two tendencies were always opposed to each other. Moreover . . . the antagonism between the Mādhyamika and the first expounders of the idealist school such as Maitreya, Asaṅga and even Vasubandhu is not so marked

as it appears at first sight. . . . The fact is that both Nāgārjuna as well as Maitreya, along with their immediate disciples, acknowledged the same fundamental tenets, and their work was determined by the same ideals, though holding quite different views in many a detail.[5]

The translator and expounder of the Prajñāpāramitā, Edward Conze, develops this view by explaining their difference of perspective:

> Mādhyamikas and Yogācārins supplement one another. They come into conflict only very rarely, and the powerful school of the Mādhyamika-Yogācārins demonstrated that their ideas could exist in harmony. They differ in that they approach salvation by two different roads. To the Mādhyamikas "wisdom" is everything and they have very little to say about *dhyāna*, whereas the Yogācārins give more weight to the experience of "trance." The first annihilate the world by a ruthless analysis which develops from the Abhidharma tradition. The second effect an equally ruthless withdrawal from everything by the traditional method of trance.[6]

Edward J. Thomas agrees with Conze:

> While the school of Nāgārjuna started from the standpoint of logic, and showed the impossibility of making any statement free from contradictions, the *Laṅkāvatāra* [according to the writer "the chief canonical text for the doctrine of subjective idealism"] started from a psychological standpoint, and found a positive basis in actual experience.[7]

Last but hardly least is the historical testimony of Buddhism itself, in particular the fact alluded to by Conze that the debate between Mādhyamika and Yogācāra eventually led to their synthesis in the Mādyamika-Yogācāra school of Śāntarakṣita and Kamalaśīla. If we remember that both systems were not just philosophies but had primarily a soteriological function—that is, were meant to be paths of liberation—then the contrast between the Mādhyamika and Yogācāra viewpoints becomes comprehensible as differences in perspective. Mādhyamika emphasizes that reality is śūnya in the sense of "empty of predication." One can say nothing *about* reality because (as argued in chapter 2) that would be to superimpose concept on percept. This does not amount to an assertion of nonduality because in limiting itself to a *negative* critique of all dualities, Mādhyamika makes no positive claims. The important point is that this seems to be done in order to clear the way for the experience we have been describing as nondual. This experience must be distinguished from any claims whatsoever—ontological, epistemological, or otherwise—made on the basis of it, for from the Mādhyamika perspective any such claim would be a savikalpa attempt to determine the bare nirvikalpa percept.

The conflict with Yogācāra arises when Yogācārins call that percept "mind" (or "consciousness": vijñāna). This does not mean that Yogācāra is "subjective idealism," as Thomas and others (including Śaṅkara) have understood it to be. Rather than the world being the projection of a subjective ego, the apparent distinction between subject and object is one that arises (or seems to arise) *within* the transcendental mind (*vijñāptimātratā*)—a view consistent with our core doctrine of nonduality. Subjective idealism is not to be found anywhere within Buddhism, nor do I see how it could be there, given the common acceptance by all Buddhist schools of anātman, denial of self. Mādhyamika naturally criticizes Yogācāra for trying thus to put a label on reality ("mind") and dialectically criticizes the term by showing that it is relative and hence delusive. But all that does not refute the Yogācāra claim, which is simple nonduality. When delusions fall away and I experience reality, the consciousness that is aware of the world and the world itself are not distinguishable. At that moment all of what is experienced *is* myself, for which reason it may be called "my mind."

Here the difference between the logical and the psychological standpoint is crucial, as Conze and Thomas have pointed out. Although the goal of Mādhyamika is to transcend the intellect, its path is still intellectual. The conceptualizing mind is surmounted by exhausting it—that is, by negating all conceptual possibilities. Only by that could the leap to prajñā occur. Yogācāra, as its name suggests, is a more meditative approach. The aim of the system is not to prove the existence of transcendental mind but to initiate the practitioner into experience of it, which occurred in samādhi. Hence Yogācārins had no need to fear the concept of "mind," for their meditative practice kept them from confusing such labels with reality itself; whereas Mādhyamika, the logical path of exhausting all concepts, could not tolerate it. So the difference between these two philosophical perspectives ultimately derives from their different soteriological approaches and does not extend to the nondual experience at which they both point.

Chapter 6 also supports the compatability of the two systems by pointing out that the Mādhyamika reconciliation of impermanence with immutability, and of all-conditionality with no-causality, is equivalent to the Yogācāra relation between the *paratantra* and *pariniṣpanna* natures. Further discussion of the historical debate between Mādhyamika and Yogācāra is beyond the scope of this work.[8]

ADVAITA VEDĀNTA

Śaṅkara's Advaita Vedānta is generally regarded as having best developed and systematized the main strand of Upaniṣadic thought, which stresses the identity of Ātman and Brahman. Brahman is an infinite, self-luminous consciousness that transcends the subject–object duality. As "the Witness" (*sākṣin*), it is that which cannot be made into an object. Unqualified and all-inclusive, perhaps its most significant feature is that it is "one without a second," for there is nothing outside it. Hence Ātman—the true Self, what each of us really is—is one with this Brahman. *Tat tvam asi*: "That thou art." This is "All-Selfness":

> . . . there is nothing else but the Self.
>
> To realize the whole universe as the Self is the means of getting rid of bondage.
>
> To the seer, all things have verily become the Self.
>
> Whoever has realized and intimately known the Self, all is his Self, and he, again, is indeed the Self of all.[9]

So the Ātman should not be understood as a distinct self that merges with Brahman. To realize Ātman is to realize Brahman because they are really the same thing. One may state, in answer to the Buddhists, that a consciousness of self is needed to organize experience, but that turns out to have been Brahman itself, once Brahman is realized—that is to say, when Brahman realizes its own true nature. The world of differences and change is māyā, illusion; there is nothing but the all-inclusive Self (which must somehow incorporate māyā). Yet this sounds awkward, since the concept of a self seems to presuppose an other, a nonself from which it is distinguished—a point to which we will return later. So perhaps the term Ātman should be rejected as superfluous, because it suggests another entity apart from Brahman. Yet the two terms do serve a function, since they emphasize different aspects of the Absolute: Brahman, that it is the ultimate reality which is the ground of all the universe; Ātman, that it is *my* true nature.

For Śaṅkara *mokṣa*, liberation, is the realization that I am and always have been Brahman. My individual ego-consciousness evaporates or is realized to be an illusion, but not the pure, nondual consciousness that it was always just a reflection of. It must be emphasized that I do not attain or merge with this Brahman; I merely realize that I have always been Brahman. Śaṅkara uses the analogy of the space within a closed jar: that space has always been one with all space; there is but the illusion of separateness. That there is really nothing to attain becomes even more significant when we remember that the same is true for Sāṅkhya-Yoga and Buddhism: however else it may be characterized, one's true nature has always been pure and unstained. The Sāṅkhya puruṣa is an indifferent seer, which was always merely observing, unaffected by pain or pleasure. In Buddhism, there never was a self; it was always just an illusion.[10]

Yet, just as there are passages in the Pāli Canon which sound Vedāntic, so there are passages in the Upaniṣads which, at first encounter, seem Buddhistic. Perhaps the most famous is Yājñavalkya's instruction to his wife Maitreyī in the *Bṛhadāraṇyaka*: "Arising out of these elements (*bhūta*), into them also one vanishes away. After death there is no consciousness (*ne pretya samjñā 'sti*)." Maitreyī is amazed by this, so Yājñavalkya explains it in the well-known passage on non-duality quoted in chapter 1:

> For where there is a duality, *as it were*, there one sees another.... But when, verily, everything has become just one's own self, then what could one see and through what?... Through what could one know that owing to which all this is known? So, through what could one understand the Understander? This Self ... is imperceptible, for it is never perceived.[11]

In his commentary, Śaṅkara interprets this passage as meaning that when one realizes Brahman there is no more particular or dualistic consciousness. But perhaps there is the same problem with consciousness as with the self. Just as our concept of a self normally presupposes a nonself, so consciousness is usually understood to require an object. In fact it is very difficult to conceive of what consciousness could be without an object, a problem which is of course very much the heart of the issue. In English, for example, all the verbs for consciousness are normally intentional, requiring both subjects and objects ("I am conscious *of* . . . ", "you are aware *of* . . . ", "he knows *that* . . . "). Advaita does not deny that our normal "I-consciousness" is intentional: "There is no manifestation of the 'I' without a modification of the mind directed to the external" (Sureśvara).[12] The claim of Advaita is rather that only the pure consciousness which is Brahman is self-luminous and nondual. But if there is nondual consciousness without an "I" that *has* it, and without an object that "I" am aware *of*, can that still be called consciousness? Perhaps either reply, yes or no, could be justified, which suggests that the difference between these opposed standpoints may be merely linguistic. We return to this crucial point in the next chapter.

The similarities between Mahāyāna Buddhism and Advaita Vedānta are so great that some commentators conceive of the two as not really distinct from each other.

> Buddhism and Vedānta should not be viewed as two opposed systems but only as different stages in the development of the same central thought which starts with the Upaniṣads, finds its indirect support in Buddha, its elaboration in Mahāyāna Buddhism, its open revival in Guaḍapāda, which reaches its zenith in Śaṅkara and culminates in the post-Śaṅkarites.
>
> So far as the similarites between Buddhism and Vedānta are concerned, they are so many and so strong that by no stretch of the imagination can they be denied or explained otherwise. So far as the differences are concerned, they are few and mostly they are not vital. Most of them rest on a grave misunderstanding of Buddhism.
> (Chandradhar Sharma)[13]

Surendranath Dasgupta agrees in the conclusion of his study of Śaṅkara's system:

> His Brahman was very much like the śūnya of Nāgārjuna. *It is difficult indeed to distinguish between pure being and pure nonbeing as a category.* The debts of Śaṅkara to the self-luminosity of the Vijñānavāda Buddhism

can hardly be overestimated.... I am led to think that Śaṅkara's philosophy is largely a compound of Vijñānavāda and Śūnyavāda Buddhism with the Upaniṣad notion of the permanence of the self superadded.[14]

Lalmani Joshi also argues for this:

> In [Gauḍapāda's] *Āgamaśāstra* we find an endeavour to synthesize and bring about a concord between Mahāyāna Buddhism and Advaita Vedānta. In this endeavour seem to have crept into Vedānta certain basic tenets of Mahāyāna philosophy, and the result was the nondualistic Vedānta of Śaṅkara.
>
> ... The Advaita turn in Vedānta in and after Gauḍapāda can reasonably and satisfactorily be explained only by recognizing the debt of Gauḍapāda and Śaṅkara to the Mādhyamika and Vijñānavāda systems of thought.[15]

The objectivity of this conclusion is further supported by the different sympathies of their proponents: Sharma is an Advaitin, Dasgupta a Hindu critical of Śaṅkara, and Joshi is sympathetic to Buddhism.

It is undeniable that Śaṅkara was much influenced by Mādhyamika dialectic, which he employed in his own criticisms of other systems. But the similarities go far deeper, to the extent that Śaṅkara's rather shrill condemnation of Buddhism begins to sound like a family quarrel between two brothers—which arguments are often the most violent.

> The Buddhist doctrines of non-origination (*ajātivāda*), of phenomenal world as illusion or mere appearance (*māyāvāda*), of twofold division of truth into ultimate (*paramārtha*) and temporal (*vyavahāra*), and of Reality (*tattva*) being without attributes (*nirguṇa*) and beyond fourfold description have become so completely Vedāntic that their origins have nearly been forgotten.[16]

Śaṅkara's main criticism of Mādhyamika, that it espouses nihilism, certainly misses the point of Nāgārjuna's negations, which is the nonconceptual jump to prajñā that occurs as a consequence of negating prapañca. As T. R. V. Murti puts it, Nāgārjuna does not deny Reality, he simply denies all views about Reality. The only difference is that Mādhyamika condemns even consciousness as unreal; but I have already argued that this is relative ego-consciousness—that is, dualistic consciousness apart from its object—and not what might be called nondual consciousness. Nor, according to Sharma, are there any significant differences between Vedānta and Yogācāra, which Śaṅkara admits profoundly influenced his teacher's teacher Gauḍapāda.[17]

In conclusion, we have seen why Sāṅkhya-Yoga, Buddhism, and Advaita Vedānta are the preeminent systems in Indian philosophy: because they elaborate the three possible solutions to the problem posed by the subject–object relation. Sāṅkhya-Yoga is the most radical possible dualism. Buddhism denies the self completely by conflating it into the object, which is critically dissolved into dharma-elements. Conversely, Advaita denies the object completely, for "there is nothing else but the Self." After refuting the extreme dualism of Sāṅkhya, we are left with Buddhism and Vedānta, whose solutions to the subject–object problem seem to be diametrically opposed. But we have also suggested their compatibility. We have noticed some Vedāntic elements in Buddhism and (notwithstanding the claims of many Indian scholars, who want to see Buddhism as an offshoot of Hinduism) the much stronger Buddhist influence on Vedānta. And we have cited the opinions of several prominent scholars who argue for their affinity, indeed sometimes their identity.

But this is not enough to resolve the ontological differences between Mahāyāna and Advaita. To stop here would be to neglect what will perhaps be the most fruitful area of our inquiry into subject–object nonduality. This issue will be continued in the following chapter.

CHAPTER 6
THE DECONSTRUCTION
OF DUALISM

After rejecting the dualism of Sāṅkhya-Yoga, in chapter 5 I suggested an affinity between Buddhism and Vedānta in several ways. But the most important differences between them have not been resolved. As a starting point, we may ask why these two traditions rather than a single tradition arose in India—and traditions that are not just inconsistent with each other but diametrically opposed in their ontological categories. T. R. V. Murti summarizes this situation and the contrasting views of each party:

> There are two main currents of Indian philosophy—one having its source in the *ātma*-doctrine of the Upaniṣads and the other in the *anātma* doctrine of Buddha. They conceive reality on two distinct and exclusive patterns. The Upaniṣads and the systems following the Brahmanical tradition conceive reality on the pattern of an inner core or soul (*ātman*), immutable and identical amidst an outer region of impermanence and change, to which it is unrelated or but loosely related. This may be termed the Substance-view of reality....
>
> The other tradition is represented by the Buddhist denial of substance (*ātman*) and all that it implies. There is no inner and immutable core in things; everything is in flux. Existence (the universal and the identical) was rejected as illusory; it was but a thought-construction made under the influence of wrong-belief. This may be taken as the Modal view of reality.[1]

In this chapter, the disagreement between the Brahmanical "substance" view and the Buddhist "modal" view is analyzed by considering five categories: self, substance, time, causation, and "the Path." We examine the conflicts of all-Self versus no-self, substance versus modes, immutability versus impermanence, the Unconditioned versus "only-conditionality," and no-Path versus only-Path. That these positions are so diametrically opposed, each the mirror image of the other, suggests our approach. Both the Substance-view and the Modal-view are extreme positions, each trying to resolve these problematic relations by conflating one term into the other. Our question is whether they end up with the same thing.

The five sections that follow consider these relations, one by one, in order to answer that question. The general approach is dialectical, but in a different sense than that of Mādhyamika. Nāgārjuna uses dialectic to demonstrate that, since each of these terms is dependent upon its opposite and hence relative, any philosophical position affirming only one of them can be shown to be meaningless. My intention is rather to demonstrate that both extremes, in trying to eliminate duality, result in much the same description of nonduality—just as one may travel east or west halfway around the world to arrive in the same place. The problem, as Nāgārjuna implied, is that linguistic categories are inherently dualistic and thus inevitably inadequate when we try to use them to describe nonduality. The natural tendency, therefore, is to eliminate one or the other of the dualistic pair, yet, whichever one is removed, the resulting descriptions end up equivalent. The final section of this chapter applies this dialectical pattern to evaluate the more contemporary deconstruction of Jacques Derrida.

SELF

As long as I am this or that, or have this or that, I am not all things and I have not all things. Become pure till you neither are nor have either this or that; then you are onmipresent and, being neither this nor that, are all things.

—Eckhart

In order to arrive at being everything
Desire to be nothing.

—John of the Cross

The not-self of Buddhism eliminating the self, or the Self of Advaita swallowing the not-self: which is an accurate description of the liberation experience? Does enlightenment involve shrinking to nothing or expanding to encompass everything? A helpful hint is found in an unlikely place, the *Notebooks 1914–1916* of Ludwig Wittgenstein.

> The I makes its appearance in philosophy through the world's being *my* world.   (12.8.16)

> Here we can see that solipsism coincides with pure realism, if it is strictly thought out. The I of solipsism shrinks to an extensionless point and what remains is the reality co-ordinate with it.   (2.9.16)

> At last I see that I too belong with the rest of the world, and so on the one side *nothing* is left over, and on the other side, as unique, *the world*. In this way idealism leads to realism if it is strictly thought out. (15.10.16)[2]

The terms and problems Wittgenstein deals with in these passages are different from ours, but his conclusions are nonetheless relevant to our inquiry into the nature of nondual experience. Buddhism may be seen to emphasize the *nothing*, the extensionless point that shrinks to nonexistence, while Śaṅkara emphasizes the *unique world* which remains. But, viewed thus, they may be seen to be describing the same phenomenon.

It is well known that all versions of the spiritual path, including of course Sāṅkhya-Yoga, Buddhism, and Advaita Vedānta, emphasize nonattachment. One should not identify oneself with any physical or mental phenomenon. In other words, one learns to relax and literally "let go of" everything. But what happens when one does this? The sense of self "shrinks to an extensionless point," and when that point abruptly disappears, "what remains is the reality co-ordinate with it." On the one side nothing, not even the extensionless point, is left; this is the Buddhist anātman, the absence of an ontological self. On the other side remains everything, the whole universe, but transformed since it now encompasses awareness within itself; this is the nondual Brahman of Vedānta.

This will become clearer if we reflect on the implications of the koan meditation process. In contemporary Zen, the two best-known techniques are the koan method of the Rinzai school and the *shikan-taza* (just sitting) method of the Sōtō school. The Sōtō approach will be discussed in the fifth section; what is relevant here is the Rinzai technique for working on a koan such as "Jōshū's *Mu*," the first case of the *Mumonkan* and one of the best known of all koans. The main case is also one of the shortest:

> A monk in all seriousness asked Jōshū: "Does a dog have Buddha-nature, or not?" Jōshū retorted: "Mu!"

The koan-point—the problem of the koan—is: What is "Mu"? The monk of the story seems to have heard that, according to Mahāyāna philosophy, all sentient beings have (or, as Dōgen would put it, are) Buddha-nature, but he could not understand how a half-starved mongrel could have the same nature as the Buddha. Literally, *mu*, like the original Chinese *wu*, is by itself a negative particle. Within ancient Chinese cosmology, *wu* sometimes refers to the Void from which the universe originated. But it is a mistake to take Jōshū's cryptic answer as denying the Buddha-nature of a dog, or as making any conceptual statement about Buddha-nature or the origin of the universe or anything else. The value of this dialogue as a koan is that, once this point is understood, little room is left for speculation. There is nothing left for the conceptualizing mind to grasp.

The old way of working on this koan must have been very frustrating, which is why it could be so effective. The Zen master pressed the student for the correct answer, rejecting all his attempts. Eventually the student would run out of replies, and then he might be encouraged simply to repeat the sound "Muuuu . . ." over and over again. Nowadays the process is usually shortened. Students are informed at the beginning that all conceptual answers are unsatisfactory, and they are instructed to treat "Mu" as a kind of *mantram*, to be repeated mentally in coordination with the breathing. The thought or rather, the internal sound of "Mu" is used to eliminate all other thoughts. In his commentary on this koan, Yasutani Hakuun-rōshi elaborates:

> Let all of you become one mass of doubt and questioning. Concentrate on and penetrate fully into Mu. To penetrate into Mu means to achieve absolute unity with it. How can you achieve this unity? By holding to Mu tenaciously day and night! Do not separate yourself from it under any circumstances! Focus your mind on it constantly. . . . You must not, in other words, think of Mu as a problem involving the existence or non-existence of Buddha-nature. Then what do you do? You stop speculating and concentrate wholly on Mu—just Mu!
> . . . At first you will not be able to pour yourself wholeheartedly into

Mu. It will escape you quickly because your mind will start to wander. You will have to concentrate harder—just "Mu! Mu! Mu!" Again it will elude you. Once more you attempt to focus on it and again you fail. This is the usual pattern in the early stages of practice.... Absolute unity with Mu, unthinking absorption in Mu—this is ripeness. Upon your attainment to this stage of purity, both inside and outside naturally fuse.... When you fully absorb yourself in Mu, the external and internal merge into a single unity.[3]

Notice what is not encouraged here. One should not cultivate a blankness of mind, in which no thoughts arise, nor should one try to push thoughts away, which divides one into two—that which is pushing the thoughts away and the thoughts pushed away. Instead, the principle is to concentrate on one thing—in this case, "Muuuu..."—in order to become absorbed into it and literally *become one* with it. It is important to see how such a practice is implied by the claim of nonduality developed here. If the sense of duality is a delusion, then nothing needs to be attained. Only that illusory sense needs to be dispelled, and the way to do that is to concentrate on something so wholeheartedly that the sense of an I that is *doing* it evaporates. The principle here was summarized by Dōgen in the first fascicle of his *Shōbōgenzō*:

To learn the Buddhist Way is to learn about oneself. To learn about oneself is to forget oneself. To forget oneself is to perceive oneself as all things. To realize this is to cast off the body and mind of self and others.[4]

What distinguishes this from an Indian mantram is the *seeking* quality generated by the need to solve the koan. Usually (although not always) it is emphasized that "great doubt" is necessary. *Great doubt* here refers to a state of perplexity which becomes so intense that it is experienced physically as well as mentally, and which functions to block conceptualizing.

When working on Zen, the most important thing is to generate the *I chin* ("doubt sensation"). What is this doubt-sensation? For instance: where did I come from before my birth, and where shall I go after my death? Since one does not know the answer to either question, a strong feeling of "doubt" arises in the mind. Stick this "doubt-mass" onto your forehead (and keep it there) all the time until you can neither drive it away nor put it down, even if you want to. Then suddenly you will discover that the doubt-mass has been crushed, that you have broken it to pieces.   (Po-shan)[5]

It would be interesting to contrast this "great doubt" with the Cartesian doubt that stands at the beginning of modern Western philosophy. Briefly, the main difference seems to be that Cartesian doubt is something the self *has*, whereas the great doubt becomes something the self *is*: the self becomes so preoccupied with its koan that it literally "forgets itself" in its puzzlement. So Cartesian doubt has the effect of reifying the sense of self, while the great doubt leads to the evaporation of that sense of self.

Another way to understand this technique is to see it as working to "produce" precisely that "unsupported thought" recommended in the Diamond Sutra and discussed in chapter 4: "a thought that is nowhere supported" because it is *just "Muuu..."*

At the beginning of Zen practice, there are many distracting thoughts and it is difficult to focus on "Mu," but if the student perseveres then the stream of inner dialogue eventually weakens as "Mu" grows stronger. The sense of self is slowly attenuated as the mental phenomena that sustain it—desires and expectations, ideas about oneself, and so on—fade away. Eventually meditation deepens to become samādhi, in which "both inside and outside naturally fuse" because there is no longer an awareness of duality, of an I that is reciting "Muuuu..." There is *only* "Muuuu..." This stage is sometimes described by saying that now "mu" is doing "mu." Without the attendant sense of an I, it is just "mu" that sits, "mu" that stands up and walks, "mu" that eats. If one perseveres, there may arise the sensation of hanging over a precipice and dangling by a single thread. "Except for occasional feelings of uneasiness and despair, it is like death itself" (Hakuin).[6] The solution is to "let go" by throwing oneself completely into "Muuuu..."

> Bravely let go on the edge of the cliff.
> Throw yourself into the abyss with decision and courage.
> You only revive after death.[7]

Kenshō, the first stage or glimpse of Zen enlightenment, occurs when the student does "let go" of himself. "All of a sudden he finds his mind and body wiped out of existence together with the koan. This is what is known as 'letting go your hold'" (Hakuin).[8] Dōgen described it by saying that one's body and mind drop away, and thereafter there is an empty, "fallen-away" body and mind. Here the Zen master may help by cutting the last thread. An unexpected action, such as a blow or a shout or even a few quiet words, may startle the student into letting go. Many of the classical Zen stories tell of students being enlightened by such actions. What happens in such cases is that the shock of the unexpected noise or pain penetrates to the very core of the student's being—that is, it is experienced nondually. When Yün-men (Jap., Unmon) broke his ankle, he was enlightened because he forgot himself and everything else as his universe collapsed into one excruciating but empty pain.

It can hardly be coincidental that similar techniques are found in Yoga and Vedānta. The stages of meditation discussed above also describe the last three stages of the Yogic path, according to the *Yoga Sūtra: dhārana, dhyāna* and *samādhi.* Patañjali distinguishes the last two as follows:

> *Dhyāna* is the uninterrupted concentration of thought on its object. This itself turns into *samādhi* when the object alone shines and the thought of meditation [i.e., the thought that "I" am *doing* it] is lost, as it were.[9]

As described above, in Zen practice "mu" is often treated like a mantram to be recited internally. The most common mantram in India is the "sacred seed word" *Om*, highly recommended in the Upaniṣads:

> When a Vedic teacher wishes to obtain Brahman, he utters *Om*; thus desiring Brahman, he verily attains Brahman.

> By making the body the lower piece of wood, and *Om* the upper piece, and through the practice of the friction of meditation, one perceives the luminous self (*ātman*), hidden like the fire in the wood.[10]

Om, unlike *Mu*, is usually recited aloud, but this need not be a significant difference. In a Zen sesshin students sit together and such noise would be a distraction. Even then, Zen students have sometimes been encouraged to vocalize *Mu*, especially if they stay up late the last night to continue their practice uninterrupted. A more serious difference is that Zen students now are usually told that the sound *mu* itself has no meaning; that is, one should simply concentrate on "Muuuu..." without having any other thoughts about it. In contrast, the

Upaniṣads present *Om* as the primordial sound from which the universe arose. It is not only a verbal symbol of Brahman but has great power in its own right. To repeat *Om*, therefore, is to attune oneself to the ground of the universe. From the Zen point of view, any such meaning can only be a distraction from the process of single-mindedly becoming one with that particular sound. But it is doubtful whether, in actual practice, the difference is very great. If one persists in reciting *Om* for a long period, eventually the sound tends to lose its connotations and become a "pure" sound divested of any meaning—at which point there would be no difference between reciting *Om* and reciting *Mu*.

Finally, the following description of Advaitic meditation brings out its similarity to both Yoga and Zen:

Usually the mind is concentrated on the object of meditation through a symbol. In deep meditation [*dhyāna*] the mind becomes focused on the object and stays still without flickering like a steady flame of (candle) light in a windless cell. This culminates in samādhi, which closes the gap between the meditator and the object of meditation, his innermost self, and unites the two. In meditation there is the tripartite distinction of the meditator, the object of meditation, and the act of meditation; in other words, of the knower, the knowable, and the process of knowledge. But in samādhi this distinction subsides. The three are fused into an integral consciousness. The less marked the distinction, the deeper is the samādhi.   (Satprakāshānanda)[11]

The assumption necessary for all these techniques is the nondualist claim that the ontological self is a delusion, and that this delusive sense of self is the fundamental duḥkha (frustration) which distorts our experience and disturbs our lives. Contrary to all schools of ego psychology, such a self can never become secure because its very nature is to be insecure. As mentioned in chapter 4, the sense of self is not a thing but a *lack*, which can conceal its own emptiness only by keeping ahead of itself—that is, by projecting itself into the next thought, action, and so on—which process *is* craving or desire. We see later in this chapter how these two aspects of the sense of self— ceaseless deferral and ceaseless desire—generate time and causality.

■

We are now ready to return to the comparison between Buddhism and

Śaṅkara. What is experienced through these meditations, as Wittgenstein implies, is the evaporation of the self, and what remains is the world without a self. Hence it is a radically transformed world. The familiar, everyday world of material objects was formerly balanced by an ego-consciousness that was supposed to be observing it. The disappearance of that discrete consciousness requires a new explanation of what awareness is. The awareness that was previously understood to be observing the world is now realized to be one with it. No longer do "I," as the locus of consciousness, see something external. Rather, the nondual, self-luminous nature of the world stands revealed. When we want to describe this experience, what shall we say? My point is that this phenomenon can be described either as no-consciousness or as all-consciousness. Early Buddhism chooses the former, claiming that consciousness is nothing more than all those things that are experienced. Śaṅkara opts for the latter, insisting that all those things are the manifestations of consciousness. Buddhism says there is no self, there is only the world (dharmas); Śaṅkara says the world is the Self. To say that there is no self, or that everything is the self, are then equally correct—or false, depending on how one looks at it. Both descriptions amount to the same thing. What is clear in each case is that there is no longer a duality between an object that is observed and a consciousness that observes it, or between the external world and the self which confronts it. Neither tradition is denying one side of the dualistic relation in order to assert the other relative side. Both are attempts to describe nonduality, and because each makes absolute a relative term, neither is more or less satisfactory than the other. In fact, they imply each other in response, which is why Buddhism and Vedānta developed in relation to each other. One would expect that a metaphysics based on denying the subject—the element of stability in a statement—would result in a more fluid and dynamic view of reality than a metaphysics that denies the predicate, and that too we find in the contrast between Buddhism and Vedānta.

Why there are these two contradictory ways of trying to describe nonduality is now obvious. Just as our usual understanding of experience is dualistic, so is the language that expresses this understanding. An attempt to describe the nondual experience will naturally tend to eliminate one or the other term. Western mystical experience too is often classified into two parallel types: the "inward way" of withdrawal from the world and the "outward way" of merging into the One. For example, Rudolf Otto, in his comparative study *Mysticism East and West*, emphasized the divergence between the mysticism of introspection and that of unifying vision and commented that "to the non-mystic their extreme difference is striking." Yet he concluded his book on these two types by acknowledging that for the mystic there is no such duality, although Otto himself was unable to go beyond "the contrast between inward and outward."[12] Perhaps here also the difference is merely in description rather than in experience.

But why is there no Brahman in Buddhism? Early Buddhism refers not to a monistic One but to a plurality of dharmas, which later Buddhism emphasized are relative and hence śūnya, empty of any self-nature. As we have seen, in Mahāyāna *śūnyatā* not only refers to the absence of a self but becomes the most fundamental "characteristic" of reality. In function it is the category which corresponds most closely to the Vedāntic concept of Brahman, serving as the standard by which the reality of phenomena is negated. But how can śūnyatā be reconciled with Advaita's "One without a second"?

My answer to this is prompted by the remark of a contemporary Zen master: "Essentially, there is only one thing...*not even one*."[13] The interesting implication of this statement is that if there were only one thing, with nothing "outside" it, then that one would not be aware of itself as one. *The phenomenological experience would be of no thing / nothing.* To be aware that there is only One actually implies that there are two: the One, and that which is aware of the One as being One. That is because awareness of a self implies another from which it is distinguished—just as a child, for example, acquires a self-identity only as he or she gains a sense of what another person is. In brief, *one* thing requires another; it is a thing because it is distinguished from something else.

This implies that, if Brahman is truly One without a second, it cannot be experienc*ed* as One. And this is suggested by the much-emphasized claim that the ātman of Vedānta is not self-conscious in the Cartesian sense:

> He is never thought of, but is the thinker; He is never known, but is the knower. There is . . . no other thinker than He, there is no other knower than He.

Through what should one know that owing to which all this is known—through what, my dear, should one know the Knower? —(Bṛhadāraṇyaka Upaniṣad)[14]

Śaṅkara explains what this means:

That which is unknown can be made known and requires proof, but not the self (the knower). If it be granted that the self requires proof, then who will be the knower (because the self becomes one of the knowables, and without a knower there can be no application of proof)? It is settled that the knower is the self.[15]

What makes this equivalent to Mahāyāna is that *a self which can never be objectively experienced*, because by definition it is the experiencer, *can just as well be described as śūnya*. However, then this will be not a nihilistic emptiness (which was Śaṅkara's mistaken criticism of Mādhyamika) but a śūnyatā that can be cherished as the Buddha-nature essence of all things.

∎

So there are two paradoxes: to shrink to nothing is to become everything, and to experience everything as One is again equivalent to nothing—athough a different sense of nothing. These paradoxes provide the common ground where the two opposed traditions meet. From the differing perspectives of the Substance-view and the Modal-view, different metaphysical systems are derived. But we may still wonder why they opt for those respective perspectives. Why does Vedānta prefer to speak of the One and Buddhism of emptiness?

Perhaps the answer to this lies in the nature of philosophy itself. In referring to Brahman as the One without a second, Śaṅkara tries to describe reality from outside, as it were, because that is the only perspective from which it can be described as One. And this of course is what philosophy generally tries to do: to look upon the whole of reality objectively and comprehend its structure, as if the philosophizing intellect were itself outside that whole. But the view of the Buddha is that we cannot get outside reality and experience it as an object; our efforts as well as our viewpoints are inevitably contained within that whole. Thinking and its conclusions are events in and of the nondual world, although they are carried on as if they were outside, an independent and fixed measure. We should remember that the Buddha was not really a philosopher, although we inevitably try to force him into that mold. As he never ceased to insist, he was interested only leading others to the experience of nirvana. Of course, Śaṅkara too emphasized the intuitive experience of Brahman and pointed out that philosophy has a role only from the empirical standpoint. But the Buddha was not interested in philosophy even from that empirical perspective, except insofar as philosophical statements could be conducive to the attainment of nirvana. From his perspective, philosophy is only so many words and conceptual structures; if one accepts them as accurate descriptions—clings to those ideas—they act as an obstruction to enlightenment. Meditation is learning how to let them go. Philosophically—from the fictional "outside"—we might say that there is only One Mind which encompasses all, but we must remember that phenomenologically there is no such thing, because, as we have seen, such a One Mind could not be aware of itself as a self-contained mind in the sense that each of us is self-consciously (but delusively) aware of his "own" mind.

What does this imply about how attaining nirvana/mokṣa would be experienced? Only fools rush in where Buddhas fear to tread, but the above analysis implies that there would not be a sense of merging into the One. Instead, it would seem to be a disintegration, although not an annihilation. The boundaries of my ego-self, which distinguish me from others, would simply dissolve as "my mind" was realized to be not something separate from the world but a "focal point" of the world. It would be a loss of all tension and dualistic effort, a relaxation of the whole being. Letting go of all those things previously clung to, one would become the everything that in fact one always was. According to Sāṅkhya-Yoga, the puruṣa in its true form is ubiquitous. The arhat, said the Buddha, is "deep, immeasurable, unfathomable, like the mighty ocean." The Vedāntic Brahman is an infinite pure consiousness pervading everywhere.[16]

SUBSTANCE

Another disagreement between Vedānta and Buddhism is indicated by Murti's terms to distinguish the two main traditions, the Substance-view and the Modal-view. Śaṅkara exemplifies the former extreme. Static Nirguṇa Brahman, without any attributes, is the only Real and hence the changing phenomenal world of particulars is unreal (māyā), just the illusory appearance of Brahman. In diametric contrast, Buddhism provides the extreme Modal-view. Reality is dynamic and momentary; objects are analyzed away into clusters of interacting and constantly changing dharma-attributes that inhere in no substance, permanent or otherwise.

I defer until the next section the temporal disagreement between immutable Brahman and impermanent dharmas, in order to focus on the conflict between Substance-view and Modal-view. The issue is whether either extreme is tenable by itself, given that substance and mode are independent terms that seem to have meaning only in relation to each other. Just as the elimination of subject (or self) transforms the object, and vice versa, so one cannot eliminate the reality of modes without transforming the concept of substance, and vice versa. It is revealing that this points precisely to where the problem arises for each tradition, and in order to make themselves consistent these two opposed traditions end up asserting what amounts to the same thing.

In order to deny the reality of all impermanent phenomena-attributes, Śaṅkara is reduced to defining substance so narrowly that it ceases to refer to anything—to *be* anything. Absolutely nothing can be predicated of Nirguṇa Brahman, which can only be approached through the *via negativa* of *neti, neti*: "Not this, not this . . ." Although Śaṅkara would deny it, his Being, "that vacuous infinitive of the copula" (Schopenhauer), ends up as a completely empty ground, an unchanging Nothing from which all phenomena arise as an ever-changing and hence deceptive appearance.

Buddhism, of course, faced exactly the opposite problem. The elimination of any substance gives dharma-attributes nothing to inhere in. Thus early Buddhism tends towards conceiving of dharmas as self-existing substances, a view that Mahāyāna refutes by pointing to their interdependence. Mahāyāna in turn resolves the problem by emphasizing and finally hypostatizing śūnyatā, the emptiness that signifies the lack of any self-nature to things and that came to be looked upon as their "true nature."

From the perspective of Buddhism, Vedānta reifies this emptiness into an unqualified substance which, since it has absolutely no characteristics of its own, cannot really be said to *be*. From the perspective of Vedānta, Buddhism ignores the fact that some such ground is necessary, for, as Parmenides pointed out, nothing—not even appearances—can arise from nothing and it is meaningless to deny all substance: *something* must be Real. This is the point of Śaṅkara's only telling criticism of Mādhyamika: "It is not possible to negate the empirical world without the acceptance of another reality" (*Brahmasūtrabhāṣya* II, ii.31). For the Advaitin this lack of a substance seems (Buddhist denials notwithstanding) nihilistic, or, to say the least, unattractive in comparison with an eternal, immutable, all-encompassing Absolute. As in the previous section, this conflict too may be resolved by understanding the difference between an ontological perspective and a phenomenological one. Ontologically we may agree with Advaita that there must be *some*thing. There is no logical necessity to this—from a purely logical standpoint there could be absolutely nothing—but the simple fact that there is experience contradicts such an ontological nothing. Yet at the same time there is no phenomenological necessity for there to be some*thing*—no a priori need for that Real to be anything objective that can be experienc*ed*. This is the point of intersection between the conflict of categories, and from there we can see how the two approaches had to meet: attributeless Brahman purified itself into emptiness as śūnyatā was reified into that which gives birth to all phenomena. The inner dynamism in each tradition led to much the same understanding of nonduality.

Of course there is still a difference in emphasis. Although the Nirguṇa Brahman of Advaita cannot be characterized in any positive way, Saguṇa ("with attributes") Brahman is most essentially pure *cit*, that is, nondual consciousness. It is surely no coincidence that this is also the main point of difference between Mādhyamika and Yogācāra, and the synthesis between them which occurred later related the two in the same way. Yogācāra idealism became accepted as a phenomenal, "lower-truth" description of the "higher truth," an account of why the absolute truth is inexpressible: "no truth has been taught by any Buddha, for anyone anywhere."

TIME

All beings are impermanent, which means that there is neither impermanence nor permanence.

—Nāgārjuna, *Śūnyatāsaptati*

The categories of permanence or impermanence cannot be applied to unborn things.

—Gauḍapāda, *Āgamaśāstra*[17]

One of the more interesting parallels between Eastern and Western philosophy is the same disagreement within each regarding the nature of time. More precisely, it is an ontological disagreement expressed in terms of time: Is ceaseless change the "ultimate fact" or is there an immutable Reality behind or within such impermanence? The importance of this issue can hardly be exaggerated. In the former case, nothing escapes from the ravages of time; in the latter, time itself is in some sense illusory and unreal.

For both East and West, the answers given to this question have been fundamental to the subsequent development of philosophy and hence of civilization itself. In ancient Greece, this disagreement found its sharpest expression in the Presocratic difference between Heraclitus and Parmenides.[18] Heraclitus claimed that the cosmos is a ceaseless flux, which he understood metaphorically as an ever-living fire. Because of this, we cannot step into the same river twice—a view amended by his disciple Cratylus, who argued that we cannot step into the same river even once, since it is changing as we dip our foot into it.[19] In contrast and perhaps in response, Parmenides argued that "what is" is whole, immovable, unborn and imperishable—hence nontemporal—in sharp distinction from "what is not," which is literally unthinkable.[20] This implied another distinction: one should not depend on the senses, which present the illusion of change, but evaluate with reason.

Plato's "synthesis" was to combine these two alternatives into a heirarchical dualism favoring Parmenides. For example, the *Timaeus* distinguishes the visible world of changing and hence delusive appearances from the invisible and timeless world of mental forms that can be immediately apprehended by the purified intellect. His nod to Heraclitus is to grant the sensory world a derivative reality—things are the "shifting shadows," as it were, of forms—thus setting up a "two-truths" doctrine which would have been anathema to Parmenides. How mystical Plato was—what he meant by the "purified intellect" and its "immediate apprehension"—is a controversy which may never be settled,[21] but Western thought has yet to escape from the intellect-versus-senses duality that he reified. Few still accept the reality of such immaterial forms, but in a sense all the subsequent history of Western philosophy, until very recently, has been a search for the Being hidden within the world of Becoming. Even science is a "footnote to Plato," for the same dualism can be observed in its enterprise of extracting atemporal (e.g., mathematical) truths from changing phenomena. In many ways contemporary Western culture has reversed Plato's hierarchy, but we nonetheless remain largely determined by it.

Of course, the Eastern parallel to this is found in the opposition between the impermanence of the Buddhist Modal-view and the immutable Brahman of the Vedāntic Substance-view. But when we look for a resolution of these two extremes, we find a view of time very different from Plato's: a "middle way" that denies not only the dualism of Plato's synthesis but also the two original alternatives. Rather than accepting the reality of both permanence and change by combining them in a hierarchy, I follow Mādhyamika in criticizing and dismissing them both by revealing their conceptual interdependence. This leaves a paradox denying the very dualism that the problem takes for granted. One way to express this paradox is to say that, yes, there is nothing outside the flux of change, but there is also that which does not change. Rather than being a contradiction, the first alternative implies the second, because in this case to make time absolute and to negate it turn out to be identical.

The arguments in the previous two sections were dialectical. Simply to make either term absolute by eliminating the other does not work, because each half of the duality is dependent upon the other. If one is negated, so must the other be. If permanence and change are susceptible to the same approach, what does this imply about the possibility of another way of experiencing time?

Consider a solitary rock out of an ocean current, protruding above the surface. Whether one is on the rock or floating past it, it is the relation between the two that makes both movement and rest possible. Obviously, the current will be measured by the rate of movement past the rock, but the rock can be said to be at rest only if there is something else defined as moving in relation to it—a point made in physics by emphasizing the relativity of perspective. Analogous to this, the concept of impermanence—"time changing"—also requires some fixed standard against which time is measured, although "temporal juxtaposition" is very different. I am able to determine that precisely one hour has passed only because, in looking at a clock, I compare the hand positions now with my memory of where they were before. Conversely, the concept of permanence is dependent upon impermanence because permanence implies that which persists unchanged through time—while other things change. But what is the phenomenological significance of this interdependence?

In Indian philosophy, the rock represents more than permanence and unchanging substance; it also symbolizes the self. For both Vedānta and Buddhism the self is that which does not change, although of course they disagree about whether this concept corresponds to anything actually existent. But what is more important for us is that they agree in denying any dualism between rock and current. They negate this dualism in opposite ways. Buddhism denies that there is any rock, asserting that there is only a flux. The rock is a thought-construction and the sense-of-self might better be compared to a bubble which flows like the water because it is part of the water, or because it is what might be called a function of the water. In contrast, Advaita denies that there is anything really flowing. Change cannot be completely ignored, but ultimately it is subrated as illusory with the realization of immutable Brahman. But notice that neither Buddhism nor Advaita affirms the rock in relation to the current. Both deny the self-existence of the rock as jīva, an ego-self conterposed to something objective. Vedānta does this by making the rock absolute: the rock negates the flux by expanding to incorporate it—phenomena are māyā because they are only transient name-and-form manifestations of Brahman—but the rock can do this only by divesting itself of all rocklike and all other characteristics.

In terms of the analogy, then, Advaita and Buddhism end up with much the same thing. Whether the rock disappears or expands to encompass everything by becoming nothing, all that can be experienced in either case is *the water flowing*, although devalued to a greater (māyā) or lesser (śūnya) degree. But now the dialectic reverses. If there is no rock at rest relative to the water (permanence), what awareness could there be of any current (change)? If everything is carried along together in the current, then phenomenologically there is no current at all. This is the crucial point, to which we shall return in a moment.

•

The Buddhist claim of impermanence does not accept time and change as we usually experience them. For all its schools, saṁsāra is literally the temporal cycle of birth and death which is in some sense negated in nirvana. For both Advaita and Buddhism, as in the "illuminative" traditions generally, time is a problem, and not an abstract problem but a very personal and immediate one. One way to express the basic anxiety of our lives is in terms of the contradiction between permanence and impermanence. Despite the efforts we make to deny our temporality, we are all too aware of aging and death; yet on the other hand, "we nevertheless feel and experience that we are eternal" (Spinoza).

The genesis of this problem is in the ways our minds usually work. "Time is generated by the mind's restlessness, its stretching out to the future, its projects, and its negation of 'the present state.'"[22] But there is no future without a past. Our expectations and intentions are determined by previous experiences—more precisely, by the seeds (vāsanās) and mental tendencies (saṁskāras) that remain from them. As we have seen, Vedānta and Buddhism both emphasize the role of memory "wrongly interpreted." Identifying with memories provides the illusion of continuity—a "life history"—necessary to reify the sense of self. Thus past (memories) and future (expectations) originate and work together to obscure the present, usually negating it so successfully that we can hardly be said to experience it—which is ironic, of course, since from another perspective all experience can only be in the present: "No man has lived in the past, and none will ever live in the future" (Schopenhauer). But the ceaseless stream of intentionality devalues the present into simply one more moment in the sequence of causal relations, as an effect of past causes and a cause of future effects. For example, thinking (as we saw in chapter 4) usually consists of linking thoughts in a series, but this misses something about the origin and nature of *this* thought because it is understood only in logical (which in effect is also temporal) relation to other thoughts.

The consequence of this devaluation of the present is that time becomes objectified via a reversal that takes place. Instead of past and future being understood as a function of present memories and expectations, the present becomes reduced to a single moment within a "time-stream" understood to exist "out there"—a container, as it were, like space, within which things exist and events occur. But *in order for time to be a container, something must be contained within it: objects. And for objects to be "in" time, they must in themselves be nontemporal*—i.e., *self-existing*. In this way, a delusive bifurcation occurs between time and "things" generally, as a result of which each gains a spurious reality.[23] The first reified "object," and the most important thing to be hypostatized as nontemporal, is the I, the sense of self as something permanent and unchanging. So the "objectification" of time is also the "subjectification" of self, which thus appears only to discover itself in the anxious position of being a nontemporal entity inextricably "trapped" in time.[24]

The best philosophical expression of this intuitive notion of "objective" time is found in Newton's conception of an absolute linear time which flows smoothly regardless of what events occur, and which is infinitely divisible. This goes beyond the devaluation of the present and eliminates it completely. The present becomes a durationless instant—or rather, a mere dividing line—between the infinities of past and future. But such a conception, although no more than an extrapolation from our "commmon-sense" view, is still too counter-intuitive, and time was rescued (but only psychologically) by the "specious present" (an ironic term indeed) of E. R. Clay and William James.

■

If we are thus trapped in time, how can we escape? The paradoxical nondualist solution is to eliminate the dichotomy dialectically by realizing that I am not *in* time because I *am* time, which therefore means that I am *free from* time.

Much of our difficulty in understanding time is due to the unwise use of spatial metaphors—in fact, the objectification of time requires such spatial metaphors—but in this case a spatial comparison is helpful. We normally understand objects such as cups to be "in" space, which implies that in themselves they must have a self-existence distinct from space. However, not much reflection is necessary to realize the the cup itself is irremediably spatial. All its parts must have some thickness, and without the various spatial relations among the bottom, sides, and handle, the cup could not be a cup. One way to express this is to say that the cup is not "in" space but itself *is* space: the cup is "what space is doing in that place," so to speak. The same is true for the temporality of the cup. The cup is not a nontemporal, self-existing object that just happens to be "in" time, for its being is irremediably temporal. The point of this is to destroy the thought-constructed dualism between things and time. When we wish to express this, we must describe one in terms of the other, by saying either that objects are temporal (in which case they are not objects as we usually conceive of them) or, conversely, that time is objects—that is, that time manifests itself in the appearances that we call objects. We find beautiful expressions of this in Dōgen. "The time we call spring blossoms directly as an existence called flowers. The flowers, in turn, express the time called spring. This is not existence within time; existence itself is time."[25] This is the meaning of his term "being-time" (*uji*):

> Being-time" means that time is being; i.e., "Time is existence, existence is time." The shape of a Buddha-statue is time. . . . Every thing, every being in this entire world is time. . . . Do not think of time as merely flying by; do not only study the fleeting aspect of time. If time is really flying away, there would be a separation between time and ourselves. If you think that time is just a passing phenomenon, you will never understand being-time.[26]

Time "flies away" when we experience it dualistically, with the sense of a self that is outside and looking at it. Then time becomes something that I have (or don't have), objectified and quantified into a succession of "now-moments" that cannot be held but incessantly fall away. In contrast, the being-times that we usually reify into objects cannot be said to occur *in* time, for they *are* time. As Nāgārjuna would put it, that things (or rather "thingings") are time means that there is no second, external time that they are "within."

This brings us to the second prong of the dialectic. To use the interdependence of objects and time to deny only the reality (svabhāva) of objects is incomplete, because their relativity also implies the unreality of time. Just as with the other dualisms analyzed earlier—self and object, substance and modes—to say that there is only time turns out to be equivalent to saying that there is no time. Having used temporality to deconstruct things, we must reverse the analysis and use the lack of a thing "in" time to negate the objectivity of time also, for when there is no "contained" there can be no "container." If there are no nouns, then there are no referents for temporal predicates. When there are no things that have an existence apart from time, then it makes no sense to speak of things as being young or old. "So the young man does not grow old nor does the old man grow old" (Nāgārjuna).[27] Dōgen expressed this in terms of firewood and ashes:

> We should not take the view that what is latterly ashes was formerly firewood. What we should understand is that, according to the doctrine of Buddhism, firewood stays at the position of firewood.... There are former and later stages, but these stages are clearly cut.

Firewood does not *become* ashes; there is the "being-time" of firewood, then the "being-time" of ashes. If there are no nontemporal objects, then the present does not gain its value or meaning by being related to past or future: each event or being-time is complete in itself. But how does this free *us* from time?

> Similarly, when human beings die, they cannot return to life; but in Buddhist teaching we never say life changes into death.... Likewise, death cannot change into life.... Life and death have absolute existence, like the relationship of winter and spring. But do not think of winter changing into spring or spring into summer.[28]

Because life and death, like spring and summer, are not *in* time, they are in themselves timeless. *If there is no one nontemporal who is born and dies*, then there is only birth and death. But if there are only the events of birth and death, with no one "in" them, *then there is no real birth and death*. Alternatively, we may say that there is birth-and-death in every moment, with the arising and passing away of each thought and act. Perhaps this is what Heraclitus meant when he said that "both life and death are in both our living and our dying."[29] Dōgen: "Just understand birth-and-death itself is *nirvāṇa*.... Only then can you be free from birth-and-death."[30]

In temporal terms, this paradox can be expressed in either of two apparently inconsistent ways. We may say that there is only the present: not, of course, the present as usually understood—a series of fleeting moments that incessantly fall away to become the past—but a very different present that incorporates the past and the future because it always stays the same.

> We cannot be separated from time. This means that because, in reality, there is no coming or going in time, when we cross the river or climb the mountain we exist in the eternal present of time; this time includes all past and present time.... Most people think time is passing and do not realize that there is an aspect that is not passing.   (Dōgen)[31]

Dōgen's "eternal present of time"—which may fruitfully be compared to the "standing now" (*nunc stans*) of medieval Western philosophy—is eternal because there is something that does not change: *it is always now*. Alternatively, this nondual way of experiencing time may be described as living in eternity: again, not eternity in the usual sense, an infinite persistence *in* time that presupposes the usual duality between things and time. There is an "eternity on this side of the grave," as Wittgenstein too realized:

> For life in the present there is no death.

> Death is not an event in life. It is not a fact of the world.

> If by eternity is understood not infinite temporal duration but non-temporality, then it can be said that a man lives eternally if he lives in the present.[32]

∎

So the eternity we seek has always been "with" us—closer to us than we are to ourselves, to paraphrase Augustine, for all that we need to do is to "forget" ourselves and realize what we have always been. But because of the habitual restlessness of our minds, we are now not able to experience the present—to *be* the present—and so we overlook something about it. What would such a nondual experience of time be like? Not the static "block universe" that has been unfairly attributed to Parmenides, for my point here is that *the immutability of the Now is not incompatible with change*. There would still be transformation, although experienced differently since one *is* the transformation rather than an observer *of* it. Such change would be a smoother, more continous flux than we are familiar with, since without anxious thought-construction and thought-projection the mind would not be jumping, staccato-fashion, from one perch to another in order to fixate itself. In one way, nothing would be different: "I" would still rise in the morning, eat breakfast, go to work, and so on. But at the same time there would also be something completely timeless about all these activites. As with the

wei-wu-wei, "in changing it is at rest" (Heraclitus, frag. 84a). In place
of the apparently solid I that *does* them, there would be an empty and
immutably serene quality to them. The experience would be not of a
succession of events (winter does not turn into spring) but just-this-
one-effortless-thing (tathatā) and then another just-this-one-thing.[33]

So Heraclitus/Buddhism and Parmenides/Vedānta are both right.
There is nothing outside the incessant flux, yet there is also something
that does not change at all: the "standing now." What transcends time
(as usually understood) turns out to be time itself. This breathes new
life into Plato's definition in the *Timaeus*: time is indeed the moving
image of eternity, provided that we do not read into this any dualism
between the moving image and the immovable eternity. In Buddhist
terms, life-and-death are the "moving image" of nirvana. This paradox is possible because, as with all other instances of subject–object
duality, to forget oneself and become one with something is at the
same time to realize its emptiness and "transcend" it.

CAUSALITY

*That which, taken as causal or dependent, is the process of being born and passing
on, is, taken non-causally and beyond all dependence, declared to be nirvāṇa.*
                              —Nāgārjuna, *Mūlamadhyamikakārikā*

*As long as a man persists in the belief in causality he will find the working of cause
and effect. But when attachment to causality vanishes, cause and effect become
nonexistent.*
                              —Gauḍapāda, *Āgamaśāstra*

The same dialectical approach has been used in each of the three
previous sections. In the controversies over Self versus nonself, substance versus modes and immutability versus impermanence, we have
seen that simply to make either term absolute by eliminating the other
is unsatisfactory, because the two terms are interdependent. We may
grant the Mādhyamika point that both Vedānta and Buddhism are
finally inadaquate as descriptive systems, but more interesting at the
moment is that, when developed and made self-consistent, the Substance-view and the Modal-view intersect in their claims about nonduality. The importance of this can hardly be overemphasized. It
means that, rather than the opposition between these two traditions

weighing against the view that they are describing the same experience, their congruence offers considerable support to the possibility of that experience.

■

The fourth disagreement that we will consider—really a fourth expression of the same basic disagreement—is over the category of causality. Can the parallel contrast between the unconditioned Brahman of Vedānta and the "all-conditionality" (pratītya-samutpāda) of Buddhism be subjected to the same dialectical resolution? Can causality be made absolute and then negated in the same way that time has been? An affirmative answer will not be surprising, given the interdependence between temporality and causality. Just as time requires that the past cause the future, so causality requires that the cause precede the effect. They are two aspects of the same delusive bifurcation, and our plight can be expressed in either terms. Even as we feel that we are (or should be) timeless but realize we are mortal, so we feel that we are (or should be) free, although we know that our lives are physically and psychologically determined. In order to deconstruct any of these dualisms fully, we must deconstruct the others as well.

Śaṅkara's account of causality constitutes part of his more general māyā doctrine, according to which all phenomena (including space and time) are due to the indescribable and indefinable ajñāna (delusion) superimposed upon Brahman. Like Nāgārjuna before him, his examination (e.g., in Brahmasūtrabhāṣya II.i.14–20) concludes that we cannot derive the real nature of causal relations from the series of discrete cause-and-effect phenomena. As a Vedantin, however, Śaṅkara decides that the true cause of all effects must be Brahman, which provides the permanent substratum that persists unchanged through all experience. All effect-phenomena are merely illusory name-and-form superimpositions upon Brahman, the substance-ground. Since Brahman is the only real and any phenomena existing distinct from it are illusory, this is a version of satkāryavāda: the effect preexists in the cause. But to distinguish this view from that of Sāṅkhya (which identifies cause and effect in a different way, by granting the reality of prakṛti, a material substratum that does not change although its forms vary), Śaṅkara's theory of causality is more precisely labeled satkāranavāda (or *vivartavāda*), since the effect (māyā) has a different kind of being from the cause (Brahman).

This amounts to a denial of causal relations as we know them: the relation between two discrete phenomena—cause and effect—is deemed incomprehensible and unreal. In predictable contrast, the emphasis in early Buddhism seems to be completely the opposite. Rather than negating causal relations in favor of an immutable Self, Buddhism dissolves the self and everything else into an impermanent sequence of cause-and-effect phenomena. We see this most clearly in the crucial doctrine of pratītya-samutpāda (dependent origination), in which each of the twelve factors is conditioned by and conditions all the others. Pratītya-samutpāda might be called "all-conditionality" because it explains all phenomena by locating them within a set of cause-and-effect relationships, according to the formula "when X exists, then Y arises."

Yet in this case we find a duplicate of the controversy between all-conditionality and the Unconditioned within Buddhism itself.[34] The problem of causality is especially important in the Mādhyamika dialectic, but at first glance there seems to be a contradiction in Nāgārjuna's analysis. On the one hand, causal interdependence is clearly a crucial concept, so important that Nāgārjuna identifies it with the most important concept śūnyatā: "We interpret the dependent arising of all things (pratītya-samutpāda) as the absence of being in them (śūnyatā)."[35] The undeniable relativity of everything is the means by which self-existence (svabhāva) is refuted. At the same time, however, Nāgārjuna redefines pratītya-samutpāda in such a way as to negate causality altogether. This is apparent even in the prefatory dedication of his *Mūlamadyamikakārikās*, in the eight negations that Nāgārjuna attributes to the Buddha:

> Neither perishing nor arising in time, neither terminable nor eternal,
> Neither self-identical nor variant in form, neither coming nor going;
> Such is *pratītyasamutpāda* ...[36]

Consistent with this, the first and most important chapter of the *Kārikās* concludes that the causal relation is inexplicable, and later chapters go further to claim that causation is like māyā. "Origination, existence, and destruction are of the nature of māyā, dreams, or a fairy castle."[37] The last chapters seize on this issue as one way to crystalize the difference between saṁsāra and nirvana, and what is perhaps the most important verse of all (XXV.9, the epigraph to this section) distinguishes between them by attributing causal relations only to saṁsara. In his commentary on the previous chapter, Candrakīrti defines samvṛti (the lower truth) and duḥkha (suffering) in the same way: "to be reciprocally in existence, that is, for things to be based on each other in utter reciprocity, is *samvṛti*." "It is precisely what arises in dependence that constitutes *duḥkha*, not what does not arise in dependence."[38]

How are we to understand this obvious contradiction? That is, how do we get from interpreting pratītya-samutpāda as dependent origination to what has been well described as "nondependent non-origination" and, what is more, reconcile the two? Following the line of argument used in the previous sections, I claim that all-conditionality is phenomenologically equivalent to a denial of all causal conditions. That is, a view so radical as to analyze things away into "their" conditions offers an interpretation of experience which becomes indistinguishable from a view that negates causality altogether. Again, the argument is made in two steps. Looking at the commonsense distinction between things and their cause-and-effect relationships, Nāgārjuna first uses the latter to "deconstruct" the former and deny that there are any self-existing things. Less obvious is the second stage, which reverses the analysis. The lack of "thingness" in things implies a way of experiencing in which there is no awareness of cause or effect because one *is* the cause/effect. Things and their causal relations stand or fall together, because our notion of cause-and-effect is dependent on that of objectively existing things. As with the previous dualisms of Self and nonself, and so on, the basic problem is that this bifurcation is untenable. Nāgārjuna shows that it is delusive by demonstrating how, once it has occurred, it is not possible to relate the two terms back together again without a contradiction. The inconsistency in our ordinary way of understanding objects is that they are taken to be both self-existent and causally contingent.

∎

In order to understand the Mādhyamika critique, we must remind ourselves of what is being criticized. This is our ordinary, common-sense understanding of the world, which sees it as a collection of discrete entities (including myself) interacting causally "in" space and time. Nāgārjuna attacks more than the philosophical fancies of Indian metaphysicians, for there is a metaphysics inherent in our everyday view. It is one or another aspect of the commonsense view that is made absolute in systematic metaphysics. This commonsense understanding is what makes the world saṁsāra for us, and it is saṁsāra that Nāgārjuna is concerned to "deconstruct." This is why we must beware of making Mādhyamika into an "ordinary language" philosophy by interpreting śūnyatā merely as a "meta-system" term. By no means does the end of philosophical language-games "leave everything as it is" for Nāgārjuna, except in the sense that saṁsāra has always really been nirvana.

It is the consequence of prapañca "thought-projection" that I now perceive the room I am writing in, not nondually, but as a collection of books and chairs and pens and paper...and *me*, each of which is unreflectively taken to be distinct from the others and to persist unchanged unless affected by something else. Just as space and time, if they are to function dualistically as containers, require something understood to be nonspatial and nontemporal for them to contain, so the causal relation is normally used to explain the interaction between things that are distinct from each other. If causality explains the interaction among things, then things must in themselves be "noncausal," and by no coincidence this is precisely our commonsense notion of what an object is: a thing whose continued existence does not need to be explained—once created, it "self-exists." The objectivity of the world (including the objectification of myself) depends upon this dualism. This constitutes saṁsāra because it is by hypostatizing such "thingness" out of the flux of experience that we become attached to things—again, the primal attachment being (to) the sense of self. In causal terms, the conclusion of chapter 2 is that what we experience as objects are thought-constructed automatizations, a shorthand way of remembering that our perceptions tend to have a certain stability, which allows us to relate them together causally and form expectations.[39] But in the automatization process we forget that objects are a "causal shorthand" and we create the delusive bifurcation between objects and their causal relations—corresponding to the bifurcation between objects and their appearances.

The point about the effect of prapañca is important because without it one might conclude that Nāgārjuna's critique of self-existence (svabhāva) is a refutation of something that no one believes in anyway. But one does not escape his critique by defining entities in a more commonsense fashion as coming into and passing out of existence. There is no tenable middle ground between self-existence independent of all conditions—an empty set, since there are no such entities—and the complete conditionality of śūnyatā. Nāgārjuna's arguments against self-existence (e.g., *MMK* chaps. I, XV) demonstrate the inconsistency in our everyday way of "taking" the world. We accept that things change, yet at the same time we assume that somehow they also remain the same—necessary if they are to be "things." Recognizing this inconsistency, other Indian philosophers have tried to solve it by making one of these absolute at the expense of the other. But the *satkāryavāda* Substance-view of Advaita and Sāṅkhya emphasizes permanence at the price of not being able to account for change, while the *asatkāryavāda* Modal-view of early Buddhism has the opposite problem of not being able to provide the connecting thread necessary for continuity. Nāgārjuna arranges these and the other solutions that have been proposed into a "tetralemma" which exhausts the possible alternatives and then rejects them all. Any understanding of cause-and-effect that tries to relate these two *separate* things *together* can be reduced to the contradiction of both asserting and denying identity. He concludes that their "relationship" is incomprehensible and unreal.

It does not suffice to answer this Hume-like critique of identity[40] with an "ordinary language" rejoinder that we should become more sensitive to the ways we use our permanence-and-change vocabulary, for the Mādhyamika position is that our usual experience is deluded and this ordinary use of language is deluding. As the first prong of his attack, Nāgārjuna refutes our everyday distinction between things and their causal relations simply by sharpening the distinction to absurdity. If things are self-existent, then they must be distinguishable from their conditions, but their "existence" is clearly contingent upon the conditions that bring them into being and eventually (when those conditions no longer operate) cause them to disappear. If it is objected that one cannot live without reifying such fictitious entities, at least to some extent, the Mādhyamika response is to agree. The lower truth is not negated altogether, but it must not be taken as the higher truth, as a correct understanding of the way things really are.

So the first stage of the Mādhyamika critique negates the bifurcation between things and their causal relations by using the latter to deconstruct the former. This repeats the early Buddhist rejection of substance, but it is only the first step. Now the critique dialectically reverses and employs the deconstructed thing to deny the reality of causal conditions. Just as things are dependent upon their causal conditions, so the category of causality turns out to be dependent upon things. Our concept of causality presupposes a set of discrete, "noncausal" entities, for it is their interrelation that we explain as causation. A collection of self-existing objects does not make sense unless they are related together in some way. As mentioned in chapter 3, our commonsense notion of compulsion is one thing pushing another. Cause-and-effect requires some thing to cause and some thing to be effected. If this is so, then a complete conditionality so radical that it "dissolves" all things must also dissolve itself.

In order to make this point, it will be helpful to transpose the argument from the too-general category of causal conditions to the more specific one of motion-and-rest. Nāgārjuna analyzes motion and rest in chapter 2 of the *Kārikās*, immediately after his initial treatment of causality, and it is clear that the second chapter is meant to apply the general conclusions of chapter 1 to a particular case. The other advantage of shifting to motion-and-rest is that we may illuminate what is otherwise a puzzling chapter. The basic problem is that it is not always clear what Nāgārjuna is actually doing in chapter 2. Like Zeno, he denies the reality of motion, but this is not done to assert a Parmenidean immutability, since rest is also denied. As a result, Nāgārjuna has been criticized for making an "arid play on words" that "resembles the shell game" in its logical sleight-of-hand—that is, he is accused of basing his argument on subtle distinctions between words that have no empirical referent—and for committing the fallacy of composition in arguing that what is true for the parts (in this case, traversed, traversing, and to-be-traversed) must be true for the whole.[41] But such criticisms miss the point of Nāgārjuna's arguments. Their import is that our usual way of understanding motion, which distinguishes the mover from the act of moving, simply does not make sense, because the interdependence of mover and moved reveals that the hypostatization of either is delusive. Nāgārjuna's logic in stanzas 2–11 demonstrates that once we have reified a distinction between them, it becomes impossible to relate them back together again—a quandary familiar to students of the mind–body problem, the result of another reified bifurcation. The difficulty is shown by isolating this hypostatized mover and inquiring into its status. In itself, is *it* a mover, or not? That is, is the predicate *moves* intrinsic or contingent to this mover? The dilemma is that neither way of understanding the situation is satisfactory. If the mover in and of itself already moves, then there is no need to add an act of motion later; the predication of such a second motion becomes redundant. But the other alternative—that the mover by itself is a nonmover—does not work either because we cannot thereafter add the predicate, it being a contradiction for a nonmover to move. In neither way can we make sense out of the relation between them. It follows that the mover cannot have an existence of its own apart from the *moving* predicate, which means that our usual dualistic way of understanding motion is untenable. To summarize this in contemporary terms, Nāgārjuna is pointing out a flaw in the everyday language we use to describe (and hence our ways of thinking about) motion: our ascription of motion predicates to substantive objects is unintelligible.

At first encounter the above argument is unconvincing. The options seem so extreme that we suspect there must be some middle ground between them. Of course we cannot accept a double-movement, but is it really such a contradiction for a nonmover to move? What else *could* move? But no such appeal to everyday intuitions, or to the ordinary language that shapes and embodies them, is successful against the Mādhyamika critique of those intuitions, which spotlights the inconsistency that is ignored (and that to some extent must be ignored, of course) in daily life. One can elaborate on this by applying the logic that was used earlier to deconstruct the difference between things and their causal relations. Just as (the general rule) complete interdependence dissolves the thing into its relational conditions, with no residue of substance remaining, so (a specific case) the "completeness" of movement—the fact that no part of me stays unmoved in the chair when "I" go to lunch—means that no unchanging and hence no self-existing thing remains to move. Our way of thinking about the relation between mover and moving is another instance of the dualistic and deluding "contained–container" metaphor. Again, Nāgārjuna needs only to sharpen the dichotomy. Despite our intuitions, which want to postulate some "unchanging core" in order to save the mover, there is no middle ground between a self-existent, unmoving thing and the compete dissolution of the thing that does the moving. Understood in this way, it becomes obvious why his arguments work just as well against the intelligibility of rest. The bifurcation between the thing and its being-at-rest is just as delusive, for the same reasons.

•

So far, we have effected only the first stage of the dialectic, both in the general analysis of causal conditions and this more specific instance of motion-and-rest. We have deconstructed the thing which moves / is caused, and what remains is a constantly changing world of causal interactions. The second stage of the dialectic is easy to state but harder to understand. Granted, if there is only cause-and-effect, then there is no thing that causes and nothing that is effected; but if there is no*thing* to cause / be effected, we will not experience the world in terms of cause-and-effect. Implicit in our concept of change is the notion that a thing is becoming other than it was, so unless one reifies something self-existent and noncausal (cf. nontemporal) in order to provide continuity through these different conditioned (cf. temporal) states, there is nothing outside the changing conditions to *be changed*. The concept of change needs something to bite on, but the first stage of the dialectic leaves nothing unconditioned to chew. If a colleague I join for lunch cannot be called the "same" person I spoke with earlier, because there is no substratum of permanence to "him," then it also makes no sense to say that he "has changed." As with birth-and-death, if there is *only* coming-and-going—with no thing that comes or goes— then there is no real coming-and-going. Without a contained there can be no container. As the bifurcation dissolves, the poles conflate into a whole that cannot be represented; it remains philosophically indeterminate, since language, in order to describe at all, must distinguish subject and predicate, mover and moved, cause and effect.

Nonetheless, we must try to get some sense of what such a way of experiencing would be like. Otherwise it will remain unclear how, except by some logical sleight-of-hand, all-conditionality can be phenomenologically identified with no-conditionality. I attempt to satisfy this need with the help of a well-known Zen story. The following example discusses the causal relations of a nondual physical action, but what is said may be applied just as well to the causation of nondual sense-perception and nondual thought.

Lin-chi was a monk in the monastery of Huang Po. Three times Lin-chi asked the Master, "what is the real meaning of Bodhidharma coming from the West?" and each time Huang Po immediately struck him. Thereupon, discouraged, he decided to leave and was advised to go to Master Ta-yü. Arriving at his monastery, Lin-chi told Ta-yü of his encounters with Huang Po, adding that he didn't know where he was at fault.

Master Ta-yü exclaimed: "Your master treated you entirely with grandmotherly kindness, and yet you say that you don't know your fault." Hearing this, Lin-chi was suddenly awakened and said: "After all, there isn't much in Huang Po's Buddhism!"[42]

What did Lin-chi realize that awakened him? If (again rushing in where Zen masters will not tread) we distort his experience into an idea in order to gloss this story, we may say that Lin-chi must have realized that Huang Po had been answering his question. The blows he had received were not punishment but a demonstration of *why* Bodhidharma came from the West. On the commonsense level the answer to Lin-chi's stock question is obvious: Bodhidharma was bringing Buddhism to China. But this is a relative lower-truth explanation. Since this is a Zen question designed to initiate a dialogue, it goes without saying that what is sought is the higher truth, and on that level there is no "why." For the deeply enlightened person, each experience is complete in itself, the only thing in the universe, each action is "just this!" Without prapañca thought-projection everything is perceived afresh, for the first time. As Bodhidharma walked from India there was no thought of why in his head; "he" *was* each step. In the same way, there was no why to Huang Po's blows: "he" too *was* that spontaneous, unselfconscious action. Lin-chi's sudden realization of this overflowed into his exclamation. "So, there isn't much to Buddhism after all!" (Only "just this!") Upon returning to Huang Po, he demonstrated that his understanding was more than just an intellectual insight by not hesitating to give Huang Po a dose of his own medicine.

The paradox that makes the above story relevant to this section is the fact that, at the same time, Bodhidharma's and Huang Po's actions are intentional. Huang Po's blow may be immediate and spontaneous, but there is also a reason for it. It is not a random or irrelevant gesture, but a very appropriate response to that particular question, drawn forth by that situation. If we translate this point about intention back into our more general category of causality, here we have a case of an act which is *both* completely caused (perfect *upāya*, "skillful means": glove fitting hand tightly, to use the Zen analogy) *and* yet is also uncaused. This paradox is impossible according to our usual understanding of causality, which uses that category of thought to relate together the supposedly discrete objects into which prapañca carves the world. That understanding would apply to the story in question if Huang Po, prapañca-deluded, were to perceive Lin-chi dualistically: Lin-chi is sitting there, a person-object that needs to be enlightened, and I, Huang Po sitting here, am the person who will try to enlighten him. Then "my" blow is reified into a deliberated effect that I hope will cause Lin-chi's awakening.

But if, as all schools of Buddhism agree, there is no self to make these causal relations among things, then that understanding of the situation cannot be correct. So Huang Po must have experienced it differently and causality must be understood differently. Causality is not denied. On the contrary, without the sense of self and other prapañca-reified objects to serve as a counterfoil, it expands to include everything. (Applying causality to the mental realm as well results in the doctrine of *karma*.) From the perspective of Mādhyamika's all-conditionality, which deconstructs all self-existing things, Huang Po's blow is part of a seamless web of conditions that can be extended, as in Hua Yen, to encompass the entire universe. As one interstice in the infinite, interdependent web of Indra, the blow reflects or rather manifests everything everywhere. But if every event that happens is interdependent with everything else in the whole universe, what a different way of experiencing is involved! It suggests a Spinozistic acceptance of whatever happens, as a product of the whole, but more deeply it implies the irrelevance of causality as usually understood. We find ourselves in a universe of śūnya-events, none of which can be said to occur for the sake of any other. Each nondual event—every leaf-flutter, wandering thought, and piece of litter—is whole and complete in itself, because although conditioned by everything else in the universe and thus a manifestation of it, for precisely that reason it is not subordinated to anything else but becomes an unconditioned end-in-itself. As argued in chapter 3, the dualism between freedom and determinism becomes deconstructed at the same time. If "liberty or freeedom signifies properly the absence of opposition," then such unimpeded interdependence implies freedom, since there is not only no thing that *does* the event but also no other to oppose it. If it is the self-caused universe-as-a-whole that makes every event happen or, better, that *is* the event, then whenever anything occurs it occurs freely. In this way, the Absolute or higher truth for Mahāyāna turns out to be *every event that ever happens in the whole universe.* That is why the Buddha could "turn the wheel of the Dharma" just by twirling a flower, and why Huang Po could teach by striking Lin-chi.

But what does all this imply about the way the Buddha twirled that flower? How did Huang Po experience his own action? Because he did not perceive the situation dualistically, the action was not "done *by* him." That the blow was appropriate to the situation was not due to any prior deliberation, however quick. On the contrary, the action was so appropriate precisely because it was not deliberated, just as the best responses in dharma-combat are unmediated by any self-conscious "hindrance in the mind." Then why did Huang Po strike rather than shout "ho!" as Ma-tsu often did, or utter a few soft words, as Chao-chou probably would have done? This is the crucial point: *he does not know.* ("Not knowing is the most intimate" said Master Lo-han, precipitating Wên-i's awakening.) His spontaneous actions are traceless, "like the tracks of a bird in the sky."[43] They respond to a situation like a glove fits on a hand because whatever "decisions are made" (if that phrase can be used here) are not made by "him." If one nondualistically is the cause/effect, rather than being a hypostatized self that dualistically *uses* it, then there is not the awareness that it is a cause/effect. It is experienced as free, whole, and "traceless." Without the interference that the self creates, Indra's all-encompassing web of causal conditions is indeed seamless. When "the bottom falls out of the bucket" and the barrier between consciousness and subconsciousness dissolves, thought and actions are experienced as welling up nondually from a source unfathomably deep—or, what amounts to the same thing, from *nowhere.*

In order to bring all this down to earth, the most important question is whether Huang Po experienced his blow as determined (caused) or freely done (uncaused). The answer is: both. If the action were dualistic, done by an ego-self, as we usually understand it, this would be impossible. But is is not a contradiction for one whose acts are śūnya. We are reminded of Nietzsche's description of his own inspiration (quoted more fully in chapter 4): "Everything happens *involuntarily* in the highest degree but as in a gale of a feeling of *freedom,* of absoluteness, of power, of divinity." The act is determined because it is not the act of an ego-self, whose only role is to let itself be absorbed into the process. The act is free because it flows spontaneously from somewhere much "deeper." The paradox of involuntary freedom points to another aspect of wei-wu-wei, action that is no action when it is experienced as springing up nondually from a boundless, unknowable source which one is, as it were, "plugged into." "As it were," because all such metaphors—springing up from, plugging into—are inescapably dualistic. Again and again, our attempts to describe nonduality must bump up against the limits of language.

•

So there turn out to be only two alternatives: *either* cause-and-effect relationships between discrete thought-constructed objects, manipulated by/manipulating a thought-constructed subject, *or* nondual all-conditionality (pratītya-samutpāda) that is experienced as unconditioned freedom (tathatā). In order to move from the first to the second alternative, the heirarchy that causality constructs must collapse into an interpenetration in which each event is equally conditioned by the whole and manifests that whole as the only thing in the universe. Causal relations form a hierarchy because the most important hypostatized thing is *me,* the subject who craves other objects and needs an understanding of causal relationships in order to manipulate circumstances and obtain what he wants. All-conditionality, in completely negating anything to be attached to, offers no practical utility, because there is no longer any object to be obtained nor any self to crave it; whereas a hypostatized self that wants to obtain some other hypostatized thing will need to construct a causal chain of events leading to it. Because each event in such a chain is experienced not in itself, but only for the sake of the next, and the next, and so on, the śūnya nature of each is overlooked in our eagerness to obtain the objectified goal. This dissatisfaction with each particular event in hurrying to the next is essential to the sense of self, which is why causality is the root category of thought and thus the one most in need of deconstruction. Man is a cause-seeking creature, said Lichtenberg. We look for compulsion in the world and therefore find it, because freedom explains nothing and gains us nothing.

This way of resolving the time and causality paradoxes (only-time is no time, all-conditionality is the Unconditioned) is important for understanding the *trisvabhāva* (three natures) doctrine of Yogācāra too, and thus the general relation between Mādhyamika and Yogā-cāra. The prapañca-world of discrete objects causally interacting "in" space and time corresponds to the *parikalpita-svabhāva*, the "imagined nature." Only-time and all-conditionality correspond to *paratantra-svabhāva*, the interdependent or "other-dependent nature." The unconditioned Eternal Present corresponds to the *pariniṣpanna-svabhāva*, the absolutely-accomplished nondual nature. Read in this way, Vasubandhu's *Trisvabhāvanīrdeśa*, for example, is completely consistent with the Mādhyamika approach. For both Mādhyamika and Yogācāra, an understanding of all-conditionality, with its negation of the self-existence of discrete things, is the crucial hinge whereby we move from delusion to enlightenment.

We are finally ready to return to Vedānta and relate this to the Advaitic analysis of causal relations. The significant point is that, despite the ontological differences, there is no disagreement between Mahāyāna and Vedānta over the noncausal nature of the nondual experience. Since Brahman is qualityless and imperceptible, there is no phenomenological difference between a Mahāyāna interpretation of Huang Po's blow and an Advaitic one. In both cases, the arm movement is experienced nondually, with no bifurcation between a self-conscious subject and "his" action. In both cases, therefore, that mysterious śūnya action is involuntary yet free, inexplicable in terms of efficient causality and having no reality in itself (nor of course does Huang Po or anything else). The only difference is that Mahāyāna stops here, while Advaita asserts that there must be an immutable ground that is the source of all the changing phenomena. But since this source by definition cannot be experienced, the difference is reduced to a more abstract (although not trivial) one of emphasis. Concluding that phenomena are illusory māyā seems to devalue them somewhat more than if phenomena are merely śūnya without any Brahman "behind" them. To repeat a point made in chapter 2, the difference becomes one of attitude towards the nondual experience rather than anything in the experience itself. The Advaitin, distinguishing between Brahman and māyā, will be more eager to negate the phenomenal world than the Buddhist Bodhisattva, for whom there are only empty forms and events.

PATH

If anyone imagines he will get more by inner thoughts and sweet yearnings and a special grace of God than he could get beside the fire or with his flocks or in the stable, he is doing no more than trying to take God and wrap His head in a cloak and shove Him under the bench. For whoever seeks God in some special Way, will gain the Way and lose God who is hidden in the Way. But whoever seeks God without any special Way, finds Him as He really is . . . and He is life iself.

—Eckhart

When we want something, normally we know well enough what needs to be done to get it. But what if the object I desire is something that can never become an object, because it is prior to the subject–object dichotomy? What if it can never be an effect, because it is always unconditioned? What if it can never be gained, because it is unattainable? Then I find myself in a dilemma. If I make no effort to do anything, it seems that the result will also be nothing and there will be no progress toward the desired goal. But to the extent that I exert myself to attain it, I don't, for in this case all effort seems to be self-defeating. This is the paradox of spiritual practice, for, as we have seen, ātman, Brahman, nirvana, Buddha-nature, and so on, are unobjectifiable (because nondual), unoriginated (beyond causal and temporal relations), and hence unobtainable. How can we escape this double bind?

Our treatment of the Advaitic all-Self versus Buddhist no-self controversy included a discussion of one form of Zen practice: the Rinzai technique for working on a koan such as Jōshū's Mu. That was illuminating, but it ignored this very pressing problem, which may be summarized as follows: Expecting a nondual experience to happen *to* you is still dualistic and therefore self-stultifying. In response, we must distinguish between two perspectives on practice: the phenomenal view, according to which we move from delusion to enlightenment, and the essential view, according to which there is no dualism between delusion and enlightenment—or between phenomenal and essential.

The former view was presented in the first section of this chapter; here I present the latter by considering the views of Śaṅkara and Dōgen on the relation between practice (samādhi, yoga, zazen, etc.) and enlightenment (mokṣa, nirvana, satori, etc.). Once again, their views about this relation seem to be diametrically opposed. Later Advaita came to incorporate yogic practices that cultivate samādhi, but Śaṅkara himself does not recognize the necessity for any practice, except perhaps for those "of inferior intellect." In contrast, for Dōgen, zazen is nothing less than enlightenment itself. But both are reacting against the same problem, the thought-constructed dualism between practice as means and enlightenment as goal, which objectifies the nondual Self / Buddha-nature into something that, insofar as it is understood to be something separate from us, can never be attained. Both came to the same insight about the necessity to overcome this bifurcation; the difference between them is in how they overcome it. The two main ways are to subsume the means into the ends, or vice versa. Śaṅkara, in denying the need for any practice, exemplifies the first. Dōgen, arguing that zazen *is* enlightenment, prefers the second. More important than this difference, however, is that in both cases we end up with a nonduality between the two terms, which might be called "the path of no-path." But the emphasis is certainly different, as we shall see: For Śaṅkara, *no-path* is indeed the path, while for Dōgen no-path is very much *the path*.

It comes as no surprise that this mutual understanding about the paradox of practice reflects their agreements regarding the nature of nondual experience—namely, that it "transcends" both temporal and causal relations. One profound implication of this is that all possible means are severed from any ends. In the thought-constructed everyday world we can and to some extent must ignore this, but the consequences for spiritual life are inescapable. It means that *no* religious practice—be it ritual, prayer, yoga, zazen, or anything else—can ever cause or lead to enlightenment, because enlightenment is understood as that experience which cannot be characterized by such temporal or causal relations. From this perspective, we can see that the usual attitude toward spiritual practices is therefore not a solution to the problem but simply another version of the problem itself. Any method or technique understood to lead to an enlightenment experience maintains the very present $\rightarrow$ future, cause $\rightarrow$ effect dualism that it is trying to escape. Projecting such a thought-constructed goal into the future sacrifices the present at its altar and thus loses *the now*, which is the only possible locus for liberation. The crucial insight for both Śaṅkara and Dōgen is that *there is nothing to attain*, which is not to deny that this insight is something that must be realized clearly. The difference between attainment and such realization is that only *now* can I realize I *am* that which I seek. Since *it is always now*, the possibility is always there, but that possibility becomes real-ized only when causal, time-bound, goal-directed ways of thinking and acting evaporate, to expose what I have always been: a formless, qualityless mind that is immutable because it is *nothing*, that is free because it is not going anywhere, and that does not need to go anywhere because it does not lack anything.

•

There is no dissolution, no birth, none in bondage, none aspiring for wisdom, no seeker of liberation and none liberated. This is the absolute truth.
—Gauḍapāda, *Māṇḍūkyopaniṣad*

For Śaṅkara, liberation (mokṣa) is realizing the true nature of the Self (ātman), which is identical with the ground of the universe (Brahman). As we have seen, the distinctive feature of Śaṅkara's Advaita is the way it understands the relationship between this spiritual ground and the concrete phenomenal world we live in—or understand ourselves to live in. Śaṅkara resolves the issue in one bold stroke by denying that there is a phenomenal world. There is only ātman/Brahman, which is and always has been unconditioned, unoriginated, all-pervasive, devoid of any modifications, self-effulgent and ever-content. Anything that seems different from this—including all temporal and causal relationships—is māyā, and such experience is avidyā, delusion involving ignore-ance of Brahman.

As a preemptive strike this is a brilliant solution to the problem of creation, but it creates its own problems, notably the difficulty of accounting for the nature of māyā, which is left unexplained in a never-never-land neither inside (no delusion in Brahman!) nor outside (nothing outside!) the Absolute. However, it determines what the nature of liberation must be for Śaṅkara: since there is *only* ātman/Brahman, nothing needs to be attained or done. Śaṅkara devotes much effort to refuting the Mīmāṁsā view that the purport of the Vedas is to inculcate dharma, defined in this instance as "that which, being desirable, is indicated by Vedic injunction."[44] On the contrary, says Śaṅkara, no action is necessary to realize Brahman, and no action can be required of one who has realized Brahman, for that realization puts an end to all activity by revealing the nondual true Self as that which never acts. At best, Vedic rituals can only lead to a better realm of saṁsāra, never salvation. Śaṅkara even denies that such Vedic statements as "the Self alone is to be meditated upon" are genuine injunctions, because "except the knowledge that arises from that dictum...there is nothing to be done, either mentally or outwardly."[45]

Actions can produce effects in one of four ways: something is produced, acquired, modified, or purified; none of these can apply to Brahman, which has no origin, cannot be attained, is immutable, and transcends any possible defect. "Even if Brahman were different from oneself, there can be no acquisition of Brahman, since being all-pervasive like space, It remains ever attained by everybody."[46] Like the sixth Ch'an patriarch, Śaṅkara does not accept even the metaphor of the Self as a mirror whose inherent brilliance needs to be cleaned by rubbing, "for no action can take place without bringing about some change in its locus" and that would make the Self subject to impermanence.[47] Like seeing a rope in the grass as a snake, we "bind ourselves without a rope," and eliminating such delusions is what reveals the awareness of Brahman, or (less dualistically) Brahman-awareness, which has no degrees, does not come from any other place, and (unlike the dirty mirror) has never been obscured, although It has been unnoticed in our preoccupation with apparently objective phenomena. It is not necesary to get rid of the body, for the Self has always been bodiless; "the idea of embodiedness is a result of false nescience."[48] This explains *jivanmukti*, how complete liberation is possible even before physical death: because there is no real embodiment to escape.

Nevertheless, most of us do not know this unattainable Brahman; instead, we suffer due to our many delusions. How can we eliminate them and realize the ever-present Self? This brings us back to the question of practice. According to Radhakrishnan, "Śaṅkara accepts the principle of the yoga practice, which has for its chief end *samādhi*...which consists in withdrawing the senses from everything external and concentrating them on one's own nature." These and the

various outer limbs of yoga "bring about the rise of true knowledge."[49]
This is accurate as an account of Gauḍapāda, and in Śaṅkara's voluminous corpus a few passages can be cited to support such a view. But
Advaitic assimilation of such practices occurred commonly after
Śaṅkara, for the main tendency of his thought is to resist the necessity
for any practice or means for the realization of Brahman. He does not
deny that they can sometimes be of limited value, as in his comment on
Gauḍapāda's approval of yogic practice—"for those of inferior intellect." Meditative repetition can be helpful because "people do not
always understand the first time."[50] Karmic factors may be stronger
than the operation of knowledge and interfere with it; then, he says,
"there is need to regulate the train of remembrance of the knowledge
of the Self by having recourse to means such as renunciation and
dispassion; but it is not something that is to be enjoined, being a
possible alternative."[51]

It is clear that the limited value of such practices lies in their
tendency to re-collect the mind from its preoccupation with various
sense- and thought-objects, to help it focus itself. But liberation is that
unconditioned and unconditionable moment when the mind
becomes aware of itself as a formless, qualityless, nongraspable consciousness, which is what it has always been. Here, as so often with such
matters, we bump up against the limits of language. To say "the mind
becomes aware of itself" implies a reflexive process, whereas for
Śaṅkara realization is just the opposite: the sense of self is the result of
just such reflexivity, and liberation occurs when the mind stops trying
to grasp its own tail.[52] At that instant, it is not the case that bonds are
broken: rather, one realizes that there never were any bonds to be
broken. Such liberation can be eternal only because it never had a
beginning.[53] This implies—the logic is inescapable—that from the
liberated point of view there is not even such a thing as liberation. As
Gauḍapāda concludes his commentary on the *Māṇḍukyopaniṣad*, "all
dharmas [here, selves] are ever free from bondage and pure by nature.
They are ever illumined and liberated from the very beginning."[54]
Śaṅkara agrees:

> Brahman cannot logically be a goal to be attained. The supreme
> Brahman can never become a goal which pervades everything, which is
> inside everything, which is the Self of all. . . . For one cannot reach where

one already is. The well-known fact in the world is that one thing is
reached by something else.[55]

•

*Subhūti said to the Buddha: "World Honored One, does your attainment of
Supreme Enlightenment mean that you have not gained anything whatsoever?"
The Buddha replied: "Just so, Subhūti, just so. I have not gained even the least
dharma from Supreme Enlightenment."*

—Diamond Sutra

*There is no ignorance, no end of ignorance, and so forth, until we come to, there is
no decay and death, no end of decay and death; there is no suffering, no cause of
suffering, no end of suffering, and no path; there is no wisdom, no attainment and
no non-attainment.*

—Heart Sutra

We find no disparagement of practice in Dōgen. On the contrary,
zazen (he emphasizes that other techniques such as *nembutsu*, sutra
reading, penances and rituals, etc., are unnecessary) is elevated to the
status of enlightenment itself—without, however, denying the importance of his own experience under Ju-ching in China. The heart of his
teaching is this *shusho itto* (or *ichinyo*), "the oneness of practice and
enlightenment." Whereas Śaṅkara resolves the delusive dualism between means and end by denying the need for any practice, Dōgen
resolves the same dualism by incorporating enlightenment into practice. In both cases the duality collapses, because without a means we
cannot objectify the end, and if there is no end then the means becomes more than a means.

Śaṅkara allows us no comfortable refuge in any technique where we
can feel secure, having delegated to it our responsibility to realize and
having thought-projected the wonderful, resolving-all-problems
event of enlightenment sometime into the future. For Śaṅkara, practice becomes sharply concentrated into the simple need to realize,
which can happen only *now*, which does happen when we cease
objectifying liberation into an effect that *will* occur. Dōgen does not
deny enlightenment, but he transforms zazen so that it is no longer
self-stultifying. The type of zazen he recommends is *shikan-taza*, "just
sitting," which is characterized by awareness that is without any
striving for a goal. The mind dwells serenely in its formlessness, and
since it is precisely this formless, goalless character of the mind that

needs to be realized, such practice is not to be distinguished from its goal.

Although arising from Chinese Mahāyāna philosophy, the problem that came to obsess the young Dōgen evokes Śaṅkara's Advaita just as much: if, according to both exoteric and esoteric schools of Buddhism, man is already endowed with the Buddha-nature by birth, why do we need to seek enlightenment and engage in spiritual practices? If we are all "originally enlightened" (hongaku), why do we need to acquire enlightenment (shikaku)? Dōgen finally realized the answer to this in China, and he expressed it in Bendōwa, his first work in Japanese and one of his most important writings. Replying to the question of why someone who has realized the Buddha's Dharma should need to do zazen, he says:

> In the Buddha Dharma, practice and realization are identical. Because one's present practice is practice as realization, one's initial negotiation of the Way in itself is the whole of original realization. Thus, even while one is directed to practice, he is told not to anticipate realization apart from practice, because practice points directly to original realization. As it is already realization in practice, realization is endless; as it is practice in realization, practice is beginningless. Thus Śākyamuni and Mahā-kāśyapa were both taken and used by practice within realization. Bodhidharma and patriarch Hui-nêng were likewise drawn in and turned by practice in realization. The way of maintaining the Buddha Dharma has always been like this.[56]

The first thing to notice about this seminal passage is a profound agreement with Śaṅkara: the need for practice is not due to any lack or defect in "original enlightenment," for there is absolutely nothing that needs to be produced, acquired, modified, or purified. In the Shōbōgenzō Dōgen tirelessly emphasizes this point. "As for the Buddha way, when one first arouses the thought [of enlightenment, which initiates one's practice], it is enlightenment; when one first achieves perfect enlightenment, it is enlightenment. First, last and in between are all enlightenment" (Sesshin sesshō). If the first thought of enlightenment is understood as a seed, then full enlightenment is the fruit, but Dōgen denies this relationship: "There is no time of the past or present when the truth is not realized. Therefore, although the unenlightened standpoint may be presupposed, root, stem, branch and leaf must simultaneously realize Buddhanature as the very same whole being" (*Busshō*, "Buddhanature"). In the same fascicle, Dōgen reinterprets the Nirvāṇa Sūtra. It is not that all sentient beings *have* the Buddha-nature, for that is still dualistic; they and even nonsentient beings *are* the Buddha-nature. It is not that enlightenment will occur "when the time comes," for "there is no time right now that is not a time that has come." Just as there is nothing but ātman/Brahman for Śaṅkara, there is nothing but Buddha-nature for Dōgen. "My" Buddha-nature is not something hidden that awaits polishing, nor a potential that will manifest itself sometime in the future: "There is no Buddhanature that is not Buddha-nature fully manifested here and now."[57]

Up to this point, then, we see a remarkable agreement between Dōgen and Śaṅkara that we are all "originally enlightened" (Dōgen) and that liberation is eternal (Śaṅkara). But this of course does not resolve Dōgen's puzzle about the relation between original and acquired enlightenment. On the contrary, it seems to make the problem more acute, and we can almost hear Śaṅkara asking the obvious question: "Yes of course; but then why do we need to practice? If Buddha-nature is not something that needs to be acquired, transformed, produced, or purified, because it is already completely manifested, then what is the point of doing zazen?"

Immediately after discussing the oneness of practice and enlightenment in the *Bendōwa* (quoted above), Dōgen considers what he calls the "Senika heresy." According to it, the way to escape birth-and-death is to realize that your mind-nature is eternal and immutable, for the body is only its temporary form. "Those who fail to grasp this are ever caught up in birth and death. Therefore, one must simply know without delay the significance of the mind-nature's immutability. What can come of spending one's whole life sitting quietly, doing nothing?"

Although presented as the view of a heretical Buddhist school, a better description of Śaṅkara's Advaita would be hard to find. Dōgen criticizes it in the strongest possible terms. The gist of his reply is that "the Buddha Dharma from the first preaches that body and mind are not two, that substance and form are not two." Therefore we should not speak of the body perishing and the mind abiding. This does not limit the Buddha-nature-without-a-second, for Dōgen concludes by emphasizing that the Buddhist teaching is that "all dharmas—the myriad forms dense and close of the universe—are simply this one Mind, including all, excluding none."[58]

This difference from Śaṅkara becomes clearer when we consider Dōgen's own enlightenment experience. During zazen his teacher Ju-ching said "body and mind must fall away" (Jap., *shinjin-datsuraku*) whereupon Dōgen's did. This may appear contrary to the Advaitic claim that there is no need to escape the body, since the Self has never really been embodied. But this was not a falling away in the sense that Advaita criticizes as unnecessary, for that would be physical death. What Dōgen experienced thereafter was not an immutable Self voided of any attributes but "the fallen-away body and mind" (*datsuraku-shinjin*): body and mind now empty, but not further negated or dismissed as *avidyā*. Many fascicles of the *Shōbōgenzō* emphasize that enlightenment is as much physical as mental, for with it the duality between them is overcome: "Your whole body is Mind in its totality" (*Ikka-Myōju*, "One Bright Jewel").

This attitude toward the body shows the "other half" of Dōgen's teaching, which is incompatible with Śaṅkara. We find it embodied in those paradoxes wherein Dōgen affirms both of two apparently contradictory aspects, juxtaposing nondual Buddha-nature with the relative, dualistic aspect of things. Thus there are many prominent passages that emphasize the importance of attaining enlightenment, even though these seem to contradict what is said—often in the same place—about the unattainability of Buddha-nature. The *Bendōwa* was cited earlier to present Dōgen's view that practice and realization are identical, but he also distinguishes them there: "The dharma is amply present in every person, but unless one practices, it is not manifested; unless there is realization, it is not attained." He goes on to quote a Ch'an patriarch: "It is not that there is no practice or realization, only that you should not defile them." In *Busshō*, just after emphasizing that everything *is* the Buddha-nature, he continues: "The Buddhanature is not incorporated prior to attaining Buddhahood; it is incorporated upon the attainment of Buddhahood" and immediately repeats the point.[59] Buddha-nature may be as complete in the seed as in the fruit, but we should not confound the two. While the seed lacks nothing, it is only the fruit that realizes that the seed lacks nothing—and yet that realization adds nothing. Each stage is *zenki*, "the total dynamic working" of Buddha-nature, and as such is not dependent upon any other stage; nonetheless, to ignore completely all temporal and causal relationships is to replace one form of blindness with another.

But what does this difference between Śaṅkara and Dōgen imply for the relation between practice and enlightenment? How does it resolve Dōgen's puzzle? We find our answer in the story with which Dōgen concludes "Genjō-kōan," the first fascicle of the *Shōbōgenzō* and his single most important work:

> As Zen master Pao-ch'ê of Ma-ku shan was fanning himself, a monk came up and said: "The nature of the wind is constancy. There is no place it does no reach. Why do you still use a fan?" Pao-ch'ê answered: "You only know the nature of the wind is constancy. You do not know yet the meaning of it reaching every place." The monk said: "What is the meaning of 'there is no place it does no reach'?" The master only fanned himself. The monk bowed deeply.[60]

The monk's question was Dōgen's: If everyone already possesses the Buddha-nature, why is there need for practice? Pao-ch'ê's answer is to the point, but it is easy to misunderstand. It is not the case that "without the actual movement of the fan the wind's constancy is only a latent, empty reality,"[61] for that amounts to another dualistic view according to which Buddha-nature must be transformed from a state of latency to actuality. If Buddha-nature is fully manifested here and now, we must overcome any notion of duality between wind and master and realize that the master's fanning himself *is* the wind's constancy, that *his activity is itself the manifestation of the wind*. What did the Bendōwa passage say about Śākyamuni and Mahākāśyapa? They "both *were taken and used by* practice within realization"; Bodhidharma and Hui-nêng "likewise *were drawn in and turned by* practice in realization." The passive verbs take on new significance in the light of Pao-ch'ê's fanning.

The heart of the *Bendōwa* passage is the obscure sentence, "As it is always realization in practice, realization is endless; as it is practice in realization, practice is beginningless." This may now be understood as meaning: "since 'original realization' is already implied by and embodied in all our practice, practice is the way that realization actualizes itself endlessly, for our practice is endless. In the same way, since practice is already inherent in realization and 'original realization' has no beginning, so our practice too has no beginning." Thus practice is not a means to the attainment of enlightenment. But that does not mean it is dispensable, for *practice is the natural way in which one's "original enlightenment" manifests itself.* In this way Dōgen avoids any dichotomy between practice and enlightenment, means and ends. For Śaṅkara, however, such a view was not possible, because he does not accept any manifestations of Brahman: they are all delusive māyā which obscures nirguṇa Brahman. For the Buddhist, emptiness is *not other* than form, and Buddha-nature is not to be found elsewhere than in its manifestation as myriad phenomena. Therefore, what is to be realized is not something apart from phenomena—some Absolute that indifferently transcends them—but their true nature which is also my true true nature. This leaves each to function freely as *ippō-gujin,* "the total exertion of a single thing" embodying the whole universe. And for Dōgen zazen is the example par excellence of the ippō-gujin manifesting human Buddha-nature.

When I do not attempt to *get* anything *from* my zazen, then it can be realized as the complete, lacking-nothing manifestation of "my" Buddha-nature. This does not deny the reality and importance of enlightenment from the relative standpoint. Done in such a fashion—not seeking or anticipating any effects—zazen in itself gradually transforms my character, and eventually I am able to realize clearly that the true nature of my mind and that of the universe are nondual. Zazen, however, cannot be said to cause this experience: enlightenment is always an accident, as Chögyam Trungpa has said, but practice undeniably makes us more accident-prone. Nonetheless, the way in which this no-seeking mind thereafter cultivates and manifests itself is through practice, for this no-seeking mind can deepen itself endlessly. "We have already been told: 'It never, never ends. Reaching Buddha, it is ever more assiduous" (*Nyorai-zenshin*).[62] Even the empty sky needs to be beaten with a stick; even the Buddha is only halfway there. And since there is therefore no "there," no final resting point, no-seeking mind is "there" at every moment and always has been.

THE CLÔTURE OF DECONSTRUCTION

One senses Derrida is indeed on the verge of someway else, if not a something else, but surely he has not yet broken out of the turn. Derrida is in the turn of language, but he has logically demonstrated language to be not a turn but a labyrinth.
—Robert Magliola[63]

Our deconstructions of time and causality have enough similarity to the deconstructions of Jacques Derrida that they benefit from a comparison. From the nondualist perspective, the problem with Derrida's radical critique of Western philosophy is that it is not radical enough: his deconstruction is incomplete because it does not deconstruct itself and attain that *clôture* which, as we have seen, is the opening to something else. This is why Derrida remains in the halfway-house of proliferating "pure textuality," whereas deconstruction could lead to a transformed mode of experiencing the world.

Any notion of a clôture for deconstruction seems incongruous with Derrida's project, whose *différance*, in deconstructing any proffered "transcendental signified," allows the dissemination of endless supplementation. Nonetheless, I argue for this by contrasting his method and claims with the dialectic I use to undermine the "commonsense" dualities between objects and their temporal/causal relations. Earlier in this chapter those temporal and causal relations were used to deconstruct the notion of a "thing" and deny that there is anything self-identical or self-present. Derrida's demonstration of the ineluctability of différance makes the same point. But that alone is incomplete. We saw that the interdependence of both terms in such dualities implies that the negation of one must also lead to negation of the other. It is the necessity for this second and reverse movement that Derrida does not see. Expressed in his categories, Derrida, although aware that each term of a duality is the différance of the other, does not fully realize how deconstructing one term (transcendental signified, self-presence, reference, etc.) must also transform the other (différance, temporization, supplementation, etc.).

What is the result of this double-deconstruction of "commonsense" dualities? Derrida's single-deconstruction leads to the "temporary" reversal of their hierarchy, and/or to a discontinuous, irruptive "liberation" from reference grounded in the search for unattainable origins, into the dissemination of a free-floating meaning beyond any conceptual clôture. For the nondualist, this can be only the illusion of liberation, while remaining trapped in a textual "bad infinity" that tends to become increasingly ludic. What is needed is not just "a change of style," however seductive or frustrating that may be. Rather, the complete deconstruction of such dualities can lead, not merely to their more self-conscious "reinscription," but to a mode of experience which is not governed by them. The nondualist agrees that such dualities are ineluctably inscribed in language and thus are fundamental categories of thought; however, this means not that they are inescapable, but that their deconstruction points finally to an experience beyond language—or, more precisely, to a nondual way of experiencing language and thought.

In other words, the ultimate irony is that deconstruction ends in the elusive "origin" that metaphysics has always sought and that Derrida believes that he has refuted. They are both right. Philosophy will never come to rest in such an origin, for no "transcendental signified" can be located with/in language, and philosophy is a language-game. The rhetorical operations that produce supposedly logical proofs cannot be eliminated. Philosophy, like all language, is basically metaphorical. This is Derrida's positive and, I hope, lasting contribution. But Nāgārjuna's deconstruction of thought via language offers a different mode of approach to the problem. "There is nothing outside the text" may be true, but it need not be true. In order to understand this, let us remind ourselves what is the paradigm "transcendental signified," according to Buddhism: not nirvana, as two centuries of Western commentators have led us to believe, for nirvana is neither transcendental ("the ontic range of nirvana is the ontic range of the everyday world. There is not even the subtlest difference between the two"; MMK, XXV, 20) nor signified ("no truth has been taught by a Buddha for anyone, anywhere"; XXV, 24). On the contrary, the paradigm transcendental signified is *the thing*—here meaning not only physical objects but also the objectified subject. What most needs to be deconstructed is the apparent objectivity of the world, which is due to taking perceptions as "signs" of the object. The relationship between names and things is the archetypal signifier/signified correspondence, and the nondualist goal is nothing else than its complete deconstruction. Nirvana is nothing other than "the utter dissipation of ontologizing thought," "the non-functioning of perceptions as signs of all named things" (Candrakīrti).[64]

Unarticulated and delusive ontological commitments underlie even the most everyday uses of language. Suddenly, language/thought is no longer the means (as according to metaphysics), nor even the end (according to Heidegger and Derrida, in very different ways), but the problem itself. Philosophy cannot grasp what it seeks in any of its categories, but, as language becoming self-conscious of its function, it can learn to "undo" itself and cease to be an obstruction, in that way allowing what we have long sought to manifest itself. This "origin-that-cannot-be-named" has always been the most obvious thing, but all ways of thinking about it—whether metaphysical or deconstructive—can only conceal it by dualistically separating us from it.

Classical Indian philosophy was a quest to determine the Real, understood as that which is self-existent, not dependent upon anything else. Anything that can be shown to be relative to something else is thereby refuted as a candidate. So Nāgārjuna's task was quite simple: to take all the proposed candidates for Reality and demonstrate their relativity (śūnyatā), leaving nothing—not even śūnyatā, since that term too is relative to the candidates. "Śūnyatā is the exhaustion of all theories and views; those for whom śūnyatā is itself a theory are incurable" (*MMK*, XIII, 8). Rather than attempt to construct a new theory of language with śūnyatā as the key term, Nāgārjuna, while understanding that ordinary language is full of deluding ontological commitments, accepts it and deconstructs it from within: "Śūnyatā is a guiding, not a cognitive, notion, presupposing the everyday" (XXIV, 18). No privileged language is created in this deconstruction, and his goal cannot be expressed or pointed to without the delusive logo-centrisms of language; but, like Derrida, Nāgārjuna thus uses it "under erasure," without committing himself to its categories.

It is here that we find the deepest resonance with Derrida, whose deconstruction also proceeds by demonstrating the inescapable dif-férance infecting all Western metaphysical candidates for a transcendental signified. Deleuze's cryptic remark about Foucault—that he is a new kind of map-maker, constructing maps for use rather than to mirror the terrain—is equally true for both Nāgārjuna and Derrida.[65] The fundamental presupposition of metaphysics—that we can mirror the whole terrain from some Archimedean point of pure, self-contained thought—is the illusion they subvert, and their weapons are śūnyatā/différance. These mirror nothing because they have no referent apart from their subversive function; to fix them within a given system is to use them in ways that suppress that function. Their divergence, as we shall see, is in their understanding of the result of this subversion.

▪

The nondualist dissolution of self-existing objects "into" time antici-
pates the critique of self-presence that Derrida makes in textual terms,
by showing that every process of signification is an economy of temporal differences:

> The play of differences supposes, in effect, syntheses and referrals,
> which forbid at any moment, or in any sense, that a simple element be
> present in and of itself, referring only to itself.... There are only, every-
> where, differences and traces of traces.[66]

But, despite realizing that each term of such dualities is only the
différance of the other, Derrida does not see the second phase, in
which the dialectic reverses. In Dōgen's "being-time," lack of *self*-
presence is not incompatible with "the eternal present of time,"
because without self-existing objects time is not composed of a succession of "now-moments." Such moments can only exist in relation to
objects, as their successive modulations. The nondualist ends up with
a distinction between the commonsense understanding of objectified
time and the nonmetaphysical Eternal Now. In contrast, Derrida
reacts against the commonsense understanding of the present (as a
succession of falling-away moments) by redefining the present in
terms of past and future.

Derrida's most detailed examination of time, and Heidegger, is in
"Ousia and Grammē: Note on a Note from *Being and Time*."[67] Its point
of departure is a footnote from *Being and Time* in which Heidegger,
having differentiated his own view of time from the traditional and
metaphysical one, argues that the "fallen" conception of time is
implicit in all Western metaphysics from Aristotle through Hegel and
Bergson. It originates in an *aporia* found in Aristotle's *Physics* IV, in
which the nature of time is determined as "nonbeing" because it is
composed of a succession of elementary parts—"nows" (*nun*):

> But in order to be, in order to be a being, it [time] must not be affected
> by time, it must not become (past or future). To participate in beingness,
> in *ousia*, therefore is to participate in being-present, in the presence of
> the present, or if you will, in presentness.

The circularity of this definition remains "unthought" until Heidegger. For the nondualist, this aporia is merely another version of the
delusive bifurcation between things and time. Aristotle's metaphysical

demonstration is only a more explicit determination of the duality already latent in ordinary language. Whether both terms resulting from the bifurcation are taken to be real (both "container" and "contained" being real, as discussed earlier) or the reality of one is used to deny the reality of the other (as with Aristotle) is irrelevant to the main point.

From a nondualistic perspective, what is most interesting about Aristotle's passage is that it will allow us to see how Derrida takes for granted the very metaphysical determination of time that both he and Heidegger unsuccessfully attempt to question. Ironically, Derrida quotes passages that seem to point to the second and reverse movement, a move that Derrida himself does not see. One example:

> This Hegelian determination of time permits us to think the present, the very form of time, as eternity.... Eternity is another name of the presence of the present. Hegel also distinguishes this presence from the present as now.

Derrida introduces Heidegger's footnote by placing it in its context:

> The Note belongs to the next to last section of the last chapter ("Temporality and Within-Time-ness as the Source of the Ordinary Conception of Time"). Time is usually considered as that *in which* beings are produced. Within-time-ness, intratemporality, is taken to be the homogeneous medium in which the movement of daily existence is reckoned and organized. This homogeneity of the temporal medium becomes the effect of a "leveling off of primordial time."

For Heidegger, the ordinary (or "vulgar") understanding of time as a homogeneous sequence of succesive "nows," *within which* we move, is inauthentic. Authentic, primordial temporality "temporalizes itself *primarily* in terms of the future" because otherwise the full structure of the present is lost: "The 'now' is not pregnant with the 'not-yet-now,' but the Present arises from the future."

In accordance with this, Derrida, too, calls into question not some *conception* of the present but, simply, "the present":

> Has not the entire history of philosophy been authorized by the "extraordinary right" of the present?... How could one think Being and time otherwise than on the basis of the present, in the form of the present, to wit a certain *now in general* from which no experience, by definition, can

ever depart? The experience of thought and the thought of experience have never dealt with anything but presence.

Derrida, like Heidegger, is concerned to overthrow the privilege granted to the present, but merely relegating presence into a function of past and future différances misses the deeper point of Nāgārjuna's critique. What is taken for granted in "Ousia and Grammē" is nowhere obvious there, but it becomes explicit in a much-quoted passage from the earlier essay "Différance":

> *Différance* is what makes the movement of signification possible only if each element called "present," appearing on the stage of presence, is related to something other than itself, but is retaining the mark of the past element and is already letting itself be hollowed out by the mark of its relation to the future element,—the trace relating no less to what is called the future than to what is called the past, and constituting what is called the present by this very relation to what is not; that is, not even to a past or a future considered as a modified present. *In order for it* [the present element] *to be, an interval must separate it from what it is not;* but this interval that constitutes it in the present must also, with one and the same stroke, divide the present in itself, thus dividing, along with the present, everything that can be conceived on its basis, that is, every being,—in particular, for our metaphysical language, the substance or subject.[68]

An interval must separate the present from what it is not in order for the present to be itself. But how does an interval function to make the present "be itself"? It can only be by distinguishing one now-moment from another, which is not-yet or already-was. What remains "unthought" in this is the usual and apparently innocuous assumption that the present is a series of such now-moments successively falling away. Doesn't any such conception of the present presuppose another present that each now-moment successively "occupies"? For what else can determine that one now-moment is *now* present, while another is not-yet or already-was? But this begins to sound oddly familiar. What did Derrida say about Aristotle's aporia?

> Time is defined according to its relation to an elementary part, the now, which itself is affected—as if it were not already temporal—by a time which negates it in determining it as a past now or a future now. The *nun*, the element of time, in this sense is not in itself temporal.

Derrida's attack on "the privilege granted to the present" should not distract us from realizing that his own conception of time constitutes another version of the everyday and "commonsense" conception of time. Ironically, both are versions of the circular aporia that Derrida criticizes in Aristotle!

This shows us again that it is not only or primarily formal metaphysics that must be deconstructed but also the ontological commitments sedimented in the categories of ordinary language and thus in our everyday, taken-for-granted understanding of experience. Otherwise our analysis, although deconstructing the explicit transcendental signifieds of systematic metaphysics, also reinstates (*relever*) the implicit, concealed ones of common sense. Derrida concludes his essay by suggesting, "perhaps there is no 'vulgar concept of time.'"

> The concept of time, in all its aspects, belongs to metaphysics, and it names the domination of presence. . . . an *other* concept of time cannot be opposed to it, since time in general belongs to metaphysical conceptuality.

This is more true than Derrida realizes: because his own conception of time, like that of common sense, like *any* conception, is metaphysical. A view of time, and thus a metaphysics (whether articulated or latent), is unavoidable as long as the delusive bifurcation between time and things has not been eliminated through ending prapañca thought-construction. However much Derrida may "solicit" the history of Western metaphysics, this example suggests that his "de-sedimentation" finally functions to justify a commonsense view which does not become aware of its own metaphysical assumptions. But this does not recuperate Heidegger, for *Being and Time* just replaces one common-sense view (dispersion in the moment) with another (goal-oriented) in its claim that authentic temporality "temporalizes itself *primarily* in terms of the future." In a note, Heidegger refers to the traditional image of eternity as *nunc stans*, but he says that this is derived from the ordinary way of understanding time, hence it "does not need to be discussed in detail." So he never sees the possibility of "being-time" in Dōgen's sense.[69]

•

What must be the nature of philosophical discourse that wants to announce the inability of thought and language to re-present reality?

Simply trying to represent that inability is self-defeating and "risks sinking into the autism of the closure." But not to represent at all leaves us either with silence or with a ludic free play of discourse, neither of which in itself is of much help to anyone else. The Mahāyāna solution is to adopt a "double-strategy" which produces a theory about the delusiveness of thought and also dismisses that theory by turning it back against itself. The Prajñāpāramitā contains countless formulations of the following form: "X is X, but it is not really X." Nāgārjuna's more rigorous deconstruction is a classic example of how the second strategy devours the first: head swallows tail, and nothing remains— no nirvana, no Buddha, no teaching at all. One result of this was Zen, whose practice negated any theory, even though it was a particular theory that justified that practice and made it possible. Only meditative practice can actually end prapañca and open up a new mode of experience.

Derrida too has a double-strategy, but his works very differently. His first strategy—his theory of why theory cannot re-present—is différance and the grammatological critique of self-presence; the second is the "dissemination" that this opens up, allowing "the seminal adventure of the trace." Again, the first strategy justifies and requires the second. There is an inevitable tension within both double-strategies, but Nāgārjuna's deconstruction is finally resolved in a clôture whose silence reveals an alternative to the superimpositions of thought-construction. In contrast, the contradiction within Derrida's deconstruction, rather than devouring itself, becomes an ambivalent "bad infinity" in which what is unsatisfactory about each strategy is disguised by alternately having recourse to the other.

Derrida understands that all philosophy, including his, can only "reinscribe," but for him the sole solution is to disseminate wildly, in the hope of avoiding any fixation into a system that will subvert his insight.[70] One wonders what freedom can be found in such a need to keep ahead of yourself. In contrast, we have the nondualist example of a Zen master, who plays with language—moving in and out of it freely—because he is not caught in it. His laconic expressions emerge from / are one with an unrepresentable ground of serenity, and although they cannot directly point to this ground, there are ways to suggest it for someone else. In comparison with this freedom, to rejoice in being caught in a language that has lost its ability to repre-

sent any truth brings to mind Bernard Shaw's comment on the plea-
sures of an endless holiday: "a good working definition of hell."

The same criticism can be made from another direction. Our discussions of causation and time led to paradoxes: if there is only
causation, then everything is unconditioned; if there is only time, then
there is no time. Derrida's conception of interpretation and supplementation may be deconstructed into another version of the same
paradox: if there is no pure and simple "origin" but only the deferral
of supplements ("the trace is the origin of the origin"), then there is no
supplementation either, because each supplement becomes its own
origin. In one sense this indeed liberates interpretation, but in a more
fundamental sense it refutes the possibility of interpretation. If the
text disappears under its interpretation, as Nietzsche said, then so
must the interpretations. As before, Derrida begins a deconstruction
but does not complete it. By turning the deconstructed term back
against the deconstructing one, dissemination may be deconstructed
into "the end of prapañca."

Poststructuralism was inaugurated by the linguistic realization that
in the functioning of the sign it is not possible to distinguish the order
of the signified from the order of the signifier. The role of the signified
is played by a set of signifiers. "The ontological consequences for such
a view are immense. The rigid metaphysical distinction between
empirical signifier and ideal signified becomes obliterated in a general circulation of signs, i.e., in the play of signifiers."[71] The literary
consequences are equally immense. The sharp distinction between
the original text-in-itself and its interpretations becomes obliterated in
a "disseminating" discourse that can "decenter the text" by appending
its own commentary as "textual graft." "The hermeneutic project
which postulates a true sense of the text is disqualified.... Reading is
freed from the horizon of *the* meaning or truth of Being," and so on.[72]
This "liberation" of the signifier also establishes a democracy among
them; in the general circulation of signs, they become equal. By
eliminating the intentions of the author (another signified "origin"),
Nietzsche's cryptic remark on a scrap of paper—"I have forgotten my
umbrella"—becomes "no more or less significant than any other passage." "Dissemination... *affirms* (I do not say produces or controls)
endless substitution, it neither arrests nor controls play."[73]

Who likes to stop someone else from playing and having fun? But there is something odd here. Why does one interpret? The original motivation presupposed a search for truth, understood as a signified that language could come to signify. Supplementation and interpretation were necessary because previous attempts to signify this truth were inadequate: the old categories needed to be adjusted or, more radically, new paradigms substituted. But why supplement *now*, if we are no longer trying to discover some conceptual truth that can be signified? Derrida offers an alternative view of interpretation: there is not only "deciphering to end exile," but also "affirming play." If there is no pure origin then there is no exile to return from; but in what sense can such play still be called interpretation, if the chain of supplementation is not rooted in some to-be-signified?

The poststructuralist response is that this objection is based on a confusion. Because other signifiers function as signifieds for each other, there is always reference—not to some mythical origin, but to other supplements. There is only the interpretation of other interpretations. This is why deconstruction is necessarily parasitic: not believing that there is nonmetaphorical truth-in-itself to be signified, it needs as "host" another text that attempts to provide such a signified. Then it is not only the host that makes truth-claims, but also the deconstruction, which gains a derivative truth-signifying ability of its own from its critique of the proffered signified.

The irony in this is that Derrida, while believing that he has refuted any transcendental signified, has in effect reconstituted an equivalent in the truth-claim of the host text, because that is the only way his own deconstruction can make any truth-claim. The motivation behind all interpretation is the belief that there is some truth to be discovered in the text, or—what amounts to the same thing—that some truth is to be derived from criticizing it. As Śaṅkara argued, the demonstration of error presupposes some truth, and whether that truth is a transcendental signified or a function of other signifiers makes no difference. Derrida eliminates the presumed origin of supplementation without realizing that this origin was also the origin of all truth, and this second loss infects all subsequent supplements all the way back to him.[74]

This is not a difficulty for the nondualist, who realizes that his own deconstruction implies the refutation of all truth as well as error, including any truth that might be called his own. Any conceptual "truth" derived from deconstruction is no less deluding prapañca than error. He does not mind this—on the contrary, he is happy for others to realize the ultimate meaninglessness of his statements as long as they realize the meaninglessness of all others as well.

The purpose of this section has been to show that, although Derrida's différance constitutes a major philosophical insight, his employment of it does not develop its most radical implications. There is no transcendental signified that language can point to, because every signified is only a function of other signifiers; all we can ever have in language is a general circulation of signs. The importance of this can hardly be overemphasized, but from this sudden checkmate of all philosophy there are two directions to go. One is to make the reasonable but solipsistic assumption that, because language cannot point outside itself, we must remain forever inscribed in its sign-circulation. This may "liberate" the proliferations of dissemination, but such "free play" must be called nihilistic if it is motivated by having nothing else to do.[75]

The other possibility is that perhaps what metaphysics has sought in language can be found in some other way. Needless to say, contemporary Western philosophy is not sympathetic to such a possibility; but isn't that too a consequence of the frustration of its own attempt to point outside itself? *In language, such a possibility cannot be proven or disproven*, but the nondualist Asian traditions that are the topic of this work are predicated on that possibility. Of course, examples are not lacking in the West either.

■

Self, substance, time, causality, the path . . . What began as a question in the introduction became the "core doctrine" of part 1 and in this chapter has been elaborated into a full-fledged metaphysical system. Or has it? If I have constructed a metaphysical system, it is a very odd one. Certainly attempts have been made to describe various aspects of the nondual experience, but the main concern has been quite different. Like Mādhyamika—perhaps I should say, as a contemporary restatement of Mādhyamika—I have tried to deconstruct the metaphysics inherent in our commonsense understanding of the world. It has not been an attempt to extrapolate from our experience, but to undo it. The basis of this is the claim that our ordinary experience is not "self-evident," for what we uncritically accept as common sense is permeated with metaphysical beliefs.

I have characterized the metaphysics of common sense as based on dualistic opposition: in this chapter we have looked at the dualisms of self versus nonself, substance versus modes, immutability versus impermanence, freedom versus conditionality, spiritual ends versus means. In daily life the contradictions within these dualisms are usually apparent only in the various kinds of duḥkha they lead to. But the nondual experience cannot be expressed in these dualisms and that has prompted attempts to resolve the oppositions. The "great divide" of Indian philosophy has been over which term of each pair to assimilate into the other. More generally, traditional metaphysical systems try to absolutize one aspect of our experience and subsume the others. The alternative chosen here is to highlight these contradictions in order to demonstrate that our taken-for-granted world, based on the confrontation between an anxious self and its unsatisfying object, is thought-constructed. The testimony of Buddhism, Vedānta, and Taoism, among many others, is that what has been thought-constructed may be thought-deconstructed.

In support of the claim that Advaita Vedānta and Mahāyāna Buddhism are describing the same nondual experience, chapter 6 argued at some length that their mirror-image categories are phenomenologically equivalent. Because our linguistic categories and ordinary ways of thinking are inherently dualistic, it is natural to try to describe nondual experience by eliminating either the subject or the object. So we have seen how Vedānta makes absolute the unchanging Self-substance, Buddhism the impermanent world that is experienced—yet, I suggest, the experience they attempt to describe is the same.

But such a comparison needs to be supplemented. Advaita Vedānta and Mahāyāna Buddhism are by no means the only Asian philosophies that purport to explain the enlightenment experience. The Indian tradition, in particular, encompasses a very wide variety of systems—nondualistic, dualistic, pluralistic, idealistic, phenomenalistic, materialistic, and so on—which with very few exceptions accept the possibility of personal liberation and attempt to explain that experience within their own categories. Some reference has been made to Sāṅkhya and Yoga, but the argument will be strengthened if analysis of the nondual experience can be expanded in a way that will allow us to account for "non-nondualistic" systems as well. This chapter attempts to do that analogically. I invent a "nondual experience" subject to a wide variety of ontological interpretations; then we notice that these divergent and inconsistent interpretations correspond to the different category-systems of the major Indian metaphysical systems.

Let us begin by returning briefly to one of the topics discussed in chapter 6: the nature of time, more specifically the question whether change is real or not. The well-known simile of water and waves may be used to show how the same experience can be subject to different and inconsistent interpretations. Which is real, the water or the waves? Water here represents the empty (nirguṇa) Absolute, and waves are its phenomenal manifestation "in" time and space. In these terms, the prajñāpāramitā claim that "form is no other than emptiness" means that the waves never lose their intrinsic nature as water, since they have no self-nature of their own, being simply a form or manifestation of the water. Yet it is also true that "emptiness is no other than form": to emphasize only the immutability of water is to miss the fact that water never exists in an undifferentiated state but appears only as waves, currents, clouds, and so on. So what *really* exists? Many answers are possible; the important point is that the difference between these answers is not a disagreement about what is perceived but about how one chooses to interpret it. One might say that there is only one thing, the water, and that waves do not really exist, since they are just the forms that water takes. Conversely, one might claim that there are only waves, since there is no such thing as undifferentiated, formless water. The answer one gives also determines whether or not there is permanence. If there is only the water, and the waves are dismissed as mere forms, then there is no change; water remains the same despite any oscillations that may occur. But if there are only waves and if the immutability of water is rejected as a thought-construction, then there is only change and no permanence.

Of course, this analogy has its limitations. We can identify water because we can differentiate it from other things (earth, air), whereas the śūnyatā of Buddhism and the Nirguṇa Brahman of Vedānta cannot be characterized in any way. The simile would work better if water were so all-pervasive that we were completely *in* it and *of* it, and thus unable to distinguish it as an *it*. And this suggests another analogy—which may or may not be something more than an analogy.

Comparing the Absolute to empty space is a metaphor that naturally suggests itself when we want to describe "something" which in itself has no characteristics. In Buddhism, space has been used as a simile for the Yogācāra *pariniṣpanna*, the *dharmadhātu*, and the Pure Land; both the Chāndogya Upaniṣad and the Brahmasūtra declare that space (*ākāśa*) is Brahman, and Śaṅkara agrees, with the important clarification that it is not "material space" that is being referred to.[1] An important paper by the Japanese Zen scholar Hisamatsu lists the spacelike characteristics of "Oriental Nothingness": like empty space itself, it is all-pervasive, unobstructed and unobstructing, pure, formless, unattainable, stable, empty, unattached, impartial, voiding voidness (beyond the distinction between void and nonvoid) and without any distinction between inner and outer.[2] Thus space seems to be an excellent analogy for "empty nonduality." The analogy breaks down— that is, we are reminded it is only an analogy—in that our usual understanding of space conceives of it as an objectively existing medium that things are "in" and as having neither life nor awareness, whereas śūnyatā for Mahāyāna, Brahman for Vedānta and the Tao for Taoism are the ground of everything including all consciousness. Of course, this is nothing other than the two sides of our familiar duality, the commonsense but problematical bifurcation between object (in this case, "material" space) and subject.

But let us use our imagination to eliminate this duality, by supposing that space *is* conscious. Let us suppose that as a result of some experience I realize that "my" consciousness is not mine at all but is an aspect of space itself. This follows a Vedāntic analogy which compares liberation to realizing that the space inside a sealed pot is not and never has been separate from the infinite space around it.[3] However, in one sense this empty Mind-space (as I rather inelegantly refer to it) is not completely void: there are various things in the Mind-space, which makes the term "in" problematical. This infinite Mind-space encompasses all things, so rather than speaking of things as being "in" space, it seems more appropriate to say that they *are* space—that is, they are what Mind-space is "doing" at that particular time in that particular place. As Śaṅkara would say, consciousness is now not "of" something but "as" something; all phenomena are therefore the various ways this empty Mind-space manifests itself. Chapters 2–4 may be understood as explicating what this "consciousness-as" means in the cases of perceiving, acting, and thinking. Although in itself this Mind-space has no attributes (Hisamatsu's list of characteristics is really a series of *neti, neti*: "it is not limited, it is not obstructed, it is not defiled, it is not attainable..."), a multitude of phenomena arise within it and of it in this fashion. Yet, paradoxically, the Mind-space remains unchanging and unchanged by these phenomena, for their appearing and disappearing do not disturb the peaceful Mind-ground "from" which they arise. These phenomena, of course, are not objects in the usual sense: they have no "self-nature," for they are not material and do not persist in themselves but are better described as processes in constant transformation.

Last but not least, this experience of Mind-space seems to reveal "The Way Things Really Are." But if "I," having had this experience, were to be asked what I had realized, how would I answer? The point of this chapter is that this "Mind-space experience" lends itself to very different and contradictory ontological descriptions. In the following section I imagine some of the responses that might occur during a conversation among people who have had this experience and who have drawn metaphysical conclusions from it.

Speaker A: "There are two very different substances, both of which are uncaused and eternal and omnipresent, although they do not seem to interfere with each other or even interact. One is immutable and attributeless consciousness (Mind-space), which, I now realize, is what my mind has always been. The other is more difficult to characterize. I suppose we can call it an 'energy-stuff,' or perhaps a fine 'matter-stuff,' except for the fact that it is dynamic, constantly transforming, taking different forms which do not actually change its nature since these are just the forms that it temporarily assumes. The difference between these two substances is now clear to me. The problem before was these two were confused because 'my' consciousness tended to fixate on various forms of the energy-stuff and so was not aware of its own true attributeless nature. But now I realize that immutable consciousness and the constantly changing energy-stuff are quite different from each other and always have been."

This is largely the view of Sāṅkhya and Yoga, whose dualistic metaphysics distinguishes puruṣa (pure consciousness) from prakṛti (all phenomena, which means anything that can be experienc*ed*). However, this characterization of the Sāṅkhya position is not quite satisfactory, for two reasons. First, the analogy had to be constructed in such a way as to falsify the Sāṅkhya claim that prakṛti is an independent substance. In order to allow for Sāṅkhya dualism, the relationship between Mind-space and phenomena would need to be left undetermined and ambiguous, but in practice it is impossible for any description to avoid a bias toward either the dependence or the independence of these two; here too, all description is also interpretation. So a nondual prejudice has been built into the analogy: phenomena and Mind-space do not simply coexist, but phenomena are a manifestation of Mind-space. This is to presuppose that the dualism of the Sāṅkhya-Yoga interpretation is erroneous, but that does pinpoint the problem with this system, which in chapter 5 was shown to be the insurmountable contradiction of how to relate two completely independent substances.

The second problem with my characterization is that it assumes there is only one Mind-space, whereas Sāṅkhya-Yoga postulates an apparently infinite number of omnipresent yet discrete puruṣas. Again, this is an inevitable deficiency of the analogy, which must commit itself to viewing separate minds as merely different aspects or facets of an all-encompassing Mind. But, here again, this is a place where the Sāṅkhya-Yoga interpretation runs into difficulties, for how can all these omnipresent puruṣas occupy the same space (as it were) and have no distinguishing characteristics (for the "attributelessness" of each is exactly the same as every other), yet be characterized as distinct and different? The main argument for a plurality of puruṣas is that if it were otherwise, when one person became enlightened all would have to become enlightened. But there are other ways around that difficulty—such as the nondualist notion that we are all *intrinsically* already enlightened.

Despite these problems, I have included the Sāṅkhya-Yoga view because it too is a possible interpretation of the experience given in the analogy: the duality-in-nonduality of phenomena "in" Mind-space. Its response is to distinguish both as independent substances, which is a plausible reaction, however unsatisfactory it finally proves to be.

Speaker B: "Speaker A is mistaken. Only one thing is real: this immutable, attributeless Mind-space, which is what I and everything else really are. The constantly changing forms that arise within and from this Mind-space are simply illusions which delude us about what really is; they have no substance or reality of their own, for they are only phenomena that represent nothing but merely manifest the Mind-space. Before, 'I' was clinging to these forms and reified them into things that seemed to exist objectively—something speaker A still seems to be doing—but now I realize that is an error. There is only this Mind-space, which is birthless and deathless and has no characteristics of its own."

This is obviously the view of Advaita Vedānta. Unlike the previous speaker, it emphasizes the dependence of phenomenal forms upon the Mind-space (Brahman), to the extent that it denies phenomena any reality at all. But from one perspective the similarity between these views is greater than their difference, for they both reveal a strong bias toward Mind-space and against the phenomenal. Vedānta shows this by devaluing phenomena into mere appearances, but Sāṅkhya may be said to go even further: although prakṛti is granted the status of an independent substance, there is an insurmountable gap between it and puruṣa, which is what "I" really am. Both views reflect a general Indian prejudice against phenomena, which will be discussed later in this chapter.

Speaker C: "What the others have called 'Mind-space' cannot really be said to exist, because it has no characteristics at all. It is so 'empty' that it is literally *nothing*, and how can nothing be 'real'? What 'I' have realized is that there is no 'I' and never was. All that does exist are those constantly transforming phenomena—or rather the 'attribute-elements' of which things are composed and which are now experienced clearly. I agree with the others that there are no self-existing physical objects, for these attributes do not depend upon or represent any material substance; but these constantly changing attributes are themselves real. It is quite right to say that a cluster of red patches does not really represent a red flower, but those patches do exist—how could that be denied? 'I' am not aware of the red patch, for there is no 'I' to be aware of it, but the patches themselves do appear and disappear and seem to interact with each other. However, it doesn't matter anymore what attributes arise or pass away, now that the sense of 'I' has evaporated and there is the deep peace of emptiness in its place."

This turns the previous view upside-down: early Buddhism denies reality to the Mind-space but grants it to phenomena—not to objects, of course, but to the dharmas that compose them. In terms of the analogy, such a denial of the Mind-space may seem perverse, but this is also due to the fact that the description given at the beginning is an interpretation, although one that may be more easily corrected in this case. In chapter 6, I argued that a consciousness which pervades everywhere and encompasses everything might just as well be characterized as an emptiness; if there were only one thing, with nothing outside it, then there would not be even one thing, but nothing. The difference in description is due to whether it is more phenomenological ("nothing") or from the fictional "outside" ("One"), but—what is important for our analogy—there need be no difference in the experience itself.

In contrast to the first two views discussed, this third one is not so prejudiced against phenomena—although nirvana is still characterized as a peaceful, unchanging condition detached from the incessant interaction of the composite dharmas. There is an important similarity between this view and that of Sāṅkhya-Yoga (discussed by speaker A). Prakṛti too is composite, a plurality of three *guṇas* which interact to compose the *tanmātras* which then interact to compose the *mahābhūtas* which also interact to compose "material objects" and mental phenomena. Both views agree that objects as we normally understand them are mental constructions (according to Sāṅkhya, under the catalytic influence of puruṣa) from a plurality of distinct "bits" of experience. The path of liberation in Yoga seems to involve reversing this evolutionary process in order to experience the tanmātras and eventually the guṇas as distinct from each other and, finally, as distinct from the puruṣa. Similarly, the *vipassanā* meditations of early Buddhism teach one to distinguish the various skandhas and not to identify with any of them. It is significant that Advaita Vedānta accepts the guṇa theory of Sāṅkhya and Mahāyāna accepts the dharma theory of early Buddhism, but in both cases these elements are relegated to a subordinate position and denied any reality of their own: for Vedānta the guṇas are ultimately māyā, and for Mahāyāna the dharmas are śūnya.

Speaker D: "I agree with speaker C that speakers A and B, by referring to mind-space, have made something out of nothing—that is, they have hypostatized emptiness into a substance. Yet I must also agree with speaker B that phenomena are not real, for they too are empty. Speaker B says they have no self-nature because they are only appearances of Mind-space, but I say they have no self-nature of their own because they are mere appearances that refer to *nothing*. The various attribute-elements arise from nowhere, interact with each other, and disappear—how can such interdependent and momentary phenomena be said to be real? Except for speaker A, we all agree that these appearances do not represent any material substratum, but speaker C still tries to make these attributes into little substances of their own. Emptiness is their source and ground; but to say that emptiness is their ground means that they have no ground. Because everything is groundless, nothing can be said to exist or be real.

"However, merely to say that everything is empty would be one-sided. There is not the voidness of a completely empty space, for myriad phenomena do arise. To denigrate and dismiss these phenomena as illusion only is 'clinging to emptiness' (or 'clinging to Mind-space'). Perhaps this is a reaction to the earlier and opposite problem of attachment to form, but one should cling to nothing. Phenomena are illusory only if we are deluded into taking them as self-existing; now that we have realized they are empty appearances, we should accept them for what they are and be able to play with them freely. The dance may have no meaning, but there is still the empty dance."

The Mahāyāna standpoint is distinguished into two viewpoints. Speaker D may be said to reflect the "relative" (saṁvṛti) truth, and speaker F presents (insofar as it can be presented conceptually) the "absolute" or "highest" (paramārthika) standpoint. Speaker D agrees with early Buddhism that the Mind-space cannot be called real and agrees with Vedānta that phenomena (dharmas) cannot be said to exist either, since they are interdependent and thus relative. However, because the dualistic category of nonexistence is dependent upon the category of existence (and hence perishes with it) and because the interdependence of phenomena means that they have causal effects, phenomena should not be said *not* to exist either.

In Mahāyāna we generally see more of a balance in perspective between empty Mind-space and phenomena, for neither is negated in favor of the other. The Prajñāpāramitā says that form is not only emptiness, for emptiness is also form. However, to say that emptiness manifests as form is not quite right; as the Heart Sutra continues, form is *not other than* emptiness, and emptiness is *not other than* form—that is, one must be careful not to reify emptiness into something that phenomena arise *from*, as Śaṅkara and our Mind-space analogy do. A more accurate phenomenological description is that *empty phenomena appear and disappear*. That brings us to the familiar Mahāyāna equation between saṁsāra and nirvana: nirvana is not something other than saṁsāra; it simply involves realizing the emptiness of the samsaric field. This implies a different attitude towards change, as we saw in chapter 6. The Vedāntic Brahman transcends time, the early Buddhist dharmas are impermanent, but the Mahāyāna view is more paradoxical: changing yet unchanging, since "things" change although their nature as empty does not. It is a more dynamic conception than that of Vedānta, which is prejudiced against phenomena, and conceives of the Absolute as static. Because "emptiness is not other than form," Mahāyāna tends to understand the Dharmakāya as more active and creative. In the history of Zen Buddhism for example, certain masters—such as Te-shan Hsüan-chien (A.D. 782–865)—have been criticized for being "too empty"—that is, emphasizing the emptiness of form too much, and not realizing sufficiently the form of emptiness. Śaṅkara would not have considered this an error, but the Five Degrees of Tōzan (Tung-shan Liang-chieh, A.D. 807–69) and the Ten Oxherding Pictures of Kakuan Shien (Kuo-an Shih-yuan, 12th c.)—which codify the various stages of Zen enlightenment—both depict such enlightenment as incomplete. The deep satori of the eighth oxherding picture—rendered as a simple circle representing empty unity—is followed by "Returning to the Source," which depicts a flowering branch representing particularity. Emptiness at this stage is found *in* the phenomena of the everyday world. According to Kakuan's commentary, one "observes the waxing and waning of life in the world while abiding unassertively in a state of unshakable serenity. This [waxing and waning] is not a phantom or illusion [but a manifestation of the Source]."[4] In the Five degrees, Tōzan represents the stage of empty unity by the third degree, *sho-chu-rai* (Ch., *cheng chung lai*), "the One alone" or "enlightenment emerging from universality"; the fourth degree, *hen-shu-chi* (*p'ien chung chih*), is "the Many alone" or "enlightenment arriving from particularity."[5] (In the fifth and highest degree, form and emptiness, the many and the One, interpenetrate so completely that there is awareness of neither.) The syncretic systems of T'ien-T'ai and Hua Yen make the same distinction.

This contrast between Brahman and śūnyatā also applies to both Hindu and Buddhist tantra:

Both the Hindu and the Buddhist Tantras have another fundamental
feature common to them [the first feature was emphasis on the human
body as the means of liberation]—a theological principle of duality in
nonduality. Both the schools hold that the ultimate nondual reality
possesses two aspects in its fundamental nature—the negative (*nivṛtti*)
and the positive (*pravṛtti*), the static and the dynamic—and these two
aspects of the reality are represented in Hinduism by *Śiva* and *Śakti* and
in Buddhism by *Prajñā* and *Upāya* (or *śūnyatā* and *karuṇā*).... The
ultimate goal of both the schools is the perfect state of union—union
between the two aspects of the reality and the realization of the nondual nature of the self and the not-self.   (S. B. Dasgupta)[6]

Speaker E: "I agree with speaker D, but he does not go far enough. He
too is still one-sided. We have realized that the world is nondual, but
we should not be so infatuated with this new way of experiencing that
we become prejudiced against the more usual dualistic mode. That
too would be an overreaction against duality—and in another sense
still dualistic. I grant that nonduality is revelatory of the truth in a way
that duality is not, but this does not imply that we should 'cling to
nonduality.' Subject–object duality and the plurality of phenomena
are also aspects of the world, and we should not dualistically reject
one mode in favor of the other. Let us accept that there are these two
ways of experiencing, without prejudice against either. Our aim
should be to understand fully the relation between these two modes
in order to be able to experience both."

A view such as this is consistent with my explication of the first
chapter of the *Tao Tê Ching* (in the second section of chapter 3). Lines
1, 3, 5, and 7 of that first chapter were seen to describe the nameless
Tao, the source of heaven and earth, which is the world apprehended
nondualistically when there are no intentions and therefore no self;
in contrast, lines 2, 4, 6, and 8 refer to the dualistic everyday world
experienced as a collection of interacting objects, due to the superimpositions of language and intention. The spiritual path leads us from
the delusions of the latter to an appreciation of the former, but
dualistic experience is not thereby rejected:

Therefore when you give up intentions you will see the wonder [of Tao]
When you have intentions you will see the forms

The experience of nonduality, with its apparent revelation of "The Way Things Really Are," should not lead to the opposite extreme of completely rejecting duality. From this point of view, we end up with two modes of experience, neither of which should be permanently negated for the sake of the other. In Zen Buddhism, for example, there is a return to the world of "delusion," if only to fulfill one's Bodhisattva Vow to save all beings, for in the nondual experience itself there are no sentient beings to be saved and nothing at all that needs to be done.

This implies an ultimate acceptance of the phenomenal world of plurality that did not occur in India, even though one might expect this as a further development of the Mahāyāna or tantric viewpoint. That is why Mahāyāna took root in China whereas Vedānta and early Buddhism could not, and it is part of a more general contrast between India and China that has had deep philosophical implications. The Indian preference for abstract, negative universals and transtemporal otherworldliness is at the opposite end of the spectrum from Chinese (and Japanese) pragmatism, which favors particular phenomena and the pattern of their transformation. [7] For example, the Chinese love of nature and their desire to unite with it (as expressed in poetry and painting) must be contrasted with Indian alienation from nature, which, given Indian geography and climate, was perhaps inevitable. Consider too the contrast between the Indian ideal of ascetic renunciation and the ragged, jovial, chubby, barefoot, and perhaps inebriated Han-shan, for whom "ordinary mind is the Tao"; the tenth and final oxherding picture depicts such a Bodhisattva "Entering the Market Place with Helping Hands." In terms of our analogy, the difference is between a general Hindu bias toward the empty Mind-space and a general Chinese bias for nondual phenomena, with Mahāyāna Buddhism somewhere between these two, which may be why it was the main bridge between these two cultures.

Speaker F: "I disagree with all the previous speakers, for this experience does not enable us to draw any ontological conclusions. Instead, this experience demonstrates what is misguided about all such ontological questions, by revealing that 'place' where all such questions and concepts have disappeared—where there are no solutions because there are no problems. From this experience we should not deduce that anything exists or not, is real or not. We cannot characterize our experience in any way, not even as nondual, for to label the experience is to represent it, whereas the experience is what occurs when we are not re-presenting. Yet re-presenting is what philosophy always does and cannot help doing. If what is important is to have this experience, we should rather be concerned to demonstrate the inadequacy of philosophy, both as a description of this experience and as a method for attaining it."

This represents what might be called the "highest" (paramārthika) standpoint of Mahāyāna, that one should not make ontological or any other philosophical inferences from the experience. In particular, it expresses the approach of Nāgārjuna, who confined himself to refuting all possible philosophical accounts of reality. This reflects the "perspective" of the experience itself, which denies the adequacy of any intellectual perspective on "it." All philosophical views are attempts to grasp the nature of this nondual experience from the conceptual and hence dualistic standpoint, therefore by definition all such perspectives must be unsatisfactory. In answer to the question about what is real, the "highest" response is to remain silent, like the Buddha. This does not evade the question but rather manifests the answer in a different dimension.

Speaker G: "All the previous speakers, including even speaker F, have assumed something that may be challenged: that this experience reveals 'The Way Things Really Are.' But we may accept the importance of the experience without taking it as revelatory in that sense. What I, at least, experienced was a miracle: God manifested Himself to me and then we merged together into what Eckhart has described as the blissful voidness of the Godhead. But this was only a temporary irruption of God into the natural order, His material creation. Later—how can I say when?—He withdrew to end the experience, leaving the physical world to operate as usual according to the scientific laws that He has established to order it. To presuppose that this brief union of my soul with Him reveals something about the nature of this world overlooks another possibility: that it was the experience of something 'Other' which completely transcends the world."

This last speaker is included to suggest that the Mind-space experience might even account for the theistic mystical experience—particularly in its "complete" form of union with God. This issue is discussed more fully at the end of the next chapter, where an attempt is made to account for the curious parallel between the Saguṇa and Nirguṇa Brahmans of Śaṅkara and the Deus and Deitas of Eckhart: there I suggest that Saguṇa Brahman and Eckhart's Deus both refer to the awareness of a consciousness pervading everywhere and encompassing everything (such as the Mind-space), while Nirguṇa Brahman / Deitas is the deeper experience of merging with that consciousness and realizing that it is "my" consciousness, whereupon even the last trace of duality disappears. However, other theists might disagree with Eckhart that the nondual experience is at all revelatory of "The True Nature of Things." Instead, they could see it as a miraculous event in which God temporarily interferes with the natural order in order to manifest Himself through it. This reminds us of the importance of cultural conditioning upon our expectations. If one had been raised in a culture which interpreted the nondual experience in this way, one would probably expect a temporary, blissful union without any such philosophical implications and might well draw no ontological conclusions afterward, except to confirm one's belief in a God who is yet understood to exist (normally) apart from the phenomenal world, His creation. The presupposition of one's own essential sinfulness—for example, "original sin" as opposed to God, who is infinitely perfect, might keep one from making any inferences about one's true nature as nondual. We should not confuse this position with the paramārthika viewpoint of Mahāyāna. For Mahāyāna, the experience indeed reveals the true nature of reality, but this is such that language cannot express it; no philosophical categories can truly grasp it. We must also be careful not to assume from this alone that the theist is wrong or misses something that the nondualist does not, for both interpretations are culturally conditioned: the nondualist too is conditioned to expect an ontologically revelatory experience—although the rest of this work can be seen as an attempt to support the nondualist's conclusions by developing and systematizing his claims.

∎

This possible theistic response is our final reaction to the Mind-space experience. Other intelligent responses may be possible, but there is reason to believe that the reactions considered above include all the philosophically important ones. This may be seen by tabulating these various responses according to their ontological views about the status of the Mind-space and of phenomena, respectively:

	Is Mind-space Real?	Are Phenomena Real?
A. Sāṅkhya-Yoga	yes	yes
B. Advaita Vedānta	yes	no
C. Early Buddhism	no	yes
D. Mahāyāna Buddhism (saṁvṛti-satya)	no	no
E. Taoism (Tao Tê Ching, chap. 1)	duality and nonduality both "Real"	
F. Mahāyāna Buddhism (paramārtha-satya)	revelatory, but no ontological claims (silence)	
G. Theism	not ontologically revelatory	

Arranged in this way, the "logic" of the responses is quite striking. The first four reactions cover the four "primary" possibilities which involve an unequivocal yes or no answer. The Mahāyāna "highest" view negates the ontological question by refusing to respond to it at all. What has been termed the Taoist view (E) urges that we not "cling" to the Mind-space experience to the exclusion of our more usual dualistic experience. A final possibility is to deny that the experience reveals the true nature of things.

Examined in this light, we are able to notice three important things. First, responses A though F exhaust *all* the major possibilities. It is difficult to conceive of any other responses that could not be classified into one of these main categories. Second, it can hardly be a coincidence that there is such a perfect correspondence between all these various possible ontological decisions and the categories of all the major metaphysical systems. This seems to imply the third and most important point, that all these metaphysical conclusions may indeed be different interpretations of the same nondual experience. This elaborates on the comparison between Buddhism and Vedānta in the previous chapter and further defends our "core doctrine" of nonduality from the criticism that a difference in ontology must reflect a difference in experience. It also raises a question. If the Mind-space analogy works so well to account for all these varied philosophical reactions, is it *more* than an analogy? At the end of chapter 2, it was noted that we can "think" nonduality only in one of two inconsistent and unsatisfactory ways: either we conceive of consciousness as pan-psychically residing "in" material objects, or we idealistically reduce the object to an image "in" the mind. The Mind-space analogy is an instance of the former, and the same qualifications apply. We must not overvalue the analogy, which cannot give us any true taste of the nondual experience; yet, just as obviously, there must be something to it.

One could take issue with the conclusions of the above paragraph by arguing that any ontological claims made on the basis of such an experience are obviously questionable. If the nondual experience is subject to such a diversity of possible interpretations, how can it be said to "enlighten" us regarding "The Way Things Really Are"? The consequence is rather that the experience is thereby devalued. However, we can turn this criticism upside-down and maintain that the consequence is to devalue not the nondual experience itself, but the ontological question and metaphysics generally. This experience may be valid as revelatory, but the revelation is one that cannot be suc-cessfully represented because it introduces us into an altogether different dimension, ungraspable by language. This of course is consistent with the "highest" view of the various nondual philos-ophers themselves, who generally acknowledge that what is most important is not the philosophical conclusions derived from the ex-perience but the experience itself.

But such a sweeping condemnation of philosophy would be an ungenerous conclusion. In *Sense and Sensibilia* J. L. Austin pointed out that *real* is one of those words whose negative use "wears the trousers"; a definite sense attaches to an assertion that something is real only in relation to a specific way it might *not* be real. Nietzsche has shown how ethical motivations often stand disguised behind meta-physical conclusions. We may apply these remarks here by asking: what have all these systems wanted to label as "unreal," and what ethical motives are latent in their attempt? In this way we may recover an appreciation for what they have tried to do. In our preoccupation with the differences among these systems, we should not overlook their even more basic agreement. We can realize the main concern of all these philosophical systems has been to devalue the same thing. Even those systems that, in our tabulation, accept the reality of phenomena (i.e., Sāṅkhya-Yoga, early Buddhism) do not uncritically accept the commonsense reality of the pluralistic world. The point is that, on the basis of what I argue is a nondual experience, all of these systems challenge the reality of the objective world that we naively discover ourselves to be "in" and otherwise take for granted: a collection of material objects (including me), each supposedly discrete yet interacting causally in space and time. However inadequate their own ontological categories may finally prove to be, that should not keep us from valuing their critique of those "commonsense" dualities which not only delude us but keep us from even becoming aware that we are deluded.

In our discussions of the metaphysical differences between India and China, we saw that the positive ontological claims of the various systems can be placed on a spectrum that ranges from exclusive preference for the empty Mind-space, on the one extreme, and preference for nondual phenomena, on the other. Applying Nietzsche's dictum, we can conclude that some nondualist systems are more world-negating and others are more world-affirming. If we want to evaluate this difference, we should not forget a final point: each of these Asian systems has not only based its categories upon the liberation experience, but also traditionally included some kind of meditative praxis aimed at recreating that experience. This means that any negative effect from clinging to ontological claims can be offset by this built-in, self-correcting, and even "self-transcending" mechanism. In this way they ensure that we will go beyond all concepts, including their own.

$\rm A$ final test for our model of nonduality uses it to interpret one of the most important and popular Advaitic texts. We are particularly concerned to see the implications of nonduality for the two main philosophical problems that the *Bhagavad-gītā* raises: the interrelations among the various *yogas* or *margas* ("paths to God"), and the relationship between personal God and impersonal Absolute. Neither issue is unique to the *Gītā*, but it does raise both in a particularly clear and inescapable way. Its widespread appeal must have been due to its apparent success in synthesizing what were previously perceived as distinct yogas and goals, but is this synthesis philosophically successful as well? Is the *Gītā* truly synthetic or merely syncretic? The question about the relation between God and Absolute is a problem that recurs in later Advaita, within other traditions such as Eckhart's Christian mysticism, and more recently in the dialogue between Semitic and Asian religions. What may be unique to the *Gītā*, and what does not seem to have been noticed, is that it demonstrates a connection between these two apparently discrete problems. The second section of this chapter suggests that understanding how the yogas work may give us some insight into the relation between theism and nondualism.

THE NONDUAL YOGAS

Different commentators have extracted different numbers of yogas from the *Gītā*, but there seem to be three major ones: *jñāna*, the path of knowledge; *bhakti*, the path of devotion; and *karma*, the path of action or service.[1] Which is the most important one? That centuries of textual and philosophical analysis—of what is, after all, a popular work—have not led to agreement about their priority implies that the question is misconceived. Later I argue for the unity of the yogas and show that ultimately they must be practiced together, but my first task is to demonstrate how and why the yogas work. All commentators try to explain what the various yogas involve—for example, pointing out that karma-yoga is not renunciation *of* action (*naiṣkarmya*) but *in* action (*niṣkāma karma*). But by themselves such explanations are incomplete because they take the yogas out of the context that makes them meaningful. My intention is to demonstate with greater precision the relations among the yogas, the respective problematic aspects of our experience that each works on, and the transformed mode of experience that they lead to.

To do this requires a less ambiguous metaphysical infrastructure than we find in the *Gītā*, which incorporates several sets of philosophical categories usually understood to be inconsistent—most notably, Sāṅkhya and Vedānta. Our nondualistic approach is obviously incompatible with the radical dualism of Sāṅkhya, whose puruṣa and prakṛti play an important role in the *Gītā*. Following the critique of Sāṅkhya made in chapter 5, which concluded that its dualism fails, I reinterpret Sāṅkhya categories and presuppose that the goal of the spiritual path is a nondual way of experiencing the world in which there is no distinction between subject and object. Then the corresponding problem is dualism: experience, apparent or real, in which there is a polarity between my consciousness and the external world. What light does this shed upon the *Gītā*? We may see the three traditional yogas as types of spiritual practice that work to transform different dualistic modes of experience into their respective nondual mode. Jñāna-yoga transforms or "purifies" the dualistic intellect, karma-yoga the dualistic physical body, and bhakti-yoga dualistic emotions. Jñāna changes the way I perceive the world, karma changes the way I live and act in the world, and bhakti changes the "affective tone" of my being-in-the-world—all from a dualistic to a nondualistic mode.

The Problems

There is an unmistakable parallel between these yogas and the "three roots of evil" or Buddhism's "three unwholesome roots": delusion and ignorance (*moha*), desire and greed (*rāga* or *lobha*), hatred and resentment (*dveṣa* or *dosa*). From the nondualist perspective, these "three evils" are what happen to the three above-mentioned nondual aspects of our being when they have been warped into a dualistic mode. Each aspect is liable to a particular type of distortion.

Moha is easily explicable as the mind deluded into a dualistic understanding of the world, the root delusion being that "my" mind is a consciousness separate from the pluralistic objective world. The *Gītā* states that this is because awareness has become fixated upon sense-objects. How this fixation began is not explained; as in Buddhism and Advaita no "first cause" is postulated. But we are told that dwelling on such objects produces attachment, which in turn causes desire, anger, bewilderment, loss of memory, and the destruction of intelligence. "When the mind runs after the roving senses, it carries away the understanding, even as a wind carries away a ship on the waters" (II 62–67).[2] Once I identify with "my body," I become preoccupied with the relation between that object and all the other objects in the world. Since my body is naturally the "gravitational center" of my world, I try to rearrange those objects into an alignment most satisfactory to its desires. Thus the implicit perspective used to evalute each situation is dualistic: what do I want out of this? What can *I* get from these *objects*?

It is hardly necessary to point out that this also involves a distortion of emotional life, the "affective tone" of my being. To live in the world in such a self-centered way, as only one among a plurality of beings, means that I relate to others as means to my ends or as competitors for those same ends. To the degree that I have a sense of self, I will try to "use" others—if not directly to satisfy physical desires, then less directly to satisfy more subtle psychological ones, such as the need to be loved or respected. All of these desires feed the insatiable sense of self. When other objects resist such manipulation, I feel frustrated and resentful. In contrast with compassion and unattached love, in which we are more *at one* with that which is loved, the various "negative emotions" reinforce the dualistic sense of separation from others. I become more isolated in what may become the hell of my own private consciousness.

The Paths

This description of the "three roots of evil" shows how they reinforce each other. Yet we know, for example, that some people are more emotional than intellectual (to the extent of "thinking with their feelings," we sometimes say), and some vice versa. This suggests that the above problems afflict different people in different proportions, which in turn suggests that the "primary path" for each person may vary. For the emotional person it would be bhakti, for the intellectual jñāna, and for the man of action karma-yoga. But the above description, in its emphasis on the interdependence of these three aspects of being, also implies that the three yogas cannot be separated—a point to which we shall return.

Jñāna-yoga is described in the *Gītā* as the development of equanimity. The true yoga is that which brings about spiritual impartiality (*samatvam*) (II 48, VI 19–26). The liberated person is not interested in achieving or not achieving anything. Gold and pebbles, praise and blame, friends and foes, saints and sinners are all the same (XIV 24–25, VI 9). This is because one sees God in all beings and knows the indestructible in all that is destructible. Krishna pervades everything. "I am the taste in the waters ... the lights in the moon and the sun ... the sound in ether and manhood in men. I am the pure fragrance in earth and brightness in fire"—to quote part of a beautiful passage (VII 8–10). Whatsoever being there is has sprung from a fragment of Krishna's splendor (X 41). So the sage regards all things with an equal eye (XIII 28).

This equanimity is not due merely to cultivating an attitude of indifference to the world—which would be incompatible with both bhakti- and karma-yoga—but is the result of a transformed way of perceiving the world. For this to occur, one must "draw away the senses from the objects of sense on every side as a tortoise draws in his limbs into his shell" (II 58). Through this, attachment to the various sense-objects can be attenuated. In the more systematic Yoga system of Patañjali, a "devolution" of prakṛti then occurs, purifying the buddhi-mind until it is able to realize its distinction from the omnipresent and unchanging puruṣa.

As we have seen, meditation is also important for the nondualistic paths of Advaita and Buddhism, where it also leads to equanimity from realizing an omnipresent and immutable "ground": Brahman or the emptiness (śūnyatā) of all form. But in both these cases, unlike in Sāṅkhya-Yoga, no duality is accepted between this immutable ground and changing phenomena—despite the obvious contradiction this seems to involve.[3] It is significant that we find this same paradox in the *Gītā*, where the omnipresence and immutability of Krishna—who is our true self—are similarly emphasized. Krishna claims, for example, that His lower nature is always engaged in work while His higher nature is incapable of work (III 22, IV 13)—in other words, that He is both immanent in the world and transcendentally indifferent to it (IX 4, 5). I have already argued that there is a phenomenological agreement beneath these various descriptions. One experiences an omnipresent "something"—not really a "thing", since it has no characteristics in itself (nirguṇa)—which does not change at all although its phenomenal manifestations do, and this realization subrates phenomena so completely that all differences among them become insignificant in comparison. The most important point is that this "something" is realized to be *me*: my own mind, birthless, deathless, and blissful. That is why "he who knows the supreme Brahman truly becomes Brahman." Jñāna-yoga—which stops the mind from seizing on sense-objects and reifying the sense of self—is able to lead to such an experience because our consciousness has always been nondual (Sāṅkhya equivalent: the puruṣa has never been in bondage), so that only the delusion of duality needs to be dispelled. The equanimity of the sage is due to the nondual experience of such an immutable ground, however variously characterized as puruṣa or Brahman or śūnyatā.

To realize that "my" actions are also empty, and to develop this way of acting in the world, is the goal of *karma-yoga*.

Perhaps in response to Buddhism, the *Gītā* transformed karma-yoga from the "orthopraxy" of early Vedic ritualism into a new way of doing all work: as a sacrifice (*yājña*) to Krishna. "Let not the fruits of action be thy motive, neither let there be any attachment to inaction" (II 47). This strikes at the heart of the self-centered dualistic attitude, which is preoccupied with obtaining such fruits and therefore with manipulating situations to one's own advantage. Instead, we are told to "act with a view to the maintenance of the world" (III 9). Selfish habits are to be worn down by directing one's physical activity into doing one's duty (*dharma-yoga*) instead of trying to satisfy incessant cravings.

But, if the argument of chapter 3 is valid, there is much more to karma-yoga than this usual description. Our discussion of jñāna above followed chapter 2 in giving a nondualist interpretation of perception. Śaṅkara's critique of karma-yoga (e.g., in his *Gītā* commentary on III.1) contrasts the nonduality of such jñāna, which is free from all distinctions and from any need to act, to karma-yoga, which presupposes plurality and assumes that the ātman is an agent. He fails to consider whether there might also be nondual action with non-differentiation between agent and act. Because such action is empty it is also nonaction, which is how Krishna describes the acts of both himself and "the man of understanding":

> He who in action sees inaction and action in inaction—he is wise among men, he is a *yogin*, and he has accomplished all his work.
> Having abandoned attachment to the fruit of works, ever content, without any kind of dependence, he does nothing though he is ever engaged in work.   (IV 18, 20)

As we saw in chapter 3, the sense of duality occurs because action is done with reference to the *fruit* of action; intentions "superimpose" thoughts upon actions. Without such superimposition, the "true nature" of action becomes manifest: "I" do not perform an act, but it arises spontaneously from the empty, immutable ground described earlier. In the vocabulary of the *Gītā*, although the higher nature of Krishna is eternally inactive, His other nature is the source of all action that occurs in the world.[4]

The *Gītā* does not recommend avoiding all intentional activity. Krishna says that action to maintain the world should be performed with a mind fixed on Him, and as a sacrifice to Him (XII 8, III 9, IV 23, IX 27). But to fix one's mind on Krishna and perform all action as a sacrifice to Him is an intention so unchanging (thus cutting through all self-ish motivation) that in practice *it is really equivalent to no intention at all*—especially when Krishna's higher nature is the transcendent nirguṇa ground of all phenomena, with no intention of Its own. When one's physical energy is not preoccupied with trying to satisfy cravings, and thus the world is not approached as a set of situations to be manipulated to satisfy those cravings, then we experience great freedom and "the world is vast and wide," as Ch'an master Yün-men said. When I am not preoccupied with going *to* some place, the going itself can become joyous. In Buddhist terms, life becomes a dance without a dancer; in terms of the *Gītā*, my body is realized to be Krishna's body. Without the sense of duality, the same energy that moves my body activates everything else too. All the individual dances are part of His cosmic dance.

Bhakti "is clearly the most troublesome discipline for philosophy,"[5] which reveals as much about philosophy as bhakti. Commentators from Schweitzer to Danto have claimed that complete surrender to the Divine seems inconsistent with the concept of socially meaningful action and jeopardizes the autonomy of the intellect.[6] But this presupposes that we have understood what such "surrender to the Divine" means. Bhakti-yoga is devotion to Krishna—"on Me alone fix thy mind" (XII 8)—but what is the phenomenology of such devotion when its object is not to be distingushed from worldly phenomena, since all is a fragment of His splendor? (X 41). If everything is a manifestation of Krishna's lower nature (emptiness is form, and māyā too is not other than Brahman), then it is clearly impossible to love Krishna and not cherish His world. "Love gives rise to affection for all" (*Kural*, VIII, 4), especially if what is loved is the ground of all being. When one is thus fixed on God, single-mindedly devoted to Him, there is no room for any negativity toward anything. Krishna's description of the true devotee in chapter 12 begins by emphasizing this: "He who has no ill-will to any being, who is friendly and compassionate, free from egotism and self-sense..." (XII 13). Then the worship of Krishna cannot be a matter of particular actions—prescribed offerings, and so on—instead, it becomes a way of performing all actions with a certain attitude. "Whatever thou doest, whatever thou eatest, whatever thou offerest, whatever thou givest away, whatever austerities thou dost practice—do that...as an offering to Me" (IX 27). Parallel with the *Om* (or other meditation-object) of jñāna-yoga and the dharma-duty of karma-yoga, *God becomes a mantra for the emotions.*

Interpreted in this way, bhakti is the path of purifying my emotional response to the world—or, less dualistically, the "emotional tone" of my being-in-the-world. Such devotion cuts through the web of negativity that perpetuates my sense of separation from others. I do not permit myself to express or harbor any negative feelings such as hatred and resentment. There is a gradual transmutation of such dualistic emotions into feelings of love and compassion. Emotionally centered on God, my affective responses no longer reinforce the sense of self, so the emotional component of the self-delusion withers away.[7]

In contrast to the dualistic emotions of hatred and so forth, love is nondual in that it promotes a sense of oneness between lover and loved. But is it nondual to the extent of jñāna and karma, which work to deny any ontological duality between consciousness and its object, actor (mind) and action (body)? Evidently not: love seems to be the relation between lover and beloved, which requires their distinction. But perhaps the problem is again our dualistic way of understanding, which sees the emotions as transient moods that come upon us, a kind of "interior weather" or mental environment that *I* am *in*. If there is no self for the emotion to come upon, our emotional life too needs to be reinterpreted. Insofar as bhakti is understood dualistically, there is the danger of its degeneration into emotional*ism*—sentimentality, eroticism, or excess of enthusiasm, as in some Bengali Vaiṣnavism, for example. But if the parallel with jñāna and bhakti holds, perhaps the practice of bhakti leads us to the experience of some nondual emotional aspect to the empty ground of our being. Insofar as I realize my true nature, perhaps love becomes, not something that I have, but something that I participate in. Such love would necessarily be nondiscriminatory. In moving from the sense of myself as an alienated consciousness to an awareness that all phenomena are a manifestation of the same nondual ground, love and compassion would spontaneously arise for all beings. Understanding myself as a facet of the Whole, I would naturally identify with all other facets of the Whole.

This suggests that bhakti too may have an ontological basis, which has some interesting implications. If such an all-pervasive love is the nondual ground of the emotions, then (to complete the parallel with jñāna- and karma-yoga) negative emotions must be the result of its being dualistically warped. As long as there is the delusion of self apart from the world, then resentment will naturally arise from any perception of a threat to that self and its desires. But insofar as I realize my true Self to be the birthless and deathless ground of all phenomena—including that of any "other" who may want to injure "me"—then there will be no negativity. And, as all lovers know, love is blissful; then is this nondual love also the bliss associated with Brahman (Sacchidānanda)?[8] If so, is romantic love, rather than being merely the epiphenomenon of sexual attraction, perhaps a glimpse of this emotional component of selflessness?

■

The three yogas as described above have at least three common features. First, each of them leads to equanimity because the yogin gives up expectation. The purest bhakti is so completely devoted to God that it asks for nothing from him in return. Karma-yoga is simply doing one's duty, giving up concern about the fruits of action. Expectation involves certain ways of thinking in which I project myself beyond the present situation, but the meditation of jñāna-yoga "lets go" of all such thoughts. In all three cases, learning not to be preoccupied with the future allows me to perceive something previously unnoticed about the present. Some existentialist interpretations of Indian *sādhanā* (the spiritual path) see self-realization as a necessarily unfinished process and man's being as a perpetual becoming.[9] But this continual projection-beyond is precisely what the yogas counteract. It is the nature of the self to be restless, always ahead of itself. But in equanimity this flight from the present moment ends, and I am able to realize something about the here-and-now which does not change.

This brings us to the second point. None of the three paths involves gaining something new, and it might even be argued that none of them involves removing anything (i.e., a hindrance). Rather, each yoga merely transforms what already is from a dualistic to a nondual mode. Chapter 4 argued that jñāna-yoga does not involve eliminating concepts or thoughts. The problem is not thoughts per se but that thinking usually functions dualistically, as prapañca or adhyāsa to obscure the empty nature of phenomena and perpetuate the delusion of self. Meditation works to break the mutually reinforcing pattern of thoughts, so their nondual nature can also be realized: thoughts too spring, not from my mind but from "the mind"—in terms of the *Gītā*, from Krishna. Karma-yoga implies that we need not withdraw from social responsibilities in order to follow the spiritual path and that the physical body is not necessarily a hindrance. The body too is a spiritual tool if one works to overcome its selfish craving by sacrificing it to the needs of the world, rather than vice versa. To act in this way leads to the realization that such actions are not mine but Krishna's. Finally, the emotions do not need to be removed in order to achieve tranquility. Instead, dualistic negativity is to be distilled into love and compassion, which may be our point of entry into a blissful love that transcends the attraction we feel for any particular object. As tantra emphasizes, what needs to be changed is not the basic "energies" themselves—intellectual, physical, emotional—but how they manifest.

The third common feature, if my interpretation of the yogas is correct, is that it is obviously impossible to make much progress in one without practicing the others, at least to some degree. I may begin with one yoga because it corresponds to the type of person I am, but that alone will be insufficient. I could not practice bhakti very long without needing to overcome my self-centered physical habits; how can I love others as Krishna while trying to use them to satisfy my own desires? The converse is also true. I could not meditate well or be a karma-yogi while harboring hatred and resentment of others. While I might not sit in a cross-legged position, I would need to cultivate the ability to "let go" of such negative thoughts and self-centered intentions in order to practice both bhakti- and karma-yoga. The "three roots of evil" function together; what each particular yoga does is break that alliance by striking at one of the links, but the three roots mutually reinforce each other, which is why all of us have all three problems to some degree. Each needs to be transmuted, although the two subsidiary links should be relatively easy to cope with when the primary path is practiced assiduously.

THE NONDUALITY OF GOD

Parallel to the problem of path priority has been the problem of goal priority. In the terms of the *Gītā*, is Krishna subordinate to the impersonal Absolute of puruṣa, or vice versa? In Vedāntic terms, is Saguṇa subordinate to Nirguṇa Brahman, as in Śaṅkara's Advaita, or is Nirguṇa subordinate to Saguṇa Brahman, as in Rāmānuja's Viśiṣṭādvaita? Later commentators transposed this philosophical issue into a textual one. Was there a pantheistic proto-*Gītā* with theistic passages added afterward, as the earliest Western scholars thought, or vice versa, as according to Garbe? But perhaps these controversies are as much pseudo-problems as the priority of the yogas. They are based upon the plausible yet questionable assumption that the two Absolutes, personal and impersonal, are incompatible. But they are not obviously inconsistent with each other in the *Gītā* as they are, for example, in Patañjali's *Yoga Sūtra*, where Īśvara is clearly an afterthought and has no essential function within the yogic system.

Krishna and puruṣa are warp-and-woof in the *Gītā*; it is difficult to conceive of one without the other. Later (if not always contemporary)[10] Advaita is also comfortable with both. The beautiful devotional hymns of Śaṅkara show that his inclusion of Saguṇa Brahman was not merely in deference to popular sentiment,[11] and more recently Ramakrishna did not doubt the existence of his own deity Kālī. Modern interpretations of Indian philosophy have too often projected the Western model of how philosophy develops, drawing lines and finding the clash of disagreement where there is often (as in the history of Buddhism) only difference of emphasis. The parallel distinction that Eckhart made between *deus* and *deitas* (God and Godhead) suggests that we should attempt to reconcile the two by considering what possible relationship there might be between them.

Up to this point, this chapter has been hermeneutical in its effort to give an interpretation and defense of the *Gītā* by reconciling its teachings with the nondualist traditions of Advaita Vedānta and Buddhism. Now I need to speculate more freely on the *Gītā*'s implications. Regarding the yogas, the nondualist perspective led us to suggest that each yoga works to transform a particular type of experience from a dualistic to a nondualistic mode. Regarding the question of goal, this encourages us to reflect on the possibility of a nondual relationship between man and God.

Bhakti was earlier interpreted as the yoga that purifies our emotional life, transforming dualistic negativity into emotions such as love and compassion in which there is more oneness between lover and beloved. It was suggested that this might lead to the experience of an "affective aspect" to the nondual ground of our being, an all-pervasive *ānanda* in which our personal feelings "participate." But whether or not this occurs, love as ordinarily experienced and understood is undeniably dualistic in that the lover is distinct from the beloved. Love, as much as hate, seems to be the relation between two things and in order to sustain that as a relation they must remain distinct. Comparing the traditional dualistic bhakti of theism with the meditative jñāna emphasized in the nondualist traditions thus raises a question. Can we attribute the difference between personal and impersonal Absolutes to the difference in function between the emotions and the intellect? As we have seen, the emotions require a "personalized Other" on which to focus in order to be purified. The intellect, in contrast, requires an empty, qualityless (nirguṇa) impersonality because jñāna works by "letting go" of all mental phenomena, emotions as well as concepts.

This possibility seems important, but by itself it does not take us very far. It suggests that the relation between Krishna and Brahman, for example, cannot be separated from the issue of the relation between emotion and intellect. But this does no more than relate both personal and impersonal Absolutes equally to us, rather than explaining what we most want to know: what is the relation between them?

What is the nondualist objection to God? Part of the problem is the notion that God is a *person* in some sense similar to us (or vice versa, according to the Semitic religions). How much of a problem this is depends upon how this personhood is understood. If the concept of God's personality is taken as metaphorical, there may be no problem at all. If belief in the personality of God is sustained by the view that we are made in his image, then we should extrapolate one main concern of contemporary philosophy—overcoming mind–body dualism—to overcoming the duality between God and the universe. Rāmānuja's analogy between them (God is to the created universe as mind is to body) suggests that the parallel between these dualisms is no coincidence.

That God is a person may be a useful metaphor, especially if he (she) is further metaphorized as a parent—although this natural image is fraught with dangers that we are now well aware of: parental love and forgiveness may be overshadowed by a possessiveness and vanity that demands acknowledgement and obedience with the threat of punishment. But the double-aspect of the Absolute, as both transcendent and immanent, is poorly expressed in the notion that God is a person who, like us, plans, creates, expects, commands, is pleased or angry, rewards and punishes—and perhaps discriminates between peoples, choosing some of them for a privileged destiny. Well-known philosophical problems arise—for example, the "inconsistent triad" —if we try to think of God in such a way.[12]

If the intention behind the metaphor of God's personhood is to capture the beliefs that there is a moral order intrinsic to the universe and that there is a transcendental meaning to our lives that makes them incalculably valuable (compare the moral order and meaning provided for children by parents), then nondualistic systems such as Buddhism and Vedānta express both of these in a more sophisticated way. The first is embodied in the doctrine of karma, which is not the predestined fate of Greek *moira* (which dualistically happens *to* me) but the notion that the universe is ordered in such a way that cause-and-effect relationships apply not only in the physical world but also in the mind. Perhaps Newton's third law of motion—for every action there is an equal and opposite reaction—is valid for acts of consciousness (intentions) as well. The supreme importance of life is better captured (if one avoids the world-negation that arises from bifurcating transcendental ground and phenomena) in the possibility of a liberation that occurs with the realization of our true nondual nature, that I am the universe.

One apparent problem with these processes, and the general impersonality of such an Absolute, is that they seem to imply the universe is indifferent to our fate. In particular, the elimination of God-as-judge seems to eliminate morality as well, substituting a mechanical cause-and-effect which is amoral in that we are free to do anything as long as we are prepared to bear the consequences. However, such freedom eliminates not morality but the fact–value dichotomy (another correlary of the mind–body, spirit–matter distinction): morality is no longer a second-order evaluation of events but is "built into" them. The effect of an impersonal Absolute is not indifference, for God is not really eliminated but, as it were, integrated into the universe—just as the negation of mind–body dualism implies not behaviorism but a "spiritualized body." That God is not other than the universe, as Spinoza argued, does not diminish God but rather elevates the universe. The universe is spiritual because it is ordered in such a way that there is moral as well as physical order, and because those who choose to make an attempt to overcome their egoism find their efforts aided by forces outside their conscious control. Modern Advaitins such as Aurobindo have claimed that the movement toward self-realization is inherent to the structure of the universe. The Buddhist *sotapanna* is literally a "stream-enterer," an inspired image. He or she has been drawn into a current that carries one along to nirvāṇa—according to tradition, within seven lifetimes. Like the watershed system of a river valley, is there a natural "gravitational" tendency for all of us to become pulled in, resisted only by our attachments? The

Mahāyāna Dharmakāya radiates love and compassion to all, impersonally like the sun, but many are not receptive to it.[13] In reaction to Platonic dualism, Aristotle speculated that the Form of a thing is its function. Extrapolating from that, may we say that God is the function of the universe?

The nondualist difficulty with theism is not just that God is a person, but that this person is an *other* to us—"Wholly Other" as the early Barth stressed and later repudiated. Of course, the two concepts are closely related. My awareness of being a person is dependent on there being other persons; a sense of self arises only in dialectical relation to other selves. Then *is God a person only in relation to myself*? If so, what will happen if I "merge with" God—which is the goal of most theistic mystics, just as nondualists wish to realize their oneness with Brahman, and so on. In this union with God, I am of course transformed— but then won't God be transformed too? Into what?

In samādhi the meditator seems to merge with the object of his concentration; my awareness *of* the object (physical or mental) is no longer distinguishable *from* the object. Usually this is only a temporary trance state, for the mind later becomes preoccupied with thoughts again. But the nondualist claims that this is not a delusion. On the contrary, it is a glimpse of the true nondual nature of phenomena: they are not other than "my" mind. Because he was able to let his individual mind and body "drop away," Dōgen realized that "mind is nothing other than mountains and rivers and the great wide earth, the sun and the moon and the stars"—the essential Mahāyāna claim that is equally crucial to Advaita. But unlike Buddhism, Advaita finds a role for God in Śaṅkara's distinction between Saguṇa (with attributes—i.e., Īśvara) and Nirguṇa (without attributes—i.e., completely empty of any phenomenal characteristics) Brahman. The transcendental latter, like Eckhart's Godhead, is inactive and immutable, whereas the former is not immanent *in* the world but *is* the world as the totality of Brahman's self-luminous manifestations. Yet how is this description of Saguṇa Brahman equivalent to God? And, more generally, how can we understand the relation between these two Brahmans?

Śaṅkara says that Brahman reflected in māyā is Īśvara (God), whereas Brahman reflected in avidyā is the jīva (ego-self). Given that

Śaṅkara (unlike Gauḍapāda) generally seems to identify māyā with avidyā, this seminal statement must mean that the mystical experience of God as the true nature of the phenomenal world is still somewhat illusory (māyā), the "other side" of the delusion (avidyā) of myself as still other than the world. A bit of māyā persists if I perceive Brahman (Eckhart's deitas) as God, but only because I experience him as other than myself. God is the Absolute viewed from outside, as it were: still a bit dualistically. Then the Impersonal Absolute is the true nature of God—nondual because completely incorporating "my" consciousness as well. In other words, to experience God is to forget oneself to the extent that one becomes aware of a consciousness pervading everywhere and everything. To experience the Godhead/Absolute is to "let go" completely and realize that consciousness is nothing other than *me*, fully becoming what I have always been. The sense of "holiness" (Otto's "the numinous") is not something added onto the phenomenal world in such mystical experiences but is an inherent characteristic of "my" self-luminous mind, although realized only when its true nature is experienced.

Contrary to some of Krishna's own statements in the *Gītā*,[14] such a nondualist explanation subordinates the Personal to the Impersonal—or does it? Certainly the concept of God as a person is preferable to a Buddhist śūnyatā misunderstood as static or nihilistic, or to a Brahman so abstract and otherworldly that it has no relation to our lives. And even a nondualist might point out that the theist who sincerely tries to love all God's creatures might well make more spiritual progress toward selflessness than the meditator who greedily desires enlightenment. But the danger of these errors is clearly indicated within the nondualist traditions themselves.

Ramakrishna said that he preferred to taste sugar than become sugar. The above interpretation implies that, before we become completely enlightened, we shall experience the operation of the Absolute upon us as God. God is the Absolute seen from "outside," but that is the only way the Absolute can be seen, since in itself it is so devoid of characteristics that it is literally a nothing. God is God only in relation to me, but when there is no longer a "me" then the spiritual quest is over.

CONCLUSION: NONDUAL VALUES

A nondualist interpretation of the *Bhagavad-gītā* concludes part 2. Whereas part 1 developed a "core doctrine" about the nonduality of experience, derived from and compatible with Buddhism, Vedānta, and Taoism, the concern of part 2 has been to defend that core theory by resolving the main disagreements among the nondualistic (and some other) philosophical systems. I have done that in various ways. Chapter 5 addresses the ontological differences among the three most important Indian metaphysical systems (or sets of systems): Sāṅkhya-Yoga, Vedānta, and Buddhism. We noticed that the differences among them correspond to the three main ways of resolving the relationship between subject and object: sharp dualism (which fails because the two terms cannot be related back together), subject-only (the "all-Self" of Advaita) and object-only (the anātman of Buddhism). The second and third alternatives are somewhat more successful attempts to describe the nondual experience, but they adopt opposite approaches: Vedānta conflates object into subject, Buddhism conflates subject into object. The rest of chapter 5 points out the otherwise deep affinities, both historical and metaphysical, between Mahāyāna and Advaita, which need to be appreciated before turning to their disagreements.

An in-depth analysis of the main differences between Mahāyāna and Advaita is the concern of chapter 6. Their metaphysical starting points are so diametrically opposed, so much mirror-images of each other, that suspicions are aroused. We approached this disagreement through five sets of category-conflicts: self versus nonself, substances versus modes, immutability versus impermanence, the Unconditioned versus conditionality, and no-Path versus all-Path. In each instance we found that the surface conflict regarding the correct category-description masked a deeper agreement about the phenomenology of the nondual experience. What is important in each case is not to assert the superiority of either relative term (although it has often been understood that way) but to overcome the dualism between each pair of terms. Nondual experience is not characterized by the delusive dualism between self and other, between mind and world, for "my" mind *is* the world. Nor is there a dualism between substance and modes, between things and their attributes, for all phenomena are śūnya, empty, with a dreamlike māyā quality, except for that One which can never be experienced as a One. Third, the category-conflict between Parmenidean Being and Heraclitean Becoming is resolved by a double-dialectic that first dissolves all things into temporal flux and then turns that flux back upon itself, leaving an Eternal Now that is not incompatible with change when we realize that *it is always now.* "He to whom time is the same as eternity, and eternity the same as time, is free from all contention" (Boehme). Fourth, this double-dialectic was applied again to the dualism between the Unconditioned (Nirguṇa Brahman, nirvana) and "all-conditionality" (pratītya-samutpāda) to break down the dualism between self-sufficient things and the causal glue that relates them together. In nondual experience, the tension between freedom and determinism is resolved in an act that is not the dilemma of a dualistic ego but arises spontaneously from one's śūnya nature. Fifth, the disagreement between Śaṅkara and Dōgen about the role of spiritual practices was seen to reflect their deeper agreement about the need to overcome any self-stultifying dualism between means and goal, for the nondual Self is not something that can be attained. Finally, this same double-dialectic was employed to criticize Derrida, arguing that his deconstruction is not radical enough because it adopts only the first of the two dialectical moments; his deconstruction misses the opportunity to deconstruct itself and attain the conceptual clôture that would allow a true opening to something else. I underscore the importance of this chapter, for it concerns more than the category-conflicts between Mahāyāna Buddhism and Advaita Vedānta. It was pointed out that the relation between Buddhism and Vedānta on these matters corresponds to the linguistic bifurcation between subject-based and predicate-based descriptions, a dilemma that has infected much philosophy, both Eastern and Western. Even more, it is a dilemma that plagues our lives, for our duḥkha can be expressed in terms of the tensions due to the sense of a separation between ourselves and others, between awareness of temporality and our "intimations of immortality," between our sense of being determined and our need for freedom, between our meditative practices and spiritual goals.

Yet there is much more to Asian thought than the fraternal quarrel between Mahāyāna and Advaita. Chapter 7 broadened the scope of the discussion by approaching the issue of phenomenology/ description in a very different way: suggesting an analogy, the Mind-space experience, which provides the opportunity for a wide variety of ontological responses. We were able to correlate these responses with the ontological positions of the main Indian systems and, just as interesting, these correlations were revealed to encompass all the main possible ontological alternatives. This raises the question whether the Mind-space analogy might in some sense be more than an analogy, but the main point is that it supports our general claim distinguishing the phenomenology of an experience from the variety of descriptions which may be applied to it after the fact. Again, the differences between descriptions seem less important than their agreement—in this case, about the phenomenology of the nondual experience, as opposed to our usual experience of the world as a collection of discrete, self-sufficient entities causally interacting in space/time.

Finally, chapter 8 has tested our "core model" of nondual experience by seeing what light it sheds on the *Bhagavad-gītā*, that very popular but philosophically problematic Vedāntic text. We looked at the two main issues it raises: the relations among the various margas (spiritual paths) and the relationship between personal (God) and impersonal (e.g., nirvana and Nirguṇa Brahman) Absolutes. The three main margas advocated in the *Gītā* correlated very nicely with working on three different aspects of experience, intellect, emotion and action; the path in each case involves "transforming" these from a dualistic to a nondualistic mode. The second section dealt with a controversy that continues to be important within the Western religious tradition. Many modern theists (e.g., R. C. Zaehner, Jacques Maritain, Etienne Gilson, Joseph Marechal) have argued that the nondual experience of undifferentiated union is distinct from and inferior to the dualistic awareness of a loving God. Others, such as

Aldous Huxley, Evelyn Underhill, Ninian Smart, John Hick, and Frits Staal, believe that mystical experiences are basically the same, and in their complete and highest form nondual. The proponents of this view acknowledge the difference in mystical claims, particularly between theist and nondualist, but explain these differences by distinguishing between the immediate experience and its interpretations—variously termed "doctrinal structures" (Deikman), "credal ramifications" (Ninian Smart), "superstructures" (Staal) and so on. Needless to say, this study falls into the latter camp. In particular, the conclusion of chapter 8 suggests that the theistic mystical experience might be understood as an "incomplete" nondual one. In it, there is the awareness of consciousness pervading everywhere, but insofar as the experience is an awareness *of...*, it is still tainted with some delusion; whereas complete union—as in Advaita's Nirguṇa and Eckhart's godhead—is to become that ground which is literally nothing in itself, but from which all issues forth. So this chapter, too, concerns issues wider than just the *Bhagavad-gītā*. It shows how our model of nondual experience may be used to explain much about the nature of the spiritual path. And I hope that the discussion of theism may contribute to the burgeoning dialogue between religions, a conversation whose importance can hardly be overemphasized.

To complete this study, we shall briefly consider the implications of nonduality, and our model of it, for three other areas of our experience. These are the three fields of value-theory: ethics, aesthetics, and social theory. A recurring difficulty in each is what is sometimes called the Is-Ought Problem, the problem of how to derive any value claim from a factual one. We have already noticed that the value–fact distinction is another corollary of the bifurcation between mind and matter, between subject as source of value and object as brute fact, and that opens the door for new approaches to some resistant problems—or, more precisely, for a new understanding of some old approaches.

Ethics. The problem of morality has become less abstract now that we are experiencing the nihilism that Nietzsche predicted a century ago. "God is dead; now all is permitted." If God and all other transcendental principles of unity evaporate, what remains to bind our dualized selves together? There is a similarity between this and our discussion of causality. Just as our concepts of self-existing entities and their causal relations are relative to each other, so our concepts of God as the source of moral law and of ourselves as amoral (if not immoral: "original sin") agents feed on each other. If God is the only source of good, this results in the religious struggle to impose a moral code upon ourselves and others, necessary to control our sinful nature. The problem is conceiving of God (and, derivatively, morality) as an *external* (hence dualistic) relating-principle, a sort of transcendental glue sustaining the moral connections between us. Nāgārjuna deconstructed self-existing things by emphasizing their causal relativity, but our social problem, in the West at least, is becoming the opposite: society is dissolving into a collection of autonomous individuals each "looking out for number one."

The nondual experience undercuts this atomism by denying the ontological reality of the ego. "He who sees all beings as the very Self and the Self in all beings in consequence thereof abhors none" (Īśā Upaniṣad, v. 6). But this is not strong enough; Vidyaranya puts it better: "The knowledge of the Self leads to the identification of oneself with others as clearly as one identifies oneself with one's body."[1] This realization cuts through the tendency to treat others primarily as competitors or objects to be manipulated and shows that the Bodhisattva doctrine has a metaphysical basis: if one *is* the whole world, one cannot be fully enlightened unless all others are as well.

But the most important thing to notice is that the whole issue has been transposed from a matter of morality to one of understanding. The problem is no longer evil, but delusion, and the solution is not a matter of applying the will but of reaching an insight about the nature of things. (Blake: "There can be no Good Will. Will is always Evil.") Socrates is vindicated: bad conduct is indeed due to ignorance, for if we really knew the good we would do it. The catch, of course, is in the *really*, for the type of knowledge necessary is neither the "correct" moral code nor any other merely conceptual understanding. As usual, William Blake hit this nail right on the head, in *Vision of the Last Judgment*:

> Men are admitted into Heaven not because they have curbed & govern'd their Passions or have No Passions, but because they have Cultivated their Understandings. The Treasures of Heaven are not Negations of Passion, but Realities of Intellect, from which All the Passions Emanate Uncurbed in their Eternal Glory.

The Combats of Good & Evil is Eating of the Tree of Knowledge. The Combats of Truth & Error is Eating of the Tree of Life.... Satan thinks that Sin is displeasing to God; he ought to know that Nothing is displeasing to God but Unbelief & Eating of the Tree of Knowledge of Good & Evil.

I do not consider either the Just or the Wicked to be in a Supreme State, but to be every one of them States of the Sleep which the Soul may fall into in its deadly dreams of Good & Evil when it leaves paradise following the serpent.

Not Good & Evil, but Truth & Error! "If God is anything, he is Understanding."

The nondualist traditions make the same point as part of their critique of dualistic categories. The tendency to evaluate all acts as good or bad, pure or impure is a classic example of the delusive vikalpa that needs to be eliminated. To eliminate all delusion therefore means to eliminate all moral codes as well. But this does not excuse selfishness, for a true elimination of delusion will also eliminate all those self-centered ways of thinking that motivate selfish behavior. Deeper than the imperfectly flexible strictures of any moral code (which may still have value as "rules of thumb") is the concern for others that springs up spontaneously within those who have realized their true nature. This is the heart of the Taoist critique of Confucianism, which sees Confucian emphasis on such doctrines as righteousness and propriety as an attempt to close the barn door after the horse of natural feeling has already run away. Nietzsche was right when he argued that such codes are ultimately motivated by fear, which gives rise to the need to control others and to control ourselves. The alternative to that fear is love, which, if it is to be genuine, is something no moral code can legislate. "Christ acted from impulse and not from rules" (Blake). He and the Buddha exemplify how compassion arises and manifests itself naturally when we have overcome our sense of separation from the world.

Spinoza concluded the *Ethics* by proposing that blessedness is not the reward of virtue, but virtue itself. The other side of this is that suffering is not the punishment for evil, but evil itself. The essence of our duḥkha is the sense of separation—between myself and God, says the theist, who defines hell in precisely those terms; between myself and the objectified world, says the nondualist, whose doctrine of karma embodies a similar realization. The problem of "evil" is that it aggravates one's sense of alienation. Someone who manipulates the world merely for his own advantage increasingly dualizes himself from it. Those who live in this way cannot help expecting the same from others, leading to a life based on fear and the need to control situations. The vicious circle that this can entail leads to a hellish solipsism. The point of the karma doctrine is that our thought-constructions and -projections actually change the quality of the world we live in; thoughts may gain a life of their own and come back to haunt us.

> For a blissful condition of man it would by no means be sufficient that he should be transferred to a "better world," but it would also be necessary that a complete change should take place in himself. . . . To be transferred to another world and to have his whole nature changed are, at bottom, one and the same. (Schopenhauer)[2]

Enormous "moral" consequences follow from the fact (discussed in the causality section of chapter 6) that the entire universe exists just for the sake of this single flower to bloom, and for the sake of me to appreciate it. For the nondualist, life is nothing but a series of such timeless śūnya experiences: a sip of coffee, a few words with a friend, a walk down a path. Someone who cannot trust his world enough to "forget himself" and *become* these situations is condemned—or condemns himself—to watch his life ooze away.

This suggests the connection between the ethical question and the aesthetic one, for "in the mind of a man who is filled with his own aims, the world appears as a beautiful landscape appears on the plan of a battlefield" (Schopenhauer again).[3]

Aesthetics. The aesthetic experience is nondual, because nonintentional; but this is nothing new. As far as I know, Kant was the first to emphasize that the aesthetic experience is nonintentional in the sense discussed in chapter 3, where it was argued that nonintentionality is the essential quality of nondual action. Nor is it coincidental that the example of music was used, and lines of poetry cited, to discuss nondual perception in chapter 2. Schopenhauer, whose aesthetic sense was more sensitive than Kant's, also expressed the point better:

in aesthetic perception, a man "ceases to consider the where, the when, the why, and the whither of things, and looks simply and solely at the *what*."[4] We distinguish art by putting a frame around it, in various ways, to protect *this* canvas and *this* time in a theater from our usual utilitarian preoccupations; these frames help us to "keep the sabbath of the penal servitude of willing" by keeping certain ways of thinking *out* of them. (An illuminating comparison may be made with the worship of idols, which seem to function in the same way.)

For Kant, a judgment of taste cannot be cognitive, because it is not objective. With Schelling and Schopenhauer we find an appreciation of the aesthetic experience as both nondual and cognitive. For Schelling:

> Every true work of art is a manifestation of the Absolute.... Subject and object, freedom and nature, are united and made one in the work of art, so that the Absolute, the infinite identity of subject and object, is finitely represented in the artist's creation.... Beauty is thus the Infinite represented in finite form.[5]

Schopenhauer's description of subject–object union is more to the point: "both have become one, since the entire consciousness is filled and occupied with a single perceptual image."[6] His philosophy of art is brilliant but, from our point of view, somewhat vitiated by its role within his metaphysics of will and the will's negation. For a deeper understanding of the connection between the aesthetic and spiritual experiences, we must return to our nondualist philosophies.

In a recent monograph on comparative aesthetics, Eliot Deutsch comments on Indian, Chinese, and Japanese aesthetic theory. He uses the famous rock garden at Ryoanji, a Zen temple in Kyoto, to discuss the Japanese concept of *yūgen*.

> The concept of *yūgen* teaches us that in aesthetic experience it is not that "*I* see the work of art," but that by "seeing" the "I" is transformed. It is not that "*I* enter into the work," but that by "entering" the "I" is altered in the intensity of a pristine immediacy.[7]

To explain Chinese aesthetics, he quotes Chuang Tzu: "Only the truly intelligent understand the principle of identity. They do not view things as apprehended by themselves subjectively, but transfer themselves into the position of the thing viewed." Deutsch's gloss: "for the

Sung painter, following Chuang Tzu, there is no real or enduring distinction between subject and object, between man and nature, insofar as they are in perfect rhythmic accord with each other."[8]

According to Deutsch, much the same point is implied by the Indian concept of *rasa*, a Sanskrit term variously translated as "flavor, desire, beauty, that which is *tasted* in art." This naturally raises the question *where* is rasa located. Does it involve the discernment of objective qualities or is it due to a special response in the experiencer? These alternatives were put forth by classical Indian theorists but "summarily dismissed by Abhinavagupta" (whose "formulation of the theory is generally considered to be the most interesting"):

> *Rasa* is not limited by any difference of space, time and knowing subject. When we say that "*rasas* are perceived" (we are using language loosely) ... for the *rasa* is the process of perception itself.[9]

Deutsch's comment on this brings out more clearly the claim of subject–object nonduality:

> The essential quality of aesthetic experience, it is maintained, is neither subjective nor objective; it neither belongs to the art-work nor to the experiencer of it; rather it is the process of aesthetic perception itself, which defies spatial designation, that constitutes *rasa*. This view that the locus or *āśraya*, as it were, of *rasa* is nowhere, that *rasa* transcends spatial and temporal determinations is, I believe, the only way open to us to understand the nature of aesthetic experience.[10]

This explains why both objectivist explanations (e.g., formalist theories emphasizing "significant form") and subjectivist explanations (e.g., romanticist and expressionist theories) fail to account for the aesthetic experience in a satisfactory way. Deutsch also discusses the connection between the aesthetic experience, understood in this way, and the spiritual one: "*Śāntarasa* [silent *rasa*], according to Abhinava, is just that transcendental realization of unity that is joy-ful and peaceful. It is grounded in the Self and is realized as a kind of self-liberation."[11] Later Deutsch *almost* equates the two: "A work of art is not a means to a non-aesthetic state, but precisely to an aesthetic apprehension, which apprehension, when fully realized, is nevertheless spiritual in character."[12]

This is such an important point, and so well put, that I do not want to hurry past it; yet I wonder if we may take it one step further. Deutsch, who is best known for his work on Advaita Vedānta, assumes here the Advaitic distinction between Reality, understood as completely contentless, and all phenomena, including aesthetic ones. Therefore, although he says that the fully realized aesthetic apprehension becomes spiritual, he also wants to distinguish them. Whereas the highest aesthetic experience for him is still temporal, "in spiritual experience the call is from that which is Real without division or object or time. The art-work, in the fullness of its experience as *śāntarasa*, points to Reality and participates in it. In pure spiritual experience there is only the Real."[13] In contrast to this Advaitic view, we have seen that the Mahāyāna standpoint accepts no such "pure Reality" apart from the emptiness of phenomena, whether aesthetic or otherwise. The significance of this difference is that it allows us to draw a somewhat different conclusion about the meaning of the art work. The point may be made with greater effect if we first offer a more extreme version of the dualism we want to criticize. This is Heinrich Zimmer discussing the Indian work of art as a symbol pointing to and representing the spiritual:

> In India the beauty of images is not intended for the aesthetic enjoyment of the secular beholder; it is a contribution to their magical force as "instruments" or "tools" (*yantra*).[14]

It is an important insight that the Indian work of art is often used as a means to self-transformation. But what may be questioned is the assumption that the pleasure of the aesthetic experience must be denied for the bliss of the "pure" spiritual one. If we do not take for granted that all true spiritual experience is completely nirguṇa, neither do we need to assume a difference in *kind* between the aesthetic and spiritual experiences. According to Coomaraswamy, the function of art for Plato is "to attune our own distorted modes of thought to cosmic harmonies, 'so that by an assimilation of the knower to the to-be-known, the archetypal nature, and coming to be in that likeness, we may attain at last to a part in that "life's best" that has been appointed by the gods to man for this time being and hereafter.'"[15] Then perhaps the profound pleasure we sometimes experience from listening to a Bach fugue or a Mozart piano concerto is not a distraction from that process of attuning, nor even a side-effect of it, but *is* that attuning.

What is the nondual experience if not such an attunement? Nor need that enjoyment be understood subjectively. If the whole of creation groans and travails in pain together, does it not also leap for joy together, in us—or rather, as us?

This implies that there is no such thing as art for the completely attuned individual:

> Could the artist attain perfection, becoming one with God, he would share in God's creation from time everlasting, natural species would be his image in time as they are in God's, nothing would remain but the ever-present world-picture as God sees it. There would be no occasion for works of art, the end of art having been accomplished.   (Eckhart)[16]

Yes, but only because here we have another version of the paradox that has recurred repeatedly throughout this book: "To the enlightened— but only to the enlightened—all experience is *śāntarasa*." (Deutsch).[17]

Society. From the nondualist perspective, what is most striking about the present world situation is the curious parallel between it and our perennial personal situation. The personal situation is, of course, the subject–object dualism, which, as analyzed in these pages, is delusive and unsatisfactory—a problem that can be resolved only in the non-dual experience. Once the correspondence between this and the collective social problem has been noticed, the natural question is whether the latter problem too may be subject to a parallel solution.

In this century it has become clear that the fundamental social problem is now the relationship between humankind as a whole and our global environment. It is because of our alienation from the earth that we are destroying it. Philosophically, this is what Heidegger identified and criticized as "humanism." But this is nothing other than the individual situation writ large: besides the problem of the individual ego, there is now the collective problem of a "species-ego." In both cases the problem is a delusive sense of duality between oneself and the world one is "in." "The same dualism that reduces things to objects for consciousness is at work in the humanism that reduces nature to raw material for humankind."[18]

When we look for the historical roots of this problem, we must go back to ancient Judea and Greece. In classical Greece an especially dualistic way of experiencing the world was nurtured by the Parmenidean and Platonic split between the ever-changing, hence delusive senses and reason, their master; we may have misunderstood Parmenides and Plato, but they have nonetheless led to science and technology. The moral justification for transforming the world was provided, albeit unintentionally, by the Old Testament: God created the world and placed man in it. When God eventually disappeared, this trinity became a duality, and there was no longer anything to stop us from befouling our own nest. What should now be clear is that we cannot be satisfied with any religion that elevates a God above his creation without seeing the Infinite in all things. If spirit is anything other than the true nature of this world, then the world is devalued, and we too insofar as we are of it.

In both these dualisms, the self is understood to be the source of awareness and therefore of all meaning and value, which is to devalue the world/nature into merely that field of activity wherein the self labors to fulfill *itself*. Then the problem is the same for both: the alienated subject feels no responsibility for the objectified other and attempts to find satisfaction through projects that usually merely increase the sense of alienation. The meaning and purpose sought can be attained only in a relationship whereby nonduality with the objectified other is re-established. Some who despair over our collective rapacity see *homo sapiens* only as a cancer, an evolutionary error by which our ecosystem may have doomed itself. But a tendency to look upon man as merely parasitic is another manifestation of the problem, reflecting the same general feeling of alienation that causes exploitation in the first place. Only by discovering our true home, in both senses, can we realize why we are here and what we are to do.

The nondualist systems that we have studied do not provide us with ready-made models to cope with this new ecological problem, which is the product of a very different worldview. In traditional Asia, oppressive political and economic systems were taken as much for granted as the weather, an attitude that encouraged spiritual withdrawal from the social world, although a withdrawal tempered by the compassion of many Bodhisattvas. In a relatively "steady-state" social system, such indifference was possible, but it is not now. Unfortunately, when humankind collectively "forgets itself" it is not in Dōgen's sense. So perhaps new forms of spiritual practice need to be developed, which temper the yin of spiritual practice with the yang of grass-roots social activism. The last two centuries have shown us that it is naive to expect the necessary changes through political or social revolutions alone. Both the personal and the species dualisms are due to delusions that cannot be behavioristically "conditioned" out of existence but that require the desire and effort to develop an awareness that transforms one's life. Perhaps the future of our biosphere depends to some extent on the quiet, unnoticed influence of those working to overcome their own sense of subject–object duality.

NOTES

INTRODUCTION

1. Plotinus, *The Six Enneads*, trans. Stephen MacKenna and B. S. Page, The Great Books vol. 17 (Chicago: Encyclopaedia Britannica, 1952), 359–60.
2. Asaṅga, *Mahāyānasaṃgraha* II, 6; quoted in Edward Conze, *Buddhist Thought in India* (London: Allen and Unwin, 1962), 253.
3. W. T. Stace, *Time and Eternity* (Princeton University Press, 1952), 136.
4. Sebastian Samay, *Reason Revisited: The Philosophy of Karl Jaspers* (University of Notre Dame Press, 1971), 213.
5. *The Awakening of Faith*, attributed to Aśvaghoṣa, trans. Yoshito S. Hakeda (New York: Columbia University Press, 1967), 72. Hakeda's commentary on this passage emphasizes its importance: "The nonduality of mind and matter, spirit and body is the basic concept of this text and a common presupposition of Mahāyāna Buddhism."
6. Michael E. Zimmerman, "Towards a Heideggerian *Ethos* for Radical Environmentalism," *Environmental Ethics* 5, no. 2 (Summer 1983): 112.

I HOW MANY NONDUALITIES ARE THERE?

1. "Selections from the Chuang-tzu," in *Sources of Chinese Tradition*, vol. 1, ed. Theodore deBary (New York: Columbia University Press, 1964); as quoted by Francis H. Cook in *Hua-Yen Buddhism* (Pennsylvania State University Press, 1977), 27, with slight alterations by Cook. See also *Tao Tĕ Ching*, chap. 2.
2. Nāgārjuna, *Mūlamadhyamikakārikā* (hereafter *MMK*) XXIII 10–11. Unless otherwise noted all *MMK* quotations are from Candrakīrti's *Lucid Exposition of the Middle Way*, trans. Mervyn Sprung (Boulder, Co.: Prajñā Press, 1979).
3. *The Zen Teaching of Hui Hai on Sudden Illumination*, trans. and ed. John Blofeld (London: Rider, 1969), 52, 49–50.
4. *Selected Sayings from the Perfection of Wisdom*, trans. and ed. Edward Conze (Boulder, Co.: Prajñā Press, 1978), 78.
5. Blofeld, *Zen Teaching of Hui Hai*, 81.
6. *The Vajracchedikā-Prajñā-Pāramitā Sūtra*, trans. from Chinese by Lu Ku'an-Yu (Hong Kong: Buddhist Book Distributor, 1976), 18–19.

7. Nāgārjuna, *MMK*, XIII 8.

8. *The Zen Teaching of Huang Po*, trans. and ed. John Blofeld (London: Buddhist Society, 1958), 64–65, with my alterations.

9. *The Three Pillars of Zen*, ed. Philip Kapleau (Tokyo: Weatherhill, 1966), 77, 79–80. Yasutani is not giving advice on how to lead everyday life; this admonition was presented during a *sesshin* (intensive meditation retreat) in which distractions are minimized and participants are expected to concentrate on their Zen practice full-time.

10. Kaṭha Upaniṣad II.i.10–11, in *The Upanishads*, trans. and ed. Swami Nikhilananda (New York: Harper and Row, 1964), 78. Unless otherwise noted, all quotations from the Upaniṣads are from Nikhilananda.

11. Blofeld, *Zen Teaching of Huang Po*, 29.

12. My translation of chap. 25.

13. Bṛhadāraṇyaka Upaniṣad I.iv.7. The bracketed additions are Nikhilananda's.

14. "The Yoga of Knowing the Mind," attributed to Padma-Saṁbhava, in *The Tibetan Book of the Great Liberation*, trans. and ed. W. Y. Evans-Wentz (Oxford University Press, 1959), 231–32.

15. *Chuang-tzu*, with commentary by Kuo Hsiang, trans. Fung Yu-lan (New York: Gordon Press, 1975), 53.

16. Bṛhadāraṇyaka Upaniṣad IV.iv.22.

17. Chang Chung-yuan, *Tao: A New Way of Thinking* (New York: Harper and Row, 1977), 38. From Chang's translation of chap. 14.

18. Bṛhadāraṇyaka Upaniṣad I.iv.7. Nikhilananda's bracketed additions.

19. Kaṭha Upaniṣad II.ii.9.

20. Kapleau, *Three Pillars of Zen*, 205.

21. Bṛhadāraṇyaka Upaniṣad II.iv.14 and IV.iii.23. Nikhilananda's bracketed additions.

22. Īśā Upaniṣad 7.

23. Taittirīya Upaniṣad III.x.6; my bracketed additions. In a footnote to this passage Nikhilananda explains the exclamations: "An expression of extreme wonder. The cause of this wonder is that though the Seer is the non-dual Ātman, yet he himself is the food and the eater, that is to say, that he is both the object and the subject."

24. Chāndogya Upaniṣad VI.ix.4.

25. *Ātmabodha* 41, as quoted in Swāmī Satprakāshānanda, *Methods of Knowledge According to Advaita Vedānta* (London: Allen and Unwin, 1965), 276.

26. *The Bṛhadāraṇyaka Upaniṣad*, with commentary of Śaṅkarācārya, trans. Swāmī Mādhavānanda (Calcutta: Advaita Ashrama, 1975), 474–75.

27. *The Teachings of Bhagavan Sri Ramana Maharshi in His Own Words*, ed. Arthur Osborne (Tiruvannamalai: Sri Ramanasramam, 1977), 251, 13–14.

28. T. R. V. Murti, *The Central Philosophy of Buddhism* (London: Allen and Unwin, 1960), 217.

29. Candrakīrti, *Lucid Exposition*, 35. Candrakīrti (6th C. A.D.?) was Nāgārjuna's main commentator within the *prāsaṅgika* tradition.

30. Vasubandhu, *Trisvabhāvanirdeśa*, 36–37; quoted in Sangharakshita, *A Survey of Buddhism* (Boulder: Shambhala, 1980), 365. Sangharakshita's bracketed additions.

31. Vasubandhu, *Triṃśikāvijñaptikārikā*; quoted in Edward Conze, ed., *Buddhist Texts Through the Ages* (New York: Harper and Row, 1964), 210.

32. S. B. Dasgupta, *An Introduction to Tantric Buddhism* (University of Calcutta, 1974), 4, 113.

33. Evans-Wentz, *Tibetan Book of the Great Liberation*, 206, 232.

34. *Tibetan Yoga and Secret Doctrines*, ed. and trans. W. Y. Evans-Wentz (Oxford University Press, 1958), 145–49.

35. Giuseppe Tucci, *The Religions of Tibet*, trans. Geoffrey Samuel (London: Routledge and Kegan Paul, 1980), 47–48.

36. D. T. Suzuki, *Essays in Zen Buddhism*, 1st ser. (London: Rider, 1927), 125, 230. Suzuki's description of prajñā is discussed in chap. 4.

37. In D. T. Suzuki, *Zen Buddhism* (New York: Doubleday Anchor, 1956), 207, 209.

38. Ibid., 160.

39. Kapleau, *Three Pillars of Zen*, 107, 137.

40. Philipp Karl Eidmann, quoted in Sangharakshita, *Survey of Buddhism*, 340.

41. Ibid., 341.

42. Fung, *Chuang-tzu*, 34, 46.

43. Ibid., 119–20.

44. *Taoist Teachings: From the Book of Lieh Tzu*, trans. Lionel Giles (New York: Dutton, 1912); quoted in Alan Watts, *Tao: The Watercourse Way* (Pelican, 1979), 92.

45. Fung, *Chuang-tzu*, 141, 116.

46. Ibid., 15, 16–17.

47. Chang Chung-yuan, *Creativity and Taoism* (New York: Julian Press, 1963), 20, 41. Nonduality remains an important element of some important contemporary Asian philosophical systems, including what has probably been the most influential Japanese philosophical work of this century, Nishida's *A Study of Good*: "What kind of thing is direct reality before we have as yet added the complexities of thought? That is, what kind of thing is an event of pure experience? At this time there is not as yet the opposition of subject and object, there is not the separation into intellect, emotion, and will, there is only independent, self-contained, pure activity." Nishida Kitaro, *A Study of Good*, trans. V. H. Viglielmo (Japanese Government Printing Bureau, 1960), 48–49. Many others (e.g. Krishnamurti) could also be cited.

2 NONDUAL PERCEPTION

1. Eliot Deutsch defines *subration* as "a mental process whereby one disvalues some previously appraised object or content of consciousness because of its being contradicted by a new experience.... it is impossible ... to affirm ... both the previous judgement and what is learned or acquired in the new experi-

ence." *Advaita Vedānta: A Philosophical Reconstruction* (Honolulu: East-West Center Press, 1969), 15.

2. Śaṅkara, *Vivekacūḍāmani* 521, trans. Mādhavānanda (Calcutta: Advaita Ashrama, 1974), 194.

3. Quoted in Ñānananda, *Concept and Reality in Early Buddhist Thought* (Kandy, Sri Lanka: Buddhist Publication Society, 1971), 28.

4. William Blake, *The Marriage of Heaven and Hell* (1792).

5. Chandradhar Sharma, *A Critical Survey of Indian Philosophy* (Delhi: Motilal Banarsidass, 1976), 194, 195.

6. It is possible to see the distinction between nirvikalpa and savikalpa as implied in the doctrine of the five *skandhas* (lit. heaps), the components of the sense-of-self. Although the skandhas are usually interpreted only ontologically, the nature and order of the five strongly suggest an epistemological approach: they "correspond obviously to the five phases which occur in every complete process of consciousness" (Lama Anagarika Govinda, *Foundations of Tibetan Mysticism* [New York: Samuel Weiser, 1971], 71). The third, *samjñā*, clearly refers to savikalpa perception, since it includes such mental processes as identification and recognition; and it could be argued that the first, *rūpa*, refers to the bare nirvikalpa percept.

7. Conze, *Buddhist Thought in India*, 62–63, 65; emphasis is Conze's. Conze quotes from his own *Buddhist Meditation*.

8. From Searle's conversation with Magee in *Men of Ideas*, ed. Bryan Magee (New York: Viking Press, 1978), 184.

9. Conze, *Buddhist Thought in India*, 65.

10. From the translation in Philip Kapleau, *Zen: Dawn in the West* (New York: Anchor/Doubleday, 1980), 185, 187.

11. For example, the *Anattalakkhaṇa-sutta* (*Saṃyutta Nikāya* III 66) supports sense-rejection, and the *Indriyabhāvanā-sutta* (*Majjhima-Nikaya* III 298–99) recommends equanimity.

12. As quoted in Ñānananda, *Concept and Reality*, 28.

13. There is a significant parallel in the etymology of *Brahman*, which is generally agreed to come from the root *bṛh* (to burst forth, to grow). "To us, it is clear, Brahman means reality, which grows, breathes or swells." Radhakrishnan, *Indian Philosophy*, 2d. ed. (London: Allen and Unwin, 1929), 1:164n. But few post-Śankara Advaitins would accept the contention that Brahman grows!

14. The three passages are quoted in Conze, *Buddhist Texts through the Ages*. The first is from the *Vimalakīrti Nirdeśa Sūtra*; the second from Śāntideva's *Śikṣāsamuccaya*, 202–03; the third from *Aṣṭasāhasrikā VII 177*.

15. Quoted in *Survey of Buddhism*, 58; Sangharakshita's addition (in parentheses).

16. Nāgārjuna, *MMK*, XXV 24. For *śiva* I have substituted "serenity" in place of Sprung's "beatitude."

17. Ñānananda, *Concept and Reality*, 3–4.

18. Buddhaghosa relates prapañca to *pamatta* (intoxication or delay) and Dhammapala equates it with *kileśa* (taints or defilements). See ibid., 108–13.

19. See *Mahānidāna Sūtra*, in *Dīgha-Nikāya* II 62–63; also Ñānananda, *Concept and Reality*, 69–71. "Papañca is thus equivalent to *Nāmarūpa*, to end which is to reach the highest attainment." G. C. Pande, *Studies in the Origins of Buddhism*, 2d ed. (Delhi: Motilal Banarsidass, 1974), 474n.

20. Candrakīrti in *Lucid Exposition*, 273, 183. I am indebted to Dr. Peter Della Santina for his comments on the relation between vikalpa and prapañca (pers. comm.).

21. Murti, *The Central Philosophy*, 232.

22. Nāgārjuna, *MMK*, XVIII 9.

23. Vasubandhu, *Trimsatikā*, in Conze, *Buddhist Texts*, 209–10. My addition in brackets.

24. See Dharmakīrti, "A Short Treatise of Logic: Nyāya-Bindu," with commentary by Dharmottara, and "Vācaspati Miśra on the Buddhist Theory of Perception," in Stcherbatsky, *Buddhist Logic*, vol. 2 (New York: Dover, 1962).

25. Stcherbatsky, *Buddhist Logic*, 2:73, 149.

26. "Jinendrabuddhi's Commentary on Dignāga's *Pramāna-samuccaya*," ibid., 2:396.

27. Ibid., 1:151.

28. Quoted in John C. H. Wu, *The Golden Age of Zen* (Taipei: United Publishing Center, 1975), 233.

29. Blofeld, *Zen Teaching of Huang Po*, 32–33.

30. Ibid., 49–50, 31, 42; my brackets and my emphasis.

31. Kapleau, *Three Pillars of Zen*, 304.

32. Ibid., 310. Kapleau's brackets.

33. For example, Stcherbatsky, *Buddhist Logic*, 1:197–98. Needless to say, many Advaitins are unhappy with this claim.

34. D. M. Datta, "Epistemological Methods in Indian Philosohy," in Charles A. Moore, ed., *Essays in East-West Philosophy* (Honolulu: University of Hawaii Press, 1951), 78. For a more detailed discussion see Purusottama Bilimoria, "Perception in Advaita Vedānta," *Philosophy East and West* 30, no. 1 (June 1980).

35. See, for example, *Brahmasūtrabhāsya* II.ii.1–32.

36. Commentary on *Gītā* II 69.

37. *Upadeśasāhasrī* XVIII 159; quoted in Satprakāshānanda, *Methods of Knowledge*, 278.

38. Surendranath Dasgupta, *A History of Indian Philosophy* (Delhi: Motilal Banarsidass, 1975), 474.

39. Tucci, *Religions of Tibet*, 66.

40. "Relation" must be put in scare-quotes because according to Śaṅkara they are not really distinct but "nondifferent," *ananyatva*: from the transcendental standpoint there is only Brahman and from the empirical standpoint there appears to be only phenomena, so to discuss a "relation" between them is to confuse different perspectives. Notice, however, that the same could be said about the "relation" between nondual and dualistic perception. The definition of *adhyāsa* is in the preamble to the *Brahmasūtrabhāsya*.

41. Sharma, *Critical Survey of Indian Philosophy*, 274.

42. Radhakrishnan, *Indian Philosophy*, 2:565, 572.

43. Satprakāshānanda, *Methods of Knowledge*, 77.

44. Kapleau, *Three Pillars of Zen*, 107, 153. Compare the favorite koan of the Japanese Zen master Bassui: "Who is the master of [i.e., who is hearing] that sound?"

45. Simone Weil, *Waiting on God*, trans. Emma Cranford (London: Routledge and Kegan Paul, 1951), letter 4, 38.

46. See Hans Jonas, *The Phenomenon of Life* (New York: 1966), 135–36, 147; as quoted in Hannah Arendt, *The Life of the Mind* (New York: Harcourt Brace Jovanovich, 1978), 1:110–12.

47. See George Berkeley's *Essay Towards a New Theory of Vision* (1709), sec. 45.

48. David Hume, *An Enquiry Concerning Human Understanding*, sec. 4, pt. 1.

49. David Hume, *A Treatise of Human Nature*, bk. 1, pt. 4, sec. 7.

50. The first passage is from *Kaṭha Upaniṣad* II.ii.15, repeated in *Muṇḍaka Upaniṣad*, II.ii.10 and *Śvetāśvatara Upaniṣad* VI.14. See also Śaṅkara's commentary on the *Bṛhadāraṇyaka Upaniṣad*, IV.iii.7. The second is *Muṇḍaka Upaniṣad* II.ii.9 and the third is *Chāndogya Upaniṣad* III.xvii.7. Cf. William Blake: "What is Above is Within, for every-thing in Eternity is translucent" (*Jerusalem*).

51. Tucci, *Religions of Tibet*, 63–64.

52. *Aṅguttara Nikāya* I 10, Horner's trans.; quoted in Sangharakshita, *Survey of Buddhism*, 70–71.

53. Rudolf Otto, *Mysticism East and West*, trans. Bertha L. Lacey and Richenda C. Payne (New York: Macmillan, 1932), 110, 115.

54. Dasgupta, *History of Indian Philosophy*, 1:493.

55. In the first of Berkeley's *Three Dialogues Between Hylas and Philonous*.

56. Heidegger, *Being and Time*, div. 1, pt. 5, chap. 34.

57. R. J. Hirst, "Perception," in *The Encyclopedia of Philosophy*, ed. Paul Edwards (New York: Macmillan), 6:86. My emphasis.

58. Richard Gregory, "Visual Illusions," *Scientific American* 219, no. 5 (1968): 66.

59. Karl Popper, "Philosophy of Science: A Personal Report," in *British Philosophy in the Mid-Century*, ed. C. A. Mace, 172.

60. R. J. Hirst, "Phenomenalism," in Edwards, *Encyclopedia of Philosophy*, 6:131

61. Ludwig Wittgenstein, *Tractatus Logico-Philosophicus* (London: Routledge and Kegan Paul, 1961), 57, no. 5.633.

62. Nāgārjuna, *MMK*, III 2.

63. Vasubandhu, *Madhyāntavibhagabhāsya*, commentary to v. 26, in *Seven Works of Vasubandhu*, trans. Stefan Anacker (Delhi: Motilal Banarsidass, 1984), 269.

64. That is the direction in which the argument of this chapter might be developed further, to deny finally any dualism between thoughts and percepts. When the nondual percept is fully distinguished from all thought-superimpositions, maybe it is realized to be just as much a creation of "my" mind as dreams and fantasies. Then the essence of delusion is the sharp distinction we draw between the materialized objective world and the powers of our "Imagination,

the real & eternal World of which this Vegetable Universe is but a faint shadow, & in which we shall live in our Eternal or Imaginative Bodies when these Vegetable Mortal Bodies are no more" (William Blake, *Jerusalem*).

65. William Blake, *The Marriage of Heaven and Hell*.

66. Blake, frontispiece to *The Gates of Paradise*.

67. Plotinus, *Enneads* I.6.9.

68. Maurice Merleau-Ponty, *The Phenomenology of Perception*, trans. Colin Smith (London: Routledge and Kegan Paul, 1962), 205. This double-aspect approach is rich in other implications too. It is consistent with the claims of "body-work" therapies (for example, Rolfing) popular in contemporary psychology. It even casts a different light on phrenology, that discredited "science" which may yet contain a grain of truth. To infer character from the shape of the head is certainly too mechanistic, but isn't there some causal interaction between personality and body—especially with regard to the face, where the sense-organs cluster? Why does the development of a face, over the years, reveal so much?

3 NONDUAL ACTION

1. These *Tao Tê Ching* passages are from the translation in Chang's *Tao*, with modifications by me.

2. See Ludwig Wittgenstein, *Philosophical Investigations*, trans. G. E. M. Anscombe (Oxford: Basil Blackwell, 1972), 32, I.67ff.

3. Roger T. Ames, "*Wu-Wei* in 'The Art of Rulership' chapter of *Huai Nan Tzu*," *Philosophy East and West* 31, no. 2 (April 1981): 196.

4. See ibid, 196–98, and Herlee G. Creel, *What Is Taoism?* (University of Chicago Press, 1970), 44–47.

5. I have borrowed Ames's translation, "*Wu-wei*," 194.

6. Quoted in Creel, *What Is Taoism?*, 54.

7. Fung Yu-lan, *A Short History of Chinese Philosophy*, 225.

8. Arthur Waley's translation in *The Way and Its Power* (London: Allen and Unwin, 1968).

9. For example, see Wing-tsit Chan's translation in *A Source Book of Chinese Philosophy* (Princeton University Press, 1963), chaps. 36, 40, 52, 76, 78.

10. Creel, *What Is Taoism?*, 54, quoting Wang Pi on *Lao-Tzu*, Duyvendak's *Tao Tê Ching*, 10, 11 and Fung's *Short History of Chinese Philosophy*, 100–01.

11. "The important phrase, *wu-wei*, thus means 'not-having willful action.'" Sung-peng Hsu, "Lao Tzu's Conception of Evil," *Philosophy East and West* 26, no. 3 (July 1976): 303.

12. "It is important to note that 'spontaneity' is really the positive name for the negative expression of *wu-wei*." Ibid., 304.

13. Creel, *What Is Taoism?*, 74, 45–46. Creel first argued for this view in "On Two Aspects in Early Taoism" (1954) and repeated his position in "On the Origin of Wu-Wei" (1965). Both are reprinted in *What Is Taoism?*

14. Fung's *Chuang Tzu*, 40, 117, 124, 119–20.

15. Burton Watson, trans., *The Complete Works of Chuang Tzu* (New York: Columbia University Press, 1968), 83.

16. See Chang, *Creativity and Taoism*, 10.

17. *Chao Lun* IV 6:14a, as quoted in Chang's *Tao*, 122.

18. From the translation in Kapleau, *Zen: Dawn in the West*, 188, 187.

19. Chang Chung-yuan, trans. and ed., *Original Teachings of Ch'an Buddhism* (New York: Vintage, 1971), 22.

20. Conze, *Perfection of Wisdom*, 76, 101, 104, 116; Conze, *Buddhist Thought in India*, 236–37.

21. *Tibetan Yoga*, 134, 136. The interpolated brackets are by the translator, Evans-Wentz. There and in his notes he explains that this describes the nonduality of thinker and thought (and this interpretation will be discussed in Chapter 4), but nothing in the text itself excludes an interpretation in terms of nondual physical action.

22. *Bhagavad-gītā* IV 18, 20; trans. Radhakrishnan, in *Sourcebook of Indian Philosophy*, ed. Radhakrishnan and Moore (Princeton University Press, 1957), 117.

23. Conze, *Perfection of Wisdom*, 76. The "triple world" refers to the three levels of saṁsāra, the worlds of desire, form, and the formless.

24. Masao Abe, *Zen and Western Thought* (London: Macmillan, 1985), 145.

25. Martin Buber, *I and Thou*, trans. Walter Kaufmann, 2d ed. (Edinburgh: T. T. Clark, 1970), 125. This page, which describes the I–Thou relationship as "at once . . . passive and active", shows the ambivalence in Buber's approach. In order to maintain that "I-Thou" is a relationship, he must keep the *relata* distinct from each other and deny nonduality; but this passage, like many others, suggests nonduality.

26. Conze, *Perfection of Wisdom*, 66–7.

27. *Mumonkan*, case 20, trans. in Kyozo Yamada, *Gateless Gate* (Los Angeles: Center Publications, 1977), my emphasis and addition.

28. From *The Blue Cliff Record*, case 89, trans. Thomas Cleary and J. C. Cleary (Boulder: Shambhala, 1977), 571.

29. From Yasutani's "Commentary on Mu," in Kapleau, *Three Pillars of Zen*, 46–47.

30. Quoted in Chang, *Original Teachings of Ch'an*, 130.

31. Yamada, *Gateless Gate*, 86, 88.

32. From Cleary and Cleary, *Blue Cliff Record*, case 92, with modifications by me.

33. Kapleau, *Three Pillars of Zen*, 82.

34. Howard H. Brinton, *The Mystic Will* (New York: Macmillan, 1930), 218.

35. R. B. Blakney, trans., *Meister Eckhart* (New York: Harper and Row, 1941), 127, 241. See also Eckhart's sermon "Blessed are the Poor in Spirit" and *Defense* IX, 31.

36. According to Wing-tsit Chan, 350 Chinese commentaries on the *Tao Tĕ Ching* are extant, and some 350 more have been lost or survive only in fragments. (*Source Book of Chinese Philosophy*, 137).

37. Wing-tsit Chan, *The Way of Lao Tzu* (Indianapolis: Bobbs-Merrill, 1963), 99.

"This chapter both introduces and summarizes the entire *Tao Tê Ching*. The 'five thousand' words of the text are all based on this chapter." See also Chang's *Tao* 1.

38. Chan, *Way of Lao Tzu*, 99.

39. Martin Heidegger, *What Is Called Thinking?*, trans. Fred D. Wieck and Glenn Gray (New York: Harper and Row, 1968), 178.

40. My version of this chapter, constructed from a transliteration after consulting other translations.

41. For a discussion of what ineffability in the *Tao Tê Ching* does *not* mean, see Arthur C. Danto, "Language and the Tao: Some Reflections on Ineffability," *Journal of Chinese Philosophy* 1, no. 1 (1973): 45–55. For an argument that the *Tao Tê Ching* is not ineffable, see Dennis M. Ahern, "Ineffability in the *Lao Tzu*: The Taming of a Dragon," *Journal of Chinese Philosophy* 4, no. 4 (1977): 357–82.

42. See Shigenori Nagatomo, "An Epistemic Turn in the *Tao Tê Ching*," *International Philosophical Quarterly* 23, no. 2 (June 1983: 174ff. Nagatomo also sees the first chapter as referring to two different modes of experience, but, in my opinion, the subjectivism of his phenomenological categories does not allow him to illuminate the difference between them.

43. See *Mumonkan*, case 37.

44. The latter interpretation is usually described only as "ontological," but the epistemological and ontological issues here cannot be separated; it is a difference in experience that changes our understanding of what is. An account of these interpretations would encompass the whole history of Taoism. Fung Yu-lan, author of the monumental *History of Chinese Philosophy*, gave an ontological interpretation in *A Short History of Chinese Philosophy* (1948), but later (probably under pressure from the authorities) changed to a cosmological view in 1964. For a discussion of Fung's interpretations, see David C. Yu, "The Creation Myth and Its Symbolism in Classical Taoism," *Philosophy East and West* 31, no. 4 (1981): 487, 497. According to Charles Wei-hsun Fu, chap. 2 of *Chuang Tzu* refutes the cosmological interpretation. Fu has used Wang Pi's distinction between origin and function to interpret the first chapter of the *Tao Tê Ching* as distinguishing Tao-as-Origin from Tao-as-Function. "Creative Hermeneutics: Taoist Metaphysics and Heidegger," *Journal of Chinese Philosophy* 3, no. 2 (1976): 125ff.

45. Chan, *Way of Lao Tzu*, 99.

46. Chang's *Tao*, 3–4.

47. However, Lao Tzu's Non-Being should not be taken either in a Parmenidean sense or (what is more likely) as equivalent to the Mahāyāna śūnyatā. Nāgārjuna takes pains to distinguish śūnyatā from both being and nonbeing, which as relative to each other are both denied. A more fruitful interpretation of Lao Tzu's Non-Being is to see it as one way of making what Heidegger calls "the ontological difference" between beings and Being.

48. Wittgenstein, *Philosophical Investigations* I.31. For a more general discussion of the parallels between Wittgenstein and Taoism, see Russell Goodman, "Style,

Dialectic, and the Aim of Philosophy in Wittgenstein and the Taoists," *Journal of Chinese Philosophy* 3, no. 2 (1976): 145–57.

49. See Heidegger, *Being and Time*, div. 1, pt. 3, secs. 15–16. In contrast to my use of the distinction, Heidegger views *vorhanden* objects, just "lying there," as derivative from *zuhanden*; he saw his project in *Being and Time* as an attempt to overcome the error (prevalent since Parmenides) of basing a metaphysics upon *vorhanden*. Whether his later work after the *Kehre* is consistent with this is unclear to me.

50. Wittgenstein reserved the term "seeing...as" for more ambiguous types of seeing (e.g., the duck-rabbit). See *Philosophical Investigations* II.x.1.

51. P. H. Nowell-Smith, from an article "On Causation or Causality." I am acquainted with a cyclostyled copy of this article, but have not been able to trace its source.

52. Nāgārjuna, *MMK*, XXV 19–20. Yet XXV 9 distinguishes them: "That which, taken as causal or dependent, is the process of being born and passing on, is, taken non-causally and beyond all dependence, declared to be *nirvāṇa*." This issue is discussed in chap. 6.

53. Stuart Hampshire, *Thought and Action* (London: Chatto and Windus, 1960), 126, 119.

54. David Hume, *An Enquiry Concerning Human Understanding*, sec. 7, pt. 1.

55. Friedrich Nietzsche, *The Will To Power*, trans. Walter Kaufmann and R. J. Hollingdale (New York: Vintage, 1968), 295–99, nos. 551–2.

56. "The greatest difficulty faced by every discussion of the Will is the simple fact that there is no other capacity of the mind whose very existence has been so consistently doubted and refuted by so eminent a series of philosophers" (Arendt, *Life of the Mind*, 2:4). William Blake: "There can be no Good Will. Will is always Evil; it is perniciousness to others or suffering."

57. Hobbes, *Leviathan* II, 21.

58. This has important implications for our understanding of such completely deterministic systems as Spinoza's.

59. See Aristotle's *Nicomachean Ethics*, 1174a 14; also *Metaphysics*, IX. 6, 1048b 18ff.

60. Herbert A. Giles, trans., *Chuang Tzu* (New York: AMS Press, 1972), 240–41.

4 NONDUAL THINKING

1. *Phaedo* 65c.

2. In Kapleau, *Three Pillars of Zen*, 306.

3. Ibid., 205.

4. D. T. Suzuki, "Reason and Intuition in Buddhist Philosophy," in Moore, *Essays in East-West Philosophy*, 17.

5. Ibid., 29.

6. Ibid., 35.

7. *Oxford English Dictionary*.

8. Suzuki, "Reason and Intuition," 34, 17.

9. "Mahāmudrā," 136. Krishnamurti makes a similar claim: "Revolution, this psychological, creative revolution in which the 'me' is not, comes only when the thinker and thought are one, when there is no duality such as the thinker controlling thought; and I suggest it is this experience alone that releases the creative energy which in turn brings about a fundamental revolution, the breaking up of the psychological 'me.'" *The First and Last Freedom* (London: Gollanz, 1956), 140.

10. *Śikṣāsamuccaya* 233–34, in Conze, *Buddhist Texts*, 163; my emphasis.

11. Rene Descartes, "Meditations on First Philosophy," in *The Philosophical Works of Descartes*, trans. Haldane and Ross (Cambridge University Press, 1973), 1: 151–52.

12. Ibid., 153.

13. David Hume, *A Treatise of Human Nature*, bk. 1, pt. 4, sec. 6, "Of Personal Identity."

14. John Levy, *The Nature of Man According to the Vedanta* (London: Routledge and Kegan Paul, 1956), 66–67.

15. Ibid., 69. This invites comparison with Sartre's view of self-consciousness as developed in *The Transcendence of the Ego* and *Being and Nothingness*.

16. Quoted in Kapleau, *Three Pillars of Zen*, 205.

17. Blake's critique of rationality also relates it to memory:

> The Spectre is the Reasoning Power in Man, & when separated
> From Imagination and closing itself as in steel in a Ratio
> Of the Things of Memory, It thence frames Laws & Moralities
> To destroy Imagination, the Divine Body, by Martyrdoms & Wars.
>
> *(Jerusalem*, pl. 74)

There is another parallel in Owen Barfield's *Saving the Appearances: A Study in Idolatry* (New York: Harcourt Brace Jovanovich, n.d.), 154–55: "Just as, when a word is formed or spoken, the original unity of the 'inner' word is polarized into a duality of outer and inner, that is, of sound and meaning; so, when man himself was 'uttered', that is, created, the cosmic wisdom became polarized in and through him, into the duality of appearance and intelligence, representation and consciousness. But when creation has been polarized into consciousness on the one side and phenomena, or appearances, on the other, memory is made possible, and begins to play an all-important part in the process of evolution. For by means of his memory man makes the outward appearances an inward experience. He acquires his self-consciousness from them. When I experience the phenomena in memory, I make them 'mine', not now by virtue of any original participation [cf. 'nondual experience'], but by my own inner activity." Barfield's book is one of those insightful and curious works which, blithely ignorant of Asian thought, attempt to interpret Christianity into something that is more naturally compatible with Buddhism and Vedānta.

18. Nietzsche, *Will to Power*, 264, 265.

19. *Sutra Spoken by the Sixth Patriarch on the High Seat of "The Treasure of the Law,"* trans. Wong Mou-lam (Hong Kong: Buddhist Book Distributor, n.d.), 35.

20. Ibid., 49. My emphasis.

21. My version of this line; see ibid., 19.

22. Conze, *Perfection of Wisdom*, 90.

23. Quoted in Alan Watts, *The Way of Zen* (London: 1962), 102n. Compare: "The True is thus the Bacchanalian revel in which no member [i.e., no thought] is not drunk; yet because each member collapses as soon as he drops out, the revel is just as much transparent and simple repose." From Hegel's Preface to *The Phenomenology of Spirit*, trans. A. V. Miller (Oxford University Press, 1977), 27, no. 47.

24. Chang, *Original Teachings of Ch'an*, 203.

25. Śaṅkara's *Laghu-vākya-vṛtti* 9; quoted in Satprakāshānanda, *Methods of Knowledge*, 238.

26. Ramana Maharshi, *Erase the Ego* (Bombay: Bharatiya Vidya Bhavan, 1978), 28.

27. Suzuki, "Reason and Intuition," 18, 24, 41.

28. Blofeld, *The Zen Teaching of Huang Po*, 54.

29. From case 19 of the *Mumonkan*. Case 34 consists of Nan-ch'üan's simple statement: "Mind is not the Buddha. Knowing is not the Way." There are significant Christian parallels. Johannes Scotus (Erigen): "God does not know Himself, what He is, because He is not a *what*; in a certain respect He is incomprehensible to Himself and to every intellect.

30. Lu K'uan Yu, *Ch'an and Zen Teaching*, Third Series (London: Rider, 1962), 116.

31. *The Zen Teaching of Hui Hai*, trans. John Blofeld (London: Rider, 1969), 56. There is a remarkable parallel in Hegel's analysis of the "bad infinite" (or "false endlessness": *schlechte unendlichkeit*) in the Encyclopedia *Logic* (1817). There he defines "determination" as the quality of a something set off by that quality from other somethings. When it is realized that the quality of each entity depends on others because in a sense it has these others within itself as the conditions of its own determinateness (cf. the Hua Yen metaphor of Indra's Net), this becomes *alienation* because the nature of each quality varies as the others do. This is a "bad infinite" because insofar as I (for example) try to go beyond determination, I end up merely exchanging one finite determination for another. The solution involves a reversal of perspective: true infinity is that of the "free-ranging variable" which always has some finite value but is not bound to any particular one. This is "being-for-self."

32. The concept of symbolic immortality projects is well discussed by Ernest Becker in *The Denial of Death* (New York: The Free Press, 1973) and *Escape from Evil* (New York: The Free Press, 1978). This raises important questions about the nature of academic research: Is it a collective immortality project? If we understand our work as scientific, is it an attempt at the very objectivity which is challenged by the subject we study?

33. *The Zen Teaching of Huang Po*, 41.

34. Hume, *An Enquiry Concerning Human Understanding*, sec. 7, pt. 1.

35. Chang, *Creativity and Taoism*; D. T. Suzuki, *Zen and Japanese Culture* (Princeton University Press, 1959).

36. Quoted in P. E. Vernon, ed., *Creativity* (Penguin Books, 1970), 55.

37. Ibid., 57–58.

38. Arthur M. Abell, *Gesprache mit beruhmten Komponisten* (Garmisch-Parten-Kirchen, Germany: Schroeder-Verlag, 1964), 145, 156. I have lost the name of the translator of these passages from Abell.

39. Ibid., 20–21.

40. Quoted in Gordon Rattray Taylor, *The Natural History of the Mind* (London: Secker and Warburg, 1979), 225.

41. Abell, *Gesprache*, 187.

42. Quoted by Brian Inglis, "The Woman Who Saw What Others Could Not," in *The Sunday Times Magazine* (London), 2 May 1982: 51.

43. Friedrich Nietzsche, *Ecce Homo*, trans. Walter Kaufmann, in *Basic Writings of Nietzsche* (New York: Modern Library, 1968), 300–01.

44. Friedrich Nietzsche, *Beyond Good and Evil*, trans. Marianne Cowan (Chicago: Henry Regnery, 1955), 231.

45. Quoted in Peter McKellar, *Imagination and Thinking* (London: Cohen and West, 1957), 131–32.

46. Quoted in E. Harding and E. M. Rosamond, *An Anatomy of Inspiration* (Cambridge: Heffer, 1942); reproduced in Taylor, *Natural History of the Mind*, 224.

47. Milton, *Paradise Lost* 9:21–24.

48. Taylor, *Natural History of the Mind*, 224. *Jerusalem* had a divine origin: "I see the Saviour over me / spreading his beams of love & dictating the words of this mild song." (I, 4–5).

49. Goethe, Dickens, and Eliot all quoted in Taylor, *Natural History of the Mind*, 224.

50. Quoted in Arthur Koestler, *The Act of Creation* (London: Hutchinson, 1964), 166–67.

51. Quoted in Roger Sale, *Fairy Tales and After* (Cambridge: Harvard University Press, 1978), 102–03.

52. Ibid., 103.

53. Jaynes, *The Origin of Consciousness*, in *The Breakdown of the Bicameral Mind* (Boston: Houghton Mifflin, 1976), 376.

54. Thackeray and Blyton in Taylor, *Natural History of the Mind*, 224.

55. Carl G. Hempel, *Philosophy of Natural Science* (Englewood Cliffs, N.J.: Prentice-Hall, 1966), 14.

56. Quoted in Koestler, *Act of Creation*, 115–16.

57. Ibid., 117.

58. Ibid.

59. Ibid., 116–17.

60. All in Inglis, "The Woman Who Saw What Others Could Not."

61. Koestler, *Janus*, 149.

62. Lloyd Morgan, quoted in Koestler, *Act of Creation*, 145.

63. Ibid., 213.
64. Kant, *Critique of Pure Reason*, B367. For a discussion of this distinction, see Arendt, *Life of the Mind*, 1:57.
65. Brinton, *The Mystic Will*, 100–02.
66. Ibid., 124, 113, 103.
67. Eckhart, quoted ibid., 125.
68. See J. L. Mehta, *The Philosophy of Martin Heidegger* (Varanasi: Banaras Hindu University Press, 1967), 1.
69. Heidegger, "A Dialogue on Language," trans. Peter D. Hertz, in *On the Way to Language* (New York: Harper and Row, 1971), 12.
70. Heidegger, "Letter on Humanism," trans. Frank A. Capuzzi, in *Martin Heidegger: Basic Writings*, ed. David Farrell Krell (New York: Harper and Row), 215.
71. Heidegger, *What Calls for Thinking?*, trans. Frank A. Capuzzi, ibid., 358.
72. Arendt, *Life of the Mind*, 1:171.
73. The German title can be translated either "What calls for thinking?' or "What is called thinking?"
74. *What Is Called Thinking?*, 159, 168–69.
75. Mehta, *Philosophy of Heidegger*, 374. A good discussion of the *Kehre* is on pp. 369–389.
76. Heidegger, "Letter on Humanism," 199.
77. Ibid., 194.
78. Ibid., 236, 194.
79. Heidegger, *What Calls for Thinking?*, 353.
80. Heidegger, "Letter on Humanism," 222.
81. Ibid., 223.
82. Ibid., 204, 210, 210–11, 212, 211 (my emphasis in the last).
83. Ibid., 229.
84. Ibid., 242. My emphasis.
85. Heidegger, "On the Essence of Truth," trans. John Sallis, in *Basic Writings*, 140–41. Unless otherwise indicated, my emphasis in all the quotations in this section.
86. Ibid., 123.
87. Ibid., 125 (Heidegger's emphasis), 134, 135.
88. Heidegger, "Conversation on a Country Path about Thinking," in *Discourse on Thinking*, trans. John M. Anderson and E. Hans Freund (New York: Harper and Row, 1966).
89. Heidegger, "The End of Philosophy and the Task of Thinking," in *Basic Writings*, 374.
90. Heidegger, *What Is Called Thinking?*, 44, 98.
91. Heidegger, "End of Philosophy," 384–87.
92. Heidegger, "What Is Metaphysics?", in *Basic Writings*, 98, 103, 105, 106.
93. William Barrett discusses this in his introduction to the Anchor paperback anthology of Suzuki's writings, *Zen Buddhism* (New York: Doubleday, 1956), xi.
94. *Mumonkan*, case 7, in Yamada, *Gateless Gate*.

95. See *Mumonkan*, case 46, ibid.
96. Chang, *Original Teachings of Ch'an Buddhism*, 231.
97. Heidegger, "End of Philosophy," 373.

5 THREE APPROACHES TO THE SUBJECT–OBJECT RELATION

1. The subject–object dualism with which these three systems are concerned can be expressed either as a consciousness–object dualism or a self–nonself dualism. Although these dualisms are not identical, they are obviously closely related, and for our purposes they will be treated as equivalent.

2. See also *Gradual Sayings* I.8.10, in *Aṅguttara Nikāya*, where the Buddha describes consciousness (*citta*) as luminous (*pabhassara*):

   This consciousness is luminous but it is defiled by adventitious defilements. The uninstructed average person does not understand this as it really is. Therefore I say that for him there is no mental development.

   This consciousness is luminous, and it is freed from adventitious defilements. The instructed Aryan disciple understands this as it really is. Therefore I say that for him there is mental development.   (Horner's trans.)

3. Edward J. Thomas, *The Life of Buddha* (London: Routledge and Kegan Paul 1949), 201.

4. For example, see Stcherbatsky, *The Central Conception of Buddhism* (Delhi: Motilal Banarsidass, 1974), esp. 3, 73.

5. Guiseppe Tucci, *On Some Aspects of the Doctrines of Maitreya and Asanga* (Calcutta: University of Calcutta, 1930), 2–4; quoted in Sangharakshita, *Survey of Buddhism*, 345.

6. Conze, *Buddhist Thought in India*, 251.

7. E. J. Thomas, *The History of Buddhist Thought* (London: Routledge and Kegan Paul, 1933), 230, quoted in *Survey of Buddhism*, 346; Sangharakshita's addition.

8. For a brief summary of the issues in this debate, see Lalmani Joshi, *Studies in the Buddhistic Culture of India* (Delhi: Motilal Banarsidass, 1977), 178–80.

9. Chāndogya Upaniṣad VI.viii.7; Śaṅkara's *Vivekacūḍāmani* 226, 339; Īśā Upaniṣad 7; Bṛhadāraṇyaka Upaniṣad IV.iv.13.

10. The same point is made in the Zen Oxherding Pictures: the Ninth Picture is "Return to the Source," but in so doing one realizes that one never left it.

11. Bṛhadāraṇyaka Upaniṣad II.iv.12–15, in Radhakrishnan and Moore, *Sourcebook of Indian Philosophy*, 82. My emphasis. Other Upaniṣadic verses sometimes cited as Buddhist in essence are Chāndogya VI.ii.1, Kaṭha I.xxvi.28 and II.v.7, Aitareya III.3.

12. *Naiṣkarmya Siddhi*, III 58, trans. A. J. Alston, as quoted in Deutsch's *Advaita Vedānta*, 55.

13. Sharma, *Critical Survey of Indian Philosophy*, 318.

14. Dasgupta, *History of Indian Philosophy*, 1:493–94. My emphasis.

15. Joshi, *Buddhistic Culture*, 340–41.

16. Ibid., 338.
17. For further discussion of this topic, see ibid., chaps. 9, 13; and Sharma, *Critical Survey of Indian Philosophy*, chp. 18.

6 THE DECONSTRUCTION OF DUALISM

1. Murti, *Central Philosophy of Buddhism*, 10–11.
2. Ludwig Wittgenstein, *Notebooks 1914–1916*, ed. and trans. G. E. M. Anscombe (Oxford: Blackwell, 1961).
3. "Yasutani's Commentary on Mu," in Kapleau, *Three Pillars of Zen*, 79–80.
4. Dōgen-Zenji, *Shōbōgenzō*, trans. Kosen Nishiyama and John Stevens (Sendai: Daihokkaikaku, 1975), 1:1.
5. Po-shan, as quoted in Garma C. C. Chang, *The Practice of Zen* (New York: Harper and Row), 103.
6. Hakuin, quoted in Suzuki, *Zen Buddhism*, 148.
7. Po-shan, quoted in Chang, *Practice of Zen*, 103.
8. Hakuin, quoted in Suzuki, *Zen Buddhism*, 148.
9. *Yoga Sūtra* I.41.
10. Taittirīya, I.viii.1 and Śvetāśvatara I.14.
11. Satprakāshānanda, *Methods of Knowledge*, 276.
12. *Mysticism East and West*, 275, 278.
13. From a *teisho* (sermon) by Yamada Kōun given during a Zen sesshin. My emphasis.
14. Bṛhadāraṇyaka Upaniṣad III.vii.23 and II.iv.14. Compare also III.iv.2: "You cannot think of the thinker of thinking; you cannot know the Knower of Knowing." Kena Upaniṣad II.3: "It is known to him who does not know It, and it is unknown to him who knows It."
15. *Ātmajñānōpadeśavidhi* IV.10, quoted in Satprakāshānanda, *Methods of Knowledge*, 239.
16. See also Plato's *Republic*, VIII.518. After this initial experience of "returning home," would the state of nirvana/mokṣa be blissful or not? This is an important controversy. In Sāṅkhya-Yoga, the liberated puruṣa is indifferent to both pain and bliss; apparently no emotional characteristics are applicable. Yet the true self is by no means emotionally neutral in Vedānta: Brahman is sacchidā-nanda, Existence-Consciousness-Bliss; all our phenomenal happiness is but a pale reflection of this ultimate joy.
    Without attempting to resolve this issue, let me point out two passages that suggest these positions might not be irreconcilable. Chāndogya Upaniṣad IV.x.4–5: "Then they said to him: 'Brahman is life (*prana*). Brahman is joy. Brahman is the void.' Then he said: 'I understand that Brahman is life. But joy and void I do not understand.' They said: 'Joy (*ka*)—truly, that is the same as the Void (*kha*). The Void—truly, that is the same as joy.'" In one of the Pāli sutras the arhat Śāriputra, in answer to a similar question, says "that there is no sensation, is itself bliss."

17. Gauḍapāda, *Āgamaśāstra* IV.60. Previously Guaḍapāda demonstrates that all things are unborn (*ajāti*).

18. Such, at least, is the traditional interpretation of their views, which has been questioned—notably by Heidegger, who claims that there is no such disagreement between them. This section could be used to support such a reinterpretation, for it could be argued that its conclusions are compatible with the fragments that remain of both Heraclitus and Parmenides.

19. For the same reason, Cratylus also concluded that language can never describe reality, since words are an attempt to fix that which never stops changing. So at the end of his life he no longer spoke but just "wagged his finger." A Greek Zen master?

20. Aristotle's description of Parmenides is as accurate a summary of Nāgārjuna: "Some earlier philosophers, e.g., Melissus and Parmenides, flatly denied generation and destruction, maintaining that nothing which is either comes into being or perishes; it only seems to us as if this happens" (*De Caelo* 298 B14). "They say that no existing thing either comes into being or perishes because what comes into being must originate either from what exists or from what does not, and both are impossible: what is does not become (for it already is) and nothing could come to be from what is not" (*Physics* 191 A27).

21. Thomas McEvilley makes a case for Plato as a Mādhyamika in "Early Greek Philosophy and Mādhyamika," *Philosophy East and West* 31 no. 2 (April 1981): 149–52.

22. Arendt, *Life of the Mind*, 1:45. Arendt is describing Plotinus and Hegel, but the quotation also fits the nondualist Eastern traditions.

23. Heidegger finds the same duality at the origin of Greek philosophy: "even the very relation between presencing and what is present remains unthought. From early on it seems as though presencing and what is present were each something for itself. Presencing itself unnoticeably becomes something present.... The essence of presencing, and with it the distinction between presencing and what is present, remains forgotten. *The oblivion of Being is the oblivion of the distinction between Being and beings.*" "The Anaximander Fragment" in *Early Greek Thinking*, trans. Krell and Capuzzi (New York: Harper and Row, 1975), 50–51. Although Heidegger sees the interdependence of presencing and what-is-present, he does not further deconstruct the duality because, like Advaita Vedānta, he wants to maintain an "ontological distinction" between Being and beings.

24. A possible objection here, that this confuses "psychological" with "objective" (e.g., Newtonian) time, presupposes the very duality that this work is challenging.

25. Masunaga Reiho, *The Soto Approach to Zen* (Tokyo: Layman Buddhist Society Press, 1958), 68.

26. Dōgen, *Shōbōgenzō*, 1:68–69.

27. Nāgārjuna, *MMK* XIII.5.

28. Dōgen, *Shōbōgenzō*, 1:2.

29. And perhaps not. The source is Sextus Empiricus (*Outlines of Pyrrhonism* III

230): "Heraclitus says that both life and death are in both our living and dying; for when we live our souls are dead and buried in us, but when we die our souls revive and live." The gloss makes the first statement rather pedestrian, but it may not be Heraclitus' own. What Heraclitus says in frags. 67 and 65 could also be used to explain śūnyatā: "God is . . . fullness/emptiness"; "fullness and emptiness are the same thing."

30. In the "Shōji" (Birth and Death) fascicle of Dōgen's Shōbōgenzō.

31. Ibid., 1:69, 70.

32. Wittgenstein, Notebooks 75e, dated 8.7.16.

33. This suggests a "solution" to Zeno's paradoxes, which presuppose a realist (objectified) conception of time. Quantification into a succession of finitely (atomism) or infinitely (continuum) divisible moments is inevitable if time is a "thing" and thus obviously composed of parts, but no collection of such units can ever add up to the flux of an event. As Nāgārjuna also pointed out, the basic problem is that continuity can never be established between such discrete moments, regardless of their duration. The error is to presuppose that the "now" is merely a unit of time, one of a sequence of moments successively falling away. Of course, this does not refute Zeno. His paradoxes prove just what he wanted: as his teacher Parmenides argued, time as something objective, that things are "in," is unreal.

34. This is probably no coincidence, since there is little doubt that the dialectic of Gauḍapāda (believed to be Śaṅkara's teacher's teacher) was influenced by Mādhyamika. See Gauḍapāda's Āgamaśāstra IV.3–41 for an Advaitic discussion of causality obviously influenced by Nāgārjuna's.

35. MMK XXIV.18.

36. Ibid., 32–33.

37. MMK VII.34, as quoted in Murti, Central Philosophy of Buddhism, 177.

38. Candrakīrti, Lucid Exposition, 230, 236.

39. If percepts are Mind, it may be better to say that by perceiving them as objects we give them the stability that we then attribute to them.

40. See Hume's Enquiry Concerning Human Understanding, sec. 4, pts. 1–2.

41. Richard Robinson, "Did Nāgārjuna Really Refute All Philosophical Views?" Philosophy East and West 22 (1972): 325. Cheng Hsueh-li, "Motion and Rest in the Middle Treatise," Journal of Chinese Philosophy 7 (1980): 235ff.

42. This version of the story, from the Transmission of the Lamp, is given in Chang, Original Teachings of Ch'an, 116–17.

43. Tung-shan told his students to walk "in the bird's track," which is of course trackless, showing no deliberative traces before and leaving none after.

44. The Pūrva-Mīmāṁsā-Sūtras of Jaimini, trans. Ganganatha Jha (Varanasi: Bharatiya Publishing House, 1979), I.i.2, p. 3.

45. Bṛhadāraṇyaka Upaniṣad I.iv.7.

46. The Brahma-Sūtra-Bhāṣya of Śaṅkarācārya, I.i.4.

47. Ibid.

48. Ibid.; see also Kaṭha Upaniṣad I.ii.22.

49. Radhakrishnan, *Indian Philosophy* II 616. Radhakrishnan cites *Brahma-Sūtra-Bhaṣya* III.iv.27.

50. *Brahma-Sūtra-Bhaṣya* IV.1.4.

51. Bṛhadāraṇyaka Upaniṣad I.iv.7.

52. There is a striking parallel in Plato's *Republic*, from the Cave parable: "our view of these matters must be this, that education is not in reality what some people proclaim it to be in their professions. What they aver is that they can put true knowledge into a soul that does not possess it, as if they were inserting vision into blind eyes.... But our present argument indicates ... that the true analogy for this indwelling power in the soul and the instrument whereby each of us apprehends is that of an eye that could not be converted to the light from the darkness except by turning the whole body.... Of this thing, then, there might be an art, an art of the speediest and most effective shifting or conversion of the soul, not an art of producing vision in it, but on the assumption that it possesses vision but does not rightly direct it and does not look where it should, an art of bringing this about." *Republic* VII 518b–d, trans. Paul Shorey, in *Plato: The Collected Dialogues*, ed. Edith Hamilton and Huntington Cairns (Princeton University Press, 1961).

53. *Māṇḍūkyopaniṣad* IV.30.

54. Ibid. IV.98.

55. *Brahma-Sūtra-Bhaṣya* IV.iii.14.

56. "Dōgen's Bendōwa," trans. Norman Waddell and Abe Masao, *The Eastern Buddhist* 4 no. 1 (1971): 144.

57. My appreciation of Dōgen has been enriched by many secondary sources, notably Hee Jin Kim, *Dōgen Kigen: Mystical Realist* (Tucson: University of Arizona Press, 1975); Francis Cook, "Enlightenment in Dōgen's Zen," *Journal of the International Association of Buddhist Studies* 6 no. 1 (1983); Stephen Heine, "Temporality of Hermeneutics in Dōgen's *Shōbōgenzō*," *Philosophy East and West* 33 no. 2 (April 1983). The *Sesshin Sesshō* quote is in Cook, p. 18. The *Busshō* quotes are from Heine, p. 140.

58. "Dōgen's Bendōwa," 145–46.

59. Dōgen, "Shōbōgenzō Buddha-Nature, Part II," trans. Norman Waddell and Abe Masao, *The Eastern Buddhist* 9 no. 1 (May 1976): 88.

60. Dōgen, "Shōbōgenzō Genjōkōan," trans. Norman Waddell and Abe Masao, *The Eastern Buddhist* 5 no. 2 (October 1972): 139–40.

61. Ibid., 140n.

62. In Kim, *Dōgen Kigen*, p.

63. Robert Magliola, *Derrida on the Mend* (Purdue University Press, 1984), 48.

64. This is from Candrakīrti's gloss to *MMK* XXV.24.

65. Quoted in Hubert L. Dreyfus and Paul Rabinow, *Michel Foucault: Beyond Structuralism and Hermeneutics* (Brighton: Harvester Press, 1982), 128.

66. Jacques Derrida, *Positions*, trans. Alan Bass (University of Chicago Press, 1981), 26.

67. Jacques Derrida, *Margins of Philosophy*, trans. Alan Bass (University of Chicago Press, 1982), 31–67.
68. Magliola's trans., in *Derrida on the Mend*, 32–33. My emphasis.
69. This section discusses *Being and Time*, div. 2, VI, no. 81, incl. n. xiii.
70. "Both the destruction and deconstruction of the history of philosophy have the effect of leading, not to a forgetting or an overcoming of it, but to an increased preoccupation with it": David Couzens Hoy, "Forgetting the Text," in *The Question of Textuality*, ed. Spanos, Bove, and O'Hara (Bloomington: Indiana University Press), 234. It is a way to recuperate the tradition without believing in it; for what else are philosophers today to do?
71. David B. Allison, "Destruction/Deconstruction in the Text of Nietzsche," ibid., 215.
72. From Derrida's *Spurs*, quoted ibid., 211.
73. Derrida, *Positions*, 86.
74. "The task confronting a post-structuralist . . . theory of reading is to explain misreadings without generating ontological commitments of the same sort that caused previous distortions" (Hoy, "Forgetting the Text," 223).
75. Given Derrida's fondness for Nietzsche, a Nietzschean evaluation is appropriate here. For Nietzsche, nihilism is a hope for the future, because it provides the possibility for a necessary "revaluation of all values." But more immediately it is a grave danger: "God (Being, the transcendental signified, value, reference, meaning) is dead; now everything is permitted." In textual terms, what form would such nihilism take? Do we find an equivalent in the loss of the original source of meaning, experienced as a vertiginous freedom to proliferate and disseminate in any way that we want? Is it then that "I have lost my umbrella" becomes as meaningful as any other statement?

7 THE MIND-SPACE ANALOGY

1. See, for example, Vasubandhu's *Madhyāntavibhāgabhāṣya* 21, and Śaṅkara's *Brahmasūtrabhāṣya* I.i.22, I.iii.41.
2. Shin-ichi Hisamatsu, "The Characteristics of Oriental Nothingness," in *Philosophical Studies of Japan*, vol. 2, trans. Richard DeMartino (Tokyo: Japan Society for the Promotion of Science, 1960).
3. See, for example, *Muṇḍakopaniṣadbhāṣya* III.ii.5, *Brahmasūtrabhāṣya* II.i.14.
4. Kapleau, *Three Pillars of Zen*, 310. Kapleau's brackets.
5. Chang, *Original Teachings of Ch'an*, 46. Some Christian mystics have made the same point, such as Jakob Boehme, according to whom "a good act thus begins with the evil particular, passes through the empty universal and ends in a life which endows the limited particular with a universal value. . . . Like the negative mystics he [Boehme] asks us to flee the evil world and retreat to the Absolute, but unlike them he asks us to return to the same world with the Absolute in tow. The other-world ethics is discovered in an act which transcends nature but which is applied to nature." Brinton, *Mystic Will*, 213, 221.

6. Dasgupta, *Introduction to Tantric Buddhism*, 3–4.
7. For further discussion of this difference, see Hajime Nakamura's encyclopedic *Ways of Thinking of Eastern Peoples*, ed. Philip P. Wiener (Honolulu: East-West Center Books, 1964).

8 NONDUALITY IN THE *BHAGAVAD-GĪTĀ*

1. The distinction often made between *jñāna* and *dhyāna* (or *yoga* or *raja*) seems illegitimate to me, unless one confuses knowledge with scholarship—as the development of the metaphysical systems may have encouraged. But the attitude of the *Gītā* is the same as that expressed in *Muṇḍaka Upaniṣad* III.ii.9: "He who knows the Supreme Brahman verily becomes Brahman."
2. All *Gītā* quotations and citations in this chapter are from the translation by S. Radhakrishnan in *The Bhagavadgītā* (New York: Harper and Bros., 1948).
3. In relation to Advaita, I mean that māyā is not granted any reality apart from Brahman.
4. This makes possible a more sympathetic interpretation of Vedic orthopraxy. The complexity of detailed rituals requires great concentration, so, as in Japanese tea ceremony, one could look upon the goal not as "doing it exactly right" but as developing that sustained attention.
5. Robert A. McDermott, "Indian Spirituality in the West: A Bibliographic Mapping," *Philosophy East and West* 25, no. 2 (April 1975): 214.
6. Ibid.
7. The emotional fixation on the sense of self may also be broken by worshiping an object such as an idol or one's guru. The concreteness of such objects means that making them into emotional mantras is both easier and more dangerous.
8. "For truly, beings here are born from bliss, when born; they live by bliss; and into bliss, when departing, they enter" (*Taittirīya Upaniṣad* III.vi.1).
9. See, for example, Troy Wilson Organ, *The Hindu Quest for the Perfection of Man* (Athens: Ohio University Press, 1970), esp. pp. 69–70, 171–75, 336–37.
10. For example, see ibid., 255.
11. "O Lord, even after realizing that there is no real difference between the individual soul and Brahman I beg to state that I am yours and not that you are mine. The wave belongs to the ocean and not the ocean to the wave." "Nowhere exists in all the world another sinner equal to me; nowhere a Power like Thyself for overcoming sinfulness. O Goddess, keeping this in mind, do Thou as it pleases Thee." Quoted ibid., 254. However, the attribution to Śaṅkara has been questioned.
12. Three attributes often given to God—all-knowing, all-loving, and all-powerful—seem to be incompatible with human suffering.
13. In *Divine Love and Wisdom*, Swedenborg claimed that people misunderstand the nature of God's love: God's love is always active, but we are not always receptive to it. Although his writings are firmly Christian, there is much in them of great interest to the nondualist. For another example, *Heaven and Hell*

claims that after death God does not consign spirits to heaven or hell, but they choose their own habitation by how they react to him; the virtuous are attracted to His presence, the bad flee from it to the region of hell that corresponds to their own nature. This karmic interpretation suggests comparisons with the Tibetan *Bardo Thodol*.

14. For example, in XII 2–5 and XIV 27 Krishna declares his superiority over the impersonal Absolute.

CONCLUSION

1. Vidyaranya, *Pañca-pādikā* VI.285.
2. Arthur Schopenhauer, *The World as Will and Idea*, trans. R. B. Haldane and J. Kemp (London: Routledge and Kegan Paul, 1983), vol. 3, 286.
3. Ibid., vol. 3, 145.
4. Ibid., vol. 1, 231.
5. In F. C. Copleston, *Arthur Schopenhauer: Philosopher of Pessimism* (London, 1946), 10.
6. Quoted in Gardiner's *Schopenhauer* (Harmondsworth: Penguin, 1963), 192.
7. Eliot Deutsch, *Studies in Comparative Aesthetics* (Honolulu: University Press of Hawaii, 1975), 32.
8. Ibid., 46–47.
9. Ibid., 2.
10. Ibid.
11. Ibid., 17.
12. Ibid., 88.
13. Ibid., 18–19.
14. Heinrich Zimmer, *The Art of Indian Asia* (New York: Pantheon, 1955), I, 318.
15. Ananda K. Coomaraswamy, *Why Exhibit Works of Art?* (Luzac), as quoted in Bernard Blackstone, *English Blake* (Hamden, Conn.: Archon Books, 1969), 429. Blackstone's book is an excellent study of Blake's mystical philosophy.
16. Quoted in Ananda K. Coomaraswamy, *The Transformation of Nature in Art* (New York: Dover, 1956), 81.
17. Deutsch, *Studies in Comparative Aesthetics*, 19.
18. Zimmerman, "Towards a Heideggerian *Ethos* for Radical Environmentalism."

ANNOTATED BIBLIOGRAPHY

I am not familiar with any other comparative studies on subject–object nonduality, but a vast literature—Eastern, Western, and in-between—has touched on this issue. In the following, some of the most valuable resources are given as suggestions for further reading—which does not imply that reading is the only, or necessarily the best, way to pursue the matter. Needless to say, not all the following works have been consulted in the writing of this book.

For an overview of the Eastern tradition, John M. Koller's *Oriental Philosophies*, 2d. ed. (New York: Charles Scribner's Sons, 1985) is an excellent place to start. The important philosophical issues raised in the Hindu, Buddhist, and Chinese traditions are discussed there in a clear and concise manner. If there is a lack, it is the omission of the Tibetan and Japanese traditions. This is more than compensated for in Hajime Nakamura's *Ways of Thinking of Eastern Peoples* (Honolulu: University of Hawaii Press, 1968), an encyclopedic but rewarding work that contrasts the modes of thinking prevalent in the Indian, Tibetan, Chinese, and Japanese cultures by investigating the differences in language structure and in the way Buddhism was adapted.

The two best histories of Indian philosophy are Sarvapalli Radhakrishnan, *Indian Philosophy*, 2 vols. (London: Allen and Unwin, 1962) and Surendranath Dasgupta, *A History of Indian Philosophy*, 5 vols. (Cambridge University Press, 1922–55). The first is more readable, the second more detailed. Chandradhar Sharma's *Indian Philosophy: A Critical Survey* (New York: Barnes and Noble, 1962) is concise and suitable for quick reference.

Many translations of the Upaniṣads are now available. In addition to the classic edition by Radhakrishnan, *The Principle Upanisads*

(London: Allen and Unwin, 1953), there is a four-volume edition by
Nikhilananda (*The Upanishads*, New York: Harper and Row) and a
one-volume paperback abridgement with the same title (Harper
Torchbook, 1964). The Advaita Ashrama (5 Dehi Entally Road, Calcutta, India 700014), the publishing arm of the Ramakrishna Mission,
publishes English versions of all the important Advaitic texts with the
commentaries of Śaṅkara. Works by and about such modern Vedān-
tins as Ramakrishna, Vivekananda, Aurobindo, and Radhakrishnan
are also readily available in English. Especially recommended are the
teachings of Ramana Maharshi, whose dialogues often have a Zen-like
quality: *The Collected Works of Ramana Maharshi*, Arthur Osborne
(London: Rider, 1959) and Osborne's *Ramana Maharshi and the Path of
Self-Knowledge* (London, Rider).

   Advaita Vedānta: A Philosophical Reconstruction, by Eliot Deutsch
(Honolulu: East-West Center Press, 1966) is a good introduction to
the subject, and Deutsch's *A Source Book in Advaita Vedānta*, with J. A.
B. VanBuitenen (Honolulu: University of Hawaii Press, 1971) provides
translations of selected passages and a helpful introduction. *A Thousand Teachings: The Upadeśasāhasrī of Śaṅkara*, trans. and ed. Sengaku
Mayeda (University of Tokyo Press, 1979), is a well-edited version of an
important Śaṅkara text, with a valuable introduction. For serious
study, Karl H. Potter's *Encyclopedia of Indian Philosophies, vol. 3: Advaita
Vedānta up to Saṃkara and His Pupils* (Princeton: Princeton University
Press, 1981) provides invaluable summaries of the major works. I look
forward to the forthcoming volume on Mādhyamika.

   There are many fine surveys of Buddhism in English. *A Short History of
Buddhism*, by Edward Conze (Boston: Unwin Paperbacks, 1982), is a
good introduction to the vast subject. Also recommended are Conze's
more philosophical *Buddhist Thought in India* (London: Allen and
Unwin, 1962) and Sangharakshita's *A Survey of Buddhism* (Boulder,
Co.: Shambhala, 1980). A. K. Warder's detailed *Indian Buddhism*,
2d. ed. (Delhi: Motilal Banarsidass, 1980) contains an extensive bibli-
ography.

   Walpola Rahula's *What the Buddha Taught*, 2d. ed. (New York: Grove
Press, 1978) remains perhaps the best introduction to Theravāda
Buddhism, with expositions of the Four Noble Truths, Eightfold Path,
etc., and translations of selected passages from the Pāli Canon. *The*

Psychological Attitude of Early Buddhist Philosophy, by Lama Anagarika Govinda (New York: Samuel Weiser, 1974), is an excellent exposition of a sometimes dull subject, the Abhidharma. For a critical analysis of the Pāli Canon, see *Studies in the Origins of Buddhism*, 3d. ed., by G. C. Pande (Delhi: Motilal Banarsidass, 1984), which attempts to stratify these early texts.

Edward Conze's main work was with the Prajñāpāramitā literature, and his translations are the main resource for Western study. A selection of valuable passages is given in his *Selected Sayings from the Perfection of Wisdom* (Boulder, Co.: Prajñā Press, 1978). The most useful text for further study is probably the Aṣṭasāhasrikā, translated as *The Perfection of Wisdom in Eight Thousand Lines and Its Verse Summary* (Bolinas, Calif.: Four Seasons Foundation, 1973). For a scholarly overview of the whole field, see Conze's *The Prajñāpāramitā Literature* (The Hague: Mouton, 1960).

Lately there has been much interest in Mādhyamika, and several translations of Nāgārjuna's *Mūlamadhyamikakārikā* are now available. Probably the best, although incomplete, is in *Lucid Exposition of the Middle Way: The Essential Chapters from the Prasannapadā of Candrakīrti*, translated with a very helpful introduction by Mervyn Sprung (Boulder, Co.: Prajñā Press, 1979). Among the many other works by or attributed to Nāgārjuna, probably the most important is the *Vigrahavyāvartanī* (Turning the opponent's arguments against him), which as far as I know is available in an English translation only by Kamaleswar Bhattacarya, titled *The Dialectical Method of Nāgārjuna* (Delhi: Motilal Banarsidass, 1978). *Nāgārjuna's Philosophy*, by K. Venkata Ramanan (New York: Samuel Weiser, 1979), is a well-organized collection of passages from the *Mahāprajñāpāramitāśāstra*, traditionally attributed to Nāgārjuna but surviving only in Chinese. Among the many secondary materials now available, T. R. V. Murti's *The Central Philosophy of Buddhism* (London: Allen and Unwin, 1955) remains especially important, despite its "Absolutistic" tendencies. The later split of Mādhyamika into the Prāsaṅgika and Svātantrika schools is discussed in Peter Della Santina's *Mādhyamaka Schools in India* (Delhi: Motilal Banarsidass, 1986).

For Yogācāra writings, see *Seven Works of Vasubandhu*, trans. Stefan Anacker (Delhi: Motilal Banarsidass, 1984). Janice Dean Willis provides another important Yogācāra text in *On Knowing Reality: The*

Tattvārtha Chapter of Asaṅga's Bodhisattvabhūmi (New York: Columbia University Press, 1979). *Studies in the Buddhistic Culture of India*, by Lalmani Joshi (Delhi: Motilal Banarsidass, 1977), is much more than a study of Buddhism in the seventh and eighth centuries; it is a valuable resource for the influence of Mahāyāna on Vedānta, countering the common belief that Buddhism is an "offshoot" of Hinduism. Aśvaghoṣa's *The Awakening of Faith*, trans. Yoshita S. Hakeda (New York: Columbia University Press, 1967), is a terse "mentalist" text that greatly influenced the development of Mahāyāna in China. English translations of many important Mahāyāna sutras are now appearing. See, for example, D. T. Suzuki's *The Laṅkāvatāra Sutra* (London: Routledge and Kegan Paul, 1957) and his commentary on it. *Studies in the Laṅkāvatāra Sutra* (London: Routledge and Kegan Paul, 1957). For the Chinese Hua Yen tradition (the metaphor of Indra's Net), there are *Hua Yen: The Buddhist Teaching of Totality*, by Garma C. C. Chang (University Park: Pennsylvania State University Press, 1971), *Hua-yen Buddhism* by Francis Cook (University Park: Pennsylvania State University Press, 1981), and *Entry into the Inconceivable* by Thomas Cleary (Honolulu: University of Hawaii Press, 1983).

The English literature on Ch'an/Zen Buddhism has become vast, so one can only indicate a few places to start. Philip Yampolsky's translation of *The Platform Sutra of the Sixth Patriarch* (New York: Columbia University Press, 1967) makes use of the recently discovered Tun-huang texts. Highly recommended are two well-known translations by John Blofeld: *The Zen Teaching of Huang Po* (New York: Grove Press, 1958) and *The Zen Teaching of Hui Hai on Sudden Illumination* (London: Rider, 1969). Two contemporary Zen masters have supplied excellent commentaries on the Mumonkan, the most famous collection of Zen koans: Zenkei Shibayama's *Zen Comments on the Mumonkan*, trans. Sumiko Kubo (New York: Harper and Row, 1974), and *Gateless Gate* by my own teacher Kōun Yamada (Los Angeles: Zen Center Publications, 1979). A valuable introduction to D. T. Suzuki's early works is given in *Zen Buddhism: Selected Writings of D. T. Suzuki*, edited by William Barrett (New York: Anchor/Doubleday paperback, 1956). Suzuki emphasized the Rinzai approach and had little to say about Sōtō; for the other side, the writings of Dōgen are highly recommended. Several translations of Shōbōgenzō fascicles have recently appeared in English. Excellent translations by Norman Waddell and Abe Masao have been appearing irregularly in the journal *The Eastern Buddhist.* Most of the important fascicles are included in *Moon in a Dewdrop,* ed. Kazuaki Tanashashi (San Francisco: North Point Press, 1985). Among the many secondary materials, Hee-Jin Kim's *Dōgen Kigen: Mystical Realist* (Tucson: University of Arizona Press, 1975) stands out.

The tradition of D. T. Suzuki is continued today in the "Kyoto School," by such thinkers as Keiji Nishitani, who wrote *Religion and Nothingness,* trans. Jan Van Bragt (Berkeley: University of California Press, 1982), and Masao Abe, the author of *Zen and Western Thought,* ed. William LaFleur (Honolulu: University of Hawaii Press, 1985). An anthology of Kyoto School writings is presented in *The Buddha Eye,* ed. Frederick Franck (New York: Crossroad, 1982). The results of recent Ch'an scholarship, incorporating the researches of Yanagida and others into the Tun-huang manuscripts, is summarized in *Early Ch'an in China and Tibet,* ed. Whalen Lai and Lewis Lancaster (Berkeley: Buddhist Studies Series, 1983). For Zen as practiced today, see Philip Kapleau's *The Three Pillars of Zen* (New York: Harper and Row, 1969) and Shunryu Suzuki's *Zen Mind, Beginner's Mind* (New York: Weatherhill, 1970), a collection of talks given to his students at the San Francisco Zen Center. Those interested in practicing Zen are advised to read Robert Aitken's *Taking the Path of Zen* (Berkeley: North Point Press, 1982).

For Tibetan Buddhism, the early translations by W. Y. Evans-Wentz—*Tibetan Yoga and Secret Doctrines, The Tibetan Book of the Great Liberation, The Tibetan Book of the Dead,* and *Tibet's Great Yogi Milarepa*—are still useful and available from Oxford University Press. An excellent overview of the subject is *Foundations of Tibetan Mysticism* by Lama Anagarika Govinda (New York: Samuel Weiser, 1971). Another classic is *The Theory and Practice of the Maṇḍala* by Guiseppe Tucci (London: Rider, 1969). Recently Shambhala Press (now Boston and London) and Wisdom Publications (London) have released many important translations of and commentaries on Tibetan texts. One example is *Clear Light of Bliss: Mahāmudrā in Vajrayāna Buddhism,* by Geshe Kelsang Gyatso (London: Wisdom Publications, 1982), an explanation of the tantric meditation practices of the mahāmudrā.

The literature on Taoism is not as extensive, but there are more translations of Lao Tzu's *Tao Tê Ching* than can be counted. One of the most interesting is by Chang Chung-yuan: *Tao: A New Way of Thinking*

(New York: Harper and Row, 1975). It includes an introduction and extensive commentary which relates Taoist to Western thought, particularly that of Heidegger. For an alternative view there is Wing-tsit Chan's *The Way of Lao Tzu* (Indianapolis: Bobbs-Merrill Library of Liberal Arts, 1963); the same translation is included in Chan's *Source Book in Chinese Philosophy* (Princeton: Princeton University Press, 1963). Probably the best translation of Chuang Tzu is by Burton Watson, *The Complete Works of Chuang Tzu* (New York: Columbia University Press, 1968). The relevance of his "serious playfulness" for our contemporary world is explored in *Chuang Tzu: World Philosopher at Play*, by Kuang-ming Wu (New York: Crossroad, 1982). The third classical Taoist text has been translated by A. C. Graham, *The Book of Lieh-tzu* (London: John Murray, 1960).

Within the Western tradition, the works of such well-known figures as Pythagoras, Heracleitus, Parmenides, Zeno, Plato, Plotinus, Spinoza, Berkeley, William Blake, Schelling, Hegel, Kierkegaard, Schopenhauer, and Nietzsche do not need references. The Nietzsche renaissance in Europe has produced a number of interpretations interesting to the nondualist; a good anthology of them is *The New Nietzsche*, ed. David B. Allison (New York: Delta paperback, 1979). Henri Bergson, Alfred North Whitehead, and Karl Jaspers are among the modern thinkers whose works are certainly relevant but are not discussed in this study. Heidegger's magnum opus is the early *Being and Time*, translated into English by John Macquarrie and Edward Robinson (New York: Harper and Row, 1962), but it is his later essays that are generally more interesting to the nondualist. Many of them are collected in *Martin Heidegger: Basic Writings*, ed. David Farrell Krell (New York: Harper and Row, 1977). A notable exception is "Conversation on a Country Path about Thinking," which is included in *Discourse on Thinking* (New York: Harper and Row, 1966). Among the many secondary materials in English, J. L. Mehta's *The Philosophy of Martin Heidegger* (Varanasi: Banaras Hindu University Press, 1967) and Michael Zimmermann's *Eclipse of the Self*, 2d. ed. (Athens: Ohio University Press, 1986), are especially recommended. Of Jacques Derrida's works to date, the most relevant are *Of Grammatology*, trans. G. C. Spivak (Baltimore, Md.: Johns Hopkins University Press, 1976) and

Margins of Philosophy, trans. Alan Bass (Chicago: University of Chicago Press, 1982).

For investigating the nondualistic elements within the origins of the Judeo-Christian tradition, *The Other Bible*, ed. Willis Barnstone (New York: Harper and Row, 1984) provides a rich collection of noncanonical gospels, creation myths, gnostic and Manichaean texts, apocalypses, and mystical documents. *The Western Mystical Tradition*, by Thomas Katsaros and Nathaniel Kaplan (New Haven: College and University Press, 1969), is recommended for a comprehensive overview. Among the classical Western mystics that I am familiar with, the thread of nondualism is strongest in Eckhart, Jakob Boehme, the anonymous *Cloud of Knowing*, Emanuel Swedenborg, and William Blake. An excellent collection of Eckhart's sermons and tracts is translated by R. B. Blakney in *Meister Eckhart* (New York: Harper and Row, 1941). Eckhart has inspired many cross-cultural comparisons, most notably Rudolf Otto's *Mysticism East and West* (New York: Macmillan, 1932), which compares Eckhart and Śaṅkara, and D. T. Suzuki's *Mysticism Christian and Buddhist* (New York: Collier Books, 1962), comparing Eckhart and Zen. *The Cloud of Unknowing* (which lends itself to comparisons with the Zen koan process) is accessible in several modern versions; readily available and recommended is the translation by Clifton Wolters (Penguin, 1978). Jakob Boehme is less approachable. Of his many writings the most important are probably *Aurora, The Six Theosophical Points,* and *The Generation and Signature of All Things,* but in his case it is better to begin with a secondary source, such as Howard H. Brinton's study *The Mystic Will* (New York: Macmillan, 1930) or Franz Hartmann's *Jacob Boehme: Life and Doctrines* (Blauvelt, N.Y.: Steinerbooks, 1977).

The Swedish mystic Emanuel Swedenborg is little known now, but in my opinion his voluminous works provide one of the most fertile areas for East–West mystical comparison and dialogue. He claimed to have visited heaven and hell but his descriptions sound more Buddhist than Christian and his account of the after-death experience may be fruitfully compared with such Buddhist classics as the *Tibetan Book of the Dead*. If there are a heaven and hell, I hope they function in the way he describes. His best-known work is titled, appropriately, *Heaven and Hell*; recommended is the recent translation by George F. Dole. Among his other major works are *Divine Love and Wisdom, Conjugial* [sic!] *Love*, and his magnum opus, the twelve-volume *Arcana Caelestia*. All are published by and available from the Swedenborg Foundation, 139 East 23rd St., New York 10010. *The Presence of Other Worlds: The Psychological/Spiritual Findings of Emanuel Swedenborg*, by Wilson Van Dusen (New York: Harper and Row, 1974), is a good way to enter his very different reality. William Blake's father was a Swedenborgian, and Swedenborg had a profound influence on William Blake. Among the literature on William Blake himself, I found Bernard Blackstone's *English Blake* (Hamden, Conn.: Archon Books, 1966) especially insightful.

Eastern Orthodox Christianity has been generally more sympathetic to mysticism than has the Western church, and there are fruitful comparisons between its hesychasm "prayer of the heart" and such Asian techniques as mantras and koans. Highly recommended is Vladimir Lossky's classic *The Mystical Theology of the Eastern Church* (Cambridge: James Clarke, 1957). For the mystical element within Islam, see *An Introduction to Sufi Doctrine* by Titus Burckhardt (Wellingsborough, U.K.: Thorson, 1976). The best-known equivalent for Judaism is Gershom G. Scholem's *Major Trends in Jewish Mysticism* (New York: Schocken, 1961). Martin Buber's *Tales of the Hassidim*, 2 vols. (New York: Schocken, 1948) is a delightful collection, although his approach has been challenged by Scholem and others. But Buber's small *I and Thou*, 2d. ed., trans. Walter Kaufmann (Edinburgh: T. T. Clarke, 1970), is an indisputable classic that invites nondualistic readings. It is also impossible not to mention William James's early phenomenological study, *The Varieties of Religious Experience* (New York: Collier Books, 1961).

Subject–object nonduality has deep implications for the nature of creativity. *The Creative Process*, ed. Brewster Ghiselin (New York: Mentor paperback, 1961), is an anthology of first-hand reports and reflections. *The Act of Creation*, by Arthur Koestler (London: Hutchinson, 1964), is a valuable study of that process. For works focusing on Eastern art, see *Zen and Japanese Culture* by D. T. Suzuki (Princeton University Press, Bollingen Series, 1973), *Zen and the Fine Arts* by Shin'ichi Hisamatsu (Tokyo: Kodansha, 1974), and *Creativity and Taoism* by Chang Chung-yuan (New York: Julian Press, 1963). A spirit deeply informed on both Eastern and Western art is found in the writings of Ananda K. Coomaraswamy, such as *Christian and Oriental*

Philosophy of Art and *The Transformation of Nature in Art* (both New York: Dover, 1956).

The developments in contemporary physics do not figure in this study, but they too have important implications for nondualism. Suggestively nondualistic statements are found in the writings of Werner Heisenberg, Erwin Schroedinger, Louis deBroglie, etc. Recently several books have explored this in some detail: *The Tao of Physics* by Fritjof Capra (Berkeley: Shambhala, 1975), *The Dancing Wu Li Masters* by Gary Zukov (London: Fontana, 1980), *Wholeness and the Implicate Order* by David Bohm (Routledge and Kegan Paul, 1980), and *The Holographic Paradigm and Other Paradoxes*, edited by Ken Wilber (Boston: Shambhala, 1982).

One of the most exciting areas for nondualistic exploration is psychology. As the inadequacy of the reductionistic Freudian paradigm has become more apparent, interest in transpersonal approaches has grown. The works of Carl Jung are one place to start. Two classics in the field are *Zen Buddhism and Psychoanalysis*, by Erich Fromm, D. T. Suzuki, and Ralph deMartino (New York: Harper Colophon, 1960), and *Psychotherapy East and West* by Alan Watts (New York: Pantheon, 1961). Ernest Becker's *The Denial of Death* (New York: Free Press, 1973) and *Escape from Evil* (New York: Free Press, 1978) seem important to me; although pitilessly existentialist, his revision of Freudianism, which replaces sexual repression with death-denial, opens the door to transpersonal approaches. This direction has been developed by Ken Wilber, who has attempted a grand and partly persuasive synthesis in *The Atman Project* (Wheaton, Ill.: Quest Books, 1980) and *Up from Eden: A Transpersonal View of Human Evolution* (New York: Anchor/ Doubleday, 1981). Three recent East–West anthologies are *Buddhist and Western Psychology*, ed. Nathan Katz (Boulder, Co.: Prajñā Press, 1983), *Beyond Therapy: The Impact of Eastern Religions on Psychological Theory and Practice*, ed. Guy Claxton (London: Wisdom Publications, 1986) and *Transformations of Consciousness*, ed. Ken Wilber and others (Boston: Shambhala, 1986). Stanislav Grof has published several provocative books on his research into psychedelic experience, notably *Realms of the Human Unconscious: Oberservations from LSD Research* and, with Joan Halifax, *The Human Encounter with Death* (New York: Dutton, 1976, 1977).

In the search for a "new paradigm" it is not possible to ignore the writings of Carlos Castaneda, which purport to present the teachings of the Mexican Indian sorcerer Don Juan. The most important of the series are *Journey to Ixtlan, Tales of Power,* and *The Fire from Within* (New York: Pocket Books, 1974, 1976, 1985). Frankly, I don't know what to make of Castaneda. It is difficult to accept everything he writes but even more difficult to discount him completely.

The cultural bankruptcy of contemporary Western dualism has been well documented, notably by Theodore Roszak in *The Making of a Counter Culture* and *Where the Wasteland Ends* (New York: Anchor/ Doubleday, 1969, 1973); the second contains an incisive critique of Christian dualism. His *Unfinished Animal* (New York: Harper Colophon, 1977) is a sympathetic but tough-minded examination of the "consciousness revolution."

I conclude with a few works which are difficult to classify. Owen Barfield's *Saving the Appearances: A Study in Idolatry* (New York: Harcourt Brace Jovanovich, n.d.) argues that the disparity between normal and scientific consciousness shows that there is another form of consciousness which he calls "participation." *The Philosophy of Consciousness without an Object* (New York: Julian Press, 1973) is Franklin Merrell-Wolff's reflections on his own experience of subject–object nonduality, informed by his study of Vedānta. *Buddhist and Western Philosophy*, ed. Nathan Katz (New Delhi: Sterling Publishers, 1981), contains many insightful papers. Finally there are many other figures whose works are undoubtedly pertinent but whom I have not read yet, such as Krishnamurti, Mircea Eliade, Fritjof Schuon, and Hans Gadamer.

Among the relevant journals, preeminent is *Philosophy East and West* (Philosophy Department, University of Hawaii, Honolulu). *The Eastern Buddhist* (Otani University, Koyama, Kita-ku, Kyoto, Japan) publishes many fine papers on Mahāyāna Buddhism. For those more interested in psychological implications, there is the *Journal of Transpersonal Psychology* (345 California Avenue, Suite 1, Palo Alto, Calif.).

INDEX